The Aesthetic Clinic

SUNY series: Insinuations, Philosophy, Psychoanalysis, Literature

---

Charles Shepherdson, editor

The Aesthetic Clinic

Feminine Sublimation in Contemporary Writing, Psychoanalysis, and Art

FERNANDA NEGRETE

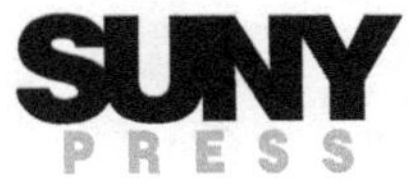

Cover: Louise Bourgeois, *Precious Liquids*, 1992. Collection Musée National d'Art Moderne, Centre Georges Pompidou, Paris © The Easton Foundation/VAGA at ARS, NY. Photo: Frédéric Delpech.

Published by State University of New York Press, Albany

Printed in the United States of America

For information, contact State University of New York Press, Albany, NY
www.sunypress.edu

Library of Congress Cataloging-in-Publication Data

Name: Negrete, Fernanda, author.
Title: The aesthetic clinic : feminine sublimation in contemporary writing, psychoanalysis, and art / Fernanda Negrete, author.
Description: Albany : State University of New York Press, [2020] | Series: SUNY series Insinuations, Philosophy, Pychoanalysis, Literature | Includes bibliographical references and index.
Identifiers: ISBN 9781438480213 (hardcover : alk. paper) | ISBN 9781438480220 (ebook)
Further information is available at the Library of Congress.

10 9 8 7 6 5 4 3 2 1

Contents

Illustrations

Acknowledgments

The inception of the aesthetic clinic goes back to discussions with my dissertation committee. I am extremely grateful to Tracy McNulty, for sparking creative freedom and enabling constraints. Anne Berger sustained a poetic and rigorous reading practice. Patty Keller gave important advice on writing about literature and visual art together. Bruno Bosteels pushed me to interrogate my love of Deleuze *and* the subject of the unconscious. At the University at Buffalo, I am especially indebted to Ewa Ziarek and Steven Miller, who have been exceedingly supportive, motivating guides. I am fortunate to be a part of the Center for the Study of Psychoanalysis and Culture, which galvanized this project. A fellowship from the Humanities Institute enabled me to present a chapter and enjoy great discussions during the 2016–17 academic year, under the superb David Castillo and Libby Otto. Thanks to all my colleagues in the Department of Romance Languages and Literatures at UB, and to Elizabeth Scarlett for granting me release from teaching duties to focus on this project in 2016–17. The UB Honors College under Dalia Muller supported this project through a Faculty Fellowship in 2018. The UB Modernisms Research Workshop provided valuable feedback on my Bourgeois material. Thanks to Carrie Bramen and the Gender Institute at UB for a Faculty Research Grant in 2018 to do research in New York City, and the invitation to present my results to the Feminist Research Alliance. The Easton Foundation, especially Maggie Wright, made working on Louise Bourgeois a dream. The Tinker Field Research Grant for Latin American Studies and a Cornell Graduate School research travel grant, to study Lispector manuscripts in Rio de Janeiro and reach Iceland, spurred the initial stages of the project. I am grateful to the Julian Park Fund for supporting this publication, and owe special thanks to Julian Park Chair Ewa Ziarek and to Melodia E. Jones Chair Jean-Jacques Thomas for generously covering image copyright costs. UB librarians Molly Poremski and Michael Kicey have been hugely helpful.

Many colleagues at UB and beyond have been examples, readers, and friends: Henry Berlin, Laura Chiesa, Jamie Currie, Sergey Dolgopolski, Caroline Ferraris-Besso, Rodolphe Gasché, Claire Goldstein, Elisabeth Hodges, David Johnson, Damien Keane, Anna Klossowska, Chad Lavin, Nicholas Lustig, James Martell, Elizabeth Mazzolini, Jesse Miller, Noam Pines, Justin Read, Sven-Erik Rose, Jonathan Strauss, Camilo Trumper, Paola Ugolini, Margarita Vargas, Audrey Wasser, and Krzysztof Ziarek. The graduate students in my seminars on this project offered valuable insights, specifically Marta Aleksandrowicz, Ashley Byczkowski, Bryan Counter, Elham Dehghanipour, Cheryl Emerson, Laura Hensch, Megan Hirner, and Matthew Skrzypczyk. Willy Apollon, Heidi Arsenault, Danielle Bergeron, Lucie Cantin, Shanna de la Torre, Jeffrey Librett, Tracy McNulty, Steven Miller, Valerie Wevers, and Daniel Wilson have been formidable teachers and interlocutors on psychoanalysis as the effect of an experience. I have also found different forms of inspiration and encouragement for this book from Guillermo Albert, Aura Bautista, Araceli Casillas, Hélène Cixous, Cyril Francès and Hedwige Claux, Caroline Gates, Kaisa Kaakinen, Gabriela Montaraz, Daniela and Carla Negrete, Jim Siegel, Carissa Sims, Daniel Stifler, Omar Tapia, Daniel Tonozzi, Anarela Vargas, and Paloma Yannakakis. Special thanks to my editor, Rebecca Colesworthy, for her faith in this project, as well as to the manuscript readers, and SUNY Press. My parents, Elsa and Jaime Negrete, offered colossal help to free time for writing in the past semesters. Finally, I would like to thank my husband and daughter, Henry and Rosa Berlin, for their brilliance, love, and patience. This book is dedicated to them, and to the women in my life.

Acquired Permissions

Portions of chapter 4, "(Re)Visions of Love: Marguerite Duras," appeared in a different form in "Duras' *Césarée* and the Subject of Love," *CR: The New Centennial Review.* 15: 3 (2015): 167–199, and in "Acts of Love and Unconscious Savoir in Marguerite Duras' Writing," *S: Journal of the Circle for Lacanian Ideology Critique* 12 (2019).

Introduction

On Freud's Couch, Dreaming of Art

During an extremely short trip to Paris in November 2003, I visited the Centre Pompidou and encountered the work of Sophie Calle, whose retrospective exhibit "M'as-tu vue" had opened a few weeks earlier. Its largest piece, the multipartite autofictional installation *Douleur exquise* (1984–2003) (*Exquisite Pain*) made a powerful impression on me, the extent of which I did not fully realize until much later. Perhaps the artwork's strong effect was partly due to having discovered it on a three-day transatlantic trip (where nothing else so memorable happened). At the time, I did not notice that my circumstances, my jet-lag, even, resembled the artwork's own structure, since the "exquisite pain" in its title was an involuntary effect of the protagonist's having left home (Paris) on a three-month trip to Japan that began on a trans-Siberian train.

I remember, upon my return, describing the work—an excruciating, drawn-out, multimedia narrative of a breakup, and of the most painful experience lived by ninety-nine other individuals[1]—in detail to a close college friend who, to my surprise, was immediately moved to tears, although she had not seen the exhibit herself. The attunement of her response to this particular artwork's logic, which is based on the transmission of unique experiences for which words fail, to subjects who did not witness them, only became clear to me after more than a decade, and this belatedness is also intrinsic to Calle's piece. That now-distant

1. See the book version: Sophie Calle, *Douleur exquise* (Arles, France: Actes Sud, 2003).

viewing experience appears to me today as an origin of this book, whose chapter 5 focuses on *Douleur exquise* (1984–2003).

The time Calle's *Douleur exquise* itself took to be completed, eighteen years, involves in profound ways the transformation of the world Sophie and her camera knew at the work's inception, when she boarded an eastbound train across communist Russia and China in 1984, to reach Japan on a three-month artist's grant to go abroad. By 2003, when *Douleur exquise* was first shown in its complete version at the exhibit I saw, not only had the Berlin Wall fallen more than a decade earlier, but so had the Kodak empire, giving way to the rise of digital images in the late capitalism we still know now. Obviously, this lapse of time must have also implied changes in its author's life (at the very least, over these years Sophie Calle had become a recognized figure in the contemporary art world). In like manner, between 2003 and now, my own reality has changed in ways I could not foresee at the time of that brief trip and art-viewing. I did not imagine then, for instance, writing on that particular artwork, let alone still thinking about it sixteen years later. My choice to do so concerns its decisive effect on my sense of what works of art and literature can do to subjects through their very opacity and singularity, a question this book develops.

The temporality of creation in Calle's artwork also resembles the infamously long years it usually takes for a psychoanalysis to reach its end. This similarity is no accident, for what causes this delay is, one might indeed say, an "exquisite pain": an excess, or, in a word Jacques Lacan introduced to psychoanalysis, a singular "jouissance" that stands at odds with shared reality, and with any preexistent path into the social link that sustains that shared reality. *Douleur exquise* is precisely about evoking such an excess, and stages its resistance to being cleared away by a daily narrative process that lasts ninety-nine days. "Jouissance," often translated into English as "enjoyment," is commonly used in French to refer to intense pleasure, including that of orgasm. But the latter famously ends quickly. To the extent that jouissance exceeds reality and emerges as "exquisite pain," its specificity escapes phenomena we can name and identify in an objective way. An intensity of this order might be felt as pain rather than pleasure, insofar as it remains a satisfaction only to itself, and not to an external criterion that establishes the limits of enjoyment. This excessive jouissance thus undyingly resists a full resolution in language (or "sex"), which is why it may be clinically defined as "untreatable," presenting itself as an unwelcome symptom that disrupts the organism.[2] Such an untreatable jouissance is of central importance in this book: *The Aesthetic Clinic* is about strategies that take the side of jouissance in an effort to create—through art, psychoanalysis, and writing—a space for it in reality, more specifically, a clinical space for the transmission of the aesthetic force such jouissance carries, each time in a unique form.

At stake in my engagement with works by Louise Bourgeois, Sophie Calle, Lygia Clark, Marguerite Duras, Roni Horn, and Clarice Lispector alongside psychoanalytic and aesthetic theories is an understanding of the function of the work of art as a process that bypasses the interests of self- and social identity, in order to access subjects of an unconscious jouissance and uphold, as the only good each subject can bring uniquely into the world, desire. Gilles Deleuze's aesthetic philosophy is particularly important to my articulation between works by these women, aesthetics, and psychoanalysis. The more common tendency among Deleuze scholars is to discard psychoanalysis as reactive, to which Deleuze's own criticism of that field contributed, although psychoanalytic thought is a crucial underpinning for his own theories. Deleuze's continual proposal—expanded with Félix Guattari—of an experimental, decidedly non-normative unconscious, certainly makes room for theorizing women's art and writing,[3] and, I believe, it also favors a discussion on female subjectivity in its specificity, and on the feminine. This proposal's break with Oedipal law enables an approach of the desire and jouissance problematic beyond a question of satisfactions that must be renounced and of the family romance as the decisive underlying element in the unconscious. Furthermore, Deleuze's grounding of this unconscious in aesthetics, a field of inquiry about sensations and the acts of thought they inspire by disrupting habit and convention, also invites one to conceive of the work of art and writing as a rigorous, necessarily nonrepresentational process that engages an untreatable excess. Reading

2. Willy Apollon, "The Untreatable," trans. Steven Miller. *Umbr(a). Incurable* (2006): 23–39. Coincidentally, in this essay Apollon explains castration, a relevant concept I will also discuss, in terms of "an irreparable cut" that "becomes the source of *an exquisite suffering*" (35, my emphasis).

3. Feminist theorists have considered the potential of Deleuze's philosophy to examine the stakes of women's writing. See examples in *Deleuze and Feminist Theory*, ed. Ian Buchanan and Claire Colebrook (Edinburgh: Edinburgh University Press, 2000), and *Deleuze and the Schizoanalysis of Feminism: Alliances and Allies*, ed. Janae Sholtz and Cheri Carr (New York: Bloomsbury, 2019).

and perceiving must, in turn, abandon interpretation and the assumption of a stable standpoint external to the work. The art and writing this book explores insist, in particularly powerful ways, on the need to renounce that position of control; reading subjects can thus instead welcome the incalculable transformations that the artwork's encounter discloses for them. Upholding desire, then—in practices of writing *and* reading, sculpting *and* viewing—is making something out of the intractable jouissance, rather than erasing it in attempts at representing and interpreting, which inevitably miss the mark. That desire would distinguish itself as aesthetic, in the sense Deleuze gave to this term: as a unique sensation with a parameter of its own.[4]

This notion of the work of art implies a methodological approach to reading that this book develops, where an irreducible opacity in the work, that is to say, its resistance to translation into common terms, leads the process and raises its own conditions, much in the way that signifiers play unique roles in each psychoanalysis. For example, in chapter 3 I explain that, in Lygia Clark's lifelong "search for a fusion between 'art and life,'" as she herself defined it in 1956,[5] her experimentation led to reconceptualizing the work of art itself. While she shared this task with conceptual artists around the world at the time, this reconceptualization involved not only acknowledging the materiality of the canvas (in the style of Lucio Fontana, for instance), or pushing its limits (as did, say, Lee Bontecou) onto other spaces (as in land art or *dérive* experiments); it also meant understanding the work as an autonomous "proposition"—one that is capable of bringing desire into a unique kind of speech act that introduces its own language and temporality, while calling for a reader, or "participant." Each work of art, then, calls to be read in its

---

4. Or as "obscure and distinct," in Baumgarten's classic formulation in the late eighteenth century, to introduce a discipline within philosophy that did not fit the ideals of light and clarity. At the end of this book I will consider a renewed sense of these two qualities with Horn and Lispector.

5. Lygia Clark, "Lecture at the Escola Nacional de Arquitetura, Belo Horizonte, Fall 1956," *Lygia Clark: The Abandonment of Art 1948–1988* (New York: Museum of Modern Art, 2014), 54. Translations of Clark's writings cited from this source are by Cliff Landers or Licia R Olivetti. Clark envisions in this text an alliance between artist, architect, and psychologist to develop "new and authentic plastic solutions" to create an atmosphere or environment for "the future habitation of man," in which he (or she) "will be the artist," as he will be able to choose and modulate his living environment (54–55).

own terms. When the reader can welcome this constraint, the analytic and theoretical dimensions of the work itself emerge through its very form or aesthetic quality, as something inseparable from the aesthetic experience that provokes those dimensions in the first place.

Indeed, Clark's writings confirm that the creation of concepts through art was an effect of what one could call (with Bataille) extreme inner experiences that preceded it. The propositions she develops throughout the 1960s and early '70s increasingly constrain participants to undergo, for their part, intense experiences, too. As Suely Rolnik aptly puts it, the propositions increasingly "depended on the process that they mobilized in the body of the participants as the basis of their realization."[6] Eventually, this priority leads Clark to leave the world of art, as she had once left the canvas, and to turn her studio into a clinic for one-on-one sessions, where her propositions support the bodily expression of its user's/patient's unconscious. Another important consequence of the work of upholding desire is the possibility the artwork opens—in Clark's participatory propositions and clinic, but also in other approaches, such as the "exquisite pain community," created by Calle's *Douleur exquise*, which I discuss at greater length in chapter 5—of getting beyond interactions between egos, to transindividual encounters between subjects of unconscious desire. Here, too, the interests of self and social identity that serve what Sigmund Freud called "civilization" are bypassed, in favor of an aesthetic expression of desire based on the truth of a different, unconscious experience beyond the limits of language that constitute perception and consciousness.[7]

This is what I previously referred to as the "exquisite pain community:" In the last of its three parts, *Exquisite pain* accompanies its repetitive tale and image with ninety-nine stories[8] of different people

6. Suely Rolnik, "The Body's Contagious Memory: Lygia Clark's Return to the Museum," trans. Rodrigo Nunes. *transversal—eipcp multilingual webjournal*. https://transversal.at/transversal/0507/rolnik/en

7. This "beyond" or "out-of-language" is, of course, an effect of the cut introduced by language into being. This inaugural status of language does not, however, eradicate everything that is not graspable within "sense" or the "sayable." Language introduces lack, which, as this book will explain, is the site of the free drive that can be harnessed in creative acts.

8. The book version features ninety-nine stories; the installation version contains thirty-six.

accounting, at Sophie's request, for the moment they most suffered in their lives, for which Calle, who never saw or lived this herself, creates ninety-nine images. The four elements form a sequence of quadriptychs, with others' pain on the right, and Calle's on the left (in chapter 5, see figures 5.3 and 5.4). On this side, the stubborn image of a red analogue phone on a twin bed in a hotel room remains intact to the very end, despite the protagonist's efforts at narrating *ad nauseam* to dissolve the painful memory at the work's core. I believe *Douleur exquise* suggests that it is this insistent element, a strange experience that cannot find its place in a given moment or word, that gives rise to a work of art, where it might find expression. The repetitive, disruptive psychic pain of absence, provoked by a romantic rupture, that *Douleur exquise* foregrounds and attempts to work through, by telling it's story ninety-nine times, indicates the relevance of the analogy I find between this piece and a psychoanalytic treatment.[9] Its distillation into a precise image of absence (in the repetitive photograph of a red, hung-up analogue telephone on a single made bed in a hotel room) and a precise formula ("exquisite pain") opens up the beautiful possibility of welcoming others' untreatable pain into the work. Moreover, the reading process that the work calls for extends the operation of transmission beyond the subjects whose stories are explicitly included on the right side of the quadriptych. These effects of embracing the untreatable closely resonate with the conviction, in contemporary psychoanalysis after Jacques Lacan, that what takes place at the end of an analysis is not only a cure, as release from the hold an underlying unconscious mental representation ("fantasy") has had on a subject's life. Rather, the analysand's own construction and transmission of an unprecedented object ("objet *a*") that causes desire also becomes possible, and often necessary. Its transmission consists in somehow evoking something that does not already have a signifier, but is unique to a subject.

Thus, I find, the transmission of *objet a* is not only a clinical matter, but also an aesthetic one. The hysteric women Freud observed and wrote about at the turn of the twentieth century attest to this aesthetic dimension through their bodies, acts, and dreams. Freud recognizes a

9. I am thinking of a Lacanian approach to the analytic process. I will discuss key moments and differences between Freud's views on the treatment he created and Lacan's proposal of a formalized conclusion, drawing on the more recent theorizations of Willy Apollon for the École freudienne du Québec (the Freudian School of Quebec).

creative talent there, but its potential to speak ethically to the aesthetic and to the concept of art comes forth a century later, in works of contemporary artists such as Louise Bourgeois, who in the 1990s, as I explain in chapters 1 and 2, launched an investigation on hysteria through sculpture and installation. Calle's *Douleur exquise* or Bourgeois' *Arch of Hysteria* (1993; figure 1.1 in chapter 1), like the other works this book explores, are not only objects that can be called aesthetic—for their unique formal, material, spatial, and temporal qualities—but also processes concerned with the clinical dimension of jouissance and desire.

A project of Sophie Calle's that preceded the 2003 exhibit where I discovered her work speaks most directly about the artist's engagement with psychoanalysis. In *Appointment with Sigmund Freud* (1999),[10] at the Freud Museum in London, which was the psychoanalyst's last home, Calle chose among the relics of Freud's life and juxtaposed them with her own objects, photographs, and stories. She placed some of these objects in Freud's actual consultation room, and in other rooms in the house, offering something like a set of fragments for her case history.[11] The following sections of this introduction will focus on a particular gesture I find Calle to make in Freud's office, a kind of correspondence between "Sophie" and "Dora." They offer an introduction to questions and concepts central to this book, as well as to the kind of conversation that can take place between contemporary art and literature by women, aesthetics, and psychoanalysis.

The wedding dress Calle spread over Freud's couch in his consultation room playfully staged two wishes: first, in her words, "the secret dream I share with so many women: to one day wear a wedding dress,"[12] and, second, to have analysis with Freud. However, in a distinctly hysterical gesture, it simultaneously posed a challenge to some of "the master's" words on female subjectivity. To better grasp this challenge, and its

10. Sophie Calle, *Appointment with Sigmund Freud* (New York/London: Thames & Hudson, 2005).

11. In the narratives that form part of her artworks in this period of her career, she frequently refers to psychoanalysis as a part of her Lebenswelt. More recently, in *Prenez soin de vous* (2007), she also makes references to the psychoanalytic clinic and theory, in a Lacanian vein. For instance, one of the participants in this piece that engages 107 women contributes the formulas of sexuation Jacques Lacan put forth in 1972–1973.

12. Calle, *Appointment*, 65.

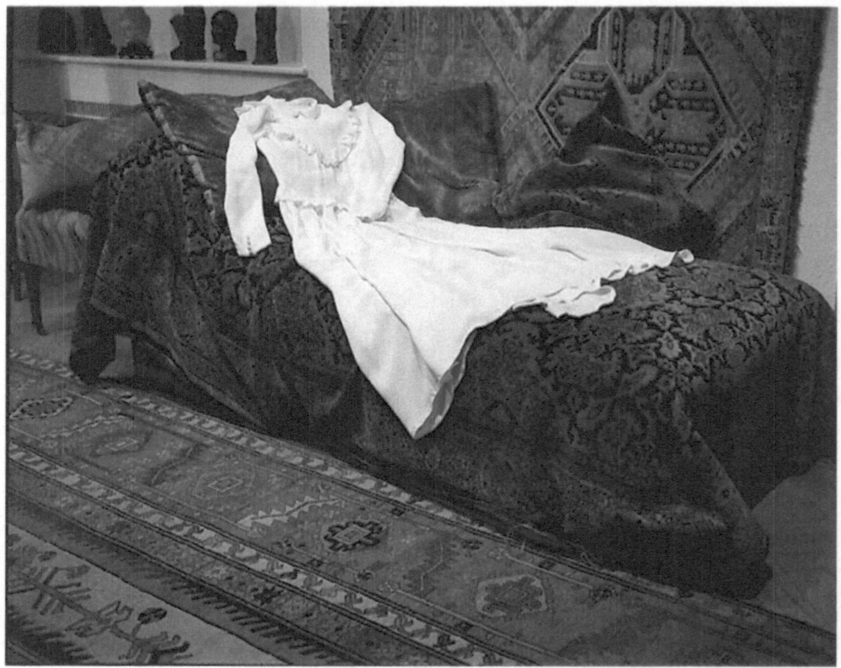

Figure I.1. Sophie Calle, *The Wedding Dress*, 1999. Image courtesy of the Paula Cooper Gallery. © 2019 ARS, NY/ADAGP, Paris.

hysterical character, let me recall a few of such words by the founder of psychoanalysis. According to Ernest Jones in the role of Freud's biographer, the famous question "What does a woman want?" "*Was will das Weib?*" comes to Freud in the context of his humble confession to one of the first women analysts, Princess Marie Bonaparte, that he has not been able to answer that question in three decades "of research into the feminine soul"[13] (an interesting formulation on what being an analyst entails). The beginning of his 1933 lecture "Femininity" resonates with that confession, although he turns his puzzle over to humankind: "Throughout history people have knocked their heads against the riddle of the nature of femininity."[14] If one takes Sophie's wedding dress on

13. Ernest Jones, *Sigmund Freud* II (New York: Basic Books, 1955), 421.

14. Sigmund Freud, The Standard Edition of the *Complete Psychological Works of Sigmund Freud*, trans. James Strachey (London: Vintage, 2001), XXII: 113. Hereafter cited as SE.

Freud's couch into consideration, with regard to the riddles of the nature of femininity and a woman's desire, her answer could seem simple. But while she displays the ultimately common "secret wish to one day wear a wedding dress," this confession raises the question of what is actually at stake in such a wish for Sophie.

Freud's terms "feminine" and "femininity" are also not to be taken at face value. Freud's theory of bisexuality (which originates around 1896 in his correspondence with Wilhelm Fliess) attributes masculine and feminine traits to both men and women.[15] The "Femininity" lecture introduces this key idea of psychoanalysis by outlining the perspective of "anatomical science"[16] at the time, which reveals the presence of both traits in both human organisms, simply in greater or lesser quantities or degrees, aside from the disjunction between ovum or sperm. Against this minimal element to distinguish bodies, the social convention he highlights, of immediately making a distinction between male or female upon "meet[ing] a human being,"[17] appears as a matter not grounded in anatomy or biology in any significant way. He thus warns the audience against simply taking the model of human reproductive sexual functions to mean that "masculine" is a name for aggressiveness, while "feminine" means passivity: "we must beware in this of underestimating the influence of social customs, which similarly force women into passive situations."[18] Freud's reasoning here cautions readers of Sophie Calle's *Appointment* too, against hurriedly concluding that the "secret wish to one day wear a wedding dress" shared with so many women is, ultimately, a wish to comply with the custom of "becoming someone's wife" (just as it would be a mistake to simply assume that if a man shares Sophie's secret wish, he feels like or wishes to be a woman).

15. See *The Complete Letters of Sigmund Freud to Wilhelm Fliess, 1887–1904*, trans. Jeffrey Moussaieff Masson (Cambridge: Belknap, 1985). For an account of the theorization of the feminine and masculine in this correspondence, and its relevance to contemporary psychoanalysis, see Daniel Wilson, "Writing the Drive: From Freud's Theory of Bisexuality to Wittgenstein and the Limits of Language." *differences: A Journal of Feminist Cultural Studies* 28.2 (2017): 65–85.

16. Freud, *SE* XXII, 113.

17. Freud, 113.

18. Freud, 116.

Enigma, Excess, and Envy

Having destabilized the meaning of the word "femininity" with his initial remarks on anatomy and social convention in the lecture, Freud still wants to present psychoanalysis as a distinctive line of inquiry with regard to this term. One of the most striking sentences in the lecture states: "And now you are already prepared to hear that psychology too is unable to solve the riddle of femininity."[19] Freud thus insists on a true enigma. It concerns not only the evolutionary question of "how in general the differentiation of living organisms into two sexes came about,"[20] but also a distinctively psychoanalytic question (which resonates with Simone de Beauvoir's most famous contribution to feminist theory): "psychoanalysis does not try to describe what a woman is—that would be a task it could scarcely perform—but sets about enquiring how she comes into being, how a woman develops out of a child with a bisexual disposition."[21] If he sees this question as more difficult than that of how a man develops out of a child, it is not only because, from his own comment that social customs force women into passive situations, it follows that he considers these customs to subjugate men less, or not as much into passive situations. Rather, the enigma has to do above all with the child's libidinal life, which does not find in female anatomy a direct path to female sexual maturity from a reproductive standpoint. Female sexual development, he thinks, involves a change of erotogenic zone (from the clitoris to the vagina) that is instead not required for the male reproductive function to operate. A different perspective on this question of erotogenic zones (one that avoids the prescriptive tone of renouncing the clitoris as an indication of maturity) might help to see what libidinal life is about, or what the concern is for psychoanalysis: for one body, orgasm is in principle tied to the possibility of reproduction, whereas for the other, it is not bound to its reproductive capacity.[22] In a way, then, the female reproductive system's "split" indicates the mobility of the body's erotogenic

19. Freud, 116.

20. Freud, 116.

21. Freud, 116.

22. For a clinical exposition of this line of thought see Willy Apollon, "Féminité dites-vous?" *Savoir: Revue de psychanalyse et d'analyse Culturelle* 2.1 (May 1995): 15–45.

zones in human beings and their independence from organic functions. They respond, instead, to the unbound drive, which, as Lacan would later point out, is not an anatomical object of study.[23]

Freud shows an awareness to feminist objections regarding the consequences for women of his account of child sexual development, where he proposes the castration and Oedipus complexes. Not only is the boy spared from having to change erotogenic zone to "reach maturity"; his discovery that the girl does not have a penis introduces for him the threat of castration, which helps him give up the mother as first love object that sets up his rivalry with his father. The threat of castration, then, allows the boy to repress and even destroy the Oedipus complex. As a result: "a severe super-ego is set up as its heir."[24] Having internalized prohibitions, the boy can now be his own authority and become an active member of society. For the girl, castration is not a threat, but a discovered fact, and Oedipus, or her change of love object from her mother to her father "through the influence of her envy for the penis," appears as a shift "as though into a haven of refuge. In the absence of fear of castration the chief motive is lacking which leads boys to surmount the Oedipus complex."[25] The consequence of remaining in the Oedipus complex for a long time is that "the formation of the super-ego must suffer; it cannot attain the strength and independence which give it its cultural significance, and feminists are not pleased when we point out to them the effects of this factor upon the average feminine character."[26] In other words, Freud considers that without an incentive to develop a strong, independent super-ego, women are generally less capable of significant cultural achievements or contributions than men.

23. Whereas Freud's take on femininity remains caught within the scientific paradigm, awaiting an organic explanation of the unconscious to be revealed in science, Lacan insists that there is no organic explanation for the unconscious. See Sarah Kofman, *L'énigme de la femme: La femme dans les textes de Freud* (Paris: Galilée, 1980); Danielle Bergeron, "Femininity" *American Journal of Semiotics*. 8.4 (1991); and Wilson, "Writing the Drive."

24. Freud, *SE* XXII, 129.

25. Freud, 129.

26. Freud, 129.

Dangers in Constructing a Clinical Aesthetics

Is abandoning psychoanalysis—as a treatment and theory—advantageous to exploring the potential of women's experimental writing and art, or art concerned with sexuality that does not conform to the Oedipal myth?[27] At a first glance, this seems like Deleuze's standpoint in his book on the paintings of Francis Bacon and aesthetics. Bacon's canvases present bodies that undergo various processes of deformation as a result of what Deleuze calls passing forces and intensities (for instance of contraction, dissipation, flight, gravity, rhythm, screaming, and sleep) that establish various unique relations with the enclosed spaces they inhabit. In painting such bodies, Bacon is known to have used late nineteenth-century photographic documents from the inpatients at the Salpêtrière Hospital diagnosed with hysteria by Jean-Martin Charcot, who was interested in charting hysterical attacks into four distinct phases, and whose investigations inspired Freud to invent the analytic cure. Deleuze follows Bacon's rejection of psychoanalytic interpretation, as incapable of seizing the relevance of the paintings' operations, as producers of original sensations and not disguised representations of unacknowledged wishes. Thus, Deleuze highlights hysteria in his logic of sensation, as a major concern and development for Bacon's painting, but also in an extended way, for painting as an artform. The thought of hysteria in this study leads Deleuze to briefly posit the idea of a correlative "galloping schizophrenia" in music, and thus to consider "constructing a clinical aesthetics": "It is true that there are numerous dangers in constructing a clinical aesthetics (which nonetheless has the advantage of *not* being a psychoanalysis)."[28] A few paragraphs later, he insists, and presents the locution that gives my book its title: "Can we speak of a hysterical essence of painting, under the rubric of a purely aesthetic clinic, independent of any psychiatry and psychoanalysis?"[29]

27. This question was provoked by the innovative critiques of phallocentrism in psychoanalysis that Hélène Cixous ("The Laugh of the Medusa," *Portrait of Dora*) and Luce Irigaray (*Speculum of the Other Woman*) launched in the 1970s with psychoanalyst and feminist activist Antoinette Fouque (founder of *Editions des femmes* in 1972).

28. Gilles Deleuze, *Francis Bacon: The Logic of Sensation*, trans. Daniel W. Smith (London/New York: Continuum, 2003), 51. Emphasis in the original text. Hereafter cited as *FB*.

29. Deleuze, *FB*, 55.

Deleuze nominally distinguishes between the aesthetic clinic he invokes and psychoanalysis, as well as an analytic cure, and it is evident that the latter's clinical frame is not in play in painting and its work with hysteria, or in the other arts and their ways of harnessing different clinical structures. An aesthetic clinic has to be something different from "applied psychoanalysis." I believe the key to this important distinction, between an application of psychoanalytic theory to a nonclinical, cultural object, and an aesthetics with clinical effects on desire that simultaneously calls for a clinic uniquely grounded in aesthetics, lies in treating works of art and writing as differential sites that offer unique, autonomous modes of thinking and reading. A simple turn away from psychoanalysis does not ensure the construction of an aesthetic clinic, nor is it the only adequate response to Freud's limited views on women's psychical capacities.

What is Sophie Calle doing in Freud's London office, exactly a century after his hysteric patient Dora spent three months in the Vienna location, as the analyst relates in *Fragment of a Case of Hysteria*? It is no accident that Deleuze formulates the construction of an aesthetic clinic within the context of a reflection on hysteria, specifically, the structure and phenomenon that Freud and before him Charcot observed, especially in women, and that gave rise to psychoanalysis. For Deleuze is concerned with creating, as the basis of aesthetics, a concept of sensation that implies a work of the senses beyond the organism, as a response to nonorganic intensities. And this is also what underlies the phenomena in nineteenth-century hysteric bodies that Bacon brings to his painting: "the famous spastics and paralytics, the hyperesthetics or anesthetics, associated or alternating, sometimes fixed and sometimes migrant, depending on the passage of the nervous wave and the zones it invests or withdraws from."[30] While one seldom reads about hysteria in Deleuze's work aside from this important late study on aesthetics, this hysteric background remains very present in the works by the contemporary women artists and writers here discussed—Louise Bourgeois, Sophie Calle, Lygia Clark, Marguerite Duras, Roni Horn, and Clarice Lispector.[31]

30. Deleuze, *FB*, 49.

31. Chapter 1 will consider the role nineteenth-century hysteria played in the invention of psychoanalysis, as well as the structure of hysteria in clinical psychoanalysis, showing how Bourgeois' art harnesses hysteria and its cultural trajectory.

Although Deleuze insists on separating the proposal to construct an aesthetic clinic from psychoanalysis and psychiatry, his very approach articulates such an aesthetics around clinical structures employed in psychoanalysis: hysteria (as one of two modes of neurosis along with the obsessional) and schizophrenia (as one of two modes of psychosis, with paranoia as the other).[32] Thus his thought cannot be understood as a simple turn away from psychoanalysis. As I will later point out, Deleuze's engagement with psychoanalysis runs deeper than he admits in his *Logic of Sensation*, and since his collaboration with Félix Guattari in *Anti-Oedipus*, from 1972. I certainly agree with his sense that the practice of art can and should steer the construction of an aesthetic system with its own concepts. I believe the fascinating question he poses, in psychoanalytic terms, of the clinical potential of artforms and bodies of work calls to be explored in unique, mixed media works of art that, like Bacon's, carry in themselves a clinical ambition. I initially mentioned, for example, Calle's "exquisite pain" as a formula (displacing a medical term) and photographic image for an untranslatable experience of stubborn psychic pain, or jouissance. "Art is a Guaranty of Sanity" is the sentence welded above the entrance to Louise Bourgeois' installation *Precious Liquids* (1992) (figure 2.1 and book cover), and it is important to find out how art might guarantee sanity, and what sanity involves from an aesthetic perspective. Lygia Clark named some of her handmade works, made for others to engage with and activate them, "Objetos relacionais," Relational Objects, evoking D.W. Winnicott's theory of the transitional object and space. Clark seeks to give participants access to another space and time, as well as to an aesthetic dimension of their body, just as playing, to Winnicott, can carry a child to a space that exceeds the limits of reality, but that is also not an isolated inner prison. These and the other clinical artworks in this book shed light on the problems of sublimation, sexuality, and the feminine, which are crucial

32. Deleuze links perversion to aesthetic productions early on, in the 1967 introductory essay to Sacher-Masoch's *Venus in Furs*, where he views the fact that the names of two modes of perversion, sadism and masochism, come from literature, as an opportunity to explore the literary (or aesthetic) and the clinical together: "The clinical specificities of sadism and of masochism are not separable from the literary values peculiar to Sade and Masoch." (Deleuze, *Coldness and Cruelty*, trans. Jean McNeil [New York: Zone Books, 1989], 14.)

to any aesthetics with clinical implications and effects.[33] So let us return to Freud's office and texts, as Calle's *Wedding Dress* invites us to do.

A Girl's Fates

Freud's theory of female sexuality discerns three fates for the girl. At worst, she remains stuck in the Oedipus complex; another, disappointed in her father's power to provide refuge, will "regress into her early masculinity complex,"[34] which may express itself in the choice of another woman; at best, she becomes a mother to a boy who will later have cultural significance directly. What about women who do achieve that significance themselves, for instance the women analysts around Freud, whom he cites, or his contemporary, Virginia Woolf, whose *A Room of One's Own* addresses problems closely linked to Freud's argument here? In the 1933 lecture, Freud reports that in current discussions about this, the answer is that women are considered "more masculine than feminine" in that regard.[35] (Woolf in 1928 would instead say that great writers, men or women, discover how to put the feminine and the masculine to work in harmony[36]). At the turn of the twenty-first century, where might the protagonist "Sophie" with her wedding dress stand, according to the psychical process Freud outlined for the girl? And what about the artist Calle, who turns that very wedding dress into an element in an art installation with Freud's couch? Calle's autofictional works highlight a split between the protagonist and the artist/narrator, and such a split makes a statement on the questions of feminine desire and "becoming a woman."

For *Appointment with Sigmund Freud*, Calle defined the project as follows: "to display relics from my own life amongst the interior of Freud's home and also to select objects from his personal collection which relate

---

33. These are, I believe, as crucial as Deleuze's turn, with Guattari, to the psychotic structure Freud kept at bay.

34. Freud, *SE* XXII, 130.

35. Freud, 117.

36. Woolf ponders upon "the unity of the mind" and resolves to "amateurishly sketch a plan of the soul so that in each of us two powers preside, one male, one female" and considers that writing requires the two to "live in harmony together, spiritually cooperating." *A Room of One's Own* (Orlando: Harcourt, 2005), 96–97.

to stories I wished to tell."[37] Her wedding dress interestingly does not relate to the story of any official marriage, but instead to the beginning of a long-awaited first rendezvous with a certain man:

> I had always admired him. Silently, since I was a child. On 8 November—I was 30 years old—he allowed me to pay him a visit. He lived several hundred kilometers from Paris. I had brought a wedding dress in my bag, white silk with a short train. I wore it on our first night together.[38]

In suggesting that her attraction to this man was not limited by her having a properly adult body, the narrative evokes Freud's important theory of childhood sexuality. The child's body may not be reproductively mature, but it is a body affected by jouissance that sets the drives in motion, "silently," beyond what the child or anyone around her can say. The story suggests that the man waited for her adult body. The long work *Douleur exquise* retells this little story, revealing that this man was Sophie's father's friend when she was a child, which invites the reader to consider a possibly Oedipal aspect of her attraction for "a substitute father." Through the act of bringing a "virginal" wedding dress, Sophie works to link this first night together to her childhood attraction for the man. The narrative tightly weaves together the child and "the 30 year-old woman" (featured in Freud's "Femininity" as one in whom desire appears to have run its full course and rigidified), as if nothing else had taken place in between those two parts of her life but this infatuation finally finding satisfaction (although the other stories in *Appointment* indicate a lot of, often disturbing, experience of sexuality in the service of repression). The wedding dress stresses the event's inaugural quality, just as the narrative stresses the long wait and distance she endured for it (even if the dress only has a "short train").

Fifteen years later, in 1999, Calle places that dress and the memory it embodies on Freud's couch. Insofar as what an analysand brings to it are unconscious wishes, the wedding dress spread over it, in replacing a living body, appears as a representation of Sophie's wish to "become a bride," which Calle's narratives in other projects indeed make explicit (but

37. Calle, *Appointment*, 9.

38. Calle, 79.

what does it involve for her?), along with Sophie's repeated tragicomic impossibility to fulfill it. This consistent failure is no accident from a psychoanalytic point of view, and Calle's narratives, which underscore this unpleasant repetition in precise ways, betray an awareness of the part it plays in an unconscious desire, alongside the more pleasant and confessable wish to wear a wedding dress, which she has no problem fulfilling.[39] Wearing it to her own wedding is another story, and not Sophie Calle's, in any case. The disembodied presence of the dress points to the fact that, while this dress traditionally symbolizes an ideal of female identity, in which a woman reaches sexual maturity and confirms her value by a man's supposedly lifelong commitment to her, the dress remains merely a layer, a coating a body can "slip into" or out of, without fully identifying with it (in a related gesture, Calle does not miss the opportunity to slip into Freud's overcoat and pose, replicating a photo of the psychoanalyst in his garden[40]). This slippery quality is indeed foregrounded again later, in Calle's story about this same wedding dress in *Douleur exquise*: "C'était un ami de mon père. Il m'avait toujours fait rêver. Pour notre première nuit, je me suis glissée dans le lit vêtue d'une robe de mariée." ("It was a friend of my father's. He had always made me dream. On our first night, I slipped into bed wearing a wedding dress.") It is relevant that *Douleur exquise* tells the end of this romantic affair, exactly, when he fails to go the required distance to meet her in a New Delhi hotel room after a three-month separation. This breakup causes the "exquisite pain" of a more fundamental absence, outlined in *Appointment* by the inert dress on the couch in a room from which Freud is missing too.

Lack

"Penis envy" in Freud's account of female psychic development names one mode of unconscious response to a fundamental experience of lack

39. In another story within *Appointment*, Calle poses in a wedding dress for a fake wedding, with a group of people and Gregory Sheppard, whom she had married, without a dress, at a drive-through chapel in Las Vegas (and soon divorced). In *Le mariage de rêve* (*Dream Wedding*) (2001) she poses in a red wedding dress at the Paris-Roissy airport, longingly staring out the window toward a departed plane in which her fiancé has flown away to China.

40. See Calle, 2–3.

that every human being is faced with. This experience is unavoidable insofar as language fails to name what takes place within the child's body on the level of drives, and Freud, taking the child's discovery of anatomical difference as an important moment, and thinking of the neurotic psychic structure, posits two kinds of response. But "penis envy" of course resonates with an unfortunate Aristotelian model of female anatomy as an incomplete or imperfect human body, since it suggests that the penis would fill the lack the girl discovers in herself, and that, logically, the male body is therefore not lacking. And indeed, the boy's "threat of castration" and repression of his Oedipal love offer the illusion of not lacking. In this light, one could consider "the wedding dress wish" Sophie brings to Freud's couch, as an instance of what he called penis envy, since both the gesture of "wearing something" and the act of marriage the dress invokes suggest images of complete satisfaction, or fulfillment of the lack that makes wishes possible in the first place. It is as if all she needed was the dress, or the man, or a baby boy, per Freud's outlined optimal fate for women. Yet both penis envy and castration anxiety are modes of resistance, and the point of the discovery of sexual difference lies, I insist, in an experience, for both the girl and the boy, of not being/having everything (to/for an Other on whose love their being depends).

Calle's intervention in Freud's office with the dress on the couch does not lose sight of that underlying experience. As her introductory narrative to the project explains, she chose to accept the invitation to create an exhibition in Freud's last home "after having a vision of [her] wedding dress laid across Freud's couch."[41] There is a significant difference between wearing a wedding dress and laying it across Freud's couch. Take another look at Figure 1.1. Facing the scarcely majestic, disembodied dress laid out flat on the empty couch, viewers are not so much invited to recognize or identify with the iconic bride figure as an ideal for a woman, as they are confronted with an absence—the absence at stake in castration. And that is the gesture's brilliance. The absence of the patient's body from the consultation room achieves two things. First, it underscores a double split: between Sophie as protagonist of the narrative and the dress, on the one hand, and, on the other, between the protagonist and the artist. She seems to have left the couch to apply her body to the tasks of writing, taking photos, and organizing Freud's

41. Calle, 9.

office in her own way, through gestures such as that of laying out the dress that, for Sophie, has never coincided with an actual wedding.[42] The second effect of the missing body is that while the dress may stand in for the patient on the couch, the subject of unconscious desire can never be fully represented by the signifiers available in a given culture, here a Western one for female sexuality. How long will the dress lie there? Will it someday realize the doctor's chair is also empty?

Femininity versus Ego

In *Analysis Terminable and Interminable* (1937), a late paper in which Freud himself asks why psychoanalytic treatment takes such a dreadfully long time, castration is discussed as a logical moment at the end of analytic treatment, which gives rise, once again, to this crucial resistance in the child's development. It emerges as "penis envy" for women and as what he calls a "masculine protest" for men, which consists in "a struggle against his passive or feminine attitude to another male."[43] In both cases, a "repudiation of femininity"[44] is at stake. The final obstacle to the analytic cure, or what makes it "interminable," is, thus, the repudiation of femininity, which sides with the drive in the latter's struggle against the ego. As Daniel Wilson points out, to Freud this struggle cannot be entirely reconciled;[45] therefore it persists, as an "underlying bedrock"[46] that makes analysis to him interminable, in a certain way.

---

42. The project in which she does get married is the film *No Sex Last Night (Double Blind)* with Gregory Sheppard. This is an edited film shot with two hand cameras, by Sophie and Greg, who take a road trip from New York to California in an old Cadillac and speak to their cameras about the lack of communication between them. Calle intermittently presents an image of the unmade hotel beds, accompanied by her words "No sex." At a certain point the sentence is reduced to "No," repeatedly, until at a certain point there is a "Yes." Along the road they decide to get married, and she is not wearing a wedding dress. This inspires her to organize a "fake wedding" photograph with Sheppard. See my footnote 37.

43. Freud, *SE* XXIII, 250.

44. Freud, 250.

45. "Writing the drive," 72. Wilson explains that attempts at reconciling the drive, or feminine, to the ego emerge in the form of "a tendency to collapse the feminine into the maternal," influenced by Melanie Klein.

46. Freud, *SE* XXIII, 252.

I pointed out earlier that Freud in the "Femininity" lecture destabilizes the meaning of this term, in order to point to something that neither science nor culture can truly grasp. As for psychoanalysis, if it cannot "solve the riddle of femininity" either, it can point to its properly enigmatic dimension, as an "inner" experience of heterogeneity that is nonetheless intrinsically human. Femininity is an unconscious experience of excess of the drive that is irreconcilable with the ego. The formalization of an end of analysis into what Lacan called "la passe" ("the pass") is concerned with breaking through the repudiation of the feminine, or "censored jouissance,"[47] by finding a way to sustain it in its very heterogeneity to the ego. To Freud, "avoiding a symptomatic reaction to a 'censored jouissance' that attributes this jouissance to an Other"[48] means periodically returning to analysis, as the only space for this jouissance that does not fit in the social link to express itself without causing too much disruption in the ego's life. But jouissance will continue its work.

To Lacan, a conclusive moment must be reached when the analysand no longer attributes the jouissance to an Other, after which she can alone construct and transmit this jouissance as a necessarily unique objet *a*. What is it like to "not repudiate" but rather embrace femininity, to take responsibility for it, and thus to "traverse castration"? Is this act restricted to a school of psychoanalysts? In a way, yes, insofar as it is part of a specific space and practice. Yet surely this shift in a subject has effects in its life, beyond the clinical context. What are the consequences of traversing castration, with regard to a human being's "cultural significance," since to Freud that function was dependent upon internalizing laws and prohibitions that fail to grasp the feminine? How might a work of art offer, as Freud's office did, a space to sustain the feminine? Each work discussed in this book engages such questions uniquely.

A Girl's *Savoir*, and Her Other Fates

I have stated that Calle's dress in *Appointment* points the viewer to a knowledge, or unconscious *savoir*, about an experience of the signifier's lack, or of language's inability to name the jouissance in the subject of

47. Apollon, *Untreatable*, 32.

48. Wilson, "Writing the Drive," 66.

the drives. The girl's early, intimate experience of this defect in language is more than a feeling of inferiority with regard to the boy's organ (which, as explained, is an attitude of resistance against the nonrepresentable that castration confronts her with), and also what poses an obstacle to Freud, as he attempts to account for female sexuality through the Oedipus complex. Calle's tale and installation underscore a feminine savoir about this experience of lack, whose excess (a lack of limits, one might say) turns the Oedipal overtones in the love affair into a humorous experiment, as if it were a matter of giving the "haven of refuge" Oedipal love promises to be an honest try, only to confirm that it does not work. Together, this savoir, the appeal to a master (the father's friend as lover, and later, Freud) who would finally set a limit on a disturbing jouissance, and the display of his solution's insufficiency are distinctively hysterical. The hysteric sustains desire in its unsatisfied form, as Freud's patient "Dora" will help to demonstrate. Since, however, all this is articulated in an artwork in Calle's case, it is not only an example of hysteria and its symptoms; it is also about art as a specific mode of dealing with the lack that sexual difference highlights. Calle's tale and dress on the couch suggest an aesthetic way of sustaining the feminine.

In his most explicitly psychoanalytic study, *Logic of Sense* (1969), Deleuze zeroed in on the feminine as the repressed force that any artist or writer must welcome in order to set forth a genuine act of creation. This is how he accounts for Lewis Carroll's choice of a little girl for his works *The Adventures of Alice in Wonderland* and *Through the Looking Glass*. Later, in collaboration with Félix Guattari[49] and drawing on Virginia Woolf, he develops the idea that the girl's prominence in English novel writing is due to the fact that she holds the key to escape the social identities that erase this girl, whose body is "stolen" in order to install identities or "the organism," inscribed within a system of oppositions:

> The question is not, or not only, that of the organism, history, and subject of enunciation that oppose masculine to feminine in the great dualism machines. The question is fundamentally that of the body—the body they *steal* from us in order to

49. It is relevant to recall here that Guattari was a psychoanalyst and co-founder, with Jean Oury, of the antinormative *La Borde* clinic for psychotics in France, which continues to operate.

> fabricate opposable organisms. This body is stolen first from the girl: Stop behaving like that, you're not a little girl anymore, you're not a tomboy, etc. The girl's becoming is stolen first, in order to impose a history, or prehistory, upon her. The boy's turn comes next, but it is by using the girl as an example, by pointing to the girl as the object of his desire, that an opposed organism, a dominant history is fabricated for him too. The girl is the first victim, but she must also serve as an example and a trap. That is why, conversely, the reconstruction of the body as a Body without Organs, the anorganism of the body, is inseparable from a becoming-woman, or the production of a molecular woman.[50]

This passage from *A Thousand Plateaus* (1980) places society or the norms, values, and ideals of culture at odds with what they refer to as "the body," whose capacity has nothing to do with its cultural codification as "organism." The body is also not simply an original state of nature before this cultural over-coding. The operation of becoming, then, or of "reconstruction of the body as a Body without Organs," which they deem "inseparable from a becoming-woman" concerns finding a path for the feminine, such as the ones they discern here in modernist novels in English by Virginia Woolf, as well as by Henry Miller and D.H. Lawrence.[51] In other words, the schizoanalysts here enter a discussion on the Freudian Oedipus and castration complexes to suggest a liberating potential for the body, through the girl, or the becoming-woman she introduces, beyond Oedipus.

Whereas the girl introduces castration anxiety in the boy, upon his discovery of their anatomical difference, where indeed she is an example of what might happen to him if he does not comply with his culture's norms, Deleuze and Guattari find the girl taking on a very different exemplary role in novels. For Freud, as mentioned, the girl's own discovery of anatomical difference with regard to the boy leads to penis envy. Deleuze and Guattari not only suggest that the girl may also

50. Gilles Deleuze and Félix Guattari, *A Thousand Plateaus*, trans. Brian Massumi (Minneapolis & London: University of Minnesota Press, 1987), 277. Hereafter cited as *ATP*.

51. Deleuze and Guattari, 277.

become a writer of Virginia Woolf's caliber, but that in order to write, "even the most virile, the most phallocratic"[52] writers need not only five hundred pounds a year and a room of their own, but must undergo a becoming-woman. An encounter with the feminine is indispensable to genuine creation beyond the cultural ideals that repress femininity or "steal the girl's body," insofar as it gives access to the body unbound from those ideals. This opens up the possibility of something new. While, according to Deleuze and Guattari, even the most phallocratic writers must welcome the becoming-woman or the differential girl beneath identity, a phallocratic work of art as its result seems to me logically less radical, in its ability to invent or bring something unprecedented into the world that does not simply reflect the traditional distribution of power.[53] I am more interested in how a woman like "Sophie" or a girl like "Dora" take the step of a becoming-woman.

In a way, a "virile" or "phallocratic" writing is less radical to the schizoanalysts too, or else it would have a prominent role in what I see as their rethinking of sublimation. The latter, a Freudian term, is a process in which the unbound bodily drives bypass repression and are able to find a creative outlet. To "reconstruct the stolen body" or "to make oneself a Body without Organs," is a process the schizoanalysts see at work in a number of different practices from various cultures and historical periods, such as medieval courtly love, Taoism, peyote rituals, and Antonin Artaud's writings. They adopt the formula "Body without Organs" from Artaud, whose proposition of a theater of cruelty is as relevant as his schizophrenic experience of the body. The "body without organs" for Artaud is directly concerned with treating an ill sexuality trapped in the service of reproduction and ideology. He invokes, under what he calls the principle of cruelty, emasculation as a solution to this problem for Western men. He declares: "There's nothing more useless than an organ. When you make him a body without organs you'll

52. Deleuze and Guattari, 276.

53. In Woolf's self-proclaimed "amateurish sketch" of the bisexual soul of the writer (see my footnote 34, where I mention Woolf), she lists examples and states that Proust "was wholly androgynous, if not perhaps a little too much of a woman. But that failing is too rare for one to complain of it, since without some mixture of the kind the intellect seems to predominate and the other faculties of the mind harden and become barren." *A Room*, 102.

deliver him from all his automatisms and give him his true freedom."[54] The schizoanalysts claim that "making yourself a Body without Organs" begins with "a becoming-woman," which can be understood as a step in the direction of embracing the censored jouissance, or of overcoming the repudiation of femininity that serves reproduction and ideology (it is significant that Taoism and courtly love develop cultures of enjoyment that bypass male orgasm, whose previously discussed tie to reproduction places it in the service of civilization). The Body without Organs then concerns the unruly drives that exceed both the work of the organism and determinations of society.

In its embrace of the girl's savoir that something of desire—"what a woman wants"—escapes the wedding dress, or the purview of the signifier, Calle's *Wedding Dress* can itself be seen as its own aesthetic practice of the Body without Organs. But "becoming" could be taken to mean escaping the dimension of fate that the Freudian account of the girl's development had instead showcased, as if the path of becoming were endless errancy without consequences, or without its movement leaving a singular trace. And this is not what is at stake for the schizoanalysts' concept of becoming. In the practices that inform their discussion on the Body without Organs, which require specific modes of asceticism and an ethics, an aimless errancy can have undesirable results, or "botch the BwO."[55] It is necessary, then, to consider what can happen to the body at stake here, a body animated by the unbound drive.

Dora and the Motive of Symptoms

If Freud cautiously recommended that individuals return to analysis every few years, it is because he was keenly aware that "the repressed material," or the drive, continues to push against any repression or suppression; it unceasingly "struggles for freedom in the human mind,"[56] as symptoms demonstrate much more often than artworks. The repressed, or "censored jouissance" activates the drives, beyond the organism and the social, yet

54. Antonin Artaud, *Pour en finir avec le jugement de Dieu* (Paris: K Éditeur, 1948), 40. Translations for this and all texts in French, Portuguese, or Spanish in this book are mine unless otherwise noted.

55. Deleuze and Guattari, *ATP*, 161.

56. Freud, *SE* XXIII, 249.

it finds expression in symptoms that may involve physical, social, deadly suffering. In "Analysis Terminable and Interminable," Freud briefly summarizes the concept of the death drive, which he introduced in 1920 with *Beyond the Pleasure Principle*; in his summary, the death drive is presented as a crucial factor in the difficulty an analysis can encounter, when this force appears in the form of masochism, "absolutely resolved to hold on to illness and suffering."[57] The symptom as a result of the drives is, then, a writing produced "to encode the scene of a jouissance that must remain censored, unsaid" and that therefore "cannot be dissociated from the jouissance."[58] Freud had first learned about the logic of this writing from hysteric women, such as "Dora."

Freud saw the eighteen-year-old patient he names "Dora" for three months in 1899, until she broke off the treatment on December 31, 1899, and he first published the incomplete case in 1905. Unlike the "grande hystérie" he had witnessed at Charcot's Tuesday lessons with demonstrations by female inpatients in the Salpêtrière Hospital or even some of the cases in the *Studies on Hysteria* with Breuer, Freud begins the Dora case by pointing out that it's a case of "petite hystérie," where no extreme phenomena occur. And yet, or precisely thanks to the absence of more spectacular occurrences, the work of listening to Dora's accounts, alongside the observation of her physical symptoms and social circumstances—which give rise to a couple of traumatic events in the way of sexual advances to her on the part of Herr K, her father's mistress' husband, provide Freud with material that brings into relief the unnamable jouissance which Dora faces, as well as her social link's failure to provide her with a space for this jouissance to emerge as anything else than illness.

In the case history, Freud offers a description of the logic of the symptom, which "comes into the patient's mental life at first as an unwelcome guest"[59]; moreover, "the motive for being ill is, of course, invariably the gaining of some advantage."[60] Freud exemplifies this by asking us to imagine "a bricklayer . . . who has fallen off a house and been crippled, and now earns his livelihood by begging at the street-corner."[61] The point

57. Freud, 242.

58. Apollon, *Untreatable*, 33.

59. Freud, *SE* VII, 36.

60. Freud, 36, n27, added in 1923.

61. Freud, 37.

of this example is that if "a miracle worker"[62] promises to heal his leg, the bricklayer would not look forward to recovering, since by then, his disability has become his way of life and would struggle without it. The analyst's task, he notes, is thus complicated by this resistance to being cured. This example of Freud's for the motive of the symptom, where a worker becomes disabled and won't let go of the illness that places him outside of productive social membership, is interesting to compare to Dora's own problems as a young, female member of society whose symptoms (from nausea to "avoidance of men engaged in affectionate conversation,"[63] to aphonia, to dragging one leg for nine months) all point to being sexually harassed by Herr K, and to having to comply with her father's denied love affair to Frau K. Indeed, Dora's situation raises the question Juliet Flower MacCannell has accurately formulated for the figure of the girl: "What is society supposed to mean to the girl, what are her obligations and duties to it, and what are the rewards it offers her?"[64] Dora's symptoms call into question what one might call women's "proper role," that is, a productive, socially recognized one, asking what this role may have to do with desire. The answer is: precious little. For, as noted previously through Freud's observations, a woman's options as she enters adulthood are quite limited, particularly in the societies he has examined.

"Symptoms have a sense and they are related to the patient's experiences," Freud claims in one of his Introductory Lectures, delivered at the University at Vienna in 1917.[65] Precisely in putting individuals out of commission, symptoms are a form of resistance to societal norms and an expression of unspeakable desires. After the 1920 theory of a "beyond the pleasure principle" where the death drive is introduced, it becomes clear that the symptom sides with the drive, at the expense of the ego's life, which seeks to fit into the social link. To obtain the sense of the symptom, the analyst must listen to its singularity and see what that benefit might be, in spite of the patient's life. Thus, if the symptom appears as "an unwelcome guest" to the patient on a conscious level, an

62. Freud, 37.

63. Freud, 23.

64. Juliet Flower MacCannell, *The Hysteric's Guide To The Future Female Subject* (Minneapolis: University of Minnesota Press, 2000), 7.

65. Freud, *SE* XVI, 257.

analyst must instead welcome that symptom, and the unknown, specific logic that determines the death drive's way of fueling it.

Dora and the Limits of Sex

In his work with Dora, Freud works with physical symptoms, acts, memories, and dreams to reveal and tease out Dora's unconscious "love currents" for her father, Herr K, Freud as her doctor under transference, and Frau K. Accepting this possibility already exceeds what is appropriate to the world around her under "love." But these remain questions about her relation to the other.[66] Meanwhile, Dora strives to find different positions to those offered to her by the social link—not only through the position of "Freud's patient lying on the couch," which allows a space from which to consider those relations, but also as "flâneuse" walking alone in the city, lakeside, or gallery, or in viewing paintings and reading. Dora speaks of all these activities in Freud's account, who, for his part, demonstrates a remarkable sensibility for disclosing coded chains of signifiers that operate across the girl's words and actions. Freud reads two of Dora's dreams, and her body's silent "speech"—in subtle gestures as she lies on the couch and in the illnesses and pains she complains about—to distill a very specific set of apparently unrelated words and scenes that all point to a question of sex. Indeed, the adolescent girl interrogates not only society and others' actions, but also the enigma of sexual difference beyond the social, on the level of jouissance. I will come back to this in relation to her interest in art-viewing.

Dora comes to analysis after telling her parents that Herr K has made indecent propositions to her. Her father discusses the matter with the Ks, and sends her to Dr. Freud, hoping he will help (him, that is) by getting rid of this idea in her (and Freud does not attempt to fulfill the father's wishes). Unlike the three characters in Dora's story (her father, who does not want to hear this, Herr K, who denies having harassed her, and Frau K, who accuses her of having a perverse mind), Freud believes the girl. Even though her father brings her to Freud's office in

66. On the limitations of Freud's role and the logic of the hysteric structure in the case, see Paul Verhaeghe, *Does the Woman Exist? From Freud's Hysteric to Lacan's Feminine*, trans. Marc du Ry (New York: Other Press, 1999).

the hope that she will stop creating obstacles against his unofficial love affair to Frau K, Freud's commitment to the truth prevails; he wants to hear not only what happened, but especially what moves her. He is ready to break social conventions in the context of treatment, so as to discuss sexual matters openly in the first place: "I call bodily organs and processes by their technical names, and I tell these to the patient if they—the names, I mean—happen to be unknown to her. *J'appelle un chat un chat*," he writes.[67] On the other hand, he remains caught within societal expectations and its codification of sex, when he unfortunately assesses Dora's reactions to Herr K's advances—disgust, when he pushes her against the wall on a stairway to kiss her, speaking sharply to him when she wakes up from a nap to discover him hovering over her bedside, a slap on his face, when he tries to kiss her again during a walk by the lake, telling her parents—as "abnormal," given that she has entered puberty and should thus feel "excited."

Dora's symptoms certainly speak of the advantage she gains from the suffering they cause her;[68] they also denounce, together with her act of putting an end to the treatment, the enduring obscenity of what Apollon calls "the cultural montage of sex," which "represses desire and constrains the drive within the limits of the receivable."[69] It is worth noting that the different characters around Dora also provide great examples of the drive limited according to this montage, notably Herr K, who feels an urge to act on his impulse to impose himself physically on the girl. This married man could come into Freud's consultation room too, to see what is causing him to act in this way (after having, perhaps tacitly, accepted his wife's affair to Dora's father). The drive, or the way in which the censored jouissance is at work in a body, gives rise to physical symptoms such as Dora's, as well as to impulsive acts such as Herr K's. What else can it stir up? At the end of Freud's account, Dora, who no longer drags her leg, visits Freud one last time, and reports that she decided to visit the Ks and to calmly confront them. While she had initially complied with them and her father (she tolerated Herr

67. Freud, *SE* VII, 48.

68. The brevity of the treatment does not allow a full analysis of Dora's fantasy. Freud had also not yet developed the concept of the primal scene at the time.

69. Apollon, "From the Cultural Construction to Desire." Schema from the GIFRIC Training Seminar "The Clinic of the Symptom" (June 5–9, 2017).

K's advances and her father's affair, as long as Frau K treated her like a close friend), she can no longer do so, now that the work of the drive in her has taken a different form to that of the symptoms in her body. The drive had initially only disrupted her body, and it now allows her to confront her social link in a new way. The consequences don't appear too destabilizing for others in this case . . . then again, a few months after she confronts the Ks, she witnesses an accident on a busy street. The victim run over by a carriage had been "Herr K," who "had stopped in front of her as though in bewilderment, and in his abstraction he had allowed himself to be knocked down by a carriage."[70] It is understandable that Freud would want analysis to "tame" the drive.[71]

Unruly Drive

To Lacan, psychoanalysis in his wake, and also to schizoanalysis, the drive is not something to avoid, but rather "the source of the fundamental, inalienable freedom and creativity of the human subject, which are responsible for the best in humanity as well as the worst."[72] "At its best," Lucie Cantin points out, the energy of the drive, or jouissance, takes an aesthetic form. At worst, it is the most destructive and violent force—and the art of "making oneself a BwO" points to exactly this risk, and these would be the true "dangers" of constructing an aesthetic clinic Deleuze invoked. As I have been stating, this book investigates how certain works of art by women put that jouissance to work in an aesthetic form. Dora's case presents different possible manifestations of the drive constrained within "the receivable," which is the site of gender identifications and the repudiation of femininity for men and women.

In "Femininity" Freud states that "there is only one libido, which serves both the masculine and the feminine sexual functions," and libido is "the motive force of sexual life."[73] But the implications of the previously discussed points of (non-)convergence between the reproductive functions

70. Freud, *SE* VII, 121.

71. Freud, *SE* XXIII, 225.

72. Cantin "The Drive, the Untreatable Quest of Desire," trans. Tracy McNulty, *differences: A Journal of Feminist Cultural Studies* 28.2 (2017): 24–45, 30–31.

73. Freud, *SE* XXII, 131.

and erotogenic zones lead him to observe that "teleologically—Nature takes less careful account of [the feminine function's] demands than in the case of masculinity. And the reason for this may lie—thinking once again teleologically—in the fact that the accomplishment of the aim of biology has been entrusted to the aggressiveness of men and has been made to some extent independent of women's consent."[74] The survival of the species biologically depends on men's but not on women's orgasm, or even consent, although it obviously does depend on women's reproductive systems. Freud is speculating on the possibility that it is perhaps because the goal of reproduction has in the past been accomplished through men's aggressiveness, and to some extent without women's consent, that women's orgasm is not guaranteed by the reproductive function. In other words, Freud sees the way in which orgasm functions in men and women as an acquired trait in the evolution of the human species.[75] Freud's observation stresses the fact that the libidinal life of individuals is *not* subordinated to the aim of biological reproduction. While "the aggressiveness of men" may be a violent expression of the drive that has served biological reproduction, this does not justify it as something biologically inevitable.

Humanity is not excused from responsibility to imagine and strive for the end of sexual violence and of gender inequality, based on the lame dialectics of her "not having" to support his illusion of "having"[76]; this only amounts to a rejection of the feminine that Freud's work instead challenged, insofar as he posited the unconscious and made a space for its expression in the clinic. As members of societies we are undoubtedly responsible for solving problems of gender and sexual violence; but why does this violence keep returning under guises new and old?

---

74. Freud, 131.

75. Freud's comment points to his "Lamarckian metapsychology," which is beyond the scope of this book, although this theory serves as a background to the phenomenon of "conversion hysteria" (how the unconscious expresses itself by transforming the body) it does discuss. See Wilson "Freud's Lamarckian Clinic" in *Psychoanalysis and Inheritance*, ed. James Godley and Joel Goldbach (Albany, NY: SUNY Press, 2018). I engage with this essay's discussion of the missing object of the drive in chapter 2.

76. Woolf brilliantly denounced this dynamic over ninety years ago in *A Room of One's Own*.

I remember asking myself this very question just a few years ago, while jogging near my home and workplace in Buffalo, New York, on a bike trail that is known for being the site where a serial killer attacked several of his female victims between 1981 and 2006. But why wouldn't sexual violence keep returning, insofar as it is a consequence of censored jouissance in the work of bodily drives, and—following Cantin's view of violence and the aesthetic as the alternatives—of its not finding aesthetic expression? And here an important difference emerges, between what different cultures repress or accept, according to their norms and ideals, and a more profoundly unconscious experience. If an extremely progressive and inclusive politics were all there is to it, a solution would have been found, and the repression that led Freud to posit the unconscious would only be an effect of restrictive societies.

Beyond the Limits of Culture

The fundamental repression, or the censored, is not a problem only for patriarchal, oppressive societies—though not because of some automatic aggressive instinct supporting biological aims. The censored jouissance instead results from "the upsurge of a pure mental representation"[77] in human beings. "Nothing corresponds in our internal or external environment"[78] to this kind of representation or "hallucination" that has effects in the organism and the world nonetheless. In fact, civilizations and cultures are collective hallucinations. Moreover, this upsurge of a hallucination in each being is "a fundamental experience that makes beings into subjects of a real that turns them definitively away from the reality of their biological and social roots."[79] Psychoanalysis sheds light on the fact that a censored jouissance is, under different, sometimes very subtle avatars, intrinsic to the existence of cultures, no matter how politically progressive or conservative they claim to be. In other words, the feminine in human beings, regardless of their gender, is continually rejected by culture in the very imposition of identities and destinies

77. Apollon, "Untreatable," 30.

78. Apollon, 28.

79. Apollon, 30.

according to the norms and ideals of different cultures. Yet, as Jacqueline Rose stated, thinking of sexual identity and femininity, and as Patricia Gherovici more recently recalls, with transgender subjectivity in mind, "there is a resistance to identity at the very heart of psychic life."[80] Perhaps it is possible to take responsibility from this site of nonidentity and of freedom—for the worst and the best.[81]

Of all the different identities and destinies promoted across different time periods and cultures, that of motherhood for women is a strikingly constant one, and this cannot be dissociated from the fact that the survival of the human species has depended on female reproductive systems to this day. Freud may seem conservative in proposing motherhood with a boy as the best possible fate for a woman, but his focus was on her libidinal satisfaction finding a solution that also works for the ego in the social link, even if, as mentioned earlier, he knew these two dimensions were not entirely compatible.[82] In the contemporary psychoanalytic line of thought this book engages with, the feminine cannot be encompassed by motherhood, which continues to function as a key cultural strategy to control the jouissance that threatens civilization. The feminine is instead the uncontrollable remainder, whose irruption as a "mental representation," in Apollon's words, or "hallucination," in Freud's, causes, for each human being, a jouissance beyond language and the organism, and also intimately linked to the aesthetic. Societies encourage the fate of motherhood through multiple strategies, among which one finds, of

80. Jacqueline Rose, *Sexuality in the Field of Vision* (London: Verso, 1986), 91. Also cited in Patricia Gherovici, "Anxious? Castration Is the Solution!" *Psychoanalytic Inquiry* 38.1 (2018): 83–90.

81. Apollon explains that the Freudian unconscious "introduces subjectivity as a veritable mutation that displaces the responsibility and intentionality of the human act outside the field of conscious perception and of the space-time defined by the neurophysiologic limits of pleasure and reality" ("Untreatable," 28). In other words, human subjectivity is the effect of a decentering out of the limits that suffice for organic functioning, and the unconscious does not exempt acts of freedom from responsibility.

82. In his discussion of the "taming" of the drive, Freud states that silencing its "demand" is impossible and undesirable; ideally, he writes, it could be "brought completely into the harmony of the ego . . . and no longer seeks to go its independent way to satisfaction" (*SE*, XXIII: 225), but this is followed by a detailed account of the tension between ego and drives in an analysis, with various possible outcomes.

course, the lovely wedding dress that has appeared throughout this introduction. Spread across Freud's couch, Sophie's dress, a cultural symbol of happiness, also appears as a complaint.

A fantasy of defloration is what a "virginal" wedding dress represents in general, as everyone knows. While it might allow a young woman to dream of an unprecedented sexual enjoyment, and, conveniently, to give her dream a valuable form in the social link, her drive could never be satisfied by the cultural apparatus that seduces girls with this signifier in exchange for their entry into the service of reproduction and motherhood, which as a set of external conditions indeed makes it less likely for her to become a great writer or psychoanalyst (or scientist, or lawmaker). In this way, Sophie's dress evokes the famous "Dora" case, where Freud insisted on imposing upon his patient the interpretation that her symptoms revolve exactly around a repressed "phantasy of defloration, the phantasy of a man seeking to force an entrance into the female genitals."[83] In Dora's "second dream," the girl walks into her room in an unknown, strange town and finds "a letter from Mother lying there."[84] This letter announces her father's death: "Now he is dead, and if you like? you can come."[85] In 1999, the wedding dress lying there, on Freud's couch in London, can be seen as a kind of letter to Dora, not from Mother, but from Calle. By introducing the classic "bride wish" as a key element in her work, Calle, who simultaneously gives shameless indications of an already active sexual life and builds on her difficulty to make marriage "truly" happen for her, highlights the fact that the unprecedented enjoyment remains unsatisfied, and that this jouissance has little to do with cultural expectations, including, importantly, that of having sex. Like a letter from another scene, beyond the limits of culture, the white bridal dress on the couch becomes strange, and thus evokes a powerful feeling Dora could only express as "her adorable white body."[86]

Dora "could find no clear answer to make" for Freud's question on what the young woman found so remarkable in a certain painting, that she remained standing in front of it, alone, for two hours. "At last she

83. Freud, *SE* VII, 100.

84. Freud, 94.

85. Freud, 94. Freud comments on the strangely placed question mark in the letter.

86. Freud, 61. Dora praises Frau K's "adorable white body."

said: 'The Madonna.' "[87] Dora's decision to break off her treatment with Freud comes shortly after a dream linked to two instances of viewing art. One of these viewings is of Raphael's 1512 *Sistine Madonna*, in Dresden a few years before the session where the previously cited dialogue took place,[88] and the other of a modern painting featuring woods and nymphs in the background, which she had seen the day before her session with Freud, on December 27, 1899, in the eighth Vienna Secession exhibit.[89] In Freud's interpretation, "The '*Madonna*' was obviously Dora herself,"[90] holding, of course, the baby boy (who will redeem the world). Furthermore, he discerns the female genitals in the Secessionist "wood" and "nymphs" that made their way into Dora's dream,[91] and he confirms that Dora knows "Nymphen" are not only the Greek mythological creatures, but also a technical term for the female inner labia (nymphae). It is relevant to Calle's gesture that "nymph" comes from *numphē*, the Greek word for "bride." Dora may have a highly specialized vocabulary to describe the female genitals, but her speechlessness before "the Madonna," and later before Freud's question on what she admired has to do, I suggest, with something strange that the experience of viewing mobilizes in her, an experience for which words are fundamentally lacking.

Calle's empty dress as mentioned earlier subtly underscores the fact that there is no identity, no adequate signifier for the subject's desire. As an adolescent, Dora is encountering the "defect in language"[92]—the lack of a name in the collective for her experience—in the form of an ethical failure in the social link, and also, through her aesthetic experience of the paintings, I find, as a hole or incompleteness in the Other that cannot be filled by simply complying with this montage (although that is exactly the illusion neurotics fall under). Dora's silence—to which Calle offers an echo, through Sophie's sustained "silent admiration" of a man since childhood in her tale of wearing the wedding dress to her

87. Freud, 96.

88. Freud, 96.

89. Freud, 99. For a historical analysis of the case, see Hannah Decker, *Freud, Dora, and Vienna* (New York: The Free Press, 1992), 82–83.

90. Freud, *SE* VII, 104 n2.

91. Freud, 99.

92. On the defect in language and an experience of an out-of-language, in connection to the development of individuals, women especially, see Lucie Cantin "The Hold of Cultural Constructs: A Mortgage on the Future of Desire" in *Correspondences*. 17.2 (2017): 65–73.

first night in bed with him—expresses the failure of her jouissance to fit into her culture's codes. Freud realizes after the fact that the adoration of the Madonna must have had to do with the girl's infatuation with Frau K.[93] But the silence and the "adorable white body" Calle's dress fittingly materializes, complete with its emptiness, point even beyond the taboos of homosexuality or incest (with Frau K as a mother substitute), to something truly unnamable.

In the dream that leads Dora and Freud to the discussion about her gallery visits, the girl, who finds herself in an unknown town, struggles to find the train station to get back to her hometown on her own. When she finally arrives (after "two and a half hours," close to the amount of time she spent in front of the *Sistine Madonna* in Dresden and that it would have taken her to walk away from Herr K to town along the lake), she does not go to her father's funeral, choosing instead to calmly read in solitude an encyclopedia, which points Freud to a source of information on sexual anatomy for the girl. Perhaps her dream, where she sees herself alone, fatherless, taking her time, and exploring an unknown place or an unknown book, as well as her absorption in front of paintings in her gallery visits are more than just an escape from reality, and more than an expression of the old Oedipal dream of killing the father to free oneself from the law. Perhaps they offer her more room to make something other than an illness out of her drives.

Feminine Sublimation

The absence of a signifier, and its emergence with the question of sexual difference, activate in a body the work of drives beyond the functioning of the organism to fulfill its basic needs. How these drives will develop a kind of writing for a free-floating jouissance that pushes forward in spite of any barriers of resistance and prohibitions is the question Freud explored throughout his career, first, in hysterical attacks, then through dreams, slips of the tongue, symptomatic illnesses, acts, and, last but not least, sublimation.

"Sublimation" was the strategy Freud discerned as one in which certain subjects—insofar as they were capable of creative acts and repression of the drives had failed in them—freed themselves from their ties

93. Freud, *SE* VII, 60–61; 104 n2; 120 n1.

to the demands of civilization, in favor of a joy that had nothing to do with those demands, all while offering these subjects cultural recognition. Leonardo da Vinci, Michelangelo, Fyodor Dostoevsky, and the biblical Moses[94] are Freud's main examples of sublimation in different moments of Western civilization.[95] As "a way out," as Freud stated, of the ego's demands, sublimation differs from both the formation of an ego ideal, and from the staging of a perverse scenario,[96] since these two depend upon an imaginary Other's demands that fix the subject into place.[97] Sublimation thus named an operation that can sometimes be achieved with the work of jouissance on the drives, the very thing or energy that can disrupt and even destroy individuals and civilizations, through artmaking and other creative undertakings.

Sublimation introduces something new into the world. The creations Leonardo, Moses, or Calle propose involve a leap beyond anything civilization has ever named and (thus) accepted. What the leap entails is unnamable—beyond anything different civilizations and cultures may prohibit or enforce—because it has to do with the encounter of the fundamental lack that turns sexual difference, femininity especially with its puzzling absence, into a riddle beyond biological or socially constructed gender difference. Yet in Freud's personal experience of civilization's discontents, through the two World Wars and the need for him and his

94. On Moses and his creative act to Freud, see Tracy McNulty, "Demanding the Impossible," *Wrestling with the Angel: Experiments in Symbolic Life* (New York: Columbia University Press, 2014).

95. Sarah Kofman examined Freud's relationship to art, its role for psychoanalysis, and a Freudian aesthetics in *L'enfance de l'art* (Paris: Galilée, 1985). Griselda Pollock has developed what she calls a "feminist virtual museum," as a response to this problem, and of the absence of masterpieces by women in Western culture, which Linda Nochlin investigated in the 1971 essay "Why Have There Been No Great Women Artists?." As a feminist intervention in trauma studies and art history, Pollock explores the potential of aesthetic experiences proposed by women's artworks, as traces of trauma that need not disappear completely. Griselda Pollock, *After-affects / After-images: Trauma and Aesthetic Transformation in the Virtual Feminist Museum* (Manchester: Manchester University Press, 2013).

96. On the relation between the neurotic's fantasy and the pervert's scenario see chapters 9 and 10 in Apollon, Bergeron, Cantin, *After Lacan: Clinical Practice and the Subject of the Unconscious*, ed. R. Hughes and K. Malone (New York: SUNY, 2002).

97. Freud, *SE* XIV, 95.

family, as Jews, to leave Vienna under Nazism, while sublimation offered joy, it was a pale glimmer of hope for humanity's search for happiness.[98]

Given the previous exposition on the feminine excess of the drive that remains incompatible with the ego, which as a position of identity complies with the demands of civilization, does sublimation not entail, precisely, a rare embrace of the usually repudiated femininity? Failure to fully repress the drive, which seems like a serious disadvantage for the girl's psychical development, allows (as Deleuze and Guattari found in literature) for the invention of a path through castration, that is, through the fundamental lack that no amount of repression, denial, or reparation can truly overcome. After all, a partial failure of repression in hysteric women is what gave rise to symptoms that made the invention of psychoanalysis possible, in the first place. Certainly, symptom and sublimation are not the same, insofar as the symptom responds to a jouissance that partially fails to be stifled but that also partially responds, like the ego ideals and the pervert scenario, to an imaginary Other that, instead, falls away for the subject who finds in sublimation, or through analysis, "a way out." The creation of psychoanalysis (one might say, Freud's own act of sublimation) involved a clinical practice of listening to women's speech that confirmed the experience of the drives in their bodies caught up in an astonishing production of symptoms. The symptom would seem to be a less fortunate outcome of the free drives than that exemplified by the extraordinary artworks of a Leonardo or Michelangelo. But the processes I described earlier, of "traversing castration" and constructing an *objet a*, as well as of "making oneself a Body without Organs" suggest far more intricate ties between symptom and sublimation.

My interest in feminine sublimation in this book concerns the ethics it can propose with regard to the conflict between the drive and the common good. The earlier point I described from Freud's theory of sexuality, that fear of castration favors male development by encouraging the internalization of the law in a strong and independent superego, shows that the outcome of sublimation is something different from the forging of a way for an individual to be fit to contribute to society. Freud

98. This search, he explains in *Civilization and its Discontents*, gives rise to the civilization that, paradoxically, becomes an obstacle to it, by prohibiting satisfactions oblivious to the common good. The repressed pushes forward, even if it is violent. Violence against bodies flagged as expressions of what is detestable appears, in this light, as an extension of sexual violence.

unfortunately concluded that women must also generally have a lower inner capacity of sublimation than men, given the relationship to lack that shaped their subjectivity early on in their lives. That assessment on lack, I find, was tied to artistic and ontological criteria that Freud's contemporaries in modern literature, art, and philosophy, were beginning to upturn. The works of Bourgeois and Clark in this book's Part I shed light on these transformations, so I consider key passages from Baudelaire and Nietzsche to point out the irruption of the feminine in them, as well as in the theories they, and Freud, inspire in later psychoanalytic thought, and in philosophers such as Pierre Klossowski and Jean-François Lyotard, in addition to those I have cited in this introduction (Deleuze, Guattari, and Lacan). The result is a transformation of the criterion of health, under the command of the aesthetic.

Oedipus offers a useful myth on the link between the encounter of sexual difference and the repressed experience of jouissance as a "lost object" upon entering language as the law of coexistence, or the symbolic. But language does not work as a true guarantee for everyone; it certainly fails to provide a reliable signifier for the feminine. This means that the subject who enters language, or the shared fiction of "symbolic" life, from a feminine position (which is not determined by gender or biology[99]) inhabits it in a way that is never entirely grounded on what Lacan calls the phallic function, that is to say, on "the word" or on language insofar as it stands for the law. A subject situated in the position of "a woman" deals with a justified skepticism with regard to the word's ability to provide a limit to the excess of jouissance, or a form of expression for it in the symbolic. While this exposes the feminine subject to a specific mode of unconscious knowledge—the previously mentioned *savoir* unanchored by the signifier[100]—Dora's story reiterates the fact that this situation has most

99. Lacan makes this claim in his seminar *Encore*, when he presents the formulas of sexuation, and several commentators have elucidated this point. See Shanna Carlson, "Transgender Subjectivity and the Logic of Sexual Difference," *differences* 21:12 (2010): 46–72; Patricia Gherovici, *Please Select Your Gender. From the Invention of Hysteria to the Democratizing of Transgenderism* (New York: Routledge, 2011); Joan Copjec, *Read My Desire: Lacan Against the Historicists* (London & New York: Verso, 2015); Alenka Zupančič, *What IS Sex?* (Cambridge, MA: MIT Press, 2017); Shanna de la Torre, *Sex for Structuralists: The NonOedipal Logics of Femininity and Psychosis* (New York: Palgrave, 2018).

100. This *savoir* is certainly linked to Nietzsche's *gai savoir*, inspired by the troubadours who developed courtly love. More on Nietzsche and the troubadours in this book's chapters.

commonly resulted in a social discredit for women's word. This typical result of the experience of a defect in language is lamentable. And yet, the confrontation of the defect in language is the stuff of creation too, and taking it to its full potential means disrupting the social link, and conceiving of symbolic existence beyond a patriarchal Oedipal model and its correlative cultural montage of sex.

Dora returned to Bergasse 19 in this spirit, to let Freud know she had confronted the Ks and her father. In *Appointment*, and, I find, also in other works, Calle returns to the clinical space psychoanalysis opened up and makes an aesthetic intervention. While the other contemporary artworks in *The Aesthetic Clinic* are not about literally occupying Freud's consultation room with objects or texts, I argue that in different, important ways, they shape what I call the aesthetic clinic. The juxtaposition of the analytic space of the clinic with women's aesthetic expression beyond cultural expectations that concerns this book aims to give a vantage point on the stakes of sublimation, to examine the effects of the aesthetic interventions these women's works make in the clinic of psychoanalysis, and, in turn, to give relevance to the distinctly analytic dimension of the aesthetic.

In the links that Louise Bourgeois (chapters 1 and 2), Lygia Clark (chapter 3), Marguerite Duras (chapter 4), Sophie Calle (chapter 5), and Clarice Lispector with Roni Horn (chapter 6) entertain in different ways with psychoanalysis, it becomes evident that a critical approach that pushes psychoanalysis away loses touch with something they instead were or are deeply invested in, beyond the understandable feminist protest. I am not interested in limiting the significance of art to psychoanalytic explanations, and while psychoanalytic approaches to contemporary art abound in which the latter merely illustrates the theory, these often also miss the unique theoretical contribution the works can make in their own terms. By sustaining a relationship between the clinical (and not only theoretical) dimension of psychoanalysis as a non-normative mode of engagement with the unconscious,[101] and the aesthetic experiences this constellation of artworks gives access to, *The Aesthetic Clinic* approaches the fields of writing, psychoanalysis, art, and speculative thought as sites of experience. Placed in conversation, they shed light on their singularity and relevance beyond the question of cultural value, as well as on their contribution to aesthetics, a theory whose bedrock resides in

101. No normative engagement with it is possible; norms presuppose resistance to the unconscious.

unique experiences, in sensations that exceed our repertoire of names, and whose shock discloses a different dimension of the body.

Part I, "The Transvaluation of Health," establishes this project's specific, uncommon sense of the clinical and the aesthetic, discerning the interventions that hysteric bodies in plastic practices can make in the notion of sublimation. Chapter 1, "Louise Bourgeois' Art of Hysteria," investigates the important return to hysteria and the birth of psychoanalysis Louise Bourgeois (1911–2010) undertakes in the 1990s, through her sculpture *Arch of Hysteria* (1993). The French-American artist's ambivalent relationship to psychoanalysis and surrealism lead to an interrogation of the "acephalous" body of the drive from the perspective the hysteric, as a structure that points to the failure of language to name a part of the subject. The concept of conversion Freud invoked in his early study of hysterical patients is expanded to consider Bourgeois' sculptural transposition of photographs and drawings of the *arc de cercle* posture, in the hysterical attacks Charcot charted. Bourgeois' late gesture toward Baudelaire in a late series of floral etchings (*À Baudelaire*, 2008) invites a turn to the writings of this contemporary of Charcot's, who in his *Fleurs du mal* poems proposed a very different set of "tableaux." Finally, I compare the looping shape of *Arch of Hysteria* to Lacan's teaching on the circuit of the drive in Seminar XI, to see how an artwork turns around an "*objet a*."

Chapter 2, "Transmuting Pain into Joy with *Precious Liquids*" explores the criterion of health Louise Bourgeois invokes through the phrase "Art is a Guaranty of Sanity" in her installation *Precious Liquids* (1992). The installation's construction of a threshold and enigmatic, intimate scene continues the investigation of a "clinical" dimension of the artwork, with the bed as a material reminder of the etymology of "clinic" *kliniké techné*, which is "beside art." The chapter shows the installation's call to a transvaluation of the criterion of health, related to the concept of "convalescence" Baudelaire set forth in his essay *The Painter of Modern Life*. Through specific passages in this classic modernist essay, as well as in Deleuze's texts, and Francis Bacon's *Three Studies for a Crucifixion* (1962), the chapter develops the concept of sensation at stake in the aesthetic experience *Precious Liquids* offers. Sensation as the signature of genuine thought in Deleuze's philosophy points directly to the hysteric body of the drives again, which Klossowski discussed in Nietzsche's "valetudinarian states." Baudelaire, with Nietzsche, by insisting on "voluptuousness," "le gai savoir," and the uncanny figures of "woman," help to further specify sensation as a transmission that confronts us with sexual difference as a fundamental experience in Bourgeois' art.

Chapter 3, "Lygia Clark on the Space–Body Problem," turns to Lygia Clark (1920–1988), a Brazilian artist who was always concerned with establishing a continuity between art and life in a way that might allow a certain work with plasticity and the body to enable the latter's vitality or vibrancy in space, which was a crucial problem in her life and production. Clark was involved with psychoanalysis throughout her life and, as previously stated, actively sought to enable with her creations others' unique experiences relating to birth, as a fundamental traumatic event for the subject. A key moment in Clark's trajectory has to do with a dream that leads to the proposition "o dentro é o fora" ("the inside is the outside"), which she formalizes through a set of plastic experiments with Möbius strips, just when Lacan begins to explore topology as well. The continuity of art and life was realized in developing a form of therapeutic treatment with the relational objects she had invented throughout her career, in a private setting that entirely dropped the ambition of exhibiting her work, in favor of facilitating her patients' access to their unconscious experience of the body where the signifier fails to account for it.

Part II, "Love beyond Pleasure," brings the question of developing new modes of relation from the standpoint of sensation into full focus, which begins to appear already in Bourgeois' installations and Clark's propositions and relational objects, as two strategies that attempt to bring alive a transmission between subjects of the unconscious rather than egos. To further investigate relation, this second part of the book highlights literature, at intersections with cinema, in Marguerite Duras, and with photography and another installation of a bedroom that places an absence as the origin of the artwork, in Sophie Calle's *Douleur exquise*. The two chapters undertake a meditation on pain, separation, and love beyond the pleasure principle.

With Duras (1914–1996) and Calle (1954–), I continue to examine the logic of transmission between unconscious subjects by focusing on love, as a privileged experience with its distinct set of symptoms for the aesthetic clinic to enable new modes of relation. The clinic of psychoanalysis offers a model for such a connection on an unconscious level, through the relation between analyst and analysand. Duras and Calle put their sensibility for the unconscious to work in their writing and their visual production through strategies such as that of placing a feminine subject at the center of their experiments. Duras and Calle emphasize a reader figure in their work, an unknown other whose position consists in a receptiveness to a traumatic inscription beyond representation. The mark of this inscription at once organizes the text or artwork and undermines the (personal) narrative dimension that is also present in their writing. Attuned to a feminine subject, this figure of the reader, we will see in "(Re)visions of Love" (chapter 4), models a renewed notion of love that in Duras' case relates to what Lacan viewed as the analyst's desire, the subject-supposed-to-know, and the end of analysis; in "Developing *Douleur exquise*: Sophie Calle et al." (chapter 5), the links I develop are to Proust's investigations of the unconscious in aesthetic and libidinal registers in *A la recherche du temps perdu*.

In Duras' and Calle's works, the stuff of the unconscious takes shape in the symptom's always precise sensorial terms, and in a peculiar treatment of words that is less concerned with the production of meaning than with the transmission of sensations, much in the way that nonverbal plastic media can focus on this very undertaking (as is the case in Part I, with Bourgeois and Clark). In terms of sublimation and its ties to the symptom, chapters 4 and 5 highlight the role of the uncanny in aesthetic experience beyond interpretation. Chapter 4 also discusses Lacan's late rethinking of sublimation through the *sinthome*, which he develops with regard to James Joyce's writing, by showing the relevance of a conversation between this concept and Duras' contributions on the letter, the uninterpretable name, and the scopic drive. The latter is examined with Deleuze's concept of the irrational cut in film. Chapter 5 additionally considers primary narcissism with Calle, as a perspective with the potential to rethink the very possibility of relation and to explore its ethics.

"For an Uncanny Ethics of Care" is Part III. Time is already present as a force in some of the artworks examined in earlier chapters. For instance, chapter 5 shows that Sophie Calle's *Douleur exquise* attunes the present investigation of the aesthetic clinic to the dimension of time, through photography, narrative, installation, and their intersections. For Lygia Clark in chapter 3, the unhinging topological discovery that "the inside is the outside" also had to do with time, in the temporality of "the now." Body, birth, love, and pain are not left behind in this third part of the aesthetic clinic, but instead organized anew, around an aesthetic experience that emerges in the process of "making Time sensible in itself" (*rendre le Temps sensible en soi*). How can such an encounter of "Time in itself," which, Deleuze states, destroys the sensory-motor schema and renders characters "absent from themselves" have to do with an ethics of care, crucial to the aesthetic clinic? How can there be care without selves? "Water, Weather, Words: *Le Temps* with Roni Horn and Clarice Lispector" (chapter 6) turns to this problem with Roni Horn (1955–) and Clarice Lispector (1920–1977), in Horn's *Vatnasafn/Library of Water* (2007) and Lispector's poetic meditation *Água Viva* (1973), to see that the receptiveness that the other artworks required is exactly about this sort of care. In this final chapter, care concerns the question of encounters between human and nonhuman environments, since *le Temps* as Deleuze, Lispector, Horn, Mallarmé, and Cézanne conceive it is also climate, weather, and mood. Cézanne wanted to paint "a passing minute of the world" and this wish gave rise to a task of painting centered on "sensations," which crucially concern aesthetics (as French phenomenology and Deleuze showed) and also (I show) the feminine. My reading of *Vatnasafn/Library of Water* with *Água Viva*, from an experience of dwelling in the installation in Iceland in 2009, allows me to locate the clinical efficacy of aesthetic experience in an opening onto "the instant of the world" as a mode of care that occurs in the passage between sensations and modes of perception that a work of art or a plastic practice can enable.

Part I

The Transvaluation of Health

CHAPTER 1

Louise Bourgeois' Art of Hysteria

1893, 1993, 2018 . . . *à l'infini*

As the centennial of Sigmund Freud and Joseph Breuer's *Studies on Hysteria* approached in the 1990s, hysteria began to make its explicit appearance in Louise Bourgeois' sculptures and drawings. Her decades-long production in these two media already revealed an involvement with psychoanalysis. In 1967–68, for instance, she named her bronze clusters of round and parabolic mounds that evoke penile ends *Unconscious Landscape*. Or consider *Fillette* (1968), a sculpture of a giant male sex organ whose French title means literally "young girl," and whose shape resembles that of the 37.5-centiliter wine flask also known as a "fillette" in France. Its play on words and shapes not only focuses on sexuality, a key issue for psychoanalysis, it also highlights the displacements and condensations through which dreams and parapraxes offer a glimpse of, precisely, an unconscious landscape, where strange confluences between what is usually understood as either male or female take place.[1] The presence of psychoanalysis in her works and writings indicates that she was keenly aware of unconscious processes, so it is not surprising to learn that Bourgeois underwent psychoanalytic treatment between 1952 and

1. Fillette gave Bourgeois a place in the feminist art of the 1970s, though her artistic activity precedes this wave by decades. The sculpture is perhaps most famous due to Robert Mapplethorpe's portraits of Louise (1982), where she playfully posed holding the sculpture in her arms. See Rosalind Krauss, "Louise Bourgeois: Portrait of the Artist as Fillette," in Weiermair, Peter, with Lucy Lippard, Rosalind Krauss, Robert Storr, Thomas McEvilley. Louise Bourgeois (Germany: Frankfurter Kunstverein, 1989), rpt. in Rosalind Krauss, Bachelors (Cambridge, MA & London: MIT Press, 1999).

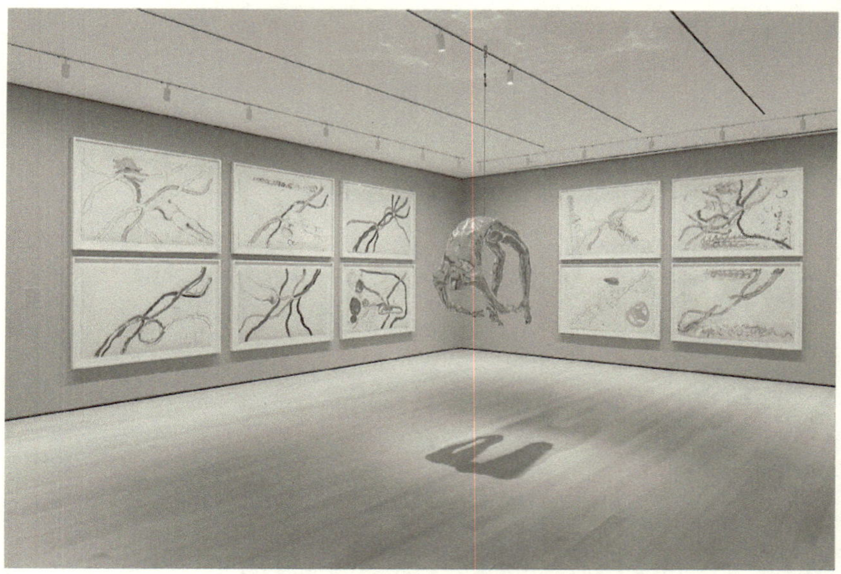

Figure 1.1. Louise Bourgeois, *Arch of Hysteria,* 1993; surrounded by À L'INFINI, 2008.

1985 in New York City.[2] What surprises, instead, is the way in which those processes find specific poetic, plastic, and visual manifestations. At stake in Bourgeois' work with psychoanalysis is a lifelong, intense engagement with the drive that materializes and is converted into graphic and sculptural form.

At MOMA's recent, extensive Louise Bourgeois retrospective (September 24, 2017–January 28, 2018), *Arch of Hysteria* (1993) was suspended exactly at the center of the final exhibit room, surrounded by a display, on three walls, of the very late *À l'infini* (2008), a set of fourteen soft ground etchings with hand additions (figure 1.1). While

2. The more intensive period of her analysis was 1952 to 1966. Bourgeois wrote a diary and intimate reflections about her life, art, and whatever was taking place, from preadolescence to the end, held by the Louise Bourgeois Archive at The Easton Foundation. These documents often mention analysis, the analyst, and problems that seem to be emerging in the treatment. Writings from that intensive period have been gathered and published under the term "psychoanalytic writings." Philip Larratt-Smith (Ed.), *The Return of the Repressed, Vol. II: Psychoanalytic Writings* (London: Violette Editions, 2012).

Bourgeois' headless creation in 1993 recalled, as I said, the centennial of the *Studies on Hysteria*,[3] the sculpture continues to make a powerful aesthetic statement now . . . "to infinity," as the title of the surrounding etchings at the exhibit indicated. Not only does the sculpture continue to matter now, and to infinity, but its statement, hysteria, can be read as speaking about a certain direction and movement ("to infinity"). How does *Arch of Hysteria* respond to the longstanding motif of decapitation that has intrigued both art and psychoanalysis, and to hysteria itself, which can also be discerned throughout the history of art? Inversely, why might hysteria, specifically, when it is so often considered and rejected as an outdated modernist construct, speak to art at the turn of the twenty-first century, and how can it shed light on the function of the aesthetic in contemporary art?

How Do You Relate to a Hummingbird?

Bourgeois declared her wish to turn to hysteria in a striking diary entry on Monday, July 16, 1990:

> Je veux considérer comme sujet:
> l'hystérieguérie—
> l'hystérie intestinale apaisée
> complètement hors de control
> Comment atteindre cette personne
> les gens ne sont pas approchable [*sic*]
> how do you relate to a hummingbird
> La Communication ne s'établie [*sic*] pas au
> niveau du conscious. You like or you do
> not like—no <u>visible</u> reason—plus tu
> parles, moins on te comprend.[4]

3. "On the Psychical Mechanism of Hysterical Phenomena: Preliminary Communication," first published in 1893, is the first section of the *Studies on Hysteria*, 1895. Freud, *SE* II.

4. "*I want to consider as subject: / hysteriahealed– /* the intestinal hysteria appeased / completely out of control / How to reach this person / people are not approachable / how do you relate to a hummingbird / Communication is not established on / the level of the conscious. You like or you do / not like–no <u>visible</u> reason–the more you / speak, the less they understand you." For this and all Louise Bourgeois writings

The note is exemplary of Bourgeois' writing style, first of all in oscillating between French and English since her relocation from France to New York in 1938, and second, in pointing to a seemingly specific situation on her mind at the time of writing that she does not explicitly describe at all. The fact that her earliest journal entries, as a French high school student, already perform this gesture betrays her search for and lifelong cultivation of a space where words and experiences are not restricted to a means of making herself understood by others, and a profound sense of everyday communication as an operation between egos, calculated to remain within what is acceptable, and therefore not taking the risk of true speech. Lacanian psychoanalysis, where hysteria remains highly relevant, calls this the structure of the address, and insists that the analytic situation must call this structure into question, and thus welcome speech beyond an ego narrative, as the analysand discovers how this structure has shaped his/her life and idea of who he/she is.[5]

In Bourgeois' note, readers do not know who "cette personne" ("this person") she wants to "atteindre" ("reach") may be, or if she is instead imagining that others ask themselves this question about her. The note is also exemplary in that it speaks of psychical pain and disturbing feelings of inadequacy. The shift from "appeased intestinal hysteria" to "completely out of control" might appear as an abrupt turn from one situation to its opposite, highlighting the common link of the term "hysteria" in relation to out-of-control behaviors and states of mind. But it may also be that the appeasing of the intestinal malfunction was completely out of Louise's control. Why is it that—after the very first phrase announces a wish to consider "l'hystérieguérie," which translates as "hysteriahealed"—the problem of reaching someone else, the impasse of approachability, relation, communication, and of being understood emerge uncomfortably, in a state that sounds far from healed? One may assume, given Bourgeois' enduring self-analytic habit in her diary, that she was exploring that intestinal complication's link to the relational conflicts, questions, and impasses she proceeds to list, and that what she calls "the hysteria" refers to a symptom that has just disappeared. Yet the number of Bourgeois' works that directly consider hysteria in the

cited in this book: © The Easton Foundation/Licensed by VAGA at ARS, NY. My translations unless otherwise noted.

5. See Jacques Lacan, "The Function and the Field of Speech and Language in Psychoanalysis," in *Écrits*, trans. Bruce Fink (New York: W.W. Norton & Co., 2006).

1990s and the emergence, during this same period, of the affirmation "Art is a Guaranty of Sanity,"[6] which she will repeatedly write on many of her late artworks, suggest that the question of "l'hystérieguérie" is much larger than the passing "intestinal hysteria" she jotted down in her diary that day.

"L'hystérieguérie" seems to concern the impossible problem of "relating to a hummingbird" and of a "Communication" Bourgeois writes in uppercase and implicitly situates on the level of the unconscious; the fact that her artworks are explicitly about hysteria and sanity indicates that the work of art indeed becomes a privileged way to take on "l'hystérieguérie." Perhaps the shift from an initial suffering to that state can be discerned in the difference between two states of suspension Bourgeois puts forth—first in frantic, hummingbird-like flutter and babble in the text, then, still suspended in the air but in precarious stillness, instead, in the polished bronze sculpture that quietly, but also uncannily, reflects the room surrounding it (figure 1.1). So "l'hystérieguérie" and its undertaking imply that hysteria and its cured or healed state remain glued together somehow. The healed state does not simply erase the hysteric symptoms. I wish to explore the crucial question of what health and sanity involve within the space of what I call an aesthetic clinic, a space that privileges the unconscious and the work of jouissance on the drives, rather than the preservation of the pleasure principle, always seeking to restore its lowest possible levels of excitation for the organism. But that question is the object of chapter 2, where *Precious Liquids* (1992) guides the inquiry. First, it is necessary to see how Bourgeois' art invites one to consider, and reconsider with a particular ethics of desire in mind, hysteria's passage across the different modern fields of medicine, psychoanalysis, and visual art, and across different time periods in art (from the Renaissance to late nineteenth-century realism, to Surrealism and Acéphale, to Francis Bacon) and literature (from the Provençal troubadours to Baudelaire).

Bourgeois' own public statements about the logic of her artworks usually proposed an autobiographical narrative with the artist's family romance as its background and explanation. This has resulted in a predominantly biographical presentation of her work and its involvement

6. One of the earliest instances of this statement appears in her diary on August 25, 1991. The same year, she embroidered the phrase on one of the fabric elements in *Cell I* (1991).

with psychoanalysis.[7] But this is not the most forceful account of the potential I discern in her works to transmit sensations, which are not concerned with personal history, and not even about personhood, but instead about transindividual, unconscious desire, that is, about what pushes us beyond limits (of the law, language, culture), to a creative act. The journal entry's insistence on an unapproachable other and on an unconscious "Communication," as well as the ambiguity regarding the subjects engaged here, suggest something broader than the classic Oedipal triangle. The text's awareness that speaking in the social link does not make room for the "hummingbird" is worthy of attention in itself, since it offers a metaphor for a living "thing" that, taking the provisional form of an upset stomach, "hums" incomprehensibly instead of speaking the common language, and flutters frenetically, making it difficult to grasp or to even want to touch. I also see the journal entry as an instigation for thinking the crucial role of hysteria in the work of art. The latter, for Bourgeois, should certainly welcome the intractable hummingbird, whatever its symptoms.

Vital Beheadings

Louise Bourgeois explores the "hysterical arch" posture in different media and techniques, but the human-sized, polished bronze sculpture *Arch of Hysteria* (1993) stands out (figure 1.2). Its long, slender, and headless human body bends back, tracing a dramatic golden bow with its limbs.[8]

7. The MOMA exhibit took a different and interesting approach, in organizing the works to trace the artist's creative process, rather than the childhood traumas. The role of her analysis and its relation to her life, writing, and art are discussed in detail by various authors in *Louise Bourgeois: The Return of the Repressed, Vol. I*. See also compelling, non-Oedipal accounts of Bourgeois' psychoanalytic works in Rosalind Krauss "Louise Bourgeois," and Mignon Nixon *Fantastic Reality: Louise Bourgeois and a Story of Modern Art* (Cambridge, MA and London: MIT Press, 2005).

8. An almost identical version of this piece exists, made with the same mold but in a nonreflective finish of silver nitrate patina. In addition, an armless variation with a less pronounced arch resting on a bed was included in two of Bourgeois' *Cell* installations (*Cell [Arch of Hysteria]*, 1992–93, and *In and Out*, 1995). I will return to these in chapter 2. "Arch of Hysteria" first appeared as a title in a series of drawings, all called *Untitled (Arch of Hysteria)*, made in 1992; one is an abstract piece in ink and watercolor, the others are red figurative gouaches on tracing paper.

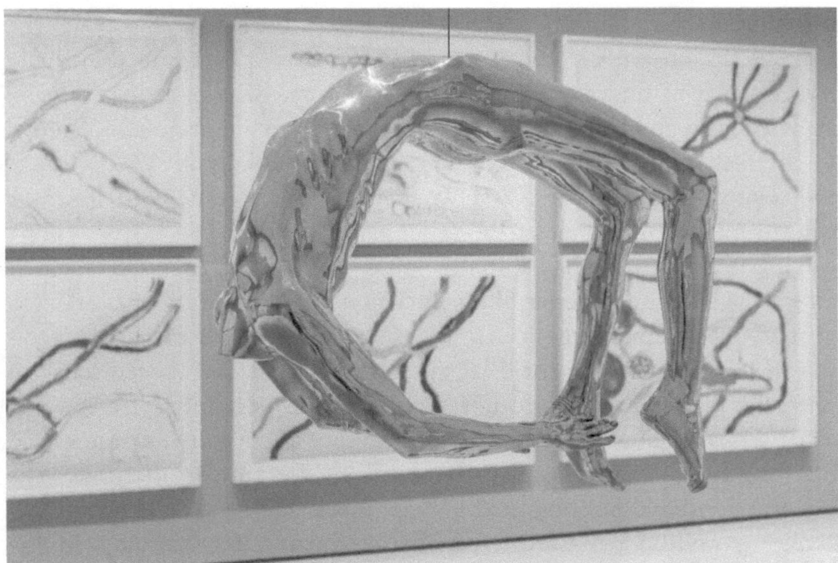

Figure 1.2. Louise Bourgeois, *Arch of Hysteria*, 1993. Installation view of the exhibition "Louise Bourgeois: An Unfolding Portrait," September 24, 2017–January 28, 2018. Photographer: John Wronn. © The Museum of Modern Art/Licensed by SCALA/Art Resource, NY. © 2019 The Easton Foundation/VAGA at ARS, New York.

Arch of Hysteria appears suspended from a single cord attached at the pelvis above most viewers' eye-level, its legs and chest hanging down to viewers' hip-height, approximately. A precarious stillness, distinctive of Bourgeois' sculpture overall,[9] is achieved by hanging the figure, thus allowing the feet to be detached from the ground in this extreme contortion. The delicate ends of the figure's limbs—its toes loosely

In *Triptych for the Red Room* (1994), the arch migrated onto engraving (with aquatint and drypoint), and in 2000 and 2004, when Bourgeois was deeply immersed in textile work, *Arch of Hysteria* reappeared suspended, in different bodies made of fabric, but in a smaller format: *Arch of Hysteria*, 2000 (with a head and arms), *Arch of Hysteria*, 2004 (two versions, male and female; both with a head but no arms), and *Arch of Hysteria*, 2004 (a merged male/female version with no arms but two heads). Plate 19, from a series of prints on cloth, *Self Portrait*, 2009, is also called *Arch of Hysteria*.

9. Some of her *Personages* from the 1940s are very slender figures standing directly on the floor, without a base, and the *Spiders* stand on very delicate legs; each is a work of complicated balance between the eight limbs.

pointing down, its fingers stretching back as though trying to reach the ankles—become more prominent, as the parts of the figure that could try to touch or find a point of support on something else. In any case, they would search blindly. But this deliberate precariousness is also due to the fact that the whole sculpture could potentially sway, or spin, as the related, small bronze *Spiral Woman* (1984) suggests, with its thick whorl replacing the upper torso and head.[10]

The condensations I initially pointed out in the title and shape of *Fillette* to show the presence of psychoanalytic thought in Bourgeois' work were also a common practice to surrealist artists, whose world Bourgeois was in touch with since the 1930s in Paris.[11] Her figures indeed speak to surrealist ideas, yet they are not limited to the principles of an avant-garde whose highest authority, André Breton, never fully acknowledged her (and her grievance against the sexist artistic milieu instantiates the hysteric's unstable position in the social link). The missing head of *Arch* evokes a well-known surrealist motif, prominent, for instance, in the *Acéphale* journal and secret society of the same name ("acephalous") that included Georges Bataille, Pierre Klossowski, and André Masson, and in Max Ernst's *La femme 100 têtes* (1929) ("The hundred-headed woman," a French pun for "the headless woman"). Coincidentally, perhaps, the diary entry one day before Bourgeois' declaration to consider "l'hystérieguérie," on Sunday, July 15, 1990, plays, like Ernst, on the homophony between "100" ("cent") and "sans":

> mes cent riens
> mes sans rien
> (je suis sans rien
> double negative)
> je suis rien, je n'ai rien[12]
> no thing

10. Both *Arch* and *Spiral Woman* lead back to an experiment with a Barbie doll that Bourgeois hung from its hair, then tried to hang horizontally and force into a backbend by immersing it in clay (*Femme maison*, 1982). I come back to this later in this chapter. *Femme maison* was also the title of several paintings from the 1940s.

11. Nixon describes Bourgeois' conflicted relationship to the surrealists in detail in chapter 1 of *Fantastic Reality*, offering a Kleinian discussion of Bourgeois' art as a feminist, anti-oedipal "rebuttal of surrealism."

12. *my one hundred nothings / my without nothings / (I am without nothing /* double negative*) / I am nothing, I have nothing*

no body
no where
no one

In this text the proliferation ("100") and lack ("sans" "without") that come together in the same phoneme are linked to "rien" "nothing," where a meeting of opposites also takes place, since in its plural form, "riens" means unimportant trinkets or words.[13] This again strikes one as a very Freudian move, given the analyst's strategy of attending to "unconsidered trifles"[14] both in the consultation room and in reading an artwork, such as Michelangelo's *Moses* sculpture. The text fluctuates between "nothing," as trivial details, and an important problem that the "double negative" (which is also the title of a 1963 Bourgeois sculpture that resembles *Unconscious Landscape* [1967–68]) "sans rien" "without nothing" allows to emerge, concerned with a real sense—bodily, spatial, relational—of "being nothing" and "having nothing" that may be experienced as lack and excess all at once, "à l'infini." This profound sense surpasses the technical concern of producing a witty condensation of images, and suggests the hysterical, at times anguished standpoint from which Bourgeois engages with the unconscious.

Bataille's vision with Acéphale was more extreme than Breton's surrealism (their collaboration ended in 1929), and might have emerged from an experience closer to the excessive lack of limits Bourgeois describes.[15] Masson illustrates the cover of the *Acéphale* journal with a beheaded male nude in the posture of Leonardo's Vitruvian man, featuring a skull in the place of the genitals. Indeed, the Nietzschean anti-fascist group seeks to ground action and thought on the Dionysian affirmation of the life of the drives rather than reason. If the Renaissance figure insisted on man as "the measure of all things," the secret society say "we must become totally other [devenir tout autres] or to cease to be."[16]

13. The pluralized "nothing" is not idiomatic in English, with the suggestive exception of the expression "sweet nothings."

14. Freud, *SE* XIII, 222.

15. Bataille's aesthetic contribution in *Documents*, another journal project, for rethinking contemporary art in the de-sublimating terms of the "informe," was explored by Rosalind Krauss and Yve-Alain Bois in *L'informe: Mode d'emploi* (Paris: Éditions du Centre Pompidou, 1999).

16. Bataille, "La conjuration sacrée" *Acéphale*, 1 (June 1936): np.

The return of hysteria Bourgeois advances in the 1990s is not a decades-delayed reaction to ideas first considered in 1930s experimental art and theory. Rather, the return stems from the unconscious as the site of what has never been said, and which therefore cannot have much to do with novelty as an ideal or a demand in the art world, or in science, the context in which psychoanalysis first emerged. Bourgeois, like Bataille, instead speaks from the perspective of the subject of the drive.[17] Both artists bear witness to the life of the drives, attending to something like a hysterical or spiritual conversion—from a sense of existence as "an agitated void" to what Bataille calls an "ecstasy and ecstatic love,"[18] which Bourgeois materializes. As Griselda Pollock has aptly noted in her analysis of Bourgeois' sculpture and traumatic past, hysteria at its core has to do with "non-being, being nothing while not dead, since the subject has to live on with the feeling of having become nothing."[19] Pollock discerns this feeling in Bourgeois' statement on the necessity of sculpting—"Every day you have to abandon your past or accept it and then if you cannot accept it you become a sculptor."[20] It concerns the fact that "some dimension of that past is so excessive that it only registers as dangerous rage."[21] That dimension, then, cannot be located in the past empirically, but is something in the body. It is interesting to consider that Freud is led by a sculpture to this very reflection in "The *Moses* of Michelangelo," insofar as the "rage and indignation"[22] that course through Moses' body and fascinate Freud as viewer cannot

17. This perspective is unrecognized by science and some of the institutions that develop around works of art, as a result of the structure of the scientific paradigm of objectivity. The latter allows, for instance, neuroscience to investigate "the mind" in a way that discards the role of unconscious subjective freedom in an individual's constitution and development. In art, the scientific paradigm that informed the history of art discipline, with Panofsky, as Didi-Huberman has explained, has a similar effect of missing the subject. See Georges Didi-Huberman, *Devant l'image: Question posée aux fins d'une histoire de l'art* (Paris: Les Éditions de Minuit, 1990).

18. Bataille, "La conjuration sacrée," np.

19. Pollock, *After-affects*, 105.

20. Bourgeois, "Child Abuse," in *Artforum*, 20.4 (December 1982): 47; quoted in Pollock, 104.

21. Pollock, 105.

22. Freud, *SE* XIII, 230.

be contained within the biblical narrative, whose sequence of events is illogical,[23] and ultimately leads to an impossible encounter with God on Mount Sinai as the origin of the new Tables of the Law Moses brings to the Israelites. The question is, how does this rage reach beauty, or "ecstatic love"?

It may depend on the act that asserts such a transformation, as well as on positions taken in the unconscious. And this is why hysteria is so important. Bourgeois' note is about a violent shift between "a hundred" and "zero" that bypasses unity: literally "no one," quite like the headless-hundred-headed woman of Ernst's title. While the latter names a published, 1929 collage novel, Bourgeois in her journal is taking private notes about something lived, and not yet offering its plastic formulation. Yet her words already speak to the specificity of hysteria that the artworks render in distilled form. *Arch*, for instance, conveys the loss, or the possession of "a nothing" with its missing head, marking, at once, through this absent body part, a split from the scene of shared reality. At the same time, the contorted figure materializes a bodily energy that, however excessive, draws an elegant bow, beyond the capacity of the most flexible human spine.[24]

Hysterics, Women, and Unintelligible Artists

A day after the meditation on "cent riens," then, the "hystérieguérie" journal entry announces an important theme in Bourgeois' late production by intertwining an unstable body and the effects of language, including, crucially, that of its inadequacy to communicate a "double negative: sans rien" bodily experience. Its result is a sense of not connecting with others, of being unintelligible and potentially disliked. In this intimate set of dissatisfactions, Bourgeois already presents distinctive traits of what psychoanalysis sees as the psychical structure of hysteria, which is not a disorder, but instead an unconscious mode of relation to the Other that gives this subject a position from which it justifies its existence. Some part of the hysteric's being seems, in her own experience, to go

23. Freud, 232.

24. I refer to the account of this sculpture's making later in this chapter.

unnamed by the culture that gives access to consciousness; the hysteric thus misinterprets the structural defect in language as a "bad" thing within that is unacceptable to others.[25]

It should be recalled that "hysteric" and "woman" are not synonyms, since the hysterical unconscious structure does not simply result from a female gender identity, even if sexual difference plays an important role in both the hysterical and obsessional neuroses. Yet the hysterics in Paris and Vienna at the turn of the century were very frequently women (as they frequently still are in the clinical setting), and the reference to female anatomy in the term "hysteria," already used by Hippocrates in Ancient Greece as the "trouble of the wandering womb," suggests a connection to female sexuality, precisely in excess of organic functions, since the myth is that the womb "wanders" out of place when it is empty, and this causes all sorts of emotional, physical, and certainly social disturbances.[26] But perhaps it could also be a cause for aesthetic expression.

In this book's Introduction, I indicated Freud's view of women as less capable of sublimation, for both external and internal reasons, whereas Calle, and the way in which her *Wedding Dress* (1999) invites us to reread Dora's case, suggest the hysteric girl's disposition toward sublimation. Bourgeois' *Arch* recalls that the birth of modern hysteria in fact relied on creative, theatrical women, as I will show in more detail. Freud himself associated what he saw in hysteric women to the work of artists, which he certainly admires: "hysterics are undoubtedly imaginative artists, even if they express their phantasies *mimetically* in the main and without considering their intelligibility to other people."[27] Freud criticizes the hysterics' opaque style—although that opacity, exactly, is the fuel of his own creative work in the clinic and in theory—and their

25. The construction of an "ideal ego" for the hysteric rests on the mistake that if only she can produce herself as an adequate object for the Other, she will find a way to survive. Instead, her entry into the seduction fantasy represses the subject. For a full discussion of this process, see Lucie Cantin, "The Borderline, or The Impossibility of Producing a Negotiable Form in the Social Bond for the Return of the Censored," trans. Mike Standish, *Konturen* III (2010), 186–201.

26. Paul-Laurent Assoun in *Le pervers et la femme* (Paris: Anthropos, 1989) traces a genealogy of the hysteric woman in Western culture, from "sorceress" to "possessed" to ill or melancholic, with Racine's Phèdre figure in mind.

27. Freud, *SE* XVII, 261. Freud in this passage is showing that "the forms assumed by the different neuroses echoed the most highly admired productions of our culture" (261).

predominantly mimetic strategies with their "phantasies." Expressions of unconscious fantasies arise in Freud's clinic in the form of symptoms, performing, in distorted ways, such fantasies with some element that remains unacknowledgeable by prevalent cultural norms and ideals.

The *arc de cercle* pose that Bourgeois' *Arch of Hysteria* recreates is an exemplary performance of this sort, though its emergence precedes the analytic couch, and the more current notion of the fantasy that supports my reading (which distinguishes between the concerns with adequacy of the ideal ego and the fundamental fantasy, without referent in reality, from which an aesthetic object can emerge). In his 1908 paper on hysterical attacks, Freud suggested that "the well-known *arc de cercle*" might be "an energetic repudiation like this, through antagonistic innervation, of a posture of the body that is suitable for sexual intercourse."[28] It is Freud's interpretation of the pose here that appears "mimetic," limited to representing sexual intercourse in a distorted way, as its opposite. But not only is the hysteric symptom not limited to the attacks psychiatrist and neurologist Jean-Martin Charcot examined and classified in the 1870s, giving this and other poses their official name; the later development of the concept of the fantasy in psychoanalysis also comes to embrace the non-mimetic core of unintelligibility Freud instead complains about here.[29] In a short text that accompanies an engraving from *He Disappeared into Complete Silence* (1947), Bourgeois returns to this problem of communicating jouissance: "Once a man was telling a story, it was a very good story too, and it made him very happy, but he told it so fast that nobody understood it."[30] Lacan writes in 1976 that when "the space of a lapse/slip no longer carries any meaning (or interpretation), only then one is sure that one is in the unconscious."[31] And this structural conception of the fantasy as mental representation

28. Freud, *SE* IX: 230.

29. Claude Landman recalls Freud's early idea, in 1897, that "Phantasien" relate to primal scenes (*Urszene*) by distorting them, and that these primal scenes always have to do with the jouissance of a father and its traumatic incidence in the subject. "Le noeud du fantasme," *La revue lacanienne* 6.1 (2010): 27–35.

30. Louise Bourgeois, *He Disappeared into Complete Silence* (New York, published by the artist, 1947), Plate 3. Text transcription from www.moma.org/collection/works/15383.

31. Jacques Lacan, "Préface à l'édition anglaise des *Écrits*" (1976). Autres *Écrits* (Paris: Seuil, 2001), 571.

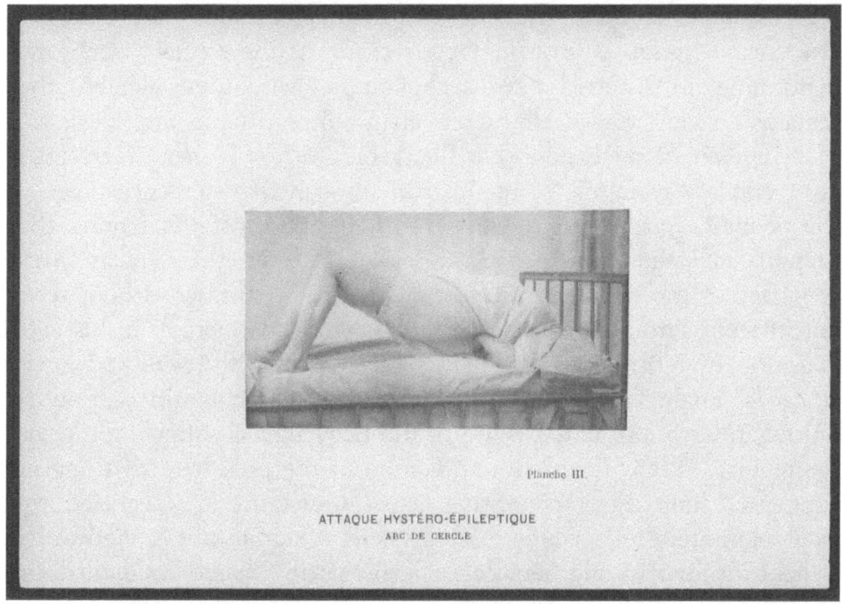

Figure 1.3. *Attaque Hystéro-Épileptique. Arc de Cercle*, 1880. Photographic plate in *Iconographie Photographique de la Salpêtrière, vol.* 3. Courtesy of the Harvey Cushing/John Hay Whitney Medical Library.

that is an effect of jouissance and has no available referent in language[32] shares its criterion with modern literature and art, which were emerging exactly during this late nineteenth-century moment of studying "la grande hystérie"—Baudelaire's and Mallarmé's poetry, or Kandinsky's abstract expressionism are some examples of this (more on Baudelaire later). Whereas Freud's taste in art was less experimental, Bourgeois inherits this inner, nonrepresentational, modernist grounding for her work.

Resurrections and Revelations

One could say, however, that Bourgeois' sculpture does "mime" or represent, and in a successfully intelligible way, an event that took place in

32. See this book's Introduction, particularly the section "Beyond the Limits of Culture."

the late nineteenth century. The pose that gives *Arch of Hysteria* its title makes clear that the term "hysteria" in Bourgeois' art directly points back to French nineteenth-century medical history, where the condition was investigated by Charcot at the Salpêtrière Hospital, which he directed between 1862 and 1893. These were also crucial years in the history of photography, and it played an important role in documenting the hysterical attacks observed in women, especially, at the Salpêtrière.[33] These documents feature the *arc de cercle* Bourgeois transposes from photography into sculpture. Chronophotography betrayed the fin-de-siècle fascination with the photographic image's ability to document the transformations of bodies in motion, and to freeze this phenomenon in still images. This was particularly helpful for Charcot's research on an illness that only manifested itself in intermittent, momentary attacks, and was otherwise invisible. Didi-Huberman points out about photography that "in its act—the shot—it is dealing with the *this*, *das Diese*: the here and the now."[34] Its violence concerns the way in which it allows another moment to interfere in the viewing present, "a punctual resurrection."[35] Yet it remains a flat image, confined to its paper support. Instead, the suspended, three-dimensional *Arch* eliminates the distance the photograph offers, mediating between the phenomenon in the image and a later moment of viewing.[36] Not only is the sculpted body materially in the room with its viewer, but its immobility might be disrupted by one's movements, which the metallic surface reflects. Indeed, although its head is missing, the suspended body might not only hang but also levitate, as in some paintings of miraculous resurrections.[37] Perhaps this, too, is the potential of hanging Bourgeois utilized, since, she found, it "allows things to turn

33. Georges Didi-Huberman has stressed that the birth of photography and the domain of the visual were inextricable from hysteria's invention at the end of the nineteenth century. See *Invention of Hysteria: Charcot and the Iconography of the Salpêtrière*, trans. Alisa Hartz (Cambridge, MA & London: MIT Press, 2003). Olivier Walusinski considers influences from academic art in Bourneville's photography. See "The Girls of the Salpêtrière," *Hysteria: The Rise of an Enigma*, ed. J. Bogousslavsky (Basel: Karger, 2014): 65–77, 69.

34. Didi-Huberman, *Invention of Hysteria*, 106.

35. Didi-Huberman, *Invention*, 106.

36. I return to photography as a medium with Roland Barthes's theory in chapter 5.

37. Paolo Veronese's *Resurrection of Christ* (ca. 1570), or El Greco's *Assumption of the Virgin Mary* (1577) come to mind.

around."[38] Whereas viewers of the *Iconographie* photographs safely look at images of hysteric bodies shot at the Salpêtrière, in *Arch* it is the viewers who appear and might be blinded by the flashing metal and their own distorted image on the sculpture's surface.

The father of neurology made it a point to track down the cause of hysteria and to find the seat of a lesion, relying on autopsies of hysterical patients to do so. Given the difficulty in finding anything, he eventually proposed the idea of a lesion of the cortex, "a 'dynamic lesion,' he said, physiological and not anatomical, 'elusive, changeable, always prone to disappear.' "[39] The ambition of visibility was thus central to his activities, where the elusiveness and ungraspability of the hysteric trait seemed to surge up repeatedly.

The *arc de cercle* pose was also sketched and painted at the time of Charcot's experiments. *Une leçon clinique à la Salpêtrière* is a realist 1887 painting by André Brouillet, a lithograph of which was owned by Freud, whose six-month internship at the Paris hospital in 1885 was decisive to his invention of psychoanalysis. The painting documents Charcot's "Tuesday lessons," during which, hypnotized by the doctor seeking to trigger hysterical attacks for the eyes of a specialized audience made up of (male) doctors and medical students, women such as Marie "Blanche" Wittman would seem to lose their heads.

Behind the lesson's attentive spectators and across from the entranced "Blanche"—whose clenched fists clash with the peacefully closed eyes and vague smile across a face turned toward the viewers of the canvas—a large sketch by Paul Richer hangs from the wall and repeats, in a more extreme version, Blanche's arched back and back-tilted head. Richer, an anatomist and sculptor in Charcot's service, helped with the ambitious project of classifying what the psychiatrist had identified as the different phases of a hysterical attack[40] in synoptic "tableaux," while Paul Régnard and Désiré Bourneville developed the photographs for the *Iconographie Photographique de la Salpêtrière* between 1875 and 1880.

38. In Nixon, *Fantastic Reality*, 170.

39. Charcot, *Clinique des Maladies I*, in Didi-Huberman, *Invention*, 77.

40. He divided the attack into four specific *périodes* or phases: *épiléptoide*, *de clownisme* (or, Freud and Breuer explain, "of large movements," such as the *arc de cercle*), *des attitudes passionnelles* ("hallucinatory," to Freud and Breuer), and finally *de délire*. Freud, *SE* II, 13.

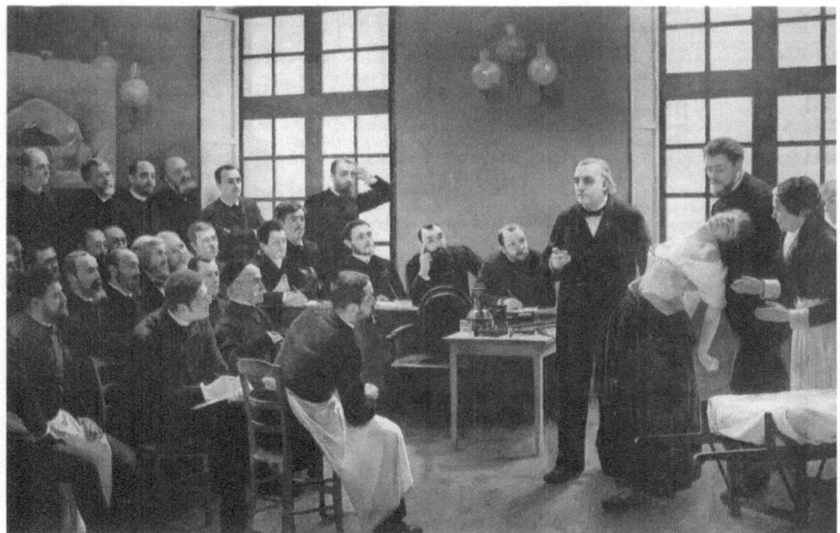

Figure 1.4. André Brouillet, *Une Leçon Clinique à la Salpêtrière*, 1887. Photograph from original oil painting; 290 × 430 cm (public domain).

As Didi-Huberman has observed in his detailed study of the *Iconography* during this period, "it just so happens" that it "does not offer a single portrait of a man,"[41] since male inpatients were not admitted to the Salpêtrière until 1881. Brouillet's painting captures well the gendered dynamics and the male gazes over a female body that seems to have surrendered self-control. While the left fist and twisted foot indicate her impairment, the décolleté exposing glowing, young-seeming skin, along with the relaxed face and arched back resting on male hands insinuate an erotic side of the scene.[42] The third of the four phases in a hysterical attack was called "attitudes passionnelles," which included "eroticism" and "ecstasy." The painting does not seem restricted to the official tableau's sequence, and thus succeeds in making visible the crucial relational dimension of Charcot's object of study. The poses and states collected in the tables and plates had a strange status, since the idea was that performing them involved losing control over and

41. Didi-Huberman, *Invention*, 80.

42. Didi-Huberman shows how this crucial aspect in Charcot's invention of hysteria as a psychiatric condition is denied.

even awareness of one's body. The use of hypnosis to trigger attacks on demand and the ambition of properly documenting them with a camera obviously implicate the specialists who conduct the experiments in the logic of hysteria. The knowledge that concerned the French psychiatrist, who saw himself as "un visuel" ("a visual type),"[43] was caught up in a dialectic of visuality that is thus indeed central to something one could call "passional," insofar as it involves the effects of looking at and being seen by another, although one might say this was his own blind spot.

Another perspective on Bourgeois' *Arch* comes forth upon looking at Brouillet's painting of Blanche with a doctor behind her, supporting her weight. This couple evoke certain *Pietà* works, such as Michelangelo's marble sculpture from 1498–99, where Mary sits, looking down compassionately at her dead son and holding his upper back, her hand emerging forth from his underarm, as his head rests on the crease of her folded arm. Similarly, in Brouillet's painting Blanche's head and upper back soften, held by a doctor's forearm and hand (with fingertips placed along the contour of her left breast). In Bourgeois' *Arch* it is instead the loose, dangling state of the legs and feet, but also the extended fingers, that evoke Michelangelo's *Pietà*. Christ's thighs rest over Mary's lap, while his calves and feet descend effortlessly, like his extended right arm onto a fold of her long robe. *Pietà* brings to mind one of the late formulations Bourgeois came up with: "Le mot pitié m'a apaisée" ("The word pity appeased me").[44] Is the change from soft languor to that "extreme tension"[45] in the back of Bourgeois' figure another conscious body to support its weight? "The base disappears," Bourgeois pointed out, reflecting on the effects of hanging (in Nixon, *Fantastic Reality*, 170). The result is that, without an external limit, the upper body of *Arch* keeps diving further and further back.

---

43. Cited in Didi-Huberman, *Invention*, 26.

44. This phrase composes a 2002 drawing (red ink and pencil on paper) with the same title.

45. *Extreme Tension* is the title of a 2007 series of etchings and mixed media on paper by Bourgeois. In the first of its eleven panels, two pairs of red, extremely long arms with extended hands stretch up to the top of the page, while the words "Extreme Tension" appear handwritten at the center. Other panels name different body parts, or physical symptoms, such as "the pains and cramps," "palpitations," and "the hot flashes," and feature additional elongated drawings that suggest nerve endings and pins. The text for this series was taken from a loose sheet of writing by Bourgeois, ca. 1959 (LB-0768).

Hysterical Expression beyond the Moral World

In 1928, Breton and Aragon published "Le cinquantenaire de l'hystérie"[46] in their journal *La révolution surréaliste*, an article celebrating the fiftieth anniversary of hysteria, which they viewed as "the greatest poetic discovery of the end of the 19th century," proposing that it be reconsidered "as a supreme means of expression," rather than as "a pathological phenomenon."[47] One readily agrees that the significance Bourgeois grants to a pose widely photographed, sketched, and called by psychiatrists at the end of the nineteenth century *arc de cercle* is in this sculpted body expressive, rather than pathological. Yet why, in the first place, do Breton and Aragon find hysteria so great and supreme in poetic and expressive terms?

By resetting Régnard's and Bourneville's 1878 "attitudes passionelles" photographs modeled by the young Salpêtrière inpatient Augustine, the Surrealists in their celebratory text strive to liberate her "passion," that is, her erotic power beyond a pathologizing medical context. They consider hysteria a transhistorical phenomenon that cannot be appropriated by the medical field that discovered it under Charcot. It is true that, unlike surrealist photographers, Régnard and Bourneville do not propose a poetic treatment of photography within the *Iconographie*.[48] Yet the Surrealists do not mention that Charcot with Richer had the ambition to gather and discuss a list of graphic artworks across Western history representing "demonic possessions" from 400 BCE to the eighteenth century, published as *Les démoniaques dans l'art* in 1887.[49] This project reveals both their appropriation of hysteria and their awareness of its expressive powers. To the authors, such possessions were nothing other than a name for hysterical attacks, predating what they viewed as Charcot's own enlightening contribution, which consisted in assigning such phenomena to the medical field, despite their unknown cause.

---

46. Aragon, Louis; Breton, André. "Le cinquantenaire de l'hystérie 1878–1928." *La Révolution surréaliste* (March 15, 1928): 20–22.

47. Aragon and Breton, 22.

48. It is relevant to consider here the point Rosalind Krauss makes on the "perverse feminization" surrealist photography embraces by blurring the image, not only explicitly, through experimental techniques such as double exposure, but also, Krauss, suggests "categorically." See the Introduction to *Bachelors*.

49. Jean-Martin Charcot and Paul Richer. *Les Démoniaques dans l'art* (Paris: Macula, 1984).

If Charcot and Richer in *Les démoniaques* focus on the pathological rather than the expressive, a closer reading of their comments betrays not just awareness of art's expressive goal, but also a sensibility, beyond medical criteria, to the very phenomena Charcot was so involved with. The painters, the authors contend, were fascinated by the expressive potential of such attacks, insofar as they opened up gestural possibilities of the body for representation that were usually limited by formal rules. "Attacks of ecstasy," Charcot writes, were of particular interest to artists for their "plastic aspect"[50] and since, to the artists, the attack "is an expressive pose, a purely passional attitude; all their effort consists of expressing, of externalizing an internal phenomenon, in a word of translating objectively, by physiognomy and corporal gestures, what happens in the regions of the mind unavailable to sight."[51]

Charcot and Richer repeatedly identify the *arc de cercle* pose among the painted figures. Such possessed bodies in fact seemed to lose their heads. According to the psychiatrist, the painters were interested in these bodies from a rigorously formal perspective. Yet it also seems that there was something contagious about this "losing one's head" that extended to the observers. Many painters, the experts in hysterical attacks observe, were inaccurate in their depictions of the contorted bodies, since, Charcot supposed, they sometimes got carried away by expressive interests before these scenes. Wouldn't the doctors triggering the attacks to study them so closely, so deeply, also be susceptible to contagion? The Surrealists insist that this had to be the case. Hysteria is not only transhistorical, but also relational. The medical field that managed hysteria denied the voluptuous dimension of the attacks to which the "specialized" observers were not only *not* immune, but in which they actively participated.[52] That

50. Charcot and Richer, 106.

51. Charcot and Richer, 108.

52. As Didi-Huberman stresses, Freud also calls this omission into question in "On the History of the Psychoanalytic Movement," where Freud recalls overhearing, as a young visiting doctor in Paris, a conversation among specialists in which Charcot says to Brouardel: " 'But in such cases, it's always a question of the genitals—always, always, always' . . . I know that for a moment I was paralyzed with amazement and said to myself: 'Well, but if he knows that, why does he never say so?' " To which Didi-Huberman responds: "because his will to know, to have a few 'plastic regularities' before his eyes, this will to knowledge was also perhaps a will to evasion" (*Invention of Hysteria*, 161). In Alice Winocour's 2012 film *Augustine*, the young patient, no

a proof of existence of hysterical attacks comes through the history of art is no coincidence. Charcot, who convinced so many doctors of his theory by presenting before them hysterical attacks triggered in women under hypnosis, knew well that looking involved a risk. Yet he and his school imagined photography, whose role in composing the medical image of hysteria was crucial, as a kind of shield against a biased, or seduced, view of the phenomena. Thanks to this technology, the psychiatrists believed they could instead achieve an accurate, undistorted grasp on the processes hysterical bodies underwent during attacks.

As one can see in Charcot's collection of artworks and beyond, the extraordinary gesturing he called hysterical, of bodies visibly assailed by invisible forces, captured the interest of a variety of fields through the course of history, with visual art keeping constant track as discursive power shifted away from a religious epistemological framework and toward a medical one. To religious, medical, and plastic-formal concerns, the Surrealists in 1928 add poetic ones, suggesting that they replace medical criteria just as, according to Charcot, the pathological understanding of hysteria replaces demonic possession (but something poetic, something of art, already dwells in Charcot's pathological understanding, and certainly in his practices). Aragon and Breton cite, as the latest medical word on hysteria, Joseph Babinski, a neurologist and favorite student of Charcot's, who in 1909 published a study that opposed and revised some of his teacher's views on the illness, which he renames as "pithianism": "Hysteria is a pathological state that manifests itself by troubles that can be reproduced under suggestion, in certain subjects, with perfect precision, and that are prone to disappear under the influence of persuasion (counter-suggestion) alone."[53]

Breton and Aragon seem to approve of Babinski's acknowledgement of hysteria's relational nature, and the poetic criterion they propose in their surrealist intervention views hysteria as pithy, too, though not pathological. They define it as "a mental *state*" (not disorder) "grounded on the need for reciprocal seduction," which is "characterized by the subversion of the relationships that are established between the subject

longer suffering from partial numbness, fakes an epileptic attack for Charcot at a make or break lecture, which is followed by a sex scene between her and the doctor, after which the film ends, when Augustine runs away from the hospital.

53. Aragon and Breton, "Le Cinquantenaire . . . ," 22.

and the moral world, which he [*il*] believes to practically depend on."[54] They end by stating that it can be considered "a supreme means of expression."[55] Their point on "reciprocal seduction" is that the medical powers of suggestion concern the needs of the patients and the doctors using this method on the patients, "whose type" is that of "the delicious Augustine."[56] Aragon and Breton provocatively ask Freud if he remembers, from his six-month internship, what went on at the Salpêtrière, denouncing the hypocrisy of its practitioners, concerning their own sexual encounters with the female patients, according to testimonies by some of the latter.[57]

The Surrealists, however, are not interested in laying bare the power dynamics between genders with this commentary; after all, they evoke the sexual encounters between doctors and patients by speaking of the latter "confusing their professional duties with their taste for love."[58] If hysteria is so supreme as a form of expression from a surrealist viewpoint, it is because it manifests a passionate intensity beyond "the moral world" and society. The hysteric body seems to guide the aesthetic criterion for Surrealism, leading Aragon in 1934 to famously proclaim "la beauté sera convulsive, ou ne sera pas" ("Beauty will be convulsive or will not be").[59] While the Surrealists certainly considered Freud's invention of the unconscious, which is more than a matter of inhibition of sexual impulses to adapt to a civilization founded on taboos, their 1928 article's approach to this subversive, sexual, passional intensity in the hysteric's body may make it seem to be a problem only in prudish social contexts, an energy that merely needs to be released and celebrated to escape pathological stigma.

---

54. Aragon and Breton, 22, my emphasis.

55. Aragon and Breton, 22.

56. Aragon and Breton, 20.

57. Aragon and Breton, 20. Jane Avril, for example, a dancer at the Moulin Rouge who spent two years in the hospital and published an autobiography in the 1930s in feuilletons, mentions the affairs some of the girls had with the doctors, and the resulting pregnancies. Avril, *Mes mémoires*, cited in Olivier Walusinski, "Les filles de la Salpêtrière," *Frontiers of Neurology and Neuroscience* 33 (2014).

58. Aragon and Breton, 20.

59. André Breton, *Minotaure*, no. 5 (1934): 8–15, 10.

Other Tableaux: "À Baudelaire" "À une passante"

Beyond celebrating and acknowledging enjoyment from hysterical or histrionic expressiveness, Louise Bourgeois' works engage in the construction of a true aesthetic clinic, which indeed surpasses the moral world, but in order to develop an ethics of desire with the drive. This means, first of all, that while the artist's hysterical arches do point back to, or "mime" a specific set of nineteenth-century medical and visual practices where the term was redefined, the *Arch of Hysteria* (1993) sculpted and suspended in space is, as I have previously mentioned, nowhere to be located in an empirical past. Instead, as a unique event, it points to "an inward passion" such as the one Freud detects in Michelangelo's *Moses*,[60] that is to say, a drive. The latter "does not arise from the external world but from within the organism itself,"[61] such that "no flight can avail against it."[62] Sculpture can remarkably bring an "inner" drive into space, as a shaped mass that modifies its surroundings. By insisting on the drive's real quality, beyond shared reality, I do not seek to minimize the suffering of the hysteric inpatients at the Salpêtrière, or Bourgeois' own childhood, during which, like Dora, she witnessed her father's sexual affair with her English teacher and nanny.[63] Although Bourgeois' art confronts the gendered power dynamics in which a certain modern portrait of the female psyche emerged, its relevance cannot be limited to a complaint or condemnation. Beyond this necessary confrontation, which, for all its advocacy of sexual liberation, the surrealist celebration of hysteria does not escape, lies the poetic power the Surrealists

60. Freud, *SE* XIII, 233.

61. Although Freud writes that a drive arises "within the organism," to distinguish it from stimuli, the drive is not merely an action of organic instincts; precisely in exceeding them the drive is felt as a displeasure that cannot be fled, as one would flee an unpleasant stimulus in the environment.

62. Freud, *SE* XIV, 118.

63. Bourgeois explores these memories in the photo essay "Child Abuse," *Artforum*, 20.4 (December 1982): 40–47. For a comparison to the Dora case, see Nixon, *Fantastic Reality*. Guided by a case study that bears significant resemblance to Bourgeois' family romance, Marie-Hélène Brousse takes another approach to the question of hysteria and sublimation, by way of Lacan's concept of the *sinthome* in "Hysteria and Sinthome," *The Later Lacan* (Albany: SUNY Press, 2007).

sought, but did not render by merely reprinting Augustine's *attitudes passionnelles*.[64]

How might the hysteric's passionate intensity and its contagiousness find poetic expression? An aesthetic clinic must engage with this problem. Bourgeois' art invites observers to take the standpoint of the hysteric, as a position for the aesthetic experiences her work enables.[65] By this standpoint I do not only mean a female, morally restricted and socially limited Victorian character (or even its contemporary edition), and certainly not an acrobatic performer of Charcotian hysterical attacks; rather, the hysteric upholds a psychic and aesthetic attitude curious about something felt that resists symbolization[66] and that psychoanalytic logic situates as feminine.

Undoubtedly, from a psychoanalytic viewpoint the hysteric's unresolved position has to do with being seen, loved, needed by an imaginary Other, too; this makes hysterics susceptible to the "mutual seduction" and to "suggestion" by whomever embodies that Other at a given moment. Their persistent feeling of "being nothing" (as Bourgeois' note put it earlier) leads them to always go further in their attempts to seduce. Yet the unsymbolizable feminine I am invoking is something different from the dynamics of seduction Charcot's service suppressed and the Surrealists instead celebrated. In my discussion on the feminine in this book's Introduction (with Freud, Sophie Calle, and Dora), I proposed that the feminine is fundamentally at odds with the ego and the enjoyment of the organ that dominates the cultural demands of sex. The feminine sides instead with the drive, however painful this may be to the ego.

A poet such as Baudelaire, who like Bourgeois had a journal-writing practice, and who had been considered by both journalists and doctors

64. As Nixon puts it, "Bourgeois acted on surrealism . . . to expose the 'epistemological fantasies' of patriarchal culture residual even in the avant-garde's most insistently antitraditional, countercultural movement." *Fantastic Reality*, 42.

65. Donald Kuspit notes that in her February 22, 1949, journal entry, Bourgeois' "identified herself as a hysteric." See "Louise Bourgeois in Psychoanalysis with Henry Lowenfeld." *Louise Bourgeois: The Return of the Repressed*, Vol. I, 24.

66. The dialogue between the Surrealists, whose definition includes several related elements (desire, sexual fantasy, the other, the moral world), and Lacan, who was involved with them in the 1930s, is implicit in his notions of psychosis, hysteria, and perversion as something more than illnesses of which to rid the subject. More on Lacan and surrealism shortly.

as "hysteric,"[67] had an intimate sense of this tension between drive and ego, as she knew. In a 1994 note on her compulsion of helping others, defending the weak, and searching for reparable objects at auctions (all useful, perhaps, against the feeling of being nothing), Bourgeois declares her kinship with the poet: "Je ne trouve les sentiments exprimés ici que dans / la poésie de Baudelaire" ("I only find the feelings here expressed in / Baudelaire's poetry").[68] In another loose sheet from circa 1961, where Louise reflects, through a "dramatic . . . black wood statue," upon the "inner conflict" between the "effort or élan or a rush from the id" and the "effort to curb instincts," she writes: "Baudelaire angoissé: 'J'ai senti passer / aujourd'hui le souffle' . . ." ("Baudelaire anguished: 'Today I felt the wind pass' . . ."), alluding to a loose sheet of Baudelaire's, intended for his autobiographical project.[69] The whole passage from the latter is remarkably on target:

> Au moral comme au physique, j'ai toujours eu la sensation du gouffre, non seulement du gouffre du sommeil, mais du gouffre de l'action, du rêve, du souvenir, du désir, du regret, du remord, du beau, du nombre, etc.
>
> J'ai cultivé mon hystérie avec jouissance et terreur. Maintenant j'ai toujours le vertige, et aujourd'hui 23 janvier 1862, j'ai subi un singulier avertissement, j'ai senti passer sur moi le *vent de l'aile de l'imbécillité*.[70]

67. See Charles Baudelaire, *Fusées. Mon coeur mis à nu. La Belgique déshabillée*, ed. André Guyaux (Paris: Gallimard, 1956), 581, n2.

68. Loose sheet of writing, c. 1994; LB-0796. Bourgeois mentioned Baudelaire in her writings across different periods, referring to him as "contrary of eternity" (diary entry, December 28, 1951), and "Prince of the Macabre" (loose sheet of writing, c, 1996; LB-0054). He is a poet who "knows and speaks of chaos" (loose sheet of writing, May 11, 1962; LB-0511: "Les poètes [Baudelaire] / connaissent et parle du / chaos." The verb agreement oscillates, referring to poets [plural], and Baudelaire [singular].). She refers to his "attraction to the morbid" (diary entry, January 6, 1993); and his "taste for ruins, and nostalgia" (diary entry, June 27, 1990; diary entry, January 6, 1993.)

69. Loose sheet of writing, c. 1961; LB-0234. I am grateful to Richard Sieburth and Françoise Gramet, translators of Bourgeois' writings for The Easton Foundation, who tracked down and pointed to this reference in the translated document.

70. In the moral as in the physical, I always had the sensation of the abyss, not only the abyss of sleep, but the abyss of action, of the dream, of memory, of desire, of regret, of remorse, of the beautiful, of numbers, etc.

The "moral and physical" sensation of the abyss, like the unique "wind of the wing of imbecility" wafting through (as Baudelaire's fear of his own mind's ceasing to function) speak to the hysteric's sense of "being nothing." But there is something in turning the suffering around, or the abyss inside out, to the simultaneously joyous and terrifying cultivation of one's "hysteria," a word in Baudelaire's time closely related to "la volupté,"[71] so dear to the poet.[72]

The *tableaux* of an aesthetic clinic must be very different from the synoptic "tableaux" through which Charcot and Richer charted poses into four phases. A very late, large Louise Bourgeois etching with hand additions bears the title/dedication *À Baudelaire* (2008) (figure 1.5).[73] Its mass of curved lines suggests a stemless flower, whose calyx wraps around three fleshy groups of lanceolate petals "turning inward," according to Bourgeois. The figure and title invite a brief turn to *Les fleurs du mal*, particularly to "À une passante" ("To a Woman Passing By"), one of Baudelaire's *Tableaux parisiens* that, like Bourgeois' drawing, is addressed to someone.[74] Through its title's dedication, the poem makes the gesture of offering itself as a gift to a woman passing by. This gift is a poem, and the poem, a "flower"—"of evil" or of fresh-cut pain, since "mal" can be both of these in French (and Baudelaire in his dedication for the entire collection of poems refers to his poems as "fleurs maladives" ["sickly flowers"]). The network of signifiers these titles weave calls

I cultivated my hysteria with jouissance and terror. Now I am always dizzy, and today, January 23rd 1862, I felt a singular warning, I felt the wind of the wing of imbecility passing over me (Baudelaire, F 86, *Fusées*, 85).

71. The *Trésor de la langue française* indicates the use of « hystérie » as « excitation, exaltation », by Sainte-Beuve in *Volupté*.

72. In "L'invitation au voyage" ("The invitation to the voyage"), for example, the destination to which the speaker invites his beloved "child, sister" ("Mon enfant, ma soeur") is the site of beauty, equated to "luxe, calme et volupté" "luxury, tranquility, and voluptuousness."

73. This hand-colored print is one of fourteen unique variants made for the edition *À Baudelaire*, in which Bourgeois collaborated with the Osiris imprint. I viewed this work at the MOMA exhibit in 2018.

74. "A une mendiante rousse" ("To a red-haired beggar") is another example within the *Tableaux parisiens*, but its perspective remains within the Surrealists' point of recognizing that the "poor girl" is an attractive sexual being.

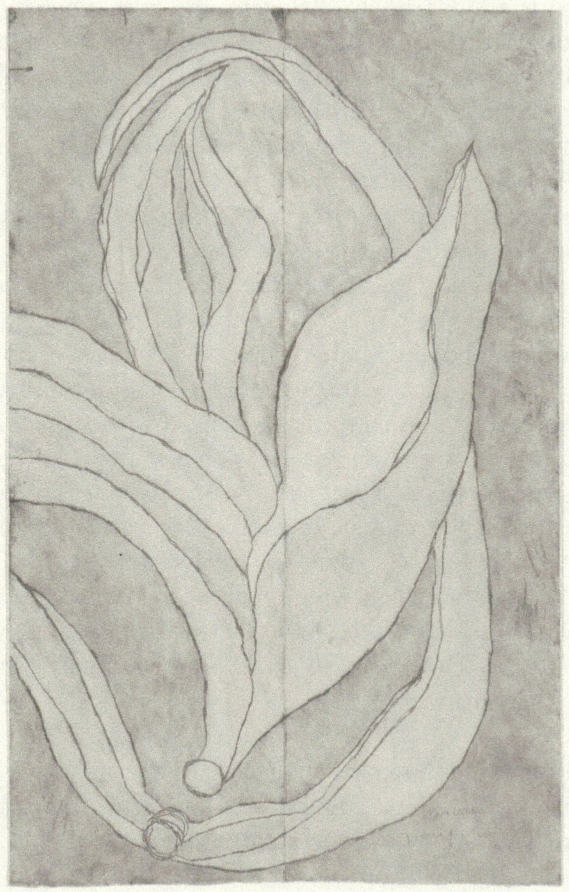

Figure 1.5. Louise Bourgeois, *Turning Inwards, Set 1 (à Baudelaire)*, 2008. Etching, watercolor, gouache, ink and pencil on paper; 59⅜ × 37¾". Collection Museum of Modern Art, NY © The Easton Foundation/VAGA at ARS, New York. Photo: Benjamin Shiff.

attention to the point I mentioned earlier, that the hysteric, whose body hosts a variety of spontaneous "maux" ("pains," "illnesses"), mistakenly believes the unreceivable part of her being to be something "bad," an "evil" that makes her inadequate, whereas it is a structural defect in language. But, as *Arch of Hysteria* suggests to Blanche in the Brouillet painting, and to the Christ in Michelangelo's *Pietà*, nobody—no doctor or virgin-mother—can carry the weight of this unreceivable, or "unaddressable." It is nothing other than the feminine, beyond cultural ideals of femininity that repress it. Perhaps it is precisely the unaddressable that Baudelaire turns into a poetic flower nonetheless, inspiring Bourgeois to address her flower etchings to him.

It is striking to realize that Baudelaire included the *Tableaux parisiens* for his second edition of *Les fleurs du mal* in 1861, just a year before Charcot began directing the Salpêtrière. Both Baudelaire's poetic investigation in the changing city and Charcot's in its largest hospital bring into focus women's bodies as sites of excess. Of the two, however, only Baudelaire's text accounts for the voluptuous—and disruptive—effects of this excess upon the viewing, speaking subject, without pathologizing or condemning it.[75] But his gesture is also different from the Surrealists' in their "50th Anniversary of Hysteria." "À une passante" places emphasis not only on the "supreme mode of expression" Surrealism recognizes in Augustine, but also on the experience it yields for the subject of enunciation affected by the sudden vision, amidst the chaotic, roaring street, of a certain gait (perhaps like Norbert Hanold in Jensen's tale, which Freud brilliantly read, the poet, too, encountered Gradiva, and was sent elsewhere by her splendor):

> La rue assourdissante autour de moi hurlait.
> Longue, mince, en grand deuil, douleur majestueuse,
> Une femme passa, d'une main fastueuse
> Soulevant, balançant le feston et l'ourlet·[76]

She passes by, standing out like a sudden, dramatic optical effect of the "deafening street," which is the subject of the poem's first verse. The

---

75. This experience is concerned with the subject of enunciation, or the split of the "I" giving rise to an unconscious dimension of being spoken beyond the ego's will.

76. The deafening street around me roared.
Long, slender, in great mourning, majestic pain,
A woman passed by, with one sumptuous hand
Lifting, swaying her scallop and hem.

In translating this sonnet I have consulted the translation by James McGowan in *The Flowers of Evil* (Oxford: Oxford World's Classics, 1993).

undulating and fleeting movement traced by this woman in mourning produces a change in the body of the poem's "moi," initially surrounded by noise. Now this "moi" is captivated by the rhythmic sway of this "majestic pain," which the fourth verse renders again audible through its words, and so the "moi" enters an intense, dangerous state of looking:

> Agile et noble, avec sa jambe de statue.
> Moi, je buvais, crispé comme un extravagant,
> Dans son œil, ciel livide où germe l'ouragan,
> La douceur qui fascine et le plaisir qui tue.[77]

It is in the eye of the woman that the poet, speaking in the first person and describing himself as "crispé comme un extravagant," which I have translated as "tense as a madman," finds a stormy sky where a hurricane is forming, and "drinks" "the sweetness that fascinates and the pleasure that kills." The second verse in this quatrain offers the split in the speaking subject through the two pronouns "Moi, je," while a dimension beyond the ego's will emerges, bringing its subject close to "the pleasure that kills."

"A une passante" draws on the centuries-older Western practice of *fin amor*, the one that inspired Petrarch's deployment of the sonnet form Baudelaire adopts here, and, a century later, Jacques Lacan's teaching on sublimation in his seminar *The Ethics of Psychoanalysis* (1959–60). The gesture of drinking from the beloved lady's eyes certainly relates this scene to the medieval tradition of courtly love, stressing, like the troubadour's songs, the bodily intensities fully at work in this subtle visual contact. Yet the Lady has been removed from her tower, still standing out as "noble," but also "nimble" and immersed like everyone else in the crowd in the city streets, making a "statuesque appearance," and soon disappearing.[78]

---

77. Nimble and noble, statuesque of leg
I, tense like a madman, drank in
From her eye, stormy sky where the hurricane forms,
The sweetness that fascinates and the pleasure that kills.

78. Anne Emmanuelle Berger has reflected on the response to the courtly situation in lyric poetry in terms of the gift, for instance through Baudelaire's "À une mendiante rousse." See "Reigning Cats or Dogs? Baudelaire's Cynicism," *Yale French Studies* (125–126). *Time for Baudelaire (Poetry, Theory, History)* (2014): 149–164.

The fascinating and deadly powers the poem's male subject finds in her eye bring the sculptural grace of her forward-moving leg close together with suffering, or beauty with "le mal." All of these powers, and their way of stirring up the two bodies in the poem, offer an idea of the feminine excess that could also result in convulsions and paralyses in Charcot's hysterics. Baudelaire's scene suggests that such an excess is not an essential property of women in general, first of all since it is his body that undergoes a shift—from the sense of hearing, surrounded by the street noises, to that of sight, where the passing woman at once maddens and revives him with her fugitive beauty:

> Un éclair . . . puis la nuit!—Fugitive beauté
> Dont le regard m'a fait soudainement renaître,
> Ne te verrai-je plus que dans l'éternité?
>
> Ailleurs, bien loin d'ici! trop tard! jamais peut-être!
> Car j'ignore où tu fuis, tu ne sais où je vais,
> O toi que j'eusse aimée, ô toi qui le savais![79]

The speaking subject in the poem ends up in a state of mourning that mirrors the one he first noticed in the woman's attire, and he mourns for their extremely subtle and brief encounter that he cannot extend, since its specificity has to do with the pace she keeps. The poem stresses the transitory and contagious character of an excess that here takes the singular form of a woman passing by, a moment's eye-contact, and a beautiful sonnet. As an example of sublimation, "A une passante" shows that the libidinal energy and its death-driven nature are not erased by

---

79. A thunderbolt . . . then night!—fugitive beauty
Whose gaze made me, suddenly, come alive again
Will I see you no longer, except in eternity?

Elsewhere, far away from here! Too late! Never, perhaps!
Since I know not where you flee, you know not where I'm going,
Oh you, who I would have loved, Oh you, who knew it, too.

(Charles Baudelaire, *Oeuvres Complètes*, ed. Claude Pichois. [Paris: Bibliothèque de la Pléiade, 1975–76] I, 92.) (Hereafter OC).

the controlled work of depicting the scene[80] or of producing the rhyming verses that wrest themselves out of the street's indistinct chaos. Charcot might have wanted to keep the feminine restrained, if not in women's wandering wombs exclusively,[81] at least inside the ward, its lecture halls, and the *Iconographie*.[82] Baudelaire instead discovers the feminine right on the streets, even "passing" across bodies, and the poet welcomes it, "drinks it" gladly, even if the fulminating passerby cannot be permanently seized and leaves him grieving (but she does remain visible to future readers in the sonnet's eternity).

Baudelaire suggested that for artists and poets, "a woman" is something else, something more, that is, than "the female of man."[83] This displacement from a logic of the complement to that of an "Other" jouissance is crucial to Lacan's formulas of sexuation, where he examines masculine and feminine subject positions, showing that "a woman" is not-all subject to the phallus, and where he famously claims that "there is no sexual relation" (on which more in chapter 4). Moving away from the logic of the complement also opens up the possibility of sublimation, out of the very thing that may seem evil or sickly. The aesthetic clinic takes on the labor of sublimation, which concerns the transmission of

---

80. In his commentary to Baudelaire's essay *The Painter of Modern Life*, more on which in chapter 2, Claude Pichois remarks that "À une passante" "is a Guys painting." Baudelaire, OC II, 1418.

81. Although Charcot chose the term "hysteria" for the illness he investigated in mysterious paralyses, seizures, trances, hyperesthesias, etc., whose meaning in Greek since Hippocrates ("illness of the wandering womb") he knew well, he also claimed that hysteria was not exclusive to women. This was in a context that disregarded his own Tuesday lessons where female patients were key to the demonstrations for an all-male medical audience.

82. Danielle Bergeron accurately assesses this problem of giving a place to this jouissance in a more recent context when, looking at the entries for "Man" and "Woman" in an encyclopedia, she discovers that whereas man is described in a struggle against nature, woman is made up of figurations that are a matter of "une monstration, de l'indexation d'un 'dehors,' d'un hors limite et d'un hors cadre" "a monstration, the indexing of an 'outside,' of an out of limit and an out of frame" "Le féminin: Un espace autre pour le désir" in *Santé mentale au Québec* 15.1 (1990), 147. Photography in Charcot's investigation subverts this control, given the reproductive nature of the medium with which he seeks a totally impartial record of hysterical phenomena. See Didi-Huberman's *The Invention of Hysteria*.

83. Baudelaire, OC *II*, 21.

feminine jouissance. Louise Bourgeois applied herself to exactly this task, which explains why during her final years she would create the etching and artist's book *À Baudelaire*. "What is feminine jouissance?" "What does a woman want?" These questions are off-target from the outset, since the question of feminine jouissance defies the object-oriented scope of "what." It only takes place as a transmission or passage of a force across bodies. *A une passante* (and before it the Provençal troubadours and trouvères[84]) convey exactly this process, through their image of the poet drinking sweetness and pleasure from the eye of the unknown woman who is paradoxically also in "majestic pain." And this brings me back to the statement that led to Baudelaire[85]: that the aesthetic experiences Bourgeois' art offers call viewers to a hysteric standpoint, insofar as it attests to the lack in language to name something feminine that continually seeks expression.

Sublime Conversions

Hysteric subjects caught up in the effort to satisfy or defy an imaginary Other are certainly not in the same situation as those who can render the feminine in an aesthetic transmission. They share the talent of "conversion" Freud theorizes from his observation of hysteric patients, such as Dora. Conversion is an unconscious investment of psychical material in the body, such that a fantasy expresses itself in physical terms, as a symptom, at the expense of the organism's regular functioning.[86] So the process of linking the work of the drive to an aesthetic expression to transmit the feminine also performs this passage from the psychic to the physical, and in that sense one can say that the sculptures of Bourgeois or Michelangelo are nothing other than sublime conversions.[87]

84. The work of *joi* means more than just joy in that poetic practice. See, for instance, Bernart de Ventadorn "Qan vei la lauzeta mover," Na Bieiris de Roman, "Na María pretç e fina valors . . . ," and Jaufré Rudel "Lanquan li jorn son lonc en may," in Jacques Roubaud, *Les troubadours: Anthologie bilingue* (Paris: Seghers, 1971). For commentary see Sarah Kay and Simon Gaunt, *The Troubadours: An Introduction* (Cambridge, UK: Cambridge University Press, 1999).

85. And to courtly love, more on which with Duras in chapter 4.

86. *SE VII*, 53.

87. For an expanded use of the term conversion in contemporary psychoanalysis that relates to my argument on a hysteric capacity for sublimation, see Jamieson

Deleuze embraces hysteria in the analysis of Francis Bacon's paintings, and of painting in general as an art form. He writes: "Painting is hysteria, or converts hysteria."[88] In stating that painting itself is hysteria or "converts" hysteria, Deleuze proposes, first, that painting has the structure and processes that define hysteria, and I will show what they consist in in his view. Second, he suggests that, through painting, hysteria itself suffers a conversion, perhaps to the terms of sensation and out of its pathological, and "mimetic" status in the *Iconographie* photographs, which Francis Bacon seems to have drawn on to produce his canvases. Deleuze privileges the nonrepresentational, "direct transmission of sensation" that Bacon sought to offer, which resonates with his own theory of destabilizing aesthetic encounters that distinguish themselves from everyday processes of recognition, as the only genuine acts of thought.[89]

According to Peppiatt's biography, Bacon said: "Everything I see gets ground up very fine. In the end one never knows, certainly I myself never know, what the images in my paintings are made of."[90] In Deleuze's view, this grinding of sources would be a step toward converting hysteria into painting's power to yield sensations, then, instead of always turning back to reference past images. The result in Deleuze's study is that Charcot's hysteria also gets ground up more or less finely. Peppiatt states that the working documents found in Bacon's studio include medical photographs, among which are lesser known photographs of male bodies suffering hysterical attacks at the Salpêtrière,[91] and illustrates this with an image of a male body lying on a bed in the *arc de cercle* posture. Peppiatt is also almost certain that Bacon "leafed through the issue of *La révolution surréaliste* (published in March 1928, while he was still in Paris) which celebrated 'Fifty Years of Hysteria' with a series of beautiful photographs of a hysterical patient at various points of 'crisis.' "[92] In this regard, one can say Bacon was not interested in his painting's making

Webster, *Conversion Disorder: Listening to the Body in Psychoanalysis* (New York: Columbia University Press, 2018).

88. Deleuze, *FB*, 52.

89. More on this in chapter 2.

90. Michael Peppiatt, *Francis Bacon: Anatomy of an Enigma* (New York: Farrar, Straus and Giroux, 1996), 30–31.

91. Several images of both male and female positions photographed by the Service Photographique de la Salpêtrière are printed in the magazine *Cimaise: Art et Architecture Actuels* 173 (Nov–Dec, 1984): 29–48.

92. Peppiat, 34.

a direct commentary on nineteenth-century hysteria, unlike Bourgeois, who brought the topic to the very titles of several sculptures and drawings. And yet, what matters is that a process of conversion is at stake through the different strategies and media that engage with hysteria, whether by "punctual resurrections" of photography, or, in Bacon's case, by "grinding up" on canvases that feature bodies deformed according to the particularity of different intensities, or by "molding," "beheading," "stretching" (the torso), and "hanging suspended" one encounters in Bourgeois' *Arch of Hysteria* (1993).

Now, coming back to the first part of Deleuze's proposition, "painting is hysteria," it has to do with the effects of painting over its viewers. To Deleuze, the process of hysteria has to do with an "excess of presence," closely related to the one I have explored in Baudelaire's tableau of the passerby. He considers that painting hystericizes, that its excessive presence overflows. If, as Lacan explained, the mirror can be considered as a site, or stage, where the subject accepts a misrecognition that founds the ego in the image of a cohesive, independent body supported by the smiling, gazing mother, the Bacon tableau disrupts that cohesive unity of the sensorimotor system and ego. The viewer thus enters the painting, accepting its effect of making a Body without Organs in her. Painting, Deleuze writes,

> invests the eye through color and line. But *it does not treat the eye as a fixed organ*. It liberates lines and colors from their representative function, but at the same time it also liberates the eye from its adherence to the organism, from its character as a fixed and qualified organ: the eye becomes virtually the polyvalent indeterminate organ that sees the body without organs (the Figure) as a pure presence. Painting gives us eyes all over: in the ear, in the stomach, in the lungs (the painting breathes . . .). This is the double definition of painting: subjectively, it invests the eye, which ceases to be organic in order to become a polyvalent and transitory organ; objectively, it brings before us the reality of a body, of lines and colors freed from organic representation. And each is produced by the other: the pure presence of the body becomes visible at the same time that the eye becomes the destined organ of this presence.[93]

93. Deleuze, *FB*, 52, emphasis in the original.

I have explained in this book's Introduction that the Body without Organs can be seen as a rethinking of sublimation, where the subject of the drive goes beyond the limits of the pleasure principle in a specific practice, whose way of moving, transforming, or reinventing the subject—according to the singularity of its jouissance investing part-objects and erogenous zones—begins with "becoming-woman," or with an embrace of the feminine, regardless of social or biological gender. If both Deleuze and Bourgeois insist on hysteria, it is because the hysteric's privileged connection to the feminine gives viewers access to this aesthetic event of the Body without Organs, which occurs in other kinds of conversions beside painting too, each time uniquely. A hysteric artwork, then, whether in painting, sculpture, or poetry, enables an aesthetic receptivity that involves an experience of the unconscious in its true complexity and elusiveness, understanding such an experience as a crucial, specific function of the artwork beyond representation.

In this sense, the headlessness of Bourgeois' bronze *Arch* and its state of suspension introduce the domain of the unconscious, a cut that opens onto what Freud called an "other scene," one that concerns the work of art and those who engage with it, *other* to the social reality upon which it has effects nonetheless. This other scene in psychoanalysis and, I contend, in the aesthetic clinic, is not just a critical space for denouncing the social order; rather, it involves unnamed intensities that insist on making themselves felt in enigmatic ways, disrupting the image of a unified persona recognized in the social scene. *Arch* thus not only evokes the photograph of the *arc de cercle* in the *Iconographie*, where the head hides, buried in a pillow, and the agitation of the attack is frozen, suspended, indeed, by the very still nature of the photographic medium. Solid, tridimensional, suspended from a cord and so susceptible to pivoting in a room reflected, complete with its observing visitors, on its metallic surface, *Arch* alters the viewing space, making room for a bodily experience of the other scene, one that is *other* even to the phenomenal aspect of hysterical attacks, whether suffered or witnessed. In *Arch*'s mirror an unfamiliar image emerges, supplanting the faces that afford us a stable social identity.

Lack and Ambivalence

Sexual difference has a fundamental place in this other scene. Bourgeois' *Arch* was modeled on a male body (that of Bourgeois' assistant, Jerry

Gorovoy), a fact that can easily be overlooked as soon as the title is read and associated with the Salpêtrière women, despite the figure's protuberant pelvis.[94] The first sculptural experiment on the hysterical *arc de cercle*, however, was with a Barbie doll that she immersed in clay from head to thigh-level, to bring it to an exaggerated arch form (*Femme Maison*, 1982).[95] The clean-cut, missing head of *Arch* certainly also suggests a well-known metaphor for castration.[96] Freud registered castration as an idea that came to children upon discovering that women's bodies "lack" a penis, a difference that introduces for both women and men the notion of not being whole insofar as there is the other sex, and with this lack, a set of psychical effects that make this difference so difficult to think and live with.[97] This is because the anatomical difference between the

94. In a 2011 interview around the exhibit *Louise Bourgeois: The Return of the Repressed* (Fundación PROA, Buenos Aires, Argentina; March 19–June 19, 2011), Jerry Gorovoy recalls the painful, violent process by which the *Arch* mold was created. He explains that he had to shave his whole body and lie on a mound of plaster, which became extremely hot as it hardened. He did this twice, to capture both sides of his body, and then Bourgeois exacerbated the mold's arch shape beyond that left by his form, by cutting the mold to pieces and twisting it. See Fundación PROA's video: www.youtube.com/watch?v=Zh6B3QzJeyo.

95. While she experimented with this doll in the arched form, the final iteration of *Femme Maison* is not arched.

96. The earlier *Cell III*, 1991, features a paper cutter, whose lifted blade threatens a small marble "arch of hysteria" figure located on its bed.

97. See my discussion on castration and penis envy in this book's Introduction. The inconsistencies regarding the masculine-feminine distinction in texts that attempt to define hysteria, such as "*Le cinquantenaire de l'hystérie*" and *Démoniaques dans l'art*, are noteworthy and symptomatic of the muddy problem of sexual difference. For instance, "the delicious Augustine," on the one hand, is the perfect example of poetic hysteria for the Surrealists, who read the girl's poses as expressions of lust; on the other hand, in their concluding definition of hysteria, the subject, strikingly, is declined in the masculine (they diagnose a "subversion of the relationships that are established between the subject and the moral world, which he [*il*] believes to practically depend on." When Charcot, for his part, states that although by its etymology hysteria unfortunately suggests an exclusively female condition the diagnosis can apply to women and men indifferently (*Démoniaques* XVI), he willingly forgets what Freud remembers from his six-month stay in Paris attending Charcot's lectures as a young doctor, that "it's always a question of the genitals—always, always, always!"

sexes entails a lack of symbolization for the feminine one, which appears only as an absence, a void, a hole.[98]

Lacan made the point in his *Ethics of Psychoanalysis*, regarding sublimation, that this void could be approached or rendered in an artistic operation. He evokes Heidegger's essay on "The Thing" to consider the making of an empty vase as a fundamental act of creation, and recalls a project his surrealist friend, the poet Jacques Prévert, developed with a collection of empty match boxes. Lacan insists on the multiplication of emptiness as that which renders manifest the Thing, beyond ordinary objecthood. Bourgeois will also explore empty vases, as I show in the next chapter, but in her work on hysteria she remains close to the problem of thinking sexual difference as the source of that proliferating void.

One of Bourgeois' later versions of *Arch of Hysteria* (made in 2004) features a suspended stitched fabric figure with two heads, one at each end of an arch made of masculine and feminine torsos that merge at its apex. Each of the heads hangs back, swiveling and looking in opposite directions. Lacan states that the structure of hysteria is essentially a question (for both female and male hysterics): "am I a man or a woman?" or "what is a woman?"[99] Insofar as the hysteric's fantasy explores all possible viewpoints, it presents an ambivalence and an ambiguity with regard to the sexual.[100] Bourgeois' sculptures especially highlight this experience of ambiguity for observers who are confronted with sculpted body parts with erotic features—tumescence, sinuousness, corrugations, orifices—that can be masculine or feminine, or that are decidedly both.[101] In the polished bronze *Arch of Hysteria*, then, the male body taking the position of "the delicious Augustine" speaks not only in feminist terms about the asymmetrical visual politics that Charcot's theater, the Surrealists' 1928 celebration, and Duchamp's *Etant données* (1946–66) all involve (and

98. Jacques Lacan, *Le séminaire. III: Les psychoses* (Paris: Seuil, 1981), 198–199.

99. Lacan, *Séminaire* III, 195–205.

100. Freud discusses this in the early paper on hysterical attacks, for instance, and Dora's analysis points to this as well. See also Verhaeghe, *Does the Woman Exist?*

101. This is prominent, for instance, in *Janus fleuri (1968)*, *Fillette (1968)*, *Cumul I (1969)*, and *Le Trani Episode (1971)*.

that Bourgeois indeed reverses[102]), but also in terms of the unconscious, where sexual difference is so unsettling. On this level, sexual difference introduces a wavering, a slight oscillation like the one suggested by the suspended *Arch*, a multiplicity of standpoints, and, at the same time, a cut that severs speaking beings from wholeness, like the missing, severed head that cannot coincide with the rest of the polished bronze *Arch*. The cut as experience rather than threat unleashes an endless process.

"Freud has written nothing on women," Louise wrote on November 1, 1954, looking for "sisters" in Viola Klein, Marie Bonaparte, and Hélène Deutsch.[103] The statement strikes one as a hysterical complaint against a master and an interrogation of other women, analysts in this case, in the hope of finding an answer to the problem of the lack of a signifier related to the girl's position. As previously mentioned, for the hysteric, the lack of a signifier from the feminine standpoint entails the repeated irruption of an excess jouissance, and, correlatively, a certain skepticism with regard to the named, social reality. Apollon writes: "As to the relation of woman to the signifier and to language, at the very least one can maintain that she does not trust them."[104] Her skepticism comes from the fact that "the signifier inserts a logic into the feminine subject that contradicts as well as obstructs the search for satisfaction,"[105] precisely because this logic is lack, and what the signifier does offer to "woman" is a position, as "mother of . . ." or "wife of . . ."[106] for which she "must lend not only her body but years of her life to the reproduction of the subject as well as social reproduction."[107]

Bourgeois is rightly unsatisfied with the kind of answer to the question of "woman" as a desiring subject that turns desire into an object to be attained (the husband, the child), and, in turn, this woman into a sexual object. Lacan changed the situation by proposing that the object

102. In conversation with her assistant and model for *Arch*, Jerry Gorovoy, she lists, among others, Lacan, Breton, and Duchamp: "ridiculous Don Juan macho father figures" who "have all motivated my work. I had a bone of contention with every one of them and I was out to call their bluff and still am" (c. 1994; LB-2191).

103. Loose sheet of writing, November 1, 1954; LB-0484.

104. Willy Apollon, "Four Seasons in Femininity or Four Men in a Woman's Life." *Topoi* 12 (1993): 101–115, 103.

105. Apollon, 103.

106. Apollon, 110.

107. Apollon, 103.

is in the position of an unconscious cause, rather than goal of desire, a point I will return to. If language establishes a collective perception taken as conscious reality, "woman" cannot help experiencing the signifier's faultiness with regard to an unspeakable excess that cannot conform itself to language, the organism, or self-preservation. Bourgeois certainly wrote about this experience. In a circa 1965 text, for instance, she writes "the diseases of the femininity" and lists a set of tasks: "try to convince the / others in order to convince myself / . . . Try to be / knowledgeable about clothes to prove that / I know everything about sex."[108] This fundamental skepticism, so closely linked to the question of sex, is a common cause for self-doubt and lack of credibility, and it is also what gives the hysteric a subversive power before the moral world (an imaginary limit), as the Surrealists highlight. If the inadequacy of language can be unsettling to a woman, it can also cause laughter. "Je suis évidemment une femme qui a des / ennuis avec sa féminité. Je ris comme / une bossue" "I am obviously a woman who has / issues with her femininity. / I cackle,"[109] writes Bourgeois around 1961. Her cackle certainly evokes the creatively contorted bodies this chapter has explored.

From Hysteric Symptom to the Arch of the Drive

The "greatest discovery" the Surrealists celebrate in 1928 was precisely what Freud received at the turn of the twentieth century, namely the *expressiveness* of the hysteric's gestures, or symptoms, which to him revealed unconscious fantasies shaped, as he writes in the Dora case, by "a psychic trauma, a conflict of affects, and a disturbance in the sphere of sexuality."[110] According to this logic, the expression of sexual impulses

108. Loose sheet of writing, c. 1965; LB-0331.

109. Loose sheet of writing, c. 1961; LB-0668. Bourgeois uses an idiomatic expression in French that literally translates "I laugh like a hunchback woman." The "cackle" preserves the sense of a deformed feminine character that relates, precisely, to the point I make here regarding being unhinged from what is socially acceptable.

110. Freud, *SE* VII, 18. Freud came to realize that fantasy does not necessarily involve a memory of an event that took place in reality and traumatized the individual; the traumatic factor that influences the hysteric symptom or the dream is thus a *psychic* event, an interpretation of an experience either coming from external reality or emerging within the body. I discuss this point in the following chapters of this book, especially chapters 2 and 4.

captured in the *Iconographie* photographs is not, then, simply "a show" where attacks were simulated to unleash, without risk of punishment, otherwise improper behavior. Symptoms (such as hysterical attacks) were welcomed by Freud as a kind of writing that gives expression to the aforementioned intensities or excitations that stand in conflict with the individual's conscious wishes.[111]

By situating the symptoms' relevance in the realm of the unconscious (the crucial nuance the surrealist text omits, perhaps to stress the rebellious, morally defiant power of hysteria they endorse), Freud made possible a distinction between, on the one hand, biology, and, on the other, the body of the drives (*Triebe*), which also stands apart from social constructions of gender and body. The drives respond, then, to another, "inorganic" and asocial life. An excess derailing the organic, instinctual functioning of biological systems and not in sync with gender identities, this other life is a central concern in both the psychoanalytic clinic and the works of Louise Bourgeois, which propose experiences that make it necessary to rethink the stakes of the aesthetic. What is this *life* of the drives that Acéphale tried to embrace and I find as aesthetic experience in Bourgeois? How do the drives concern the aesthetic? What is their specific function in the artwork? Bourgeois' *Arch* punctuates this too, by its arching gesture.

I have mentioned the fragmentary quality in some of Bourgeois' sculptures of body parts, including the headless *Arch of Hysteria* that prompted an exploration of its medical, psychoanalytic, and avant-garde references to hysteria. Such fragmentation and isolation of the part not only stresses that we are dealing here with something *other* than a complete, unified body image that might be useful for self-identity; it also indicates a certain independence of these body parts from biological systems, a realm of "inorganic life," insofar as its logic has broken away from the automatic functioning of the organism. In *Arch*, the contortion makes the body trace a curve, reaching up and back, away from the toes, and back down as far as possible. Yet the arms, instead of being

111. Monique David-Ménard has traced the development of conversion theory, from its grounding on a preexistent or coincidental organic problem that becomes invested by a psychical one, to a question of "deficiency in the subject's symbolization of her body" (44), and beyond conversion to erotogenetic zone displacement. See her *Hysteria from Freud to Lacan*, trans. Catherine Porter (Ithaca, NY: Cornell University Press, 1989).

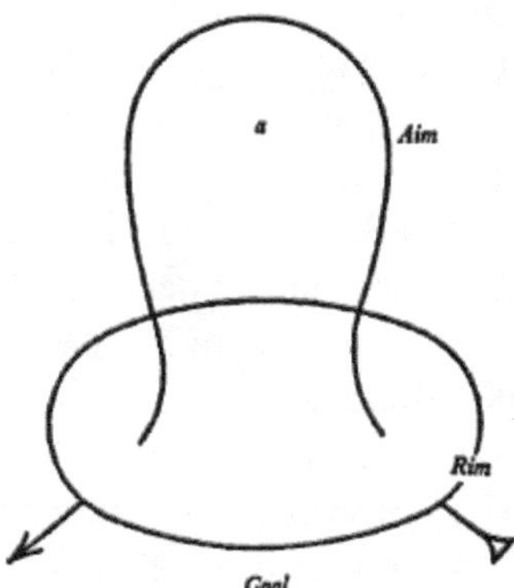

Figure 1.6. The Circuit of the Partial Drive (Lacan, *Book XI: The Four Fundamental Concepts of Psychoanalysis* [NY and London: W.W. Norton, 1981], 178).

flung up and back as well, are stretched out below the arched back, its hands extended with fingertips reaching to meet, blindly, the heels at the point of departure. This can be read as something more than the result of reproducing the photograph where the arching body is supported by a bed.[112] I'd like to point out a resemblance between the loop *Arch* draws in space and the circuit of the partial drive Lacan developed in his 1964 seminar as a commentary on Freud's 1915 paper "Instincts and their Vicissitudes" (*Triebe und Triebschicksale*).

One of the four fundamental concepts of psychoanalysis is, indeed, the drive, *Trieb*, and Lacan never tires of pointing out that "instinct" is an inaccurate and misleading translation of the German term, since instinct evokes automatic organic processes, whereas the peculiar trajectory of the drives is defined by an unconscious fantasy. In a session dedicated to the partial drive, Lacan wrote the following fragment (appropriately "partial") by Heraclitus on the blackboard: "To the bow [*arc*] is given the name of life, and its work is death."[113] Heraclitus plays on the Greek word *bíos*, both "bow," or "arch," and "life." Lacan comments: "What the

112. And in the plate the woman's elbows are bent and the visible hand makes a loose fist; see figure 1.3

113. Jacques Lacan, *The Four Fundamental Concepts of Psychoanalysis*, trans. Alan Sheridan (New York: W.W. Norton, 1981), 177. Brackets are mine to highlight Lacan's "arc."

drive immediately integrates in its whole existence is a dialectic of the bow [*arc*], I would even say of archery [tir à l'arc]. By it, we can situate its place in the psychic economy."[114] Lacan is stressing that "the dialectic of the arch" he sees in play in the drives' trajectory, vicissitudes, in other words its life, involves something of death. So the arching trajectory's peculiar effect of return to the point of departure—made visible in Bourgeois' *Arch* (1993) by the closeness between heels and fingertips—speaks to what Freud later called the death drive, in his groundbreaking *Beyond the Pleasure Principle* (1920). Bourgeois expressed harsh skepticism against Lacan ("My relationship to psychoanalysis is through writing / Lacan is a fake, a joke"[115]), although she was also ambivalent and curious. In a text from the 1970s she writes, precisely, about drive in Lacan, noting that the "erogenous zone is always a hole—failed oral satisfaction / something lacking . . . something missing,"[116] and in a diary entry of September 2 and 3, 1994, she appears to be reading Roudinesco's biography of Lacan, when she writes "topology ou l'envers et l'endroit" ("or the inside and the outside"), which makes her think of clothing, a prominent element in her own work with fabric. What I find interesting about relating Bourgeois' arching sculpture to Lacan's exposition on the circuit of the drive is that the latter responds to an aesthetic core, in an explicitly surrealist approach, as much as the former has clinical agency in the unconscious.

Lacan observes that Freud's 1915 text firmly insists on the circular character of the drives' trajectory, a movement that turns back on itself by a shift—from active to passive to reflexive—that characterizes the drive's process (through the examples of scopophilia-exhibitionism and sado-masochism).[117] Lacan insists that the drives are partial because their circuits or vicissitudes satisfy neither the ego nor the function of reproduction, but only themselves; this, precisely, distinguishes drives from instincts. The drive, he states, is "that *montage* by which sexuality participates in psychic life, in a way that must conform to the gap-like structure that is the structure of the unconscious."[118] The montage in question, a term he defines following the avant-garde surrealist collage

114. Lacan, 177.

115. Louise Bourgeois, in conversation with Jerry Gorovoy, c. 1992; LB-0837.

116. Loose sheet of writing, c. 1977; LB-1201.

117. Freud, *SE* XIV, 127.

118. Lacan, *The Four Fundamental Concepts*, 176.

technique, by the way,[119] involves an erogenous zone, which the drive—and not a biological need—invests with an intensity that overrides the homeostatic functioning of the pleasure principle meant to keep stimuli as low as possible. The participation of sexuality in psychic life thus disrupts the organism, introducing an economy of jouissance beyond pleasure. The dramatic contortion of Bourgeois' *Arch* has, indeed, nothing to do with the organism's needs, and everything to do with an unknown intensity, akin, also, to the one Saint Teresa of Ávila expressed in her mystical poetry and, as Lacan mentioned in his Seminar XX, Bernini brought to sculpture, making the head tilt back and the feet hang in *The Ecstasy of Saint Teresa* (1652).[120]

Object *a*: A Conversion of Values

To conform itself to the gap structure of the unconscious, the drive's trajectory skirts around a gap, where Lacan in his drawing situates the *objet a*, the (lost) object cause of desire (figure 1.6). Unlike any ordinary object of knowledge, the *objet a* marks the absence of a signifier for jouissance as a leftover that resists absorption into language, where the (incomplete) subject comes into being. As Lacan's drawing indicates, the object is not the target of the movement but instead an empty center shaping the trajectory's curve. In a similar way, Bourgeois' *Arch* extends and curls its metallic body back around a vacuum the figure outlines, where, as previously observed, other artworks place another body to support the main figure.[121] Lacan explains that if the satisfaction of the

119. Lacan describes the montage as a mechanism that sets off a reaction, where the drive "defines, according to Freud, all the forms of which one may reverse such a mechanism" (169). The surrealist collage as montage, whose disparate, assembled parts enter into surprising modes of connection, defies a teleological logic. He thus says the montage of the drive is initially "presented as having neither head nor tail" (169).

120. Lacan considers this Italian baroque sculpture and Spanish baroque mystical poets Saint Teresa and San Juan de la Cruz to develop the idea of "feminine jouissance" in Seminar XX, to which he gives the title *Encore*; this French word expresses this excessive jouissance since it means at once "more" and "still," and owing to its homophony with "en-corps" ("in-body").

121. It is interesting in this sense to consider Bourgeois' print suite *Triptych for the Red Room* (1994), where the arching bodies are held by another, but that "other" seems to struggle and fail to limit and contain the backbend.

drive is not merely the auto-erotism of the erogenous zone (located at the rim in the drawing), it is because of "this object—which is in fact simply the presence of a hollow, a void, which can be occupied, Freud tells us, by any object, and of whose agency we know only in the form of the lost objet, the *petit a*."[122]

This question of the drive's vicissitudes that *Arch* also evokes reveals another relation to the initially mentioned surrealist and Acéphale references. Lacan's own connection to surrealism during the 1930s is especially apparent in his discussion of the drive, in the manifestation of which he sees "the mode of an acephalous subject,"[123] with its correlative *objet a* as *trouvaille*, which is Breton's term for the object found-as-lost.[124] By taking surrealism into account in both his teaching and clinical work, Lacan highlights the relevance of the aesthetic in the experience of the unconscious. Margaret Iversen addresses the surrealist lens in Lacan's seminar, stressing the *objet petit a*'s double function of marking and covering over an absence to propose a radical idea in Lacan's text, namely "that what is really valuable in art has, paradoxically, little to do with the aesthetic pleasure we may derive from it and, further yet, that 'what one looks at is what cannot be seen.'"[125] This invisible one looks at is precisely the fading, intermittent, practically ungraspable subject of the drive[126] by which there is transgression beyond pleasure, to the realm of jouissance.

I'm interested in this daring claim Iversen locates in Lacan, about what is "really valuable in art." At the same time as Lacan sets forth the dimension of the aesthetic for psychoanalysis, he remains firmly situated in the clinical register when it comes to the concepts he describes, whose weight is intrinsic to the *experience* the analytic process and relation make possible. Such an experience, as stated at the beginning of this chapter, consists in an address that differs from that between ego and

122. Lacan, *The Four Fundamental Concepts*, 180.

123. Lacan, *The Four Fundamental Concepts*, 181, translation modified.

124. Such a link is often overlooked by anglophone readers of Seminar XI. Iversen analyzes Lacan's discussion on the "missed encounter" alongside that of the found object in Breton's novel *L'amour fou*. Margaret Iversen, *Beyond Pleasure: Freud, Lacan, Barthes* (University Park: Pennsylvania State University Press, 2007).

125. Iversen, 70. Iversen's reference is to Lacan's *Four Fundamental Concepts*, 182.

126. "The appearance of a subject" is a result ("what is new") of the satisfaction of the drive that completes its trajectory, Lacan insists. *The Four Fundamental Concepts*, 178.

other, and instead makes room for the subject to speak and reveal her mode of relation to the Other, then attempt a new way of engaging the unnamed jouissance at work in her and manifesting through the disruptive symptom.[127] Such a new way, or "conversion" of jouissance into some other medium, has no model or parameter,[128] so it is necessarily an aesthetic problem.

Thus, this act of looking, beyond pleasure, at what cannot be seen, requires a clinical lens as much as an aesthetic one, and the contribution Bourgeois' work makes at this crossroad of contemporary art and psychoanalysis lies in this very daring stance and act. The clinical dimension of experience is crucial to approach this question of the subject of the unconscious beyond aesthetic pleasure, as the thing we're involved with when we are exposed to an artwork. In the phrase Bourgeois repeatedly writes, draws, welds, embroiders, and projects onto the surfaces of her works, "Art is a guaranty of sanity," the word *art* has the status of an experience, and the sanity in play is far removed from medical criteria but intimately concerned with the body of the drives and the excess their trajectory skirts. Bourgeois' artworks, I find, give access to such an experience of the relation to jouissance,[129] not only from the standpoint of the artist (often discussed by artists themselves, as well as by critics and psychoanalysts), but also from the standpoint of the observer-reader, as one for whom the artwork constitutes an *encounter*, indeed, a kind of found-as-missed-object that elicits the drives and delineates a void.[130] The bronze *Arch* thus responds to this specific matter of the unconscious as an experience of the acephalous *trouvaille* from the hysteric's standpoint (that is, confronting the problematic absence of a feminine signifier) that gives rise to a new subject. This, perhaps, is the subject

127. Néstor Braunstein carefully discusses this operation in the Lacanian psychoanalytic clinic in *El goce: un concepto lacaniano*. Buenos Aires: Siglo XXI Editores Argentina, 2006), chapter 8.

128. On the relevance of the *objet a* to get out of a normative, necessarily phallic dichotomy, and toward the emergence of desire, see Parveen Adams, "Waiving the Phallus," in *The Emptiness of the Image* (New York: Routledge, 1995).

129. On the aesthetic and art as a unique signifier that offers direct relation to jouissance, see MacCannell, *The Hysteric's Guide to the Future Female Subject*, 52–56.

130. Deleuze discusses objects of an aesthetic encounter, beyond the pleasure principle and in relation to the Lacanian phallus as a signifier for what is always out of place, in *Difference and Repetition*, chapter 2.

of "ecstatic love" earlier invoked in Bataille's *Acéphale*, or in the set of courtly flowers offered by Baudelaire, Bourgeois, and "the woman passing by." Like "art," the concepts of "sanity" and "health" take on a new value in the aesthetic clinic. A turn to *Precious Liquids* (1992), one of Bourgeois' artworks that bear the affirmation "Art is a guaranty of sanity" is necessary to investigate them.

CHAPTER 2

Transmuting Pain into Joy with *Precious Liquids*

Louise Bourgeois' *Arch of Hysteria* (1993) and its interrogation of surrealism and the origins of psychoanalysis led, in chapter 1, to the idea that the encounter with her works of art invites viewers to adopt the hysteric's standpoint. The latter's "infinite" way of disclosing the scene of the unconscious, and with it, the life of the drives that remains inhibited or repressed as long as the ego dominates is favorable to rethink aesthetic experience. The acephalous character of Bourgeois' *Arch* propels viewers in the room with the suspended sculpture into this "other scene," as Freud first named it in *The Interpretation of Dreams*. *Arch* (1993) points to the absence of a signifier to symbolize the excess of feminine sexuality, an absence or defect that troubles the hysteric subject, and that also opens up a space for aesthetic creation beyond the limits of what already finds a referent in reality. I also emphasized the conversion of hysteria into an aesthetic form. Amidst the chaotic drives, a precise and distinct gesture, gait, or figure emerges from this other scene, transforming that of shared reality, and also transmitting something of its singularity to another subject, who therefore undergoes a conversion as well. How, exactly, does this transmission occur? An initial image of this process was discerned in courtly love and Baudelaire's *À une passante*, closer to the aesthetic clinic and to its ethics of desire than the surrealist appropriation of hysteria and convulsion as poetic categories. Bourgeois confronts the Surrealists and any psychoanalytic discourse in which the hysteric woman is held captive as an object of sexual pleasure, caught within the logic of ideological reproduction, the jouissance of the organ, and its underlying repudiation of femininity. To overcome this role, the feminine must be embraced as its own subject position. This opens up experimental connections of the clinical and the aesthetic, by way of an excess that concerns at once thought and body.

Precious Liquids (1992) proposes a turn from sculpture to installation art. Bourgeois employed both of these forms and others (for instance the soft-ground etching in the previous chapter), in multiple media. *Arch* (1993) puts some elements of installation art to work, particularly since it requires hanging and its surface reflects its surroundings. One could even argue that if hysteria is about an excess of presence that is transferred to the viewer, installation art is a form that very directly strives to make that very transference take place, by offering an atmosphere whose experience is not limited to an optical mode of attention. It is no longer the dynamics of a subject considering an object, but rather of a place being made for the subject to encounter its own strangeness in *objet a*, usually left out in other modes of attention. The presence of *Arch* in a room undoubtedly transforms the latter's atmosphere with its magnetic force—a paradoxical one, if we take the *arc de cercle* pose, as Freud did, to be an energetic rejection that unveils desire as its opposite. In the end, however, with *Arch* there is a figure, rather than a space that can potentially be entered by a visitor.[1] Instead, like the more than sixty unique installations that with it constitute the ambitious series *Cells* (1986–2008),[2] *Precious Liquids* (1992) does present itself as an enclosed, inhabitable space, conveying to viewers a direct sense of dwelling within the artwork.

In this chapter, *Precious Liquids* closes in on the convergence between the clinical—as a site concerned with that strange and specific reality that is the body of speaking beings, and the aesthetic—as a matter of sensations that provoke thought, like a shock beyond the boundaries of

1. As mentioned, visitors' reflections do appear on the sculpture's surface, but this effect is different from stepping into an environment that is the work itself. The female body in this sheltering capacity is discussed with Lygia Clark's *A casa é o corpo* (1968) in chapter 3.

2. Some works are included retroactively, since Bourgeois only began to name these works *Cells* in 1991. Louise *Bourgeois: Structures of Existence; The Cells*, the largest exhibit devoted to the *Cells* after Bourgeois' death, was organized by the Haus der Kunst, Munich, Germany, and featured thirty-two *Cells*. The exhibition travelled to Garage Museum of Contemporary Art, Moscow, Russia (September 25, 2015–January 24, 2016); Guggenheim Bilbao, Spain, March 18-September 4, 2016; and Louisiana Museum of Modern Art, Humlebæk, Denmark (October 13, 2016–February 26, 2017).

habit or the pleasure principle. The previous chapter and the Introduction have already revealed that, at this crossroads, both terms—"clinical" and "aesthetic"—slip out of common-sense frameworks. The clinic here does not focus on eradicating symptoms or on "healing," if this is taken to mean restoring the organism's equilibrium, and adjusting the psyche to what is receivable in the social link. As to the aesthetic, feelings conceptualized in philosophy as aesthetic (the beautiful and the sublime in Kant) come to grips with the problems of sexuality and feminine jouissance that place these aesthetic feelings beyond the pleasure principle. It is certainly understandable to wish for a clinic and an aesthetics that provide physical or mental "balance," and that harmonize with the cultural ideals and demands one is exposed to in everyday life, all while giving access to delight in beauty and greatness. Countless establishments in the modern world respond to such a wish under the term "clinic" (from mental health to cosmetic surgery and "beauty" centers). If I insist, with certain works of art, writing, and psychoanalysis, on an aesthetic clinic that most definitely does not promise this kind of solution, and that instead takes apart some illusions of wholeness, balance, and greatness, it is because I find these works to lay bare the corollary of such illusions—an obstruction of desire—and thus to seek different clinical and aesthetic acts.

By turning again to Baudelaire, in his essay on aesthetics *The Painter of Modern Life*, and to Nietzsche, as a proponent of "unfamiliar knowledge" or "gai savoir," and as an explorer of the drives' effects over his own body and thought, I examine a discussion *Precious Liquids* sets forth on the question of a "transvaluation of values," to put it in Nietzschean terms. The transvaluation concerns "health" and "convalescence" in the aesthetic clinic, with its understanding of aesthetic experience as the site of a transmission of objet *a*. This transmission is not only a matter of mobilizing the drives, but, beyond this, of detecting unique sensations, whose effects give rise to radical acts of thought, investing and altering a body opened up to desire, as my comparison of *Precious Liquids* to a Bacon canvas at the end of the chapter shows.

Vestibule

Precious Liquids (1992) first appears as a large cylindrical wooden water tank with a modest, human-sized entrance, placed approximately three

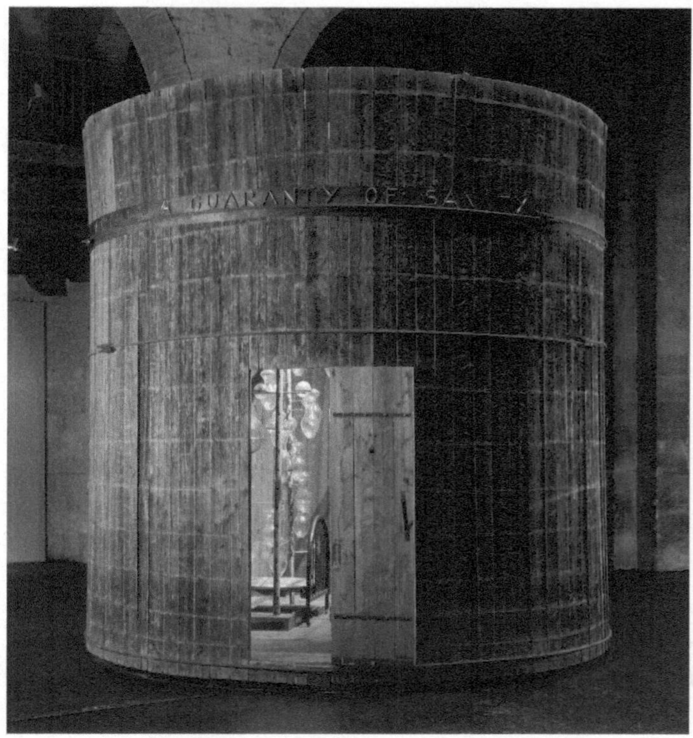

Figure 2.1. Louise Bourgeois, *Precious Liquids*, 1992. Wood, metal, glass, alabaster, cloth, and water 425.4 × 445.1 × 445.1 cm. Collection Musée National d'Art Moderne, Centre Georges Pompidou, Paris © The Easton Foundation/VAGA at ARS, NY. Photo: Frédéric Delpech.

feet below a strip of metal that wraps around the top of the barrel and reveals the sentence "Art is a guaranty of sanity." Its shape and semi-open door compel viewers to wander around its perimeter and approach the threshold that beckons one, with its lit interior. Upon turning around the gigantic barrel, another opening reveals itself, diametrically opposed to the one beneath the sign. I want to delay the moment of looking inside and describing its contents past the cylindrical wall and doors. I first stood before this piece at the Centre Pompidou in 2008, where it was the first work that came into view as one arrived to the level where works belonging to the post-1960s permanent collection are often displayed. As I was living nearby at the time, I returned often and contemplated the work many times, thinking, excitedly, that this installation would certainly have a part in my dissertation, although at the time it was water and anatomical drawings that interested me. I no longer recall how soon or late I peered inside the first time, but as I consider figure 2.1 and my impressions of this work, it now seems relevant to attend to the enigmatic quality of its façade, which will become a frame and background, once the eye turns to what is at the center of the walled circle.

From the outset, the massive tower strikes one as an odd dwelling space. But from the outset it pulls one in, since its title and container indicate liquid contents that remain invisible from this standpoint, and the door promises more to the eye. Why are they precious? And why are various kinds of liquids invoked, rather than just water, which this type of tank would usually hold in New York City? The wooden water towers, with their canopy tops, have served to provide water to buildings in New York City since the late nineteenth century,[3] a period that came up in the Paris of the Salpêtrière hysterics and Baudelaire, in the previous chapter. The tanks have therefore been present as a key element in the scenery and functioning of modern life in the city, where Bourgeois developed her body of work from 1938 to 2010.[4] Is the displacement of the barrel simply a contemporary art technique for capturing the formerly industrial/ now postindustrial city view, where an earlier modernist would have painted or photographed the skyline? The signal to modern life, cities, and industrialization, within the space of visual art, as well as the previous chapter's examination of nineteenth-century hysteric women bring to mind Baudelaire's title *The Painter of Modern Life*, to which I initially turn now.

Published in 1863, the essay offers a set of theses on aesthetics, the painter Constantin Guys, and, indirectly, Baudelaire's own work as a poet. One can also say that, like several of the latter's other texts, it is an essay on feminine jouissance, as I will later show. Baudelaire and the painters he admires are witnesses to the ways in which Paris, Europe, and the world are altered by industrial technology, urbanization, and liberal governmental institutions (Guys travels the world sketching military and

3. They can hold up to ten thousand gallons of water. www.rosenwachtank.com/about.php

4. The water tank came from the rooftop of Bourgeois' Brooklyn studio building. See Julienne Lorz, "From the Bell Jar to the Cage: The Developmental Path of Louise Bourgeois's Cells" in *Louise Bourgeois, Structures of Existence: The Cells* (Munich: Haus der Kunst, 2015), 29.

social events). But a close look at Baudelaire's famous essay shows that what he calls "modern life" is not just an effect of these factors, and the modern painter's work is not simply to represent the world altered by them. In an analogous way, *Precious Liquids*' New York water tank placed in the Paris museum is not simply a commentary about globalization. One of the crucial and daring arguments Baudelaire's essay makes resonates closely with the sentence above the front door of *Precious Liquids*, and it emerges in the title as soon as it is read differently. The painter does not portray a preexistent reality; instead, "modern life" does not exist without the painter, writer, or sculptor, as I will discuss here, when they take the vital status of their work in earnest.

After the age of commissioned works by monarchs or the church, the artist's task is not merely the representation of a world in development. In Baudelaire's essay this task appears, instead, closest to the child's exhilarating "joy of absorbing form and color" (*la joie avec laquelle l'enfant absorbe la forme et la couleur*) and to the immersion "in multitude, in the sway, in the movement, in the fleeting and the infinite" (*dans le nombre, dans l'ondoyant, dans le mouvement, dans le fugitif et l'infini*).[5] The artist abandons a focus on discrete objects or phenomena, as a way of seeing and making visible that, subordinated to a logic of identity, grasps generalities and serves recognition. By stepping out of an ordinary vision, he is able to take on "the joy," "the sway," "the movement," "the fleeting," and "the infinite." These are nothing other than sensations, even if, or especially insofar as, they defy representation. Making modern life involves going beyond what can be recognized as a referent or object of perception. This distinction has several important implications. First, it is not coextensive with that between figurative and abstract styles in painting, for instance. The nonrepresentational dimension of modern life can make as powerful an appearance in a geometric, abstract, primary-color canvas by Mondrian as in a portrait by Constantin Guys. Moreover, the operation I call "making modern life" with Baudelaire is also not defined by historical context, but by something larger, which one might call human desire. Bourgeois' *Cells* thus also *make* modern life beyond representation. Finally, the question of modes of perception and of the vision proper to sensation is not only for the artists, since

5. Baudelaire, *OC II*, 690–691.

what they undertake is the labor of relaying perceptions and visions of intensities in specific forms, or "converting" them.

By removing a bit of the skyline and bringing it indoors, an initial gesture the installation *Precious Liquids* invites its viewers to consider is one of bringing the outside in. At the same time, viewers, who in the beginning understood themselves to be indoors, within a building dedicated to art, such as the Centre Pompidou, are suddenly standing outside another building, with their view of the often clear, ample corridor blocked by this obstacle that towers up, close to the ceiling (and it is interesting to think about *Precious Liquids* inside the Beaubourg building, in particular).[6] It is as if the installation's façade said firmly to museum-goers' bodies, "you only think you know what art is, and how to look at art."

Simultaneously, the tank's open door keeps alive the hope of looking inside; it welcomes museum-goers while cutting us down to size. The modest semi-open door indicates that one's body has the appropriate dimensions for this installation to shelter it. But its way of towering over one without revealing its contents, leaving, instead, a sign one must turn one's head up to read, is not only somewhat intimidating, but also scales one's body down in the very manner of Bourgeois' gigantic steel spiders, as Mieke Bal has explained.[7] But here is a water tank in its usual dimensions, not a blown up arachnid. Then again, it was in order to reflect on the ambivalently protective and deadly mother that the largest of the spiders was named *Maman* (1999; "Mama"). And Bourgeois pondered water's deadly dangers—such as flooding and drowning[8]—alongside its virtues. In a 1995 interview with Hans-Ulrich Obrist, she stated:

6. The main Beaubourg building is itself turned inside out, as it were, with its air and water pipes, electric wiring, and escalators all running along building's façades. The photograph of *Precious Liquids* in figure 2.1 and the book cover is from an exhibit in Bordeaux, a signifier that instead highlights a play of borders (*Bord[s]-*) and "waters" (*eaux*). More on this French city's name with Duras in chapter 4.

7. See Mieke Bal's important investigation of the trope of scale in Bourgeois' *Spider* (1997). *Louise Bourgeois' Spider: The Architecture of Art-Writing* (Chicago: University of Chicago Press, 2001).

8. See her "Insomnia Drawing" and note on the back in *The Insomnia Drawings vol. I* (Zurich: DAROS, 2000), 35, as well as the drawings on the subsequent pages of that publication.

> Of all the elements, water fascinates me the most. Everything is always connected with water. The dangerous aspects of water are ice and flooding, and the benefit of water is life itself. All architecture depends on the flow of water: roofs, gutters, gargoyles, they are all connected with the channeling [of] water. Ice is very important. I'll show you drawings for a book we are about to publish called *Insomnia*. It contains more than 200 drawings, and a lot of them are concerned with water and fear, fear of the harm that water can do, floods, freezing, and the satiation that can cause you to die of thirst.[9]

So, "monstrous insect-free" as this installation may be, the ambivalence and risk remain. Life itself, and death itself. The interview discusses the river Bièvre that ran by Louise's childhood home and drainage systems during this time and until 1934, when the drains whose contents the river took were replaced by a main sewage system (shortly before she left France), as Paris and its surroundings completed the shift, begun in the nineteenth century, toward a more hygienic public space. Bourgeois's conversation with Obrist highlights the extent to which water's vital/deadly roles and the late nineteenth century return through her work.

In *Precious Liquids*, the water tank's subtle scaling down of the human body can help enable the exhilarated child's experience Baudelaire invoked. After all, something of a child's imagination is needed to turn the tanks across the skyline into shacks. Along with the tank's recontextualization, the enigmatic words welded on the strip atop the barrel and the title have already caused a city dweller's common sight to become uncanny. Together, these elements offer an initial combination of signifiers that suggests the following major concern, not only for Louise Bourgeois personally, but for art, the sentence's subject: like the water supply in a modern city, "precious liquids" are crucial elements within a system where sanity (more than sanitation) is in play.

9. "Interview with Hans-Ulrich Obrist," January 1995, in *Louise Bourgeois, Destruction of the Father, Reconstruction of the Father. Writings and Interviews 1923–1997* (Cambridge, MA.: MIT Press, 1998), 291.

This beginning—already a complex, gradual viewing and reading process—raises curiosity about this assurance, promise, or token of sanity that, in the same gesture, can no longer be taken for granted. The risk of madness is somehow involved. Otherwise, "a guaranty" would not be necessary. In this respect, too, it is interesting to turn to *The Painter of Modern Life*. What are the consequences of "absorbing" "the joy of form and color," which, linked to "movement," "sway" and "fleetingness" increasingly seem like fluid substances? The task is not at all to stop or at least tame the movement, nor is it to limit infinity. Instead, the painter's "passion and profession is *to espouse the crowd*,"[10] that is to say, to embrace the bustling multitude to which he exposes himself. Furthermore, he should be compared

> à un miroir aussi immense que cette foule; à un kaléidoscope doué de conscience, qui, à chacun de ses mouvements, représente la vie multiple et la grâce mouvante de tous les éléments de la vie.[11]

The image of the kaleidoscope places emphasis on life's multiplicity and on the movements responsible for its liveliness, incessantly producing new combinations of shapes and colors. This way of seeing the crowd and of making it visible aptly highlights the purview of sensation as something beside the identity of objects and bodies, which the movement and mixture of the crowd disturbs. Baudelaire describes the painter's activity as something as large as the life with which he is involved. "Immense." Because he "espouses the crowd" or "life" rather than observing it at a distance, which would allow its objectification, there is no simplifying or uniformizing multiplicity to the dimension of a single individual's consciousness. Since "representation" in the traditions of philosophy and the plastic arts that Baudelaire's essay criticizes puts these reductive cognitive operations to work—losing or missing life as a result—the particular work of "representing" performed by Baudelaire's painter destroys

10. Baudelaire, OC *II*, 691.

11. to a mirror as immense as this crowd; to a kaleidoscope with the gift of consciousness, which, at each of its movements, represents multiple life and the moving grace of all the elements of life (Baudelaire, 692).

the very framework that separates and preserves the individual conscious subject from its object. Baudelaire's choice of "life" as the painter's subject-object stresses the impossibility of any consciousness or object external and opposite to life, in an effort to remain identical to itself.

To welcome this mode of seeing, absorbing, making visible, is a risky exercise, for what kind of consciousness can turn itself into a mirror and endure so much difference and change within itself?[12] Does "self" even remain an accurate term for this consciousness? Baudelaire goes as far as to state that this "man of the world" is "un *moi* insatiable du *non-moi*, qui, à chaque instant, le rend et l'exprime en images plus vivantes que la vie elle-même, toujours instable et fugitive."[13] The painter, who heightens fleeting life rather than stabilizing and arresting it, in this sentence appears linked to the "moi," the "self," but in a special, atypical role. It is not a "me" in any usual sense or experience of the term.

Shortly after *The Painter of Modern Life*, for Nietzsche in 1872 aesthetic events require a Dionysian moment of *dis*-individuation or a "collapse of the *principium individuationis*"[14] that usually protects human beings from chaotic reality. He has Greek tragedy in mind, in particular music as a Dionysian force (the dithyramb). Baudelaire's painter also seems to explore this realm. Yet the point of dis-individuation for both authors is not to end up in blurry, dull indifference as the image of life. On the contrary, the result must be even livelier, so the multiplicities and the differences must become stronger in this process that ultimately seeks to "render and express" that richness to whoever is willing to engage with those images.

---

12. Baudelaire's modern painter's mirror is in this sense unlike the one found in Stendhal's *Le rouge et le noir*. If the latter famously suggests that "the novel is a mirror journeying along a high road" where a kaleidoscopic crowd like Baudelaire's might indeed gather, Stendhal's long parenthesis makes the point that the one who carries this mirror that can reflect the blue skies as well as "the mire in the puddles" is not to blame, since the road and especially the "road inspector" are responsible for the puddles. See Stendhal, *Scarlet and Black* (London: Penguin, 1953), 365–366. With Baudelaire the painter becomes himself the mirror, and intensifies or gives more life to the life being painted, so the issue is no longer one of reflecting something already there. More on Stendhal later.

13. "a self unsatiable from the *non-self*, which, at every instant, offers it and expresses it in images more alive than life itself, always unstable and fleeting." Baudelaire, OC II, 692.

14. *The Basic Writings of Nietzsche*, trans. Walter Kaufmann (New York: Modern Library, 2000), 36.

I would like to suggest that these practices of the visible closely relate to the aesthetic experience *Precious Liquids* proposes, even as the latter appears very still, silent, uncrowded. In *The Gay Science*, a title deliberately resonant with the troubadours' joyous art of *gai saber*,[15] Nietzsche denounces the fundamental criterion of habit he finds operating in the traditional concept and common use of "knowledge," wherein "something strange is to be reduced to something *familiar*."[16] Nietzsche calls instead for a process of estrangement from "what we are used to," which, he points out, is in fact "most difficult to 'know'—that is, to see as a problem; that is, to see as strange, as distant, as 'outside us.'" While "men of knowledge," the philosophers he criticizes in this aphorism, would consider "the 'inner world'" or "the facts of consciousness"[17] the most familiar, Nietzsche considers such an interiority a productive site of extreme estrangement.

Like the consciousness of the kaleidoscopic mirror Baudelaire paints, or the estrangement Nietzsche proposes, the sanity at stake in *Precious Liquids* is not a matter of building up a stable self, preserving its identity against everything and everyone around it. Still, there must be a highly efficient system to enable and sustain the absorption of "joys" without letting them stagnate. The mirror must be as large as the crowd, for instance. The water tank must have a ten-thousand-gallon capacity. The flow of absorbed fluids must continue, somehow.

Bourgeois' piece forms part of her large series of *Cells*, which were first exhibited as such in 1991. A "cell" evokes solitude, alienation, imprisonment, and *in*sanity. In *Precious Liquids* as an instance of a "cell," the enclosure and door do point to a site of solitary and possibly involuntary confinement, although the displacements and multiplications of meaning already in play, in what I have discussed of the installation thus far, also suggest a less ominous situation. "Cells" have for centuries held captive individuals (for example, the Salpêtrière's poor, prostitute, and

15. In his introduction to *The Gay Science*, Kaufmann discusses the reference to the fourteenth-century Provençal poetry competition called "consistori del gai saber" and its background in the twelfth-century Provençal troubadours. "Translator's Introduction" in *The Gay Science*, trans. Walter Kaufmann (New York: Vintage, 1974). Nietzsche makes the reference explicit in his commentary about *The Gay Science* in *Ecce Homo* (*The Basic Writings of Nietzsche*, 750).

16. Nietzsche, *Gay Science*, 300.

17. Nietzsche, 301.

"insane" women since the late seventeenth century), but they have also been monastic chambers, which suggest a possibly more meditative kind of withdrawal from public space. This religious sector certainly also has a history of participating in social systems of imprisonment, not to mention its rules of gender division and celibacy,[18] but at least in principle the monastic cell would open up a space for "inner life." After 1664, Robert Hooke adopted the name for the small rooms monks inhabited, to describe what he saw in cork with magnifying glasses.[19] "Cell" now also names the minimal unit of organic life, and the cylindrical, threshold structure simultaneously stresses the biological cell's minimal status as the limit of the organic and the inorganic.

The Inorganic Cause

The installation *Precious Liquids* is thus a *cell* in all of these ways, both in name and appearance from this initial, external perspective. As such, the cell calls to an experience of this threshold between organic and inorganic, so it is necessary to discuss what is at stake in these two terms, and to inquire about the way in which the work brings its viewer to such a threshold. In my discussion on hysteria (in chapter 1), the inorganic involved, via Deleuze, questions of bodily intensities "beyond the organism." Organs at this point are sporadic sites where "color and line," for instance, become invested.[20] This was the beginning of a concept, provoked by painting, of sensation, which followed the trajectory of the drive, rather than the ego and its correlative specular body that appears unified in the mirror stage, as Lacan points out. So, before returning to sensations as the effects of artworks, "organic" and "inorganic" need to be situated with regard to the logic of the drive that intersects with

18. Diderot's novel *La religieuse* comes to mind here, especially given its interest in exposing the management of women's sexual desire and sexual politics.

19. "Observation XVIII. Of the *Schematisme or Texture* of Cork, and of the Cells and Pores of some other frothy Bodies." *Micrographia, or Some Physiological Descriptions of Minute Bodies Made by Magnifying Glasses with Observations and Inquiries Thereupon* (London: John Martin James Allestry, 1664).

20. Deleuze, *FB*, 52. See the longer citation in chapter 1. Deleuze's thoughts in the passage are remarkably close to Baudelaire's account of the painter who absorbs "form and color" and embraces the "fleeting," just as Deleuze speaks of the "transitory organ."

biology in Freud's metapsychology. Freud indeed saw hysteric conversions from psychic to physical material as a distinct phenomenon for which "no organic cause" of illness could be found, an observation related to Charcot's problem with locating the cerebral lesion that would explain hysteria.[21] The inversion in play here is worth highlighting: Charcot seeks sensorial proof of the cause of insanity. *Precious Liquids* asserts that art—in the very destabilization of meaning and perception that forces one to think of words, objects, scenes that instead are taken for granted whenever they remain in their usual places—is a guarantee of sanity. The approach to the sensorial that turns toward a connection with something that *is not* deeply concerns psychoanalysis in terms of the object of the drive, or "objet *a*." Furthermore, Freud proposes this inexistent thing as the cause of a peculiar, perceptible manifestation in the body.

In this context, the realm of the "inorganic" is, then, not just that of "non-living matter," but also that of the imperceptible and nonrepresentable drive and object cause of desire (*objet a*). When Deleuze speaks of a painting's mobilization of a Body without Organs in the viewer, it is a matter, for example, of color or paint producing something singular upon encountering the eye (what he would call with Guattari "entering into an assemblage"). But the singularity's "inorganic" nature is not only about the paint–eye relation not depending upon an organism to do its work. It is also, crucially, about the desire that a painting is able to transmit, "investing" the eye (Standard Edition jargon would call it "cathecting") beyond the material elements paint and eye in general. The Body without Organs that art produces points, in this more profound way, to psychoanalysis, then, and to Freud's resort to biology in developing his metapsychology.

The case of unicellular organisms, precisely, allows Freud in *Beyond the Pleasure Principle* "to examine the desire that motivates life."[22] As cause of life, desire is, in some way, in a place external to the life that is its effect, inorganic in this sense. But there is more to get from the Protista. In a brilliant reading of the passages where Freud introduces unicellular organisms to examine the interaction between "germ" and "soma" (or "gene" and "individual"), Daniel Wilson explains that Freud

21. The problem, for contemporary neurology and psychiatry, of obtaining visible proof of the disorders that these fields recognize and manage remains a current one.

22. Daniel Wilson, "Freud's Lamarckian Clinic," *Inheritance in Psychoanalysis*, ed. James Godley and Joel Goldbach (Albany, NY: SUNY Press, 2019), 264.

engages closely with biological evolutionary theories and chooses the defeated Lamarckian one as his model to develop his metapsychology because there is a difference in motivation:

> Lamarckian evolution is motivated by the individual's need in excess of what is given in its biology. In the case of the Lamarckian animal—for example, the giraffe whose neck becomes longer as it stretches to reach higher branches—the individual's desire to reach the object of its instincts drives evolution. [. . .] Freud, however, uses Lamarck to theorize a response to a need that is beyond the pleasure principle, given that there is no way for the organism to modify itself to attain *das Ding*, the missing object. In response to the fact that there is no object for the drive in the environment, the organism uses its body to produce a hostile environment that explains this lack.[23]

Wilson points out that this operation of the unicellular organism models, to Freud, the human logic of the drive, beyond instinct. The organism's turn against itself in a masochistic gesture that transforms it to incarnate the cause of desire illustrates the body's distance from a mode of functioning that responds only to "organic" needs and stimuli in the environment. This, in Deleuze's theory, is the Body without Organs, and it is no accident that masochism is itself one of the ways of "making oneself a Body without Organs."[24]

The unicellular organisms in the experiment Freud considers (after Weismann) to figure out what motivates life are, fittingly, provided "with fresh nutrient fluid" as the condition for survival and reproduction. Yet "if the 'nutrient fluid' is not replaced, the organisms eventually die."[25] In *Precious Liquids*, the fluid that the environment does supply, water, is no longer available for this tank, which is also a cell and as such,

23. Wilson, 264.

24. Deleuze and Guattari in "How to Make Oneself a Body without Organs" cite from a case of masochism discussed by the psychoanalyst Michel de M'uzan. While the schizoanalysts reject the language of "lack" found in Wilson's citation (and in Lacanian psychoanalysis overall), their attack is aimed against conformist, normative, reactive understandings of desire, rather than at the structural gap that makes room for the new, which is the point of lack.

25. Freud in Wilson, 265.

to survive, must selectively manage the elements it absorbs and expels. But it is more than a cell working only to survive, and it is not even working for an organism. Its dynamics may respond, then, to something different, a more profound lack. To Freud, the organisms without the fresh nutrient fluid die from "products of metabolism which they extruded into the surrounding fluid,"[26] which Wilson explicates thus: "the organism's own biological processes are received back—by the organism—as if they originated in the environment. The protista finds its 'natural death' through a masochistic address."[27]

This operation can be compared with Bourgeois' statement about what "being a sculptor" is all about. Bourgeois in a late documentary interview starts by explaining, "you have to be quite aggressive to be a sculptor, really. To have the energy . . ." and she instantly picks up a small sheet of black paper in her hands to continue: "so when you see something like this, it doesn't hurt anybody, it's an inert thing, and [your impulse] is to look at it and say, "gee!," you see? You see immediately this twisting. That is to be a sculptor . . . It is aggressive . . . It means that: I don't like it that way, I want it my way. It is aggressive."[28] The quick, energetic twists and folds result in a small, compact spiral object that was not there initially. The sculptor's aggressive gesture in Bourgeois' demonstration responds, as she says, to an awareness of the fact that what is available in the environment does not satisfy. Bourgeois as sculptor, indeed, acts like the masochistic organism, which "does not look for something in the environment but rather transforms the environment in order to compensate for the fact that there is no object for the drive."[29] The masochistic address Wilson highlights in Freud's experiment leads the unicellular organism's misrecognized production of a toxic environment from its own body (as metabolic products) to its own death. Bourgeois' sculpture as a product of drive transforms the environment with different effects, perhaps.

A while before his essay on Bacon and painting, in *Difference and Repetition* (1968), Deleuze attacked representation as the prevailing epistemological paradigm, for its limited and limiting worldview, which

26. Freud in Wilson, 265.

27. Wilson, 265.

28. In Marion Cajori and Amei Walach, *The Spider, The Mistress, and the Tangerine* (USA: Zeitgeist Films; © Art Kaleidoscope Foundation, New York, 2008.).

29. Wilson, 265.

renders thought incapable of facing "the affirmed world of difference."[30] This happens, first of all, because "representation has only one center," whose mediatizing effect results in "not mobilizing or moving anything."[31] That center in modern philosophy is the concept of a self-identical subject of consciousness, or ipseity. Deleuze in this investigation does not propose an aesthetic clinic, but his key references to face the world of difference are Freud's death drive, Nietzsche's Eternal Return (on which more in a moment) and modern art. In his seminars Jacques Lacan often spoke of the problem of ipseity, exactly, which is not exclusive to philosophy, but a part of everyday life (or what Deleuze pejoratively calls "common sense" and "good sense"). Lacan brought this up again in Seminar XX to interrogate the ability of psychoanalysis to provoke change in a "spherical" or "Copernican" worldview with mankind at its center.[32] Lacan sees in Kepler the possibility of an "elliptical" worldview instead, which introduces two foci and is better at grasping "le point vif" "the live point,"[33] while Deleuze introduces "a painting or a sculpture"[34] in their capacity as "deformers" of representation, in order to restart the movement essential to the affirmation of difference. Deleuze's statement strongly resonates with Bourgeois' gesture to demonstrate the sculptor's aggressiveness, as does the philosopher's description of the "violence" upon thought of genuine thought. Like Baudelaire's "painter of modern life," painting and sculpture in Deleuze's account cannot be concerned with representing the preestablished world; they instead affirm the world of difference that is de-completed, driven, by the missing object discussed in the previous paragraph, to its decentering and deformation.

30. Gilles Deleuze, *Difference and Repetition*, trans. Paul Patton (London: Continuum, 2001), 78. Hereafter cited as *DR*.

31. Deleuze, 78.

32. Jacques Lacan, *Le Séminaire XX: Encore* (Paris: Seuil, 1975), 55. Hereafter cited as *E*. Roberto Harari suggests that this decentering is an epistemological position that distinguishes psychoanalysis from ego psychology. He also discusses Freud's placemenent of psychoanalysis in a chronological sequence of three "narcissistic wounds" to human beings, where the subject becomes decentered. The first wound comes from the displacement of the Earth away from the center of the universe, and the second from Darwin, who reveals the human species to be tied to the animal kingdom. Freud and Lacan, he shows, work with these two moments. *El Sujeto Descentrado: Una presentación del psicoanálisis* (Lumen: Buenos Aires, 2008), 17–18.

33. Lacan, *E*, 55.

34. Deleuze, *DR*, 78.

I believe this particular *Cell* of Bourgeois' is concerned, precisely, with the question about "the desire that motivates life," or "the missing object" that nonetheless drives a life on a unique trajectory, or a unique "Body without Organs," to the end. In the documentary Bourgeois also shares the following sequence of thoughts: "The purpose of the pieces . . . is to express emotions . . . My emotions are inappropriate to my size. My emotions are my demons . . . The intensity of the emotions are much too much for me to handle. I transfer the energy into sculpture."[35] "Emotions" or their "energy" are the metabolic products of Louise's body, and since this production is excessive, a transference is necessary (and the use of a fundamental concept of psychoanalysis here is no accident), or else this body would die from their demonic intensity, much like the masochistic organism. The risk of not transferring the demons to another support is death, and, certainly, an emotional state whose signs might suggest so-called insanity. In this precise sense, then, is art "a guaranty of sanity" to Bourgeois, then, and the "precious liquids" in question may be the death-driven body's products, on which more after the following section. But what is the difference between transferring the "demons" to sculpture, and transferring them to the environment so that they can then be misrecognized as destructive foreign agents? Also, what is the difference between a sculpture as work of art and an amulet?

Challenges of Extimate Knowledge

Precious Liquids' mode of presentation—enclosing, obstructing, beckoning in, turning "inside-out," bringing the "outside-in"—suggests, first of all, that the transference of energy does not stop, once and for all, in the sculpted materials. Like the other *Cells* and like other late, large scale installation works, (especially but not exclusively *Maman* [1999] among the other spiders, *I Do, I Undo,* and *I Redo* [1999–2000], and the giant steel mirror installation *Art is a Guaranty of Sanity* [2005–06]), *Precious Liquids* is concerned with its viewers going through the question of "the desire that motivates life," too, in the visual, poetic, plastic terms it offers. So, the installation offers a path through the question in a physical, sensorial presentation. As a complex, distinct effect of this desire, the installation recalls the working of a bodily symptom, as a writing of unconscious desire that calls to be deciphered, and points to that absolute lack that mobilizes the death drive. *Precious Liquids* thus proposes an understanding

35. Bourgeois in *The Spider, the Mistress and the Tangerine* (film).

of the artwork as a thing that comes from elsewhere—not New York City or Louise's childhood memories, not biology or the dictionary of common terms or even of psychoanalysis, not confinement practices, but somewhere further, an uncharted experience radically removed from anything in the world or its accepted history, for which Lacan proposed the word "extimate." This is what Nietzsche referred to in his previously mentioned quest for "unfamiliar knowledge" through self-estrangement.

How to avoid missing or dismissing this experience? This is a question I wish to pose as a reader of *Precious Liquids* (1992), which has already shown its oneiric character.[36] Like a dream in analysis, the work places us in a strange and specific situation within it, even before even looking in, and the various words that it offers point to multiple, simultaneous meanings that always fall short or begin to close in—as the tank's walls close in on the space within—on the uninterpretable navel that is the dream's hallmark. To Deleuze in 1968, modern painting and sculpture combine disparate points of view and movements across space,[37] renouncing the identity of the thing and of the viewing subject as its condition, in favor of something irreducible to them. An amulet, for instance a dreamcatcher, could never work in this way. The analytic dream also points to that "something," which the 1992 *Cell* sets forth through the exercise in disparate viewpoints and movements it requires of its viewer. To truly affirm the world of difference, "the thing must therefore be in no way identical, but torn asunder in a difference in which the identity of the seen object as well as that of the seeing subject vanish."[38] Furthermore, "each thing, each being must see its own identity swallowed up in difference, each no longer being more than a difference between differences. It is necessary to show difference going *differing* ('allant *différant*')."[39] What is the risk of this feeling of being "torn asunder," "vanished," and "swallowed up in difference"? Will this indeed happen upon entering the *Cell*?

Deleuze's claims on the world of difference are grounded on Nietzsche's will to embrace and affirm this encounter, particularly in

36. Mieke Bal discusses the viewer of Bourgeois' *Cells* as dreamer, with different interpretive consequences from mine, see Bal "Autotopography: Louise Bourgeois as Builder." *Biography: An Interdisciplinary Quarterly*, Honolulu, HI, 25.1 (Winter 2002): 180–202.

37. Deleuze, 78–79.

38. Deleuze, 79.

39. Deleuze, 79.

Klossowski's reading. The death of God as support for the grammatical fiction "I" must also have the effect of "swallowing up" the latter. According to Klossowski, Nietzsche's personal discovery of this correlation and the experience it provokes, of personal existence as "fortuitous,"[40] prompt Nietzsche's loss of his own identity in favor of simulacrum, in the characters Zarathustra and Dionysus, and of delirium.

In *Nietzsche and the vicious circle*, Klossowski pursued his interest in approaching Nietzsche's sickbed, through an analysis of the latter's fragments and personal letters written during the intervals of many crises described as severe migraines. Klossowski sought to interpret the connection between this writing and the crises from the perspective of Nietzsche's own theories of the body. Nietzsche distinguishes between "consciousness," "the person," and the "moral I" on the one hand, and, on the other, the body, impulses, and the *Selbst* as an unconscious force undermining the integrity and sovereignty of the mind. Klossowski highlights the migraine's function as an internal "*aggression that suspends his thinking*," proposing that "it is his own physical 'me' who *attacks to defend itself* from a dissolution: but *who* seeks to dissolve? Nietzsche's own brain."[41] The letters insist on the fact that thinking and writing is impossible for Nietzsche during the migraine attacks, so Klossowski notices in this alternation, between a crisis and a convalescent writing about the crisis that put the "brain" out of order, a clear enactment of the combat between an "I" as "consciousness" and the body as a manifold of impulses. The convalescent has become interested in observing and following the body's insurrections against the mind during his "valetudinarian states." Klossowski puts these recurrent considerations in Nietzsche's writing in terms very close to those of Freud with the hysterics, of "listening to the body": "the more he listened to his body, the more he came to distrust *the person the body supports*."[42] Nietzsche's attitude of distrusting the person or "I" while passionately observing the body responds to the following: "If the body is so much in pain, if the brain sends nothing but distress signals, it is because a *language* is trying to make itself heard at the cost

40. Klossowski, "Nietzsche, le polythéisme et la parodie" *Revue de métaphysique et de morale*. 63.2/3 (April–September 1958): 325–348, 326–327. Also published in *Un si funeste désir*, on the same year as Deleuze's *Nietzsche et la philosophie*, and cited in *DR* by Deleuze.

41. Klossowski, *Nietzsche et le cercle vicieux* (Paris: Mercure, 1969), 50.

42. Klossowski, 51.

of reason."[43] This other language speaks, then, through symptoms, at the cost of reason and of the unity of personhood.

Klossowski discerns an experience of the body qua locus of "drives" (*impulsions/Antriebe*) that destroys the person or consciousness as Nietzsche follows, from one crisis to the next, through the labyrinth of the drives what he calls "the guiding thread of the body."[44] I read Nietzsche's commitment to this "thread" that Klossowski distinguishes as "Ariadne's thread," alluding to this female figure in Nietzsche's poem "Ariadne's Lament," as the will to overcome the previously discussed repudiation of femininity Freud discerned in his patients at the end of analysis.[45] Guiding one through a disorientating coiled space toward its dangerous, life-threatening center, Ariadne's thread speaks, then, to the quest for a knowledge that embraces the strangeness of the feminine part of the subject. When *The Gay Science* repeatedly returns to body and "women," it points to their subversion of an interiority or consciousness that could be called "one's own" and provide the ground, or, rather, the necessary un-grounding for a different, uncanny knowledge: "gai saber," "joyous knowledge" or "savoir."

Ariadne's thread, Klossowski explains, leads toward "the supreme thought, but also the supreme feeling"[46] that is "the Eternal Return of the Same." Nietzsche's call to self-estrangement warns against a reading of "the same" in this formula as ipseity. Instead, this return as the "fate" or unique trajectory of the drives in symptoms gives rise to the highest act of thought, at the limit of its repository's destruction, and only by renouncing the Platonic subordination of body and emotions to the mind.[47]

---

43. Klossowski, 51.

44. Klossowski, 56.

45. See my Introduction. Tracy McNulty develops this line of thought in the final chapters of her remarkable *The Hostess: Hospitality, Femininity, and the Expropriation of Identity* (Minneapolis: University of Minnesota Press, 2007).

46. Klossowski, *Nietzsche et le cercle*, 97.

47. As a return, this highest thought comes in the form of what Deleuze calls an "original repetition" correlated to difference. While body and emotion are not at all privileged in Kant's discussion on the feeling of the sublime, this description of the Eternal Return as "the supreme thought and feeling" do evoke the extreme to which the subject's faculties are, according to Kant, pushed by this feeling, specifically the failure of the imagination to mediate for the idea of a magnitude or power that exceed the imagination. See *Critique of Judgment* paragraphs 23–29. The play of the faculties in the feeling of the sublime is also the model in *DR* for Deleuze's

This is an aesthetic subversion or transvaluation of values. Klossowski indicates that Nietzsche's exploration of the body's complicated, foreign language cultivates a *jouissance* that takes thought beyond the boundaries of self-preservation and good sense:

> Not only does he interpret suffering as energy, he wills it thus: physical suffering would be livable only insofar as it was closely connected to joy [*jouissance*], insofar as it develops a voluptuous lucidity: either it would extinguish any possible thought, or it would reach the delirium of thought.[48]

For Nietzsche, Ariadne's thread leads to either the extinction of any possible thought, or to delirium, which is where his writing ends up. Are these two the only possible fates, then, for someone who courageously follows this thread and embraces its correlative jouissance unanchored to the signifier? Are the hysteric's "unintelligible fantasies" Freud lamented condemned to either remaining unintelligible or to destroying her body?[49] In both cases, that voluptuous lucidity, another name for "gai savoir," appears untenable; it seems as though this feminine uniqueness cannot be sustained anywhere. Must the hysteric give up the foreign language of the body and adapt to common language if she wants to live? Bourgeois' installation art—which at times indeed conveys a labyrinthine exploration[50]—seems to indicate a different possibility, without turning away from the symptom or attempting to erase it.

If anything tends to fulfill the conditions of affirming difference, it is, to Deleuze, the modern work of art, which "leaves the domain of representation to become experience/experiment ('*expérience*'), transcendental empiricism or science of the sensible."[51] Is the work of art, then,

transcendental empiricism, based on pushing each faculty, not just the imagination, to its point of impossibility as the mark of genuine thought.

48. Klossowski, *Nietzsche et le cercle*, 51. Brackets are mine to highlight the word *jouissance* in the original.

49. I discuss this comment of Freud's in chapter 1.

50. Deleuze, *DR*, 79. The work of reading *Precious Liquids* toward its center proves to be something of a labyrinth. In *Cell (Arch of Hysteria)* (1992–93) the wide, inward opening door mimics the wall panels that form the rest of the enclosure, giving the impression of a labyrinth's entrance.

51. "Transcendental empiricism" later names the aesthetic system Deleuze proposes, where experience and sensation break out of limits, forcing every faculty of the

a buffer to the blow of "voluptuous lucidity" that destroys the body? Not in the aesthetic clinic. Again, the experience and experiment do not stop within the artist or the modern—or contemporary—artwork as his/her product, especially not in Bourgeois' *Cells*. If art is a matter of experience and experiment, as Deleuze suggests with the single word "expérience," derived, like "peril," from the Latin "experiri," "to try," one can think of experience as a risk of venturing outside of mastered, familiar territory. Viewing with a body receptive to the work's proposed extimacy begins with welcoming its experience; one must go through this dream, regardless of its having been sculpted by someone else. One might say that one can assume responsibility for having put oneself in front of it, as I did, several times.[52]

At the Threshold

The structure's front door reveals the right side of a small, nineteenth-century iron bed, its foot closest to the door and its head against the interior curved wall. The museum, and owner of the artwork, does not allow visitors inside the tank, so they may stand only at the threshold of the *Cell*—a name that, peering into a bedroom, is confirmed by the scene's suggestion of an intimate and solitary monastic retreat with its bare individual bed. It is, however, surrounded by four tall iron stands, from which branch horizontal rods holding empty glass vessels of various shapes and sizes. The clear clusters, in the shape of spheres, droplets, and vertically positioned hourglasses and ovals with openings on both ends hover above and around the bed, surrounding the area that would hold a mattress and a body, but instead its bare surface holds a puddle around a small drain near the bed's foot that, like the glass, glistens within the lit space (figure 2.2). The puddle could evoke some kind of secretion—

mind to "the extreme point of its dissolution" where it attains its most unique kind of action.

52. At the time I was not aware of Freud's essay on the *Moses* of Michelangelo (to which I referred in the previous chapter), where he writes about his experience of standing in front of the sculpture, or of the story about his trip to Rome and his repeated visits to see the sculpture. I had also not thought about Dora's extremely long contemplation of Raphael's *Madonna Sistina* at the Dresden gallery, which I considered in this book's Introduction.

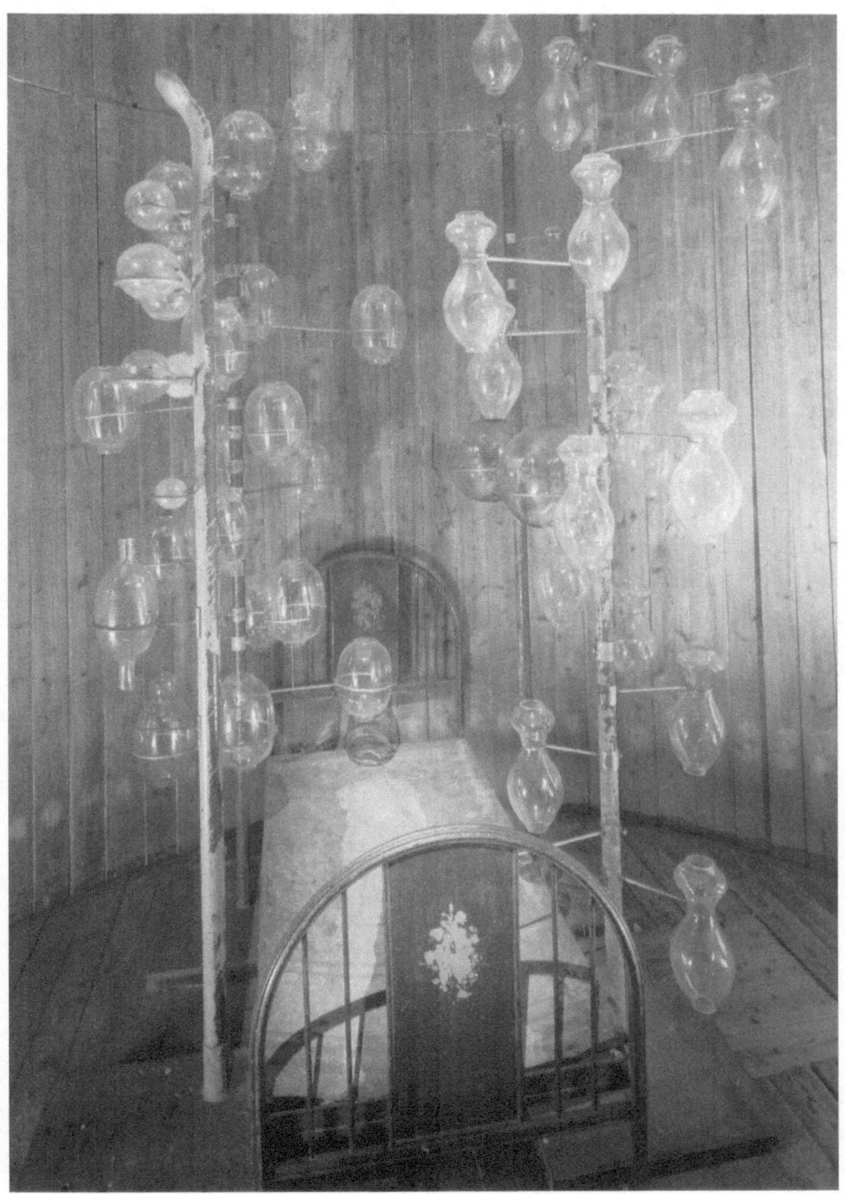

Figure 2.2. Louise Bourgeois, *Precious Liquids*, 1992. Interior view: Bed and glass vessels. Photo: Georges Meguertidtchian. Musée national d'art moderne © CNAC/MNAM/Dist. RMN-GP/© 2019 The Easton Foundation/Licensed by VAGA at Artists Rights Society (ARS), New York.

sweat and tears could have a similar aspect. Urine makes sense, since the puddle is placed where the lower part of the body would usually rest . . . Semen? Amniotic fluid? Milk? But this seems to be a child's bed; it would be too small for most human bodies capable of producing the latter two fluids. "Precious liquids" invokes all of these secretions (and still others),[53] which we do not perceive as such. The title resonates with the water on the bed and the liquid shimmer of the light on the glass bubbles and vessels. Instead of being filled with body fluids, all of these repositories present a gleaming emptiness that easily brings to mind Lacan's discussion, inspired by Heidegger, on the vase as a creative act of outlining the void of *das Ding*, the object that does not exist.[54] Donald Kuspit's claim that Bourgeois' *Cells* "monumentalize emptiness"[55] seems particularly accurate before this sight. One may have expected a monk or some other individual, sheltered by the wooden walls in the lit room. Yet the human body as a unified whole or even an incomplete figure, such as the one examined in *Arch of Hysteria* (1993), is absent here, or distributed into the multiple vases that remind of certain organs (uterus and stomach) floating, as it were, above the bed's perimeter.

Bourgeois introduced a bed into other *Cells* too. *Red Room* (*Parents*) (1994) features a full-size bed with a red rubber bedspread. *Cell I* (1991) features a single bed holding fabric elements, among which the first instance of "art is a guarantee of sanity" appears, embroidered.[56] Both *In and Out* (1995) and the slightly older *Cell* (*Arch of Hysteria*) (1992–93) contain individual beds with two stacked mattresses, each supporting a bronze

53. In a later collaborative piece with Roni Horn, whose *Vatnasafn/Library of Water* (2007) will be discussed in the final chapter, Bourgeois offers a list of what she considers precious liquids. *Wonderwater (Alice Offshore). 1. Louise Bourgeois* (Göttingen: Steidl, 2004), 51. This text for *Wonderwater* was taken from Bourgeois' diary, July 21, 1993.

54. Lacan evokes Heidegger's essay on "The Thing" to consider the making of an empty vase as a fundamental act of creation, and recalls a project Jacques Prévert developed with a collection of empty match boxes. His multiplication of emptiness evokes the Thing beyond objecthood. *Le séminaire Livre VII: L'éthique de la psychanalyse* . . . (hereafter cited as *Éthique*) (Paris: Seuil, 1986).

55. Kuspit, "Louise Bourgeois in Psychoanalysis . . . ," 22.

56. This *Cell* strongly evokes a clinical space, since, adjacent to the bed, it also features medical instruments and a bed pan. The site of a cure for an ailing—or possibly convalescent—body relates, in Bourgeois' memories, to her role of attending to her mother's long illness. Thanks to Maggie Wright for bringing this piece to my attention.

figure, from the same *arc de cercle* mold used for the sculpture discussed in chapter 1, in matte, armless versions. Something seems to spill out of the body in both of these, too. In *In and Out*, adjacent to the cubical structure that contains the arching body, a large, pink, blobby mass seems to ooze and spread, supported by its own downward flow of material (it is a pink version of the sculpture *Avenza Revisited II* [1968–69]). It is as if the body had managed to seep out of confinement, at the price of abjection, upon going through the square panels in which the translucent window panes are missing, replaced by suspended iron meat grinders at the center. In *Cell (Arch of Hysteria)*, the bed's fitted sheet is embroidered in red with the sentence "Je t'aime," repeated *ad nauseam* in columns. The repetition evokes a grade school handwriting exercise, or its torture,[57] which is echoed by the old-fashioned mechanical saw nearby. In comparison with *Precious Liquids*' wet bed, the red writing appears bloody, and it sheds light on writing itself as an insistent, bodily secretion.

There are differences in mood between the two cells I have just described and *Precious Liquids* (1992). The work of light and glass in the latter, as well as the proportions of the bed with regard to the room are key to the atmosphere's appearing less unambiguously stifling, terrifying. If the *Cells* are dreams, the ones I have just mentioned are obviously nightmares. Of course, I have not yet described everything inside *Precious Liquids*, whose more intimidating elements appear in front of the bed. But I am getting ahead of myself. I also point to the *Cells* that include an *Arch of Hysteria* figure, above all, to underscore the absence of a figure in *Precious Liquids*, which has specific, striking effects for the question of aesthetic experience as a mobilization of the drives, as the condition for transmitting sensations. The work of the drives dismantles the senses as parts of a unified body, as I have explained, and a sculpted or painted human figure can certainly set off such an experience, as *Arch of Hysteria* (1993) does, through its unique pose, traits (headless, excessively long) and effects (mirroring, hanging). Yet, as contagious as a figure can be, its presence still takes some weight off the viewer's body; some of the intensity can be returned to the tortured/enjoying figure observed.

Within the empty, huge water container of *Precious Liquids* with its semi-open doors at opposite ends, one finds empty containers floating vertically, many of which have openings at both ends. A *mise en abyme*,

57. A recurrent motif in Bourgeois. See a facsimile of *Je t'aime*, 1977 (red ink on grid paper), in *Destruction of the Father . . .* , 108–109.

then. There are no words inside to orient the reading; instead, I suddenly discover a silence that cannot be found elsewhere in the rest of the museum, and certainly not out on the deafening, roaring Paris streets. The silence is noticeable even from the threshold, and, although this viewpoint has not been established as the limit to where the viewer can step by the artist, but instead by the museum, it favors a more sustained reflection on the room's emptiness, and the almost invisible body taken apart. The empty bed has the effect of marking off a site for the body.[58] The body that is supposed to lie in bed here (as in *In and Out*) seems to have lost its external envelope, and so it hovers around the bed that would support the body, if it were there to contain the organs. My body stands by its side, too, only a bit further. Like Sophie Calle's *Wedding Dress* on Freud's couch, earlier (Introduction), this composition literalizes the "beside art" etymology for "clinic." But I am not the analyst to the individual who might lie on this bed. I have proposed that reading this work requires going through its experience in the way in which one has a dream. In this case, the bed and the softly lit bedroom could await "my" body, anticipating an overpowering impulse to lie down I did not foresee.

At the threshold of this *Cell*, marking the threshold between inorganic and organic life, my vision and hearing are split from the rest of my body. For, they have already exceeded the limits of the doorway to observe the bed and glass clusters. And transgressing the strict rules of perspective that leave me only looking from the side, not only can I assume the viewpoint of the photographer who was able to get a frontal view of the bed (figure 2.2), but also a viewpoint from the bed, and so become a strange dweller inside this room's beauty, even when I don't have permission to fully enter and lie down. Do I hear the room's silence, or mine? A loss of certainty about identities and personal belongings is precisely what the transmission of sensation involves. And perhaps this decentered dwelling is exactly what is at stake for the body, as the glass, organ-like vessels and spheres around the bed propose. Sometimes the inability to feel "comfortable in one's own skin," or in one's own room, can foreground silence as its own mode of intensity.[59]

---

58. A comparable strategy is considered by Bal in regards to the chair in Louise Bourgeois' *Spider* (1997), 14.

59. See Bourgeois' words on the fear of silence in Horn, *Wonderwater . . . 1. Louise Bourgeois*, 7.

Lying Down: From Partial Objects and Flows to *Objet a*

Like a membrane, the wooden cylinder delineates the border between inside and outside, selecting candidates to be absorbed or kept out of its precious nucleus. So, I find myself seeing the room at once as a spectator at the door, and as though lying in its bed, perhaps dreaming or hallucinating the glass vessels floating above my small resting place. Nietzsche's valetudinarian states linger on my mind. Now the vessels evoke hospital-room oxygen tanks and saline solution dispensers, although the iron bed and such hospital equipment belong to separate moments. The use of glass for these vessels fits the bed's obsolete style and echoes other works where Bourgeois highlights the medicinal use of glass. For instance, *Ventouse* (1990) is a marble structure made of two stacked rectangles whose horizontal surface holds in place a collection of glass suction cups found at a French flea market. Louise used to apply similar cupping jars on her emphysemic mother's back.[60] Glass, especially suspended in space, as it appears in *Precious Liquids*, delicately insinuates a fragile state of the body. External organs are connected to the body in order to support the organism when it is helpless. Also when it is helpless—dreaming, ailing, suffering, enjoying—the body, or its vessels now hovering around the bed, might secrete its fluids.

"When we are in a tense state," Bourgeois said, regarding *Precious Liquids*, "our muscles tighten; when they relax the tension goes down, a liquid is released." The shifts in tension and intensity are interesting to her in both a physical and emotional sense. "So it is all a matter of being in touch with that flowing of liquids. I could give you a dozen examples," she adds, "if you are terribly hungry saliva comes at the sight of a lamb chop. In this piece the liquid is suggested by the glass shapes; some are closed like drops and others, open like funnels, are metaphors for the muscles of the body."[61] Bourgeois presents the tight bond between bodily flows and emotion most concisely in her note to the Georges Pompidou museum who purchased the piece, where she

60. Lyon-Wall, Scott, "Ventouse, 1990" in *Louise Bourgeois*, ed. Marie-Laure Bernadac and Jonas Storsve (exhibition catalogue; Paris: Editions du Centre Pompidou, 2008), 304.

61. Bourgeois in "Mortal Elements: Pat Steir Talks with Louise Bourgeois," *Artforum* 32.1 (1993), reprinted in *Destruction of the Father . . .*, 235.

writes: "Intense emotions become a material liquid, a precious liquor."[62] She construes body fluids as refined products of a procedure that strongly resonates with what I have discussed on hysterical conversion, and with an understanding of the work of art also as conversion of the nonsensible missing object of the drives, which also fail to appear in the mirror stage, when the infant is propped up and presented with an image to identify with. The work of art converts this unconscious experience into material, sensorial terms that make space for the singularity of an unconscious experience of objet *a*.

As Rosalind Krauss recalls with Bourgeois' sculpture in mind, "object petit a" is Lacan's reconceptualization of the partial object[63] from Melanie Klein, where the infant, unable to perceive the mother or itself as whole individuals, depends on the breast's appearance for its survival. The partial object unleashes an experience exceeding the need to satiate hunger (whether with breastmilk or a lambchop), as Klein points out in her discussion of the infant's experiences of pleasure or pain with the internalized breast. From my previous exposition of the desire that causes life and the problem of the object missing from experience entirely and not intermittently, one can get a sense of Lacan's inflection on the object *a*. It not only registers the infant's early somatic events before they can be symbolized in language; it also implies that no one and nothing in the environment can possibly satisfy the drive. The partial objects to Lacan "only partially represent the function that produces them."[64] Beyond the part is real lack, not the whole. The trauma that determines, in excess of the organism's needs, a subject's singular modality of pleasure and pain concerns a structural loss or lack that is "the universal condition of experience . . . Because each human inherits this loss, there is no Other that can be held responsible for this loss."[65]

The infantile somatic events, where bodily flows are of key importance, can thus be understood as pointing to a true source of creativity in the subject, and become material for an original transmission on the

62. Marie-Laure Bernadac, *Louise Bourgeois* (Paris: Flammarion, 2006), 141.

63. Krauss, "Objet partiel" in *Louise Bourgeois* (2008), 211.

64. "Subversion of the Subject and Dialectic of Desire in the Freudian Unconscious" *Écrits* (New York: W.W. Norton, 2006) 693.

65. Wilson, *Freud's Lamarckian Clinic*, 265.

level of the unconscious.[66] The negative object makes room, not only for processes and feelings of persecution, fusion, disintegration, splitting, reparation, but also for the subject's singular desire, or "difference," in Deleuze's previously mentioned terms. When Deleuze and Guattari in *Anti-Oedipus* discuss cuts and flows, they examine these processes in children's cases to insist that it is of the utmost importance to consider the uniqueness of each child's "desiring machine," that is, the combinations the child develops with those processes and other unexpected elements in the environment that should not be ignored in favor of a fantasy regarding the child's relation to its parents. To eat, defecate, and sleep, "Joey," for instance, requires "machines provided with motors, wires, lights, carburetors, propellers, and steering wheels: an electrical feeding machine, a car-machine that enables him to breathe, an anal machine that lights up."[67] Bruno Bettelheim's patient Joey, they insist, repurposes these machines in an unpredictable, original way, in response to the lack of an object for his drives.

To the schizoanalysts, and to Lacanian analysis, this response of the drives cannot be forced into an Oedipal interpretation, or even understood as a way of compensating for not entering language (Joey is diagnosed with autism), since language, by definition, cannot grasp the difference that, to Deleuze, makes all the difference in the world. Bourgeois' symbolism is concerned with uniquely transmitting this differential level of experience and with making room for the viewer's singular desire, too. Bourgeois therefore works with the poetics of body fluids in response to what she calls "intense emotions" and psychoanalysis calls drives, ascribing a "precious" value to the resulting liquids as products of remarkable operations that cross over from the inorganic to the organic, or from unshared, inner experience into the sensible. Again, this can be described in terms of conversion, too (and the words "precious liquids" now also echo "the precious blood of Jesus Christ," in the Catholic ritual where wine is turned into blood and bread into a body,

66. Nixon's Kleinian reading of Bourgeois' early 1960s latex sculptures as feces is highly relevant. See chapter 5 in *Fantastic Reality*.

67. Deleuze and Guattari, *Anti-Oedipus*, trans. Hurley, Seem, and Lane (London: Continuum, 2004), 37. Hereafter cited as AO.

in transubstantiation).[68] But it turns out that, as I also noted, the only liquid materially included in the *Cell* is a small puddle of water on the bed, where I began to see organs and oxygen tanks hovering over me.

Aside from the puddle hinting at body fluids, the five senses cannot detect the precious liquids as such in the room. Why is this? Or what kind of further conversion does this trait of the installation serve? It's not exactly that the water should be viewed as converted into, say, urine, in a bathetic effect. The absence of a body in the room and of its invoked fluids not only puts me, as viewer, in its place, but also points back, through me as viewer/dweller, to the nonsensible life of the drives and that which mobilizes them.

Primal Scene

If *Precious Liquids* had initially intimidated, with its tall façade and enclosed space, it now vulnerates, with the evocations of illness and involuntary secretions that led to a discussion of the drives at stake in such processes. It was also the outdated materials with which illness or perhaps convalescence was evoked that had a vulnerating effect. I may be able to situate the iron bed frames, the New York tank that surrounds the bed, and the use of glass suction cups, or even a bit about how they related to the artist's life. But, as they mark off a site for my body, they make me face the fact that they preceded me; they take me back to a moment before my own life.

Exactly this gap is at stake in the fantasy in psychoanalysis. The unconscious fantasy, which can be deduced only from an individual's symptoms, operates in humans as a way of organizing the structural lack in imaginary terms,[69] and it involves filling in the gap for something that cannot be remembered directly with a borrowed experience. Freud developed this concept in terms of the primal scene, through work with the patient known as the Wolf Man, where Freud explains: "A child catches hold of this phylogenic experience where his own experience fails him. He fills in the gaps in individual truth with prehistoric truth;

68. Regarding the holy body and the demonic one (where Charcot saw earlier sketches of hysterical attacks), they are often difficult to tell apart, as both attempt to symbolize and control something traumatic.

69. The fantasy posits an Other in the place of the missing object (for instance, the mother who capriciously offers or withdraws the breast from the infant).

he replaces occurrences in his own life by occurrences in the life of his ancestors."[70] In his analysis, the Wolf Man remembers/constructs a witnessed *a tergo* sex scene between his parents, and the unconscious idea that his father's violence caused his mother's dysentery.

Let me pause here. Why return to the mother and father figures after the recently mentioned view, put forth compellingly by the schizoanalysts, that the singular trajectory of the drives cannot be reduced to a subject's relation to this parental triangle? Is it not, precisely, a way of denying the death of God as imaginary Other that sustained the "I," a death that, as Nietzsche claimed, needs to be encountered in the aesthetic as "voluptuous lucidity"? Yet the fantasy remains crucially relevant in contemporary psychoanalysis. Already in the Wolf Man case, Freud recognizes that not everyone actually witnessed parental coitus or seduction, yet he evinces that the primal scene has a logical function in the cause of a subject's neurosis, since it figures sex and the Other's jouissance as cause of an individual's existence. In an expanded reading of this, beyond neurosis, one can say the fantasy provides an analysis with a space for a subject's response to the structural fact that the beginning of an individual's life is the result of an Other's desire, a lacking Other, that is, who has inscribed the subject in language. While the neurotic may see the father and/or mother as responsible for its suffering or enjoyment in the fantasy, all humans are cut off from instinctual life to begin with, no matter what the surrounding conditions are. The object is missing, but a fantasy (or perverse scenario, or psychotic mission) makes up, in a specific way, for that fundamental negativity where the drives are unbound. The schizoanalysts attack the theory of the individual fantasy as an imaginary production with no revolutionary potential, or potential to fuel the Body without Organs.[71] But as Shanna de la Torre explains, "the fantasy of the primal scene is a narration of the insoluble that leaves the insoluble in place; it gives representation to a trauma that is outside language, and that representation bears the brutal residue of the real contradiction it both constructs and recalls."[72] The goal of deciphering the fantasy is thus not to constrain the unconscious within

70. Freud, *SE* XVII, 97.

71. Deleuze and Guattari, *AO* 30; 81; *ATP*, 151.

72. De la Torre, 29.

it, since this is where the subject's jouissance is already "stuck."[73] On the contrary, the ethical work of analysis is one of unbinding the drives from the imaginary constructions in the fantasy, to enable, from the "brutal residue of the real contradiction," the construction of an aesthetic object that does bring about change, or one could also say to "make oneself a BwO" that has consequences beyond the individual's private world.

Coming back to the Wolf Man's primal scene, this fantasy of coitus *a tergo*—whether or not it corresponds to what really happened or was really seen and misunderstood—serves to shape the work of the drives in his body, in a mode of jouissance that has to do with his intestines. In other words, the primal scene causes a hysterical conversion in the Wolf Man's body that speaks of his particular relationship to jouissance. The boy's immediate response to this witnessed scene at eighteen months old is a bowel movement that interrupts the parents, and later, at age three, when he observes a young female servant cleaning the floors in the position the mother assumed in the fantasy, he urinates. These events quite accurately exemplify Bourgeois' statement on *Precious Liquids*. By reading the patient's symptoms, key memories, and the dream of wolves that gives the case its name, Freud and the Wolf Man construct his primal scene, where "looking" is essential. His childhood dream features a very familiar spatial distribution for the viewer of *Precious Liquids*: the wolves, "perfectly still," "looked" through the window at the child in his bed, "as though they had riveted their whole attention upon me."[74] As the sole action in the dream, this interaction unveils the patient's memory of witnessing the sex scene, where his own "attentive looking" is in play.

A Little Girl's Scene

In the cell whose dream I welcomed, the small bed is the privileged site for an individual, a child, to look not only at the surrounding vessels,

73. Apollon writes: "The analyst's maneuver is to sustain an ethical approach rather than remitting the subject indefinitely back to the Oedipal situation by imposing himself as a third party through force. It is important that the subject escape from the trap of the false prohibition. As long as Marguerite continues to impute responsibility for the prohibited onto her mother, she will never gain access to the savoir of the impossible, where the very fact of language directly affects jouissance." "From Symptom to Fantasy," *After Lacan: Clinical Practice and the Subject of the Unconscious* (Albany, NY: SUNY Press, 2002), 134.

74. Freud, *SE* XVII, 29.

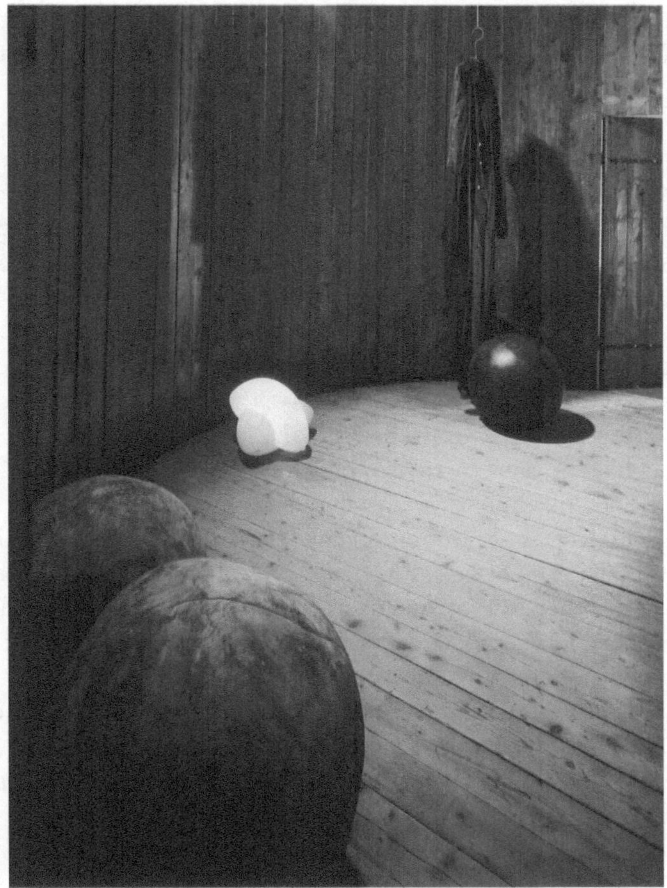

Figure 2.3. Louise Bourgeois, *Precious Liquids*, 1992. Interior view with *Le trani épisode*, 1971. Photo: Phillipe Migeat. Musée National d'Art Moderne. © CNAC/MNAM/Dist. RMN-Grand Palais/2019 The Easton Foundation/VAGA at Artists Rights Society (ARS), New York.

but also at the strange set of objects that lie and hang, perfectly still, in front of it.

Directly across from the bed, on the wooden floor, glows a small sculpture that serves as a lamp: Bourgeois' *Le Trani Episode* (1970–71) cast in alabaster. It consists of two oblong, perpendicularly superimposed lumps that suggest at once male genitals and female breasts. In the *Precious Liquids* context these body parts also suggest their corresponding fluids, but what flows out of the piece is light. Facing the right corner of the bed and against the opposite curved wall, two large, black rubber spheres sit on the floor, below an excessively long dark raincoat, suspended from a hanger along the tank's wall. The (phallic composite of) spheres and coat threaten, nightmarishly out of proportion with the small cell and bed. Under the raincoat, another layer of clothing, a light-colored shirt, peeks through. According to the work's catalogue description, embroidered on this shirt under the coat are the words *Merci/mercy*. Both "Thank you" and "mercy" presuppose the structure of the address I explained in chapter 1. Like the wolves in the Wolf Man's dream, the Other of the fantasy could "eat one up," so one would cry for mercy; a child spared from this outcome could then say "merci" to this Other. At what cost, however? What did the child give up to be spared? Did the child play the game of seduction, like the Salpêtrière hysterics? It's a good sign that both garments rest, limp and still, instead of dressing up some terrifying Other.

On the left corner in front of the bed, and closer to the cell's back door, sit a pair of light-beige, wooden spheres symmetrical to the black ones on the other side of the room. The opposition and symmetry of these two sets of objects is complementary. But the dark raincoat breaks the symmetry. Or is it, rather, that a corresponding light coat above the beige spheres is missing? And what if this absence were the more unsettling detail? Preceding affirmed, exclusive male and female identities in a binary relation, the scene's composition with *Le Trani Episode* at its center evokes the enigma of sexual difference.[75]

Bourgeois stated that in *Precious Liquids* a little girl encounters passion, rather than fear:

> *Precious Liquids* refers to a girl who grows up and finds passion instead of terror. She stops being frightened and discovers passion. Glass becomes a metaphor for the muscles of the body; representation of the emotions, of the mechanism of instability. When the muscles relax and the tension is lowered, a liquid is secreted. Inner emotions become physically liquid, release the secretion of a precious substance. Thus, when you let yourself weep, tears indicate the end of suffering,

75. For a discussion on the difference between binary, complementary oppositions and Lacan's theory of sexual difference, examined through cases of hysteria and transsexualism, see Gherovici, *Please Select Your Gender*.

> and when perspiration occurs on your back due to a state of apprehension, it indicates mastery and resolution of fear. Liquid secretion can be intensely pleasurable.[76]

How might one approach this statement together with the scene facing the bed? Is it a primal scene reduced to the male and female genital organs as aggrandized, geometrical part objects? In this case the action would be dismantled, and each "sex" sent back to its corner and adjacent door, as in public bathrooms or confinement centers. But then this would not be a very passionate encounter for the little girl. Is it a reduction of jouissance to the pleasure principle, in the good functioning of muscles and nervous and ejaculatory systems? Is that all, regarding passion? The shift from inner emotion to precious liquid the installation reflects on exceeds such mechanics, with its ambiguous *Trani Episode* sculpture occupying center stage, glowing while the floating glass vessels shimmer. The *Cell*'s strange beauty may be tied to "passion."

Consider Baudelaire's recognition of the same surprising definition of the beautiful by Stendhal as Nietzsche, in a famous passage from *Genealogy of Morals*. Stendhal "s'est rapproché de la vérité, plus que beaucoup d'autres, en disant que *le Beau n'est que la promesse du bonheur*" ("got close to the truth, more than many others, in saying that the Beautiful is nothing but the promise of happiness").[77] Both Baudelaire and Nietzsche seize upon Stendhal's formula to affirm bodily satisfactions. While Baudelaire debates with "academics" unable to recognize the contingent dimension of the beautiful, Nietzsche presents Stendhal as "a genuine spectator and artist" to take issue with Kant's "disinterestedness" as a condition for the beautiful: "If our estheticians admittedly never weary of asserting in Kant's favor that, under the spell of beauty, one can *even* view undraped female statues 'without interest,' one may laugh a little at their expense."[78] Baudelaire and Nietzsche insist that the dimension of the drives needs to be considered in the aesthetic. But if the "promesse de bonheur" follows a male parameter of orgasm,

---

76. Bourgeois in Vincent Honoré, "Precious Liquids, 1992," in *Louise Bourgeois* (2008), 235. Originally cited in *Louise Bourgeois: sculptures, environnements, dessins: 1938–1995* (Paris: MAM Ville de Paris, Éditions de la Tempête, 1995), 197.

77. Baudelaire, OC II, 686.

78. Nietzsche, *Basic Writings*, 540.

there is little room left for the aesthetic, and for the girl to encounter passion, rather than fear, or her place only as an acceptable object to an imaginary Other, playing the game of "attitudes passionnelles" and other poses, as seen in chapter 1.[79] A "genuine spectator" who comes close to "the truth" would not stop with the exhilarating fantasy, but would go further, to the lack in the Other. When Nietzsche wondered whether "perhaps truth is a woman who has reasons for not letting us see her reasons? Perhaps her name is—to speak Greek—*Baubo*?,"[80] the personification of truth as "a woman," and under this particular Greek name, a female demon who in turn personifies the female genitals brings together the registers of the looking, sexual difference, and the void it introduces in knowledge.[81] Freud also makes reference to Baubo in his short paper, "A Mythological Parallel to a Visual Obsession." He explains, additionally, that in the Greek legend Baubo lifts up her dress before the sorrowful Demeter to make her laugh.[82]

So, I argue, the "little laugh" at the "estheticians" and "academics" who deny the *jouissance* approached in the beautiful must go less against prudishness before naked women than against a treatment of the aesthetic in which "woman" remains a sexual object for a man, which is not really

79. I have discussed this position for the hysteric in the Introduction. On the distinction between this "seduction fantasy," which serves to cover up the primal scene, and the "primal scene fantasy" that exposes a fundamental contradiction, see de la Torre, 31.

80. Nietzsche, *The Gay Science*, 38.

81. On Baubo, see Nietzsche, 38, n8. Jacques Derrida addresses these connections in *Éperons*, including a psychoanalytic view of truth as fear of castration. He stresses the ambivalent question of distance and proximity from truth and the other sex, showing that "'woman' is perhaps not something, the determinable identity of a figure that announces itself at a distance, at a distance from something else, and from which one would have to distance or approach oneself. Perhaps she is, as nonidentity, nonfigure, simulacrum, the abyss of distance, the distancing of distance, the cut of the spacing, distance itself if one could still say, which is impossible, distance *herself*" (38). "La distance" is a feminine noun, and Derrida plays on distance as 'woman' which becomes in his reading of Nietzsche's claims about truth as woman, woman's action at a distance, among others, a name for irreducible difference. See Derrida, *Éperons: Les Styles de Nietzsche* (Paris: Flammarion, 1978). Nietzsche's words here are also highly relevant to Lacan's concept of semblance.

82. Freud, *SE* XIV, 338. The effect of laughter is resonant with Nietzsche's development in *The Gay Science*, and also, of course, with Freud's take on jokes' momentary lifting of repression.

subversive at all, since this old arrangement also depends on a repression of the feminine that has little to do with *gai saber* and aesthetic disindividuation. Laughter—or passion—favors, instead, releasing the dimension of feminine jouissance that corresponds to the body's heterogeneity. And, as an irruptive moment where meaningful speech breaks down, laughter can perhaps be more ideally suited to such a task than words.

Nestor Braunstein discussed sublimation in terms of the subject's "passion" of approaching *das Ding*, the missing object experienced as excess, as "an empty space" . . . "into which the subject plunges and dissolves."[83] This work of sublimation, prompted by the "unnamed jouissance, where the silence of the drives prevails,"[84] is not merely regression to a mythical, pre-subjective Thing. Rather, it is beyond the phallus: "a jouissance in the body (*en corps*)" that does not complement the masculine one by rather appears as a *plus*, something more (*encore*), supplementary, and that makes all attempts at limiting and situating it run aground."[85]

The little girl's encounter of passion instead of fear can thus be associated to discovering, in the encounter of sexual division and the absence of a signifier for the feminine, a path for "voluptuous lucidity" that does not drown her, for instance. Or a space for "supreme thought/feeling" that need not be "stolen from the little girl" in the economy of ideological reproduction, nor subjected to the possession of a penis, nor attributed to a parental figure imagined as confiscating her enjoyment. Like Ariadne, the girl at stake in *Precious Liquids* encounters, through tears, sweat, and other intense secretions, the "Dionysian transmutation of pain into joy."[86] This is the affirmation of life in Nietzschean terms, and "from the affirmation derive new values: unknown values to this day, when the lawmaker replaces the wise man, creation replaces knowledge, affirmation replaces all the known negations."[87] The lawmaker—a girl—creates new values rather than allowing reactive forces to shape thought, life, and the body. Such a creative endeavor had been considered at the beginning of this essay, through the "painter of modern life." And it is precisely what embracing the feminine involves.

83. Braunstein, *Goce*, 85.

84. Braunstein, 85.

85. Braunstein, 150.

86. Deleuze, *Nietzsche et la philosophie* (Paris: PUF, 1962), 199.

87. Deleuze, 199.

The Convalescent

"The mechanism of instability" Bourgeois invokes in reference to the previously discussed glass structures is also present in the "trani" sculpture, whose sagging lumps form a recumbent "x" and glow, indicating the ambiguity of "the sexes." The *Cell* brings us here, to this threshold where a jouissance overwrites my body, where, as Deleuze in *Logic of Sensation* cites, "I'm changing my shape, I feel like an accident."[88] If one follows the transmutation of pain into the joy *Precious Liquids* invites, one can see that the bed and vessels around it, which evoked hospital equipment, muscles, and a hallucinatory, inside-out view of internal organs, point to a subject's—a girl's—convalescence, which is aesthetic. "Supreme feeling": sublime and beautiful.

In *The Painter of Modern Life*, Baudelaire insistently stresses symptomatology to describe aesthetic feelings (as Charcot had discovered symptomatology in artistic objects). The artist's genius is epitomized in the figure of *the convalescent*, whom Baudelaire draws from his experience of both Guys' sketches and of Edgar Allan Poe's "Man of the Crowd." The latter painting, as Baudelaire prefers to call the short story, features "a convalescent" who,

> contemplant la foule avec jouissance, se mêle par la pensée, à toutes les pensées qui s'agitent autour de lui. Revenu récemment des ombres de la mort, il aspire avec délices tous les germes et tous les effluves de la vie; comme il a été sur le point de tout oublier, il se souvient et veut avec ardeur se souvenir de tout.[89]

The singularity of this condition that evokes a medical context and takes the perspective of the being recovering from illness concerns an experience of contact, even a dissolving of the limits between minds,

---

88. Deleuze cites these lines from the 1980 Talking Heads song "Crosseyed and Painless" in *FB*, 148.

89. contemplating the crowd with *jouissance*, mingles, through the medium of thought, with the turmoil of thoughts around him. Having recently returned from the shadows of death, he delightfully inhales all the germs and emanations of life; since he was on the verge of forgetting everything, he remembers and passionately wants to remember it all (Baudelaire, OC II, 690).

thoughts, and also life, presented in contagious and sensorial terms. A sensorial overflow upon the breakdown of barriers is the unique enjoyment, the *jouissance* that contemplation affords to the convalescent, as a *hypersensitive* body/psyche. To "paint modern life" is thus also to render and express a heightened way of seeing that Baudelaire defines as convalescent. It follows that such "paintings" could assist a certain viewer's recovery from some kind of illness. His subsequent explanation of convalescence as a kind of return to childhood reinforces the excess involved in aesthetic experiences, and a related subversion of values regarding health and illness that alter the stakes of the body in the aesthetic clinic.

It is in convalescence, then, that, for Baudelaire, the excess of sensibility and passion characteristic of earliest childhood perception ("nos plus jeunes, nos plus matinales impressions"[90]) becomes accessible again. He thus invites us to hark back to such "vividly colourful impressions" ("si vivement colorées"), reencountered "following a physical illness, as long as this illness has left our mental faculties pure and unharmed" ("à la suite d'une maladie physique, pourvu que cette maladie ait laissé pures et intactes nos facultés spirituelles"[91]). While Baudelaire takes a step back in the essay by adding that the painter experiences the intensity of childhood perception with an added "virility,"[92] bearing witness to his own anxiety in facing the feminine thing, it is still evident that, in Baudelaire's idea of health, the criterion to determine harm of the mental faculties unsettles the medical one:

> L'enfant voit tout en *nouveauté*; il est toujours ivre. Rien ne ressemble plus à ce qu'on appelle l'inspiration, que la joie avec laquelle l'enfant absorbe la forme et la couleur.[93]

---

90. Baudelaire, 690.

91. Baudelaire, 690.

92. Baudelaire, 690. Baudelaire's poetry exposes a male will to mastery fragilized by the socio-political-economic transformations taking place around him. See Maurice Samuels, "Baudelaire's Boulevard Spectacle: Seeing Through 'Les yeux des pauvres,'" *Yale French Studies Time for Baudelaire (Poetry, Theory, History)*. 125–126 (2014): 167–182.

93. The child sees everything in a state of newness; he is always *intoxicated*. Nothing more resembles what we call inspiration than the delight with which the child absorbs form and color (Baudelaire, *OC II*, 690).

If the child and convalescent see everything in novelty, if they are always intoxicated, if their absorption of form and color is accompanied by a remarkable joy, then the illness from which the convalescent recovers, via the painting, makes perception dull, sober, monotonous. Suffering from this illness would preclude the contagion of life's germs and emanations. And, since early childhood and convalescence are not long-lasting states, with a few exceptions (such as Guys, who is "always spiritually in the state of the convalescent"[94]) most of the individual's life, ill or not, would be spent in a sickly, blocked state of perception.

Far from idealizing a "pure and innocent" perception through the figure of the child, Baudelaire proposes a move away from common sense and toward a literal understanding of inspiration, as absorption and inhalation that may threaten the body's integrity and immunity, by putting convalescence to work in the field of artistic creation. Guys' paintings can bring nothing close to a stable state of the senses. "Healthy" and "ill" equally exclude the interstitial convalescent state of joyful, destabilizing (so perhaps also distressing) absorption of form and color. Engaging with physiological activity to reflect on aesthetic experience, the poet of modern life reveals a different, enticing kind of well-being.

> J'oserai pousser plus loin; j'affirme que l'inspiration a quelque rapport avec la *congestion*, et que toute pensée sublime est accompagnée d'une secousse nerveuse, plus ou moins forte, qui retentit jusque dans le cervelet.[95]

Inspiration, Baudelaire tells us throughout this section of his essay, is all at once a matter of expanded perception, sublime thought, and bodily symptoms. All this resonates with Nietzsche's convalescence, where Ariadne's thread of the body leads to the Eternal Return as the supreme thought/feeling while the repository of thought dissolves. Congestion is not opposed to convalescence for the aesthetic clinic, in whose development Baudelaire participates, and neither is nervous tremor, reverberating all the way to the brain, thinking its "sublime thoughts." Instead,

---

94. Baudelaire, 690.

95. I will dare to go even further and assert that inspiration has something in common with *congestion*, and that every sublime thought is accompanied by a more or less violent nervous shock which has its repercussion in the very core of the brain (Baudelaire, 690).

they attest to the violence and excess of this jouissance in the body, as well as to a connection between this jouissance and the most extreme operation of thought. The possibility of expressing life in these passages of Baudelaire's aesthetic theory depends, then, on the logic of symptoms as signs of that immense life having, indeed, been contracted by a body, with far-reaching effects for thought. His aesthetic theory thus subverts the primacy of the mind over the body, and the criterion of stability of the organism as health, based on suppressing the drives' unruly activity.

Rhythm

The glass vessels seem to rise up, like bubbles into which my body dissolves, becoming weightless and rhythmic. I encounter this *Cell* and its objects as a stranger and yet, by accepting its formal constraints, I let its stream of associations and sensations turn me into the receptacle of its forces. They constitute the artwork's rhythm: one where circles multiply within, contracting around an empty center, as a contrasting dissipation at once occurs. With these operations in *Precious Liquids*, the structure not only skirts around the empty centers it at once creates, but also engages a set of flows across thresholds in both directions, according to its rhythms, which submerge my body in the act of observing.

This dynamic of systole/diastole is also present in Bacon's paintings, caused, as Deleuze observes, by their tension between figure (body), support, and shallow background (solid color).[96] It allows us to notice a resemblance between Bourgeois' *Precious Liquids* and the cylindrical spaces of the panels in Bacon's *Three Studies for a Crucifixion* (1962), where the view is limited by this curved depth and the closed blinds and doors in the background. The central panel offers the most striking relation:

This room appears indeed walled by a cylindrical structure like the *Precious Liquids* water tank. The small bed, in a similar composition with regard to the cylinder, supports a figure, but the defaced, deformed condition of this body is made up of horizontal ovals, or elliptical circuits. It is as if Bourgeois had rotated them to a vertical position in the vessels surrounding the bed, and, across from it, to a distended sagging state, in the *Trani* sculpture. Bourgeois' shapes do not blur vision, as

96. Deleuze, *FB*, 33, 42, 82.

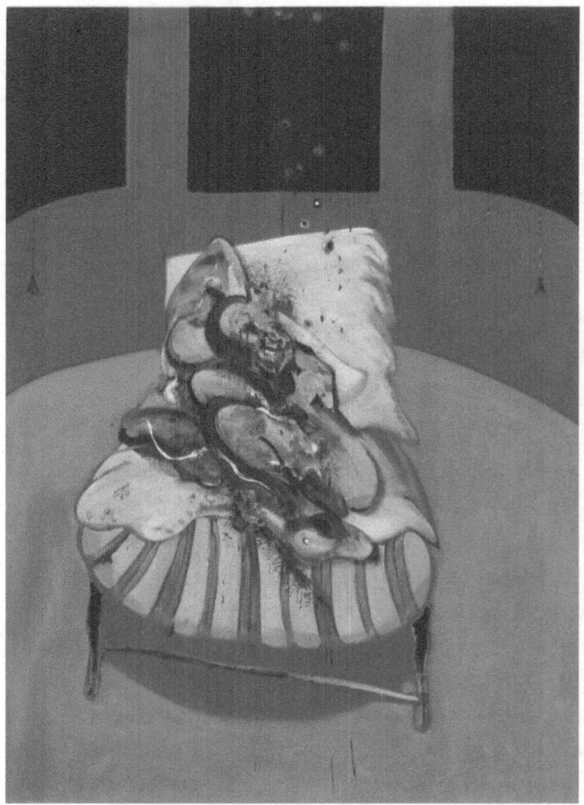

Figure 2.4. Francis Bacon, *Three Studies for a Crucifixion*, 1962. (62-04) Central Panel, 78 × 57" © The Solomon R. Guggenheim Foundation/The Estate of Francis Bacon. All rights reserved./DACS, London/ARS, New York, 2019.

Bacon's do,[97] but, as still as everything in her *Cell* may seem, the composition with its concentric circles, the movements its viewing process requires—with towering and plunging views, horizontal, slanted, at the threshold—and also the play of light, and even the silence, constitute a rhythmic interplay of speeds, tensions, distensions. In Bacon's canvas the ovals instead articulate the contorted, squeezed state of the figure bleeding out and opening its mouth to cry out, maybe laugh. The blood

97. Bacon's use of color is crucial to this and the other effects I describe, from observation of the original and a color image file. See the panel and triptych in color at www.francis-bacon.com/artworks/paintings/three-studies-crucifixion

spatter varies, from small, quick and stiff brushstrokes near the foot of the bed to the brighter, richer, smoother ones of a slower speed, close to the figure's knees. An eye socket drips dark red tears, while a fine red fizz sprays out from the figure's head. Next to it, the red paint turns into round, rising bubbles of precious, vital fluid. The figure and its secretions speak to the experience of a dissolved body image, scattered across the bed and different moments, perhaps staggered by the compressions and distensions of cylindrical space.

If we take the scene facing the bed in *Precious Liquids* as an evocation of the enigma of sexual difference, then it adds something not visible within Bacon's canvas, and whose sight is particularly difficult to bear, but that, as I stated, may also precipitate the subject to dissolve in it. And the result might be called beautiful. The unbearable lies on the bed in Bacon's painting, whose configuration as a canvas places the viewer where the scene appears inside *Precious Liquids*. But does the painting leave one out of the room? Does the figure bear the weight while one watches impassively? Bacon's canvas features closed black blinds along the walls behind the head. This redoubles the separation of this single, central figure from those in the panels at its two sides. Are the blinds attempts to cover the enclosure against the primal scene, or its underlying void? Or is it instead, as Deleuze suggests, a way of abolishing the spectacle[98] of the contorting body? The black blinds are evoked by the long black hanging coat in *Precious Liquids*, and the coat does serve the exact function of covering up a body, although, as mentioned, it is unworn. The blinds do not cover up the void, but rather close down the violence of spectacle. And this would leave the viewer, who stands in front of the bed, to encounter the painting differently, in what Bacon calls the "violence of sensation."[99]

As Michel Leiris noted, Bacon's works are unique in how they produce a closeness that introduces the viewer into the painted space, practically eliminating distance and distinction between realities: "It is as if we were no longer pure spectators, but were actually involved with the objects."[100] By attending to the paintings' "overall construction,"

98. Deleuze, 13.

99. In Deleuze, 61. Deleuze derives the idea of "two violences" from Bacon's distinction between "the scream" and "the horror."

100. Michel Leiris, *Francis Bacon, Full Face and In Profile* (New York: Rizzoli, 1983), 18.

Leiris realizes that its requirements include both "the artist building up the work and [that of] the spectator, whose eyes and mind are caught and expressly compelled into participation."[101] On her encounter with Bacon's paintings, Bourgeois stated:

> The intensity of Francis Bacon's works moves me deeply. I react positively. I sympathize. His suffering communicates. The definition of beauty is a kind of intimacy in the visual. I feel for Bacon even though his emotions are not mine.
>
> The physical reality of his works is transformed and transcended. His room does not obey the laws of perspective. To look at his pictures makes me alive. I want to share it. It's almost the expression of love.[102]

In this rich sequence of reactions, we find a reception to a vital kind of communication where suffering, beauty, and love take place upon a transformation of the works' material reality. This may just be the "Communication" Bourgeois longed for in the 1990 diary entry I cited in chapter 1, announcing her turn to "hysteriahealed." It is as a result of such a transformation, defying the laws of perspective, for instance, that Bourgeois interestingly advances a definition of the beautiful different from Breton's convulsive one, as "a kind of intimacy in the visual" that is achieved in Bacon's works, and her own. This intimacy, much like the one to which the clinical frame in analysis gives rise, is unique and not simply a moment of empathy or identification because it takes place on a different level (as Bourgeois herself wrote in that diary entry), outside a specular relation. Although Bourgeois' thoughts about her own works were usually centered on her own creative act and personal history, rather than on a communication and a transmitted sensation, such as love, life, or suffering, her own creative strategies (which are not focused on painting or on exclusively two-dimensional works) do prioritize the beautiful as "a kind of shared intimacy in the visual," achieved by a transformation, an original conversion or transmutation one might say, into material and especially spatial reality. Bourgeois in her own work

101. Leiris, 19.

102. Bourgeois, "Self-Expression is Sacred and Fatal," in Christiane Meyer-Thoss, *Louise Bourgeois: Designing for Free Fall* (Zurich: Ammann Verlag, 1992), reprinted. in *Destruction of the Father*, 229.

sought to "cut into the real," as Rosalind Krauss stressed.[103] A kind of intimacy in the *real*—the realm of the feminine without symbolization, which begins by suspending established collective "reality"—is precisely what *Precious Liquids* offers to whoever dares enter.

103. Krauss, "Louise Bourgeois: Portrait of the Artist as *Fillette*," 64–65.

CHAPTER 3

Lygia Clark on the Space–Body Problem

In the previous chapter, my discussion on Louise Bourgeois ended with a look at an exemplary installation that invites readers to witness, at the threshold of its enclosed space, a kind of primal fantasy where an impersonal transmission of sensation and an interrogation of the question of sexual difference are all at once possible. If these functions of Bourgeois' art ask the reader to stroll around the barrel walling the scene, peek through its doors, and take time to contemplate the different objects set up in the space within, with Lygia Clark the requirement of such a gesture is radicalized, to the point that there simply is no work without the reader's full immersion with certain materials in specific actions—for instance, cutting along a paper Möbius strip until it becomes shreds (*Caminhando*, 1963, figure 3.2)—within what Clark calls a "proposition." In other words, the work here is coextensive with an aesthetic experience, which Clark herself deems clinical, in the sense of enabling otherwise inaccessible desire in a subject.

Clark's propositions expand the notion of sublimation developed by Freud and others, such as Jean-François Lyotard, with whose ideas on the matter the end of this chapter will engage. Freud situated sublimation in individuals who bypassed repression and were able to redirect the drives' goal. In *The Ethics of Psychoanalysis* seminar, Lacan, reading Melanie Klein, specified that sublimation is not a matter of desexualizing the drives, but of an ambivalent *Thing* that leads to a distinction of realms. Sublimation "reveals the proper nature of the *Trieb* insofar as it is not purely instinct, but relates to *das Ding* as such, with the Thing, insofar as it is distinct from the object."[1] Lacan, furthermore, developed the notion of the *sinthome* in his late work, to consider sublimation as something that remains involved with the symptom, understood not only as a distorted expression of censored jouissance, but as the unique signature that gives a desiring subject consistency, in the way that James Joyce's writing, for instance, takes on the function of knotting the subject together.[2] Deleuze extends sublimation beyond the individual when he thinks, with Francis Bacon's paintings, of hysteria as a contagious process that dissolves boundaries between viewer, painting, painter, and painting as an art, a process, in other words, of hystericization. The latter, I showed in chapter 1, also plays an important role in aesthetic experience with Louise Bourgeois' artworks, which stress the dimension of sexual difference. Lygia Clark is well aware of hysteria's peculiar contagion too, and to harness it she is particularly interested in syncing the temporalities of the aesthetic act and experience. Lyotard's approach to the link between psychoanalysis and art and, in particular, his conceptions of the figural and plastic space underscore the abyssal and anguishing character of creation—as a confrontation of the lack of a signifier for the jouissance working in the subject's body. Clark's descriptions of the propositions' immediate effects, as well as of her own crises (directly and intimately linked to her creative propositions) indicate that, upon engaging with the propositions' constraints, a feminine subject position opens up, underscoring a natal dimension of the aesthetic experience.

Clark's production has confronted some of its best critics with the inaccuracy of the term "art" to designate her work; at the same time, it is consistently thought to concern the body.[3] Her experiments probe a variety of interactions: between body and space, among multiple bodies, between body and language, and finally across these three relations, in

1. Lacan, *Éthique*, 133.

2. I will expand on the *sinthome* in chapter 4, on Marguerite Duras.

3. A look at the exhibit publication *Lygia Clark: De l'oeuvre à l'événement*, ed. Suely Rolnik and Corinne Diserens (Nantes: Musée de Beaux Arts, 2005) (hereafter cited as *De l'oeuvre*), confirms this focal point, with article titles such as "In the end, what is there behind the corporal thing?," "Lygia Clark is not done cutting through our bodies," and "Opening the body." Clark's own titles and texts insist on the body already: "The House is the Body," "Nostalgia for the Body," "The Body is the House," "Art is the Body," etc. As for the inaccuracy of "art," the 2014 MOMA exhibit devoted to Clark's work is titled *Lygia Clark: The Abandonment of Art.*

what I, too, would prefer not to call art, but rather a distinctively *plastic* practice that guides the analysis and construction of a singular unconscious desire. Why plastic? Here I draw on the Romance languages. When French, Spanish, or Portuguese, refer to "the plastic arts," certainly a less idiomatic term in English, the emphasis is not on one of the senses ("visual art," which can include various media and techniques, such as sculpture, painting, photography, etc., is the corresponding term, but it implies that this work addresses primarily the sense of sight). Instead, to be a "plasticien" is to be involved with the plasticity of materials—from wax to words—bodies, space, time; to investigate their intensities or capacities and resistances to change—for instance, suppleness and traction—through some kind of practice that may require and beckon different senses.

Clark's plastic practice did not privilege sight—in the mid-eighties she saw it as "art for the blind, since it only communicates when it is touched," and it was profoundly skeptical of the idea of art—for instance, the same text a few lines down adds: "actually, it is no longer art, but a simple proposition to feel the body."[4] The photographic documents for *O eu e o tu* (1967, figure 3.1) aptly demonstrate both statements. Yet she is currently considered an important Brazilian avant-garde artist from the second half of the twentieth century. Her involvement with Grupo Frente's Neo-concretismo movement in Rio de Janeiro in the mid- to late 1950s, when Brazil was undergoing an important shift in cultural, aesthetic, technological, political and economic terms supports this recognition.[5] But not only is this avant-garde group a brief part of Clark's trajectory, her own sense of her work clearly exceeds the frame of art,

4. Clark, "Mid-1980s," in *The Abandonment of Art*, 243. The Brazilian art critic Mário Pedrosa makes a related statement in a text about the role of modern art and its relevance to all mental capacities and conditions, in the context of an exhibit of art by psychiatric patients at the Centro Psiquiátrico Nacional in 1947: "Modeling may cease to be a visual art given that through inner, haptic vision, the blind man, endowed with a sense of rhythm, is able to create plasticity" "The Vital Need for Art" in *Mário Pedrosa: An Anthology*, trans. Stephen Berg (New York: MOMA, 2016), 111.

5. For an synthetic account of the cultural environment in Brazil when Clark begins her production, see Paulo Herkenhoff, "Lygia Clark," in *Lygia Clark* (Fundació Antoni Tàpies, Barcelona, 1998) (hereafter *Lygia* [1998]). Briony Fer discusses the way in which Clark and Neo-concretism "salvage the work of Mondrian and other abstract artists from the universalizing principles that they espoused." "Lygia Clark and the Problem of Art" in *The Abandonment*, 226.

and even of avant-garde movements (which, by definition, consistently push the conceptual boundaries of art, and Brazil's itinerary in this regard was highly revolutionary and original since the 1920s[6]).

Clark was most recently featured as a Latin American female artist in the *Radical Women: Latin American Art 1960–1985* exhibit, organized by the Hammer Museum in Los Angeles, California. In this exhibit of 123 women artists from fifteen countries, the two selected works representing Clark were (in order of appearance in the exhibit space at the Brooklyn Museum)[7] a small set of framed photographs documenting a proposition for two participants to wear masks and connected suits entitled *O eu e o tu: Roupa-Corpo-Roupa* ("The I and the You: Cloth-Body-Cloth") (1967; figure 3.1), as enacted by Clark with Hélio Oiticica (another major Brazilian avant-garde artist and close friend of hers), and a video of a set of interviews[8] documenting the clinical practice that Clark, during the final decade of her life, developed and passed on, in order to treat "borderline individuals," as she indicates in her late writings.[9] The choice of this video accurately foregrounds the fact that Clark's practice exceeds not only the physical limits of the gallery space, but also those of the art institution as well as of its feminist critique. Specifically, Clark's long-term engagement with what I have called, to begin the previous paragraph, not art but instead "a plastic practice" that employs bodies, materials, and space, exceeds the conditions through which art becomes recognized as a cultural achievement. What I find most interesting, in addition to the much-discussed elimination of object and spectator from this practice, and to its correlative development outside the museum or gallery, is this: something of what Clark insistently grapples with and asks

6. For instance, Oswald de Andrade's "Manifesto antropofágico" "Cannibal Manifesto" is from 1929, inspired by *Abaporu* (1928), a painting by Tarsila do Amaral. This artist got her first solo exhibition at MOMA in 2018, following in the steps of two previous solo exhibitions of Brazilian women artists, Lygia Clark in 2014 and Mira Schendel in 2009.

7. The traveling exhibit was on display at the Brooklyn Museum, New York, April 13–July 22, 2018.

8. The film is Mário Carneiro (dir.) *Memória do corpo* (Brazil: Studioline, 1984).

9. In a text from the mid-1980s she writes: "my treatment is excellent for borderline personalities mainly in crisis ([the recovery time] is faster) and for ambulatory psychotics. For neurotics the treatment is long and less effective." Clark, *The Abandonment*, 239.

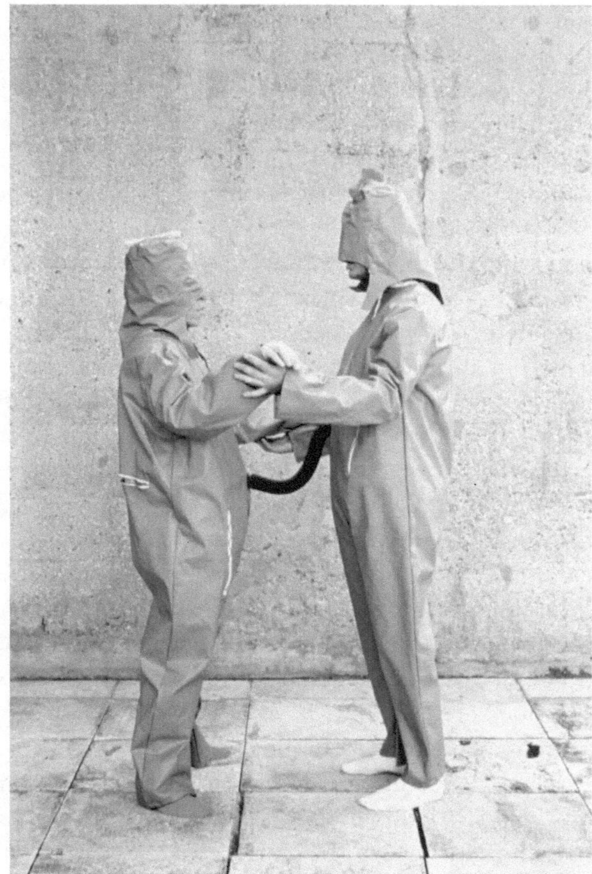

Figure 3.1. Lygia Clark, *O Eu e o Tu: Roupa-Corpo-Roupa*, 1967. (The I and the You: Cloth-Body-Cloth)—ref. no. 20374. Courtesy of "The World of Lygia Clark" Cultural Association.

her participants to confront escapes the purview of cultural recognition. Or rather, the cause and goal of that engagement for Clark concern, precisely, that which can never be fully endorsed by cultures. As I have explained in the previous chapters, cultures erect themselves on subjects' repression of the feminine, and on the related reduction of a woman to the status of partner or mother.

An important gesture outside of cultural recognition can thus be located in Clark's progressive elimination of the spectator and object—at odds with her time, which is that of the rise of the age of spectacle and the art market as part of a mass consumerist regime. Clark was not alone with these strategies, however. The poet and art critic Ferreira Gullar, Clark's friend, is perhaps best known outside Brazil for his 1959 essay "Theory of the Non-object" "Teoria do não-objeto." Both this essay and Clark's texts indicate that they had intense discussions around this idea. Ferreira Gullar defines the non-object as a "special object through which a synthesis of sensorial and mental experiences is intended to take place," and "a pure appearance" that "leaves no trace."[10] "All true works of art," he argues, are non-objects. It seems, though, that Clark's take on the elimination of object and trace exceeds the abstraction-oriented break with representation (a move she explores in an initial phase contemporary to Gullar's essay, through her geometric abstract paintings), and takes further the idea of leaving "no trace," or relic, rather, in addition to leaving behind the rather superegoic concern with qualifying as "true works of art." The point for Clark is thus not a Hegelian total *Aufhebung*, but rather to close in on the invisible subject that, mobilized by an act, surges forth in a "now" or "fatia de eternidade" (fragment of eternity).[11]

All this complicates access to Clark's work, for instance in the recent, previously described effort at including Clark among great women artists of the late twentieth century. As Yve-Alain Bois reflected in 1999, and as a small number of exhibits have proven between 1986 and now, it is certainly not impossible to display Clark's "journey . . . in all its logic,"[12] which entails requiring participants to touch and engage with her propositions and "relational objects," disrupting traditional museum etiquette. But the experiences she sought to enable through play are not merely amusing (see figures 3.1, 3.3, 3.4). The profoundly serious playfulness she proposes ultimately aims, in her own words (which resonate with those of the psychoanalyst D.W. Winnicott, whose work she knew), at "the subject's psychotic core" by awakening the subject's "ambivalence in relation to the object."[13] She thus states: "o 'objeto

10. Ferreira Gullar, "Theory of the Non-object," trans. Michael Asbury. *Cosmopolitan Modernisms*, ed. Kobena Mercer (Cambridge, MA: MIT Press, 2005), 170.

11. Clark, "O vazio-pleno" (The Empty-Full); *Lygia* (1998), 113.

12. Bois, Introduction to Clark, "Nostalgia of the Body," *October* 69 (Summer 1994): 85–88, 88.

13. Clark in *Lygia Clark*. Lygia Clark, Ferreira Gullar, and J. Ribamar. Rio de Janeiro: FUNARTE, 1980, 51 (hereafter *Lygia* [1980]).

relacional' toca direitamente o núcleo psicótico do sujeito." (The "relational object" directly touches the subject's psychotic core.)[14] Clark also considers that every subject—and not just the mentally ill or those with a psychotic structure—has a psychotic core, which necessarily escapes language as shared system of meaning. In this regard, Clark's perspective relates to the context of avant-garde psychiatry in Brazil, with Nise da Silveira, a female psychiatrist who promoted dialogue across psychiatry and contemporary art, and created the Museu de Imagens do Inconsciente "Museum of Images of the Unconscious" in 1952 at the Centro Psiquiátrico Nacional in Rio de Janeiro, which she directed.[15] The final phase of Clark's work (1976–1988), during which she develops an experimental clinic in Rio de Janeiro at the end of the dictatorship (after undergoing psychoanalysis with Pierre Fédida[16]) thus exacerbates the turn away from cultural validation, since it takes place in the absence of anyone external to the treatment (in her apartment), which is why its documentation is so limited. The sessions, furthermore, are mostly silent, allowing the patient's interaction with the relational objects, facilitated by Clark, to dominate and construct what she calls a "fantasmatica do corpo" "fantasmatic of the body" out of regressions and archaic structuring moments or reparations.[17] Even when we do read Clark's notes or view the existing documents on this mode of therapy, what can we know about another body's experience with the psychotic core, which, precisely, finds no place in language or shared reality?

Another major indication of her engagement's foundation beyond the institution of art, in a realm of "raw" psychical reality (Clark writes of "raw perceptions" ["*percepções em bruto*"][18]) lies at the origin of Clark's interest in painting, which is, in fact, a direct response to the postpartum psychosis she experienced upon giving birth to her third and last child in 1945, an event she recalls in her analysis and in writings from

14. Clark, 50.

15. See www.museuimagensdoinconsciente.org.br/#index

16. This analysis took place in Paris 1972–75, according to an interview between Suely Rolnik and Fédida. See *De l'oeuvre*, 69–70. Clark later sought the Sapir relaxation method.

17. Clark, *Lygia* (1980), 52.

18. Clark, *Lygia* (1998), 267.

different periods of her life,[19] as late as the final period of her experimental clinical practice with psychotics and borderline cases. While deeply involved with problems relevant to psychoanalysis, Clark's work was no mere application of psychoanalytic concepts to the idea of art. Her experiments sought to mobilize a clinical dimension located within the aesthetic, which she names, early on, "the inside is the outside,"[20] and whose singularities emerge only by submitting to a set of plastic constraints (spatial, material, bodily, "vibrational"[21]) that, in Portuguese philosopher José Gil's words, "open up the body" or tap into a "bodily unconscious,"[22] just as what emerges in the course of an analysis, unconscious desire, through the constraint of free association, is unpredictable and irreplaceable by preexistent theoretical statements.

Still, Clark's rigorous submission to the constraints of plasticity and their consequences for the body did not prevent her from writing extensively, in an open-ended way, about what she sought and encountered through her practice. Clark insisted that "the work is always more intelligent than the artist. It is the work that sets the direction, that shapes the concept of the thing."[23] And Clark was certainly interested in recording the direction and changing shape of the concept. Clark's attempts to transform the idea of the work at stake in a plastic practice need to be considered, I find, in both her writing and experiments. Among

19. For instance, in 1971, before starting analysis with Fédida, she writes: "How could I write my book? I ask myself every day, and see the difficulty. It would be how, through art, I left madness to go to life, and then how, stopping the making of art, I left it to go to life. [. . .] Set out in a linear way, it would be: birth of Eduardo [Clark], madness and art as a therapy." "1971," in *The Abandonment*, 234.

20. "I have always been passionate about "the inside is the outside," and it has become the subject of all my research," she writes in her final years. "Mid-1980s." *The Abandonment*, 238.

21. Rolnik develops the concept of the "vibrational body" ("corpo vibrátil") with the experiences Clark's relational objects enable, as well as with Deleuzian differences and haecceities in mind. See her remarkable "Molding a Contemporary Soul: The Empty-Full of Lygia Clark" in Susan Martin and Alma Ruiz (eds.), *The Experimental Exercise of Freedom* Los Angeles: MOCA, 1999. See also Rolnik's "Memória do corpo contamina museu" *Concinnitas* 9.1. 12 (July 2008): 15–27.

22. José Gil, "Ouvrir le corps," in *De l'oeuvre*, 64.

23. These statements took place during a meeting with therapists at the clinic Canto da Gávea, Rio de Janeiro, 1982. "Rencontre avec des psychothérapeutes," in *De l'oeuvre*, 59.

these, the next sections of this chapter will discuss the 1963 Möbius strips *Caminhando* ("Walking"), *O dentro é o fora* ("The Inside Is the Outside"), and *O antes é o depois* (The Before Is the After). To address the "abyssal and anguishing" aspects of sublimation, my discussion also highlights the significance of the act of birth in her projects, presented explicitly in propositions such as *A casa é o corpo. Penetração, ovulação, germinação, expulsão* ("The House Is the Body. Penetration, Ovulation, Germination, Expulsion," 1968).[24]

What Can a Body Do?

> Whence the importance of the ethical question. *We do not even know of what a body is capable*, says Spinoza. That is *We do not even know of what affections we are capable, nor the extent of our power*. How could we know this in advance? From the beginning of our existence we are necessarily exercised by passive affections. Finite modes are born in conditions such that they are cut off in advance from their essence or their degree of power, cut off from that of which they are capable, from their power of action. We can know by reasoning that the power of action is the sole expression of our essence, the sole affirmation of our power of being affected. But this knowledge remains abstract. We do not know what this power is, nor how we may acquire or discover it. And we will certainly never know this, if we do not concretely try to become active. The *Ethics* closes with the following reminder: most men only feel they exist when they are suffering something. They can bear existence only as suffering things; "as soon as [the ignorant man] ceases to be acted on, he ceases to be."[25]

In this passage, Deleuze foregrounds a core question in Spinoza's *Ethics* that can also be read as the ethical problem of psychoanalysis' subject

24. Other propositions from the late 1960s and early 1970s on this theme are *Cesariana* (C-section) (1967), *Arquitetura Biológica: Nascimento* (Architectural Structure: Birth) (1969), and *Túnel* (Tunnel) (1973).

25. Deleuze, *Expressionism in Philosophy: Spinoza*, trans. Martin Joughin (New York: Zone Books, 1990), 236 (hereafter cited as *EPS*).

of unconscious desire, which concerns the fact that the Other's desire is at work in a subject (as "affections from outside" [219]), inscribing itself on the body as a specific structure. In an earlier passage to the one cited here, Deleuze explains that Spinoza can consider "what can a body do?" as equivalent to "what is the structure (*fabrica*) of a body?"[26] Before I say more on the ethics of psychoanalysis that resonates here, let us further examine this Spinozian passage, in relation to Clark. With passive affections and a cut from each finite mode's power of action at the starting point of existence, the quest of attaining an original affirmation of desire (*conatus* for Spinoza) becomes a challenge, and the improbable product of an ethical work, since coming to know what a body can do supposes "concretely becoming active," and not only reasoning. It seems that, to Spinoza, among the finite modes endowed with the power to desire and reason, or humans, only few of them take the steps to exist in an affirmative way, to rise above the status of suffering things and become desiring subjects exercising their body's specific capacity. In other words, most of us merely survive, but few find a way to live beyond survival. "What can a body do" is also a question to which Lygia Clark's series of experiments between the 1950s and 1988 provide a unique answer—and one should note that, logically, the answer to the question, as Deleuze articulates it, is necessarily experimental; it only manifests as a singular existential practice, since formal knowledge of the body's capacity to be affected "remains abstract." Clark takes on the imperative to concretely try to become active, and it is an intensive process of childbirth that sets her on such a path.

Importantly, the Spinozian notion of "becoming active" as the effort of affirming one's capacity to be affected welcomes an understanding of activity and affirmation that is all at once receptive, rather than purely dominant over anything that enters into a relation with the body or "existing mode" in question. In other words, "the power of action" we have been cut off from in the beginning is not regained by cutting oneself off from everything that can affect us. After all, a body's susceptibility to being affected is in this argument itself "a power." Clark's early sculptural projects from the late 1950s and early 1960s, called *Bichos* ("Creatures"), introduce a decades-long meditation on this very problem for Clark. Unlike sculpted bodies that have achieved their

26. Deleuze, 218.

definitive pose through the artist's intervention when they come into display for viewers, the *Bichos* invite the viewer to interact with them manually. A logical step beyond Clark's painted *Superficies moduladas* ("Modulated Surfaces"), *Bichos* are metal geometric bodies of varying sizes with a number of surfaces and hinges that offer folding possibilities through which these sculpted bodies' poses change. Without this manual interaction, or affection by an external agent, the *Bichos* cannot become fully actualized. Clark thus writes:

> A kind of body-to-body takes place between two living entities. [. . .] The *Bicho* has a circuit of movements of its own that responds to the subject's stimuli. It is not composed of independent, static forms that can be manipulated at will and indefinitely, as in a game. On the contrary: its parts relate functionally, like those of a true organism, and the parts' movement is interdependent.[27]

The subject or living entity engaging with the *Bicho* is thus also affected by its movements: "the conjugation of your gesture with the *Bicho*'s immediate response creates a new relation and that is only possible thanks to the movements it knows how to perform: it is the *Bicho*'s own life."[28] The creation of "a new relation" Clark highlights, from mutual bodily receptiveness, or affection, may suggest to readers today the agenda of "relational aesthetics" Nicolas Bourriaud promoted in the late 1990s. But while artworks exemplary of Bourriaud's notion offer experiences of comfort and hospitality among viewers, and sometimes the artist,[29] the "new relation" Clark has in mind with *Bichos* and other works does not draw on experiences already available in, and even prescribed by, the social link. Thus Rolnik aptly notes, referring to Bourriaud's theories:

> Within the institutional circuit, proposals that have been qualified and theorized as "relational" (including those categorized

27. Clark, "Bichos," in *Lygia* (1998), 121.

28. Clark, 121.

29. See a full critique of this with examples and counterexamples: Claire Bishop, "Antagonism and Relational Aesthetics," *October* 110 (Fall 2004): 51–79.

> under the rubrics "interactivity," "spectator participation," and others) often limit themselves to a sterile exercise of entertainment that contributes to the neutralization of aesthetic experience—a laser engineer's thing, to paraphrase Lygia Clark.[30]

Radical (rather than neutralized) aesthetic experience requires acknowledging the consequences of truly embracing the capacity to be affected. This need not happen, according to Clark, through scandalously disturbing experiences either (she was, for instance, critical of artistic inquiries on the body through self-inflicted pain, for instance Gina Pane[31] or the Viennese Actionists). A kind of violence or shock to the senses is necessary, but this needs to be distinguished from a mere effort to horrify and thus seduce the participant to morbid curiosity—which leads back into spectacle and does not bring anything new in terms of relation, either.

In Deleuze's reading of the concept of expression in Spinoza, the body or "finite mode," understood as capacity to be affected has, as its consequence, the possibility of thorough change: "dynamic changes in the capacity to be affected," and even "'metaphysical' changes of its essence itself: while a mode exists, its very essence is open to variation, according to the affections that belong to it at a given moment."[32] In *Bichos*, Clark seemed to be considering these modes of change already in the object as well as in its participants, though she was not yet explicitly addressing change that comes through an exploration of subjects' unconscious fantasies and their traversal. As this book has been stating, the psychoanalytic clinic deals with the human body beyond anatomy and chromosomal composition, as an entity shaped by the excess of drives that result from language breaking into the organism, and the clinic is not there to control drives. In an illuminating essay that closes by calling for "a future female clinic,"[33] MacCannell clarifies:

30. Rolnik, "Memória do corpo," 19.

31. "Da Supressão do objeto (Anotações)" (On the Suppression of the Object [Notes]), 1975, in *Lygia* (1998), 264.

32. Deleuze, *EPS*, 225–226.

33. MacCannell, "Jouissance between the Clinic and the Academy: The Analyst and Woman," *Qui Parle* 9.2 (1996): 105–125, 123.

> language makes the "body" out of the organism. The clinic's aim is neither to destroy this lost excess jouissance, nor to control and/or integrate it by bringing it under the dominion of language . . . the aim is to take full cognizance of the existence and persistence of jouissance beyond the linguistic (and therefore social) realm. At its best, 'treatment' permits the subject to grasp why and where this terrifying excess (jouissance) must continually be contended with.[34]

As in *Bichos*, in psychoanalysis, "what a body can do" can only be discovered through a practice of unfolding a subject's distinct possibilities and potentialities with another who has also undergone this experiment. Does this mean that the unconscious is like a *Bicho*, with predetermined though not actualized hinges, postures, and responses, awaiting an analyst's intervention? Not in the view of psychoanalysis that most interests me. MacCannell continues to assert that the Lacanian clinic "will always demand as absolutely essential an unflagging creativeness in the use of language by both subject and analyst."[35] I would say, also, not in Clark's understanding of the unconscious. And this is why in 1963 she moves on, like Lacan, to the more slippery topology of Möbius strips and even to new operations with them. It better lends itself to the Spinozian body whose very essence, as Deleuze has just explained "is open to variation, according to the affections that belong to it at a given moment," which, I find, suits Clark's concerns too, in her concern for "the now" (*o agora*).

O *agora*: Rethinking the Work beyond Interpretation

> Somos os propositores; somos o molde; a vocês cabe o sopro, dentro desse molde: o sentido da nossa existência.
>
> Somos os propositores: nossa proposição é o diálogo. Sós, não existimos: estamos a vosso dispor.
>
> Somos os propositores: enterramos a obra de arte como tal e solicitamos a vocês para que o pensamento viva pela ação.

34. MacCannell, 107.

35. MacCannell, 107.

> Somos os propositores: não lhes propomos nem o passado nem o futuro, mas o agora.[36]

During the 1960s, Clark displaced artists to the status of *propositores—proposers*. The objects they—this "we" she speaks from—make had, in turn, the status of *propositions*, although, if this name evokes a statement with a claim to validity that logic takes as its object of study, here Clark's statements indicate the proposition's and the proposers' fragility; the *deposition* of power and mastery over the object, and their dependence on others' *disposition* ("estamos à vosso dispor"). Such others are, in the context of Clark's propositions, *participants* whose entry into the proposed dialogue by breathing into the mold was indispensable for it to come alive, and for the proposers' existence to become justified. The dialogue is thus, as Clark writes in the last of her incantatory sentences in the cited text, an experience of *o agora*, "the now." So what is the now made of? The now, one suspects in reading these phrases, cannot be the automatic sum of past moments, or even of the existent circumstances. For, an action involving a proposition and dialogue is unnecessary where everything is already given in reality. Moreover, in her statement, the proposers even bury the work of art "como tal," as everyone knows it, clearing the space for something else. That Clark's text is an invitation to rethink the function and stakes of art is perfectly logical; it speaks of the inaugural status of the now.

I am struck by the resonance between Clark's dictum—to debunk the ideal of the work of art in favor of something else, unnamed, open-ended, and immanent to the now or the act—and the ethics of psychoanalysis, as a clinical practice concerned not with the ego's self-narrative but with the subject's true speech, and I believe that considering this resonance sheds light on the ultimate concerns Clark's practice faces. Let me be clear: I am not suggesting a simple analogy between the couple sets analysand–analyst and "we, the mold–you, the breath." Yet there is

36. Clark, "Nós somos os propositores," in *Lygia* (1998), 233. "We are the proposers; we are the mold, the breath is up to you, inside that mold: the meaning of our existence./ We are the proposers: our proposition is the dialogue. Alone, we do not exist: we are at your disposition./ We are the proposers: we bury the work of art as such and call upon you so that thought may live through action. / We are the proposers: we do not propose to you the past, nor the future, but the now."

in both instances a concern with enabling unconscious "dialogue" with specific, though logically unforeseeable effects. For the effects of true speech are incalculable. Arriving at this speech in analysis is no small feat, since, as mentioned previously (in parallel to Spinoza's thought) the subject's starting point is an invasion of the Other's discourse and an adoption of ideals and prohibitions necessary to form an ego. A psychoanalysis focuses on the subject's expression through the symptom, something the body can do, indeed, which contradicts the ego narrative, since it is the way in which the repressed jouissance breaks through to consciousness. Without claiming to know what this symptom means, the analyst welcomes this expression and enables a nonhermeneutic "*process* of unknotting signifiers," which

> loosens from their grasp the object, the One . . . that had caused the signifier to "stick out" [*saille*] or appear as a *coded message*. What is discovered by the analysand in the treatment is that this One of their own discourse can neither be reconstructed nor deconstructed. It *is*, or seems *to be*; it is never convertible into a meaning or a representation. Only a "logic" of the analysand's discourse around this "One" (the *objet a*)—and motivated by it—can be grasped. By the analyst first of all. What the analyst desires is that the patient come to know this logic.[37]

The object MacCannell refers to here is Lacan's *objet a* (which we have discussed in chapter 1, in terms of the *trouvaille*) stating that it covers up and reveals at once the subject's specific lack. One could say of it, like Gullar of the non-object, that it is "a special object," not entirely in reality, in shared language, which is why it cannot be interpreted. By discovering the logic of the analysand's discourse around it—which requires the unfolding of true speech—what becomes discernable is the subject's rather than the ego's way of inhabiting, in Clark's word, "the now," and not a prescribed reality or language as "orthos-logos (the symbolic-as-moral-order)."[38]

37. MacCannell, "Jouissance between the Clinic," 113.

38. MacCannell, 110.

Topology and Psyche

By the time she wrote on the proposers and the now, Clark had made, in 1963, the Möbius-strip propositions *O antes é o depois*, *O dentro é o fora* (figure 3.2), and *Caminhando* (figure 3.3). The latter experiment introduced a new paradigm for her own practice, after the *Bichos*, whereas she still considered the former two as *Bichos* of a sort. Their titles, however, reveal the problem she was exploring in this transitional moment, and it is, precisely, a problem of finding the now of actualization, or the act. Thus in a text called "Do Ato" ("On the Act"), she describes the crisis that *Caminhando* (which I will describe in more detail) has provoked, and records the feeling: "instable in space, it seems that I'm disintegrating. To live perception, to be perception . . . my body abandons me. . . . My body left me—'walking.' Dead? Alive? I am affected by smells, by tactile sensations, by the heat of the Sun, the dreams."[39] The tension between the body's flight out of self and a heightened sensitivity to stimuli stand out here, suggesting the fall of a fairly impermeable condition, or of the perceptual boundaries keeping the body's consistency and sense of integration. A more interstitial, precarious position reminiscent of the convalescence we explored in the previous chapter (with Baudelaire and Nietzsche) takes over, raising uncertainty about being alive or dead, since something about living seems to have certainly shifted to a new state.

Clark proceeds to narrate two dreams whose effect on her seems as powerful as the heat of "o Sol" "the Sun," which she writes as a proper name.[40] I will cite the second one: "no interior, que é o exterior, uma janela e eu. Através dessa janela, desejo passar para fora, que para mim é o dentro. Quando acordo, a janela do quarto é a do sonho, o dentro que eu procurava é o espaço do fora."[41] The absence of any plot, other than the situation and "the wish to slip outside," is remarkable in this dream, as is the fact that upon waking she sees the window she had dreamt (in

39. Clark, "Do ato" (On the Act), in *Lygia* (1998), 164.

40. In this statement's context about its heat affecting the body, "o Sol" reminds of Baudelaire's *Le Soleil*, one of his "Parisian Tableaux" in *Les fleurs du mal*. There, too, the Sun powerfully awakens everything below it, the worms like the roses, the worms like the verses ("les vers comme les roses").

41. Clark, "Do ato," 164. "on the inside, which is the outside, a window and me. Through that window, I wish to slip outside, which for me is the inside. When I wake up, the window in the room is the one from the dream, the inside I sought is the space of the outside."

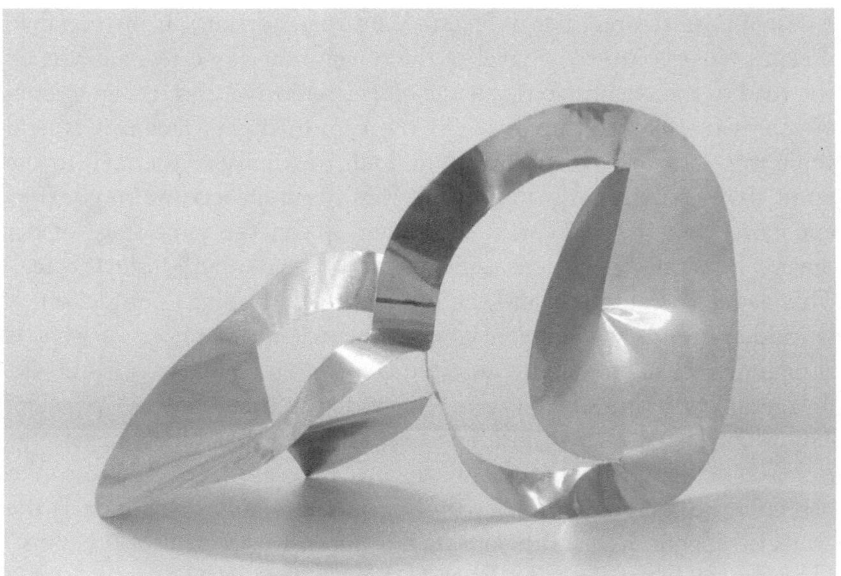

Figure 3.2. Lygia Clark, *O Dentro É o Fora,* 1963. (The Inside Is the Outside)—ref. no. 00620. Photo: Alexandre dos Santos Silva. Courtesy of "The World of Lygia Clark" Cultural Association.

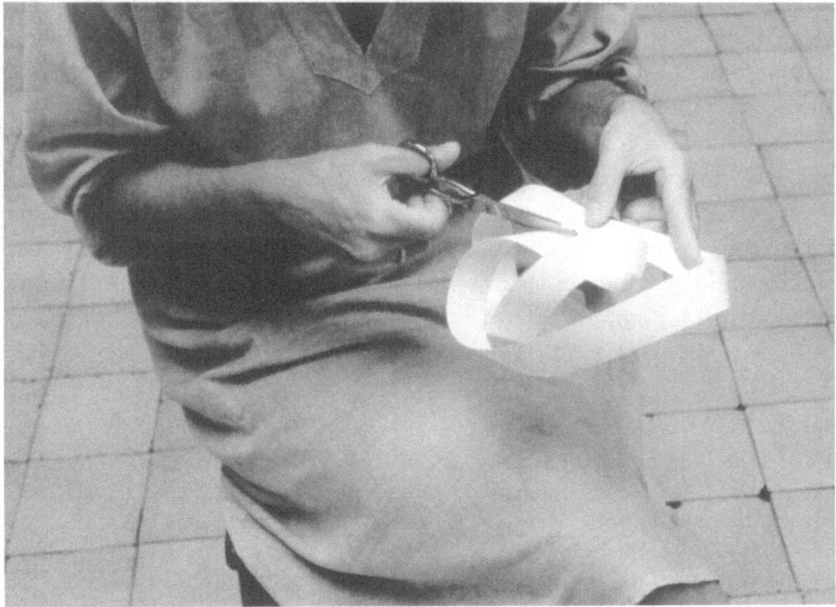

Figure 3.3. Lygia Clark, *Caminhando*, 1964—ref. no. 20243. Photo: Beto Feliciano. Courtesy of "The World of Lygia Clark" Cultural Association.

a description that reminds of Freud's Wolf Man's dream). If the Freudian dream theory points to a navel of the dream that alone sets analysis on the road to the unconscious, casting off the narrative that sets up a series of representations continuous with the ego, in Lygia's dream it is as if there were only a navel, a known and felt proximity of the real, to the point that, as nothing in the dream stops her from wishing to go to its encounter, out the window, it wakes her up, on the same stage of her dream. But waking up here does not simply "save her" from the real. This detail of waking to find the exact window leading "outside which is inside" stresses the problem of continuous movement across what is commonly considered opposite and incompatible realms: inside-outside, dreaming-wakefulness. How can a flow across them become possible? The Möbius strip that so interested Lacan offers that topology, exactly. It makes sense, then, that Clark's dream "gave birth to" ("desse sonho nasceu") the sculpted Möbius strip *O dentro é o fora* "The Inside Is the Outside" (figure 3.2) and before it, she notes, to "O antes é o depois," "The Before Is the After," a *Bicho* without hinges.

Of the sculpture's stainless steel structure, "elástica e deformável" (elastic and deformable) like her body, indeed, according to the previously cited portion of this text, Clark is especially interested in the void or emptiness existent at its center: "No meio da estrutura existe um vazio. Quando a manipulamos, esse vazio interior dá à estrutura aspectos completamente novos" (At the center of the structure there is a void. When we manipulate it, that internal void gives totally new aspects to the structure.)[42] "Internal space" or "the inside" is thus not only outside but also empty. It is perhaps unsurprising that Clark and Lacan should both be led by the Möbius strip to notice these features; what is more interesting is that it allows both of them to consider, specifically, the psyche and the unconscious in terms of "o dentro é o fora" or, in Lacan's accurate neologism, "extimité."[43] This experience of space, Clark's text

42. Clark, 164.

43. On the links between Clark's work and Lacan's theories, see Rachel Price, *The Object of the Atlantic* (Evanston, IL: Northwestern University Press, 2014); Tania Rivera "L'espace, le sujet, la psychanalyse, l'art contemporain et l'oeuvre de Lygia Clark" *Psychologie Clinique* 34 (2012): 81–94; and Christine Macel "Lygia Clark: At the Border of Art" in *The Abandonment*, 254. Lacan discusses extimacy in *The Ethics of Psychoanalysis*. For an explication of this concept as a mode of the uncanny, see Mladen Dolar "'I Shall Be With You on Your Wedding Night': Lacan and the

shows, is closely related to the feeling of her body disintegrating and fleeing, at the same time as it is opening up the possibility of a certain rhythm for the act and the now in question, which she calls an "affective space" that opens "the subject to the encounter of its own precariousness."[44] So, she adds:

> Muitas vezes acordei à janela do meu quarto procurando o espaço exterior como sendo o 'dentro.' Tenho medo do espaço—mas a partir dele me reconstruo. Nas crises, ele me escapa. É como se brincássemos—ele e eu—de gato e rato, de perde-ganha. Eu sou o antes e o depois, sou o futuro no presente. Sou o dentro e o fora, o direito e o avesso.[45]

Thus, something as crucial as the subject's (in)consistency is at stake in this distribution that is not so much between mind and body, as traditionally theorized by philosophy and religion, but rather across space and body, since, per Clark's experience, the empty center within is out in space. For Clark, the point of her plastic practice and of inviting dialogue through her propositions became to foster an encounter of this sort for its participants.

"Connect-I-cut"

Caminhando—"Walking"—is Clark's most accessible proposition, as it can be carried out very simply. It consists in the following: participants are invited to make a Möbius strip out of paper, then take a pair of scissors and begin cutting along the strip from the center, until, after several rounds, it becomes so narrow that it is impossible to cut any further. Per Clark's instructions, participants decide themselves whether to continue

Uncanny," *October* 58 (Autumn 1991): 5–23.

44. Clark, "Do ato," 165.

45. Clark, 164–165. "Many times I woke up at the window of my bedroom seeking the external space as being the 'inside.' I am afraid of space—but from it I reconstruct myself. In crises, it escapes me. It is as if we played—it and I—cat and mouse, 'give away.' I am the before and the after, I am the future in the present. I am the inside and the outside, the warp and weft" ("Mid-1980s" [1965], in *The Abandonment* 238, translation slightly modified).

cutting to the right or the left of the initial cut. Its title, a verb that signifies bodily displacement, is in the gerund, indicating the dynamic, continual temporality of the now. Yet the act itself of holding and cutting along a paper Möbius strip allows the participant to encounter that continual present, since the strip, crafted by the participant herself, features a continuity of the two sides of the paper, allowing for uninterrupted cycles of cutting. This act of holding and cutting through also presents a spatiotemporal intervention in which the sense of touch, and the physical forward-motion of the hand operating the pair of scissors, make the body intimately aware of its altering not just a strip of paper, but also space and time at each cutting "step," which splits and reshapes them. To relate these actions back to Clark's statement on the proposers, this intimate engagement, in *the now*, is the "breathing" proposition where "thought lives through the action" (*o pensamento vive pela ação*).

> Inicialmente, o *Caminhando* é apenas uma potencialidade. Você e ele formarão uma realidade única, total, existencial. Nenhuma separação entre sujeito-objeto. É um corpo-a-corpo, uma fusão. As diversas repostas surgirão de sua escolha.[46]

What does this "no separation between subject-object"—a fusion we have seen before with the painter of modern life "espousing the crowd"—involve in the paradoxical gesture of cutting? One could consider it as the elimination of a boundary, like the typical inauguration ritual of ribbon-cutting,[47] giving access to that fusion with the now. But unlike a public inauguration of a building, *Caminhando* does not lead to entering and assimilating the new space into common reality. It prompts us, instead, to inhabit the cut.

---

46. Clark, "Caminhando," in *Lygia* (1998), 151. "Initially, the *Caminhando* is only a potential. You and it will form a reality that will be unique, total, existential. No separation between subject–object. It is a body-to-body affair, a fusion. The different responses will come out of your choice." Clark, "Caminhando," in *Abandonment*, 160.

47. The abundance of rituals of cutting the human body at the beginning of life, with their many different symbolisms, come to mind here as well. For instance, on the one hand, circumcision establishes a relationship with God; on the other, cutting the umbilical cord stresses separation from the mother's body, which is necessary to the subject's existence. Both of these cuts speak of a necessary loss of jouissance that inscribes a subject in the symbolic.

Winnicott's concepts of transitional objects and space remain helpful to grasp this notion of "no separation" that Clark uses to describe the act of participation, which also applies to the subsequent *Objetos relacionais* she produced, naming them "Relational Objects" with an explicitly therapeutic application in her clinic, and object relations theory as their background. For Winnicott, the special "transitional" status of object and space appears in the scene of infancy, as essential to the child's process of developing a *self* as distinct from the external world and of coming to terms with reality. Transitional objects and space, between "inner" and "outer" worlds and free of conflict among these two realms, sustain for the child a realm of "illusion," to which Winnicott and other analysts in line with his work attribute creative value. According to Winnicott, in an optimal outcome of the child's relationship to the transitional object, the latter eventually loses its meaning without being either forgotten or mourned,[48] as the child comes to terms with not being omnipotent, relating yet distinguishing between internal and external realities, and thus between self and others.[49] For Clark, the relevance of relational objects, and of her collective, ritualistic acts *Estruturas Vivas* (Living Structures) in 1970s Paris, is totally constrained by the "ephemeral gesture"; besides this precarious temporality to which they give rise, there's nothing but a collection of "worthless materials."[50] For instance, in *Pedra e ar* (1966) an air-filled plastic bag and, positioned on one of its corners, a stone, now lifted up by the air bubble as the participant presses the bag, now sunk into the bag's fold as she lets it decompress, bring her attention to bodies' articulation of inner and outer spaces, to holding space and being held by it. "Illusion," which for Winnicott refers to the correspondence between

48. Donald Winnicott, *Playing and Reality* (London & New York: Routledge, 2005), 7.

49. Winnicott, 3. The mother–child relationship is central in all this, as the transitional object stands for the breast, which the child initially conceives as a part of itself, and at stake in the process is coming to see the mother, on whom the child depends, as "not-me," yet existent. Christopher Bollas adds the idea of a "transformational object" in adult life, in aesthetic moments of "deep subjective rapport with an object" and "an uncanny fusion" with it, reminding us of "the ontogenetic process rather than thought or phantasies that occur once the self is established." *The Shadow of the Object: Psychoanalysis and the Unthought Known* (London: Free Association Books, 1987), 16.

50. Clark, "Capturar um fragmento de tempo suspenso," in *Lygia* (1998), 187–188.

reality "and the infant's own capacity to create,"[51] is the realm where *playing* takes place. Marion Milner, whose work has many affinities with Winnicott's, explores this "creative relation to the world" for the adult as well, especially with regard to aesthetic production. She approaches this space exactly as one where "a prelogical fusion of subject and object" takes place.[52] Clark's propositions, then, invite participants to engage in playing in this rigorous sense that brings to life not only the otherwise worthless materials in the act of playing, but the subject too, whose being becomes fully immersed in that act. Or, as Clark's analyst, Fédida, notes in his observation of Winnicott's English term "playing," "the subject is hidden in the verb itself . . . *Isn't playing the* I'*s mode and time of existing*?"[53]

While ordinary time and space, where internal and external realities are not so compatible, is suspended both in Winnicott's *illusion* and in Clark's *o agora*, her propositions emphasize the disruptive dimension of this subject–object fusion. For Winnicott, the goal of the child's developmental process is to achieve and maintain the distinction of internal and external life such that survival is not caught in an either/or logic. While the state of illusion can be blissful, its implied loss of solid ground exposes its subject to the risk of madness. In a beautiful reflection on the problematic of creativity, carried out through a series of personal experiments in learning to draw and paint, Marion Milner realizes that something about seeing exceeds logical facts, which in turn keep this excess in check, and that she needed to let in this excess, along with its dangers, in order to grasp what she truly wanted to paint, even acknowledging "a fear of losing all sense of separating boundaries," since it implies "that letting go common sense appearances and letting in imagination meant letting in madnesss."[54] Importantly, this release of control begins for Milner with allowing lines to cease operating as contours between objects in the work of looking involved in sketching. This is a close point of contact with Clark's process, which began with painting, in search of a kind of line that, instead of being a contour, "becomes a hollowed-out reverse of itself, it stops being a contour that shapes or even draws things,"[55] and which Clark calls "organic." While

51. Winnicott, *Playing and Reality*, 16.

52. Cited in Winnicott, 52.

53. Pierre Fédida, "L'objeu,'" *L'absence* (Paris: Gallimard, 1978), 163.

54. Marion Milner, *On Not Being Able to Paint* (New York: Routledge, 2010), 19.

55. Briony Fer, "Lygia Clark and the Problem of Art," *The Abandonment*, 226.

the more traditional techniques of drawing and painting Milner explores reserve this direct engagement with creation to the painter, according the art-viewer more distance, Clark's decentering of these roles toward an unfinished dialogue that requires a participant aims at the exposure to madness that Milner discovers at the heart of the creative process, which, as initially mentioned, Clark considers a matter of "touching the subject's psychotic core."

Insofar as *Caminhando* offers no complete object for the participant to begin the dialogue, and instead only a set of materials to engage with in "a body-to-body affair" of connecting and cutting without the promise of a complete object at the end, it radicalizes the need for a participant to interact with the art object in a way that changes—and unravels—both. While a connection or fusion is established, so is a rupture, and opening up of a void or a discontinuity that the cut, the rhythmic acts of breathing and walking, and the distributions between proposers and participants or body and space all make present. Clark recalls *Caminhando*'s void in a 1973 essay called "L'art c'est le corps" "Art is the body," originally published in French:

> The first time I cut the *Caminhando*, I lived a ritual that was very significant in itself. And I hoped that this same action would be lived with maximum intensity by the future participants. [. . .] A concentration and a will, naïve perhaps, to learn "the absolute" by the act of making the *Caminhando*, while maintaining the gratuity of the ephemeral gesture, are necessary. The *Caminhando* left me in a sort of *void*: the immanence of the act, the abandonment of the transference to the object, the very dissolution of the concept of work and artist, all that caused in me a very serious *crisis* that I had unconsciously sought for a long time. I wonder if, after the *Caminhando* experiment, one does not gain better awareness of each of the gestures one performs—even the most ordinary ones. . . . This feeling of totality captured in the act must be perceived with much *joy* [*joie*] to learn how to live on the ground of precariousness.[56]

56. Lygia Clark, "L'art c'est le corps." *Preuves: cahiers mensuels du Congrès pour la liberté et la culture* 13 (1973): 143–145, 140–141. My emphasis.

Clark's proposition to make and then cut and dissolve the object such that no trace is left seeks to deliver its participant to what she calls in this text "the immanence of the act," which here takes the form of a walk and a cutting through space, and to "the abandonment of the transference to the object" because not only does the object not represent something else, it even dissolves in the creative act that manages to escape imaginary capture. In this sense, its shearing-shredding gesture brings to my mind the traversal of castration at the end of the analytic process. MacCannell describes it as one of "unknotting signifiers" around *objet a*, ungraspable per se. Clark adds that this experience of living "on the ground of precariousness" implies joy—a word that, especially in this connection to crisis, void, precariousness, and access to "the immanence of the act," brings us close to Spinoza's ethics of the body, where becoming "concretely active" supposes an increase of joy (a fundamental affect for Spinoza), and, of course, back to jouissance with Lacan. Where does *Caminhando* lead to, according to Clark, if not to confronting jouissance without a signifier, and to the need to find one's own way with it, a way that is not merely its repression again or its neutralization by the "*orthos-logos*" of culture?

"A coisa decisiva" / "The Decisive Thing"

The "letting go common sense" and "letting in madness" Milner invokes is not only a problem of appearances and imagination, but also, more fundamentally, of meaning and the unsymbolizable. The effects of the artwork may also bring into relief something of our core relationship to language. If we are to engage with such a disruptive *now*, we must forgo our efforts to recognize the object or word by identifying it or determining its meaning. For example, with Clark's *Caminhando* we can certainly focus on the measurements of the paper strip, describe the activity objectively, locate a set of influences that share this technique, materials, and gesture, or even try to establish an interpretation for the Möbius strip and for cutting along paper with a pair of scissors. But while we do devote attention to the proposition in these activities, they keep us removed from the continuity of *the now* on this edge of space, in the limitless time the proposition wants to bring us to in an act of cutting. The impossible statements that give titles to the two Möbius strips preceding *Caminhando*—"the before is the after" and "the inside is the outside"—invoke the perception of something different from the ordinary lived present, which Clark called in the previously cited passage "the absolute," and elsewhere "a totality in time," all while taking place alongside ordinary time, Deleuze would say.[57] These notes on *Caminhando* offer an accurate example:

> O *Caminhando*, por exemplo, só passou a ter sentido para mim quando, atravessando o campo de trem, senti cada fragmento da paisagem como uma totalidade no tempo, uma totalidade sendo, se fazendo sob meus olhos, na imanência do momento. Era o momento, a coisa decisiva.[58]

Meaning is suspended in the moment of performing the *Caminhando* activity, and only by carrying it out can Clark experience its effects, the different awareness of one's gestures she mentions in the passage before this previous one. Looking—at the landscape out the window in this case—is secondary to the peculiar walking experiment the proposition has put her through, it turns looking into something new, a transformative perception, by means of a rhythmic repetition movement enables. For, on the train, there is, again, a forward motion of cutting through space in which both body and space become reconfigured. Fédida's comparison, in an interview with Rolnik regarding Clark, between the clinical event in psychoanalysis and Clark's (early) work with autistic subjects and children, sheds light on her description of movement through space on the train. He states:

> when one tries to establish contact with an autistic subject, it is initially all of space that is disrupted. [. . .] Here is a child or an autistic adult who follows the room's volume by following a line, by turning back, and I can't say that I look at him, I can instead say that he transforms me already into the room's relationship to space where I am with him. If this

57. I expand on this matter in Part III of this book.

58. Clark, "Caminhando," in *Lygia* (1998), 152. The *Caminhando*, for example, only began to have meaning for me when, going by train across the countryside, I felt each fragment of the landscape like a totality in time, a totality being and remaking itself in front of my eyes, in the immanence of the moment. It was the moment, the decisive thing. "Caminhando," in "*Lygia Clark: The Abandonment of Art*, 161.

> disruption does not take place, there is no possible contact and if I can receive this autistic silence with the gaze's manner of scanning the room where we are, then, I can begin to be in the appropriate disposition, which is not artificial, not technically sought, where the subject will produce, in a way, with his body, forms-substances, perhaps drool, urine, even other things. . . . It's the other's body and my own body that experience the potentialities of gestures. To me, Lygia Clark seems to work with that.[59]

For Clark, the aesthetic event on the train opens up "absolute time," or totality within each fragment of landscape, beyond its function as a link to other moments lying before or after. The act precipitates us into the bodily experience beyond recognition, understanding, words, that belongs to creation, creating a body-space and body-to-body relationship, "a coisa decisiva" "the decisive thing" in Clark's account. It is not "a thing" only for psychotics or autistic children, or for a woman suffering from experiences psychiatry diagnoses as postpartum psychosis or borderline personality disorder, although it seems that these dispositions or structures with regard to the lack in the Other have less of a shield against such a "thing." Language operates as this shield. I am not suggesting that susceptibility to "the thing" is due to some disability with language on the part of psychotic or feminine structures in a Lacanian sense; rather, I am saying that these structures unveil a *savoir* of language's faultiness. Lucie Cantin refers to this problem by pointing to the hysteric, "who experiences the insufficiency of language and the fragility of the barrier it erects against the return of the censored."[60] In the holes or the area language fails to cover up, there is what Clark calls "space" as out-of-language.[61] So this *savoir* zeroes in on the link, or realm shared by "the decisive thing" and the aesthetic.

To think through the logic of "the decisive thing," I must here read one of the first scenes in Clarice Lispector's 1956 novel *A maçã no*

59. Fédida, "Ne pas être en repos avec les mots," *De l'œuvre*, 70.

60. Cantin, "The Borderline," 192.

61. In a seminar lecture, "The Quest of Desire Against the Montage," Willy Apollon reflected on the fact that "Art is in space. Space is out of language," thus the site of the censored, the unnamed. Seminar lecture notes on "The Clinic of the Dream" Annual Training Seminar, 2016.

escuro, for, the character here (a man) offers an intimate account of the experience designated by Clark and Fédida, complete with its strange "joy" and difficult implications for language and knowledge:

> E sob o sol amarelo, sentado numa pedra, sem a menor garantia—o homem agora se rejubilava como se não compreender fosse uma criação. Essa cautela que uma pessoa tem de transformar a coisa em algo comparável e então abordável, e, só a partir desse momento de segurança, olha e se permite ver porque felizmente já será tarde demais para não compreender—essa precaução Martim perdera. E não compreender estava de súbito lhe dando o mundo inteiro.
>
> Que era inteiramente vazio, para falar a verdade. Aquele homem rejeitara a linguagem dos outros e não tinha sequer começo de linguagem própria. E no entanto, oco, mudo, rejubilava-se. A coisa estava ótima.[62]

Clark, as mentioned, considered her theoretical statements to always come after submitting herself to the proposition, just like Martim in this passage of Lispector's novel, gains access to such creative not understanding, walking under the yellow sun, trying to speak to the rocks on which he sits, as a consequence of an act, "the crime," that tears him away from the social order and into the "sertão," the arid backcountry in Northeastern Brazil. The failure of language to name that other mode of perception and temporality that open up for Clark's participant, for Clark or Fédida in the room with an autistic child, and for Lispector's Martim favors not-understanding as a creation, in the latter's experience, losing the ability or automatism of understanding becomes a gift of seeing before it's too late and language, the language of others, that

62. Lispector, *A maçã no escuro* (Rio de Janeiro: Nova Fronteira, 1981), 31–32, my emphasis. "And under the yellow sun, sitting on a rock, without the slightest guarantee—the man now rejoiced as if not understanding were a creation. That precaution that a person has of transforming the thing into something comparable and thus addressable, and, only from that moment of certainty on, looks and allows himself to see because happily it will be too late not to understand—that precaution Martim had lost. And not understanding was suddenly giving him the entire world. / Which was entirely empty, to tell the truth. That man had rejected the language of others and didn't even have the beginning of a language of his own. And nonetheless, hollow, mute, he rejoiced. The thing was superb."

is, has covered up the void. "A coisa estava ótima," one reads in the passage from Lispector, "the thing was superb." The sentence initially suggests, with some humor, given the previous descriptions, that the situation was just great. So great that Martim rejoiced, the paragraph states twice. But if the "superb" and "rejoicing" states accessed by one who lost the ordinary caution that the text describes as a condition for seeing comparable and tractable things exclusively, are these pleasantly relaxing states? Far from it. "A coisa" the thing, literally, without its usual occlusion by understanding to keep a person safe, was in this scene unusually "ótima," uncanny, strangely causing Martim to rejoice as he sits in the middle of nowhere having lost his past, his future, his words, which were not really his own, and for once receptive to a paradoxical "mundo inteiro . . . inteiramente vazio" "entire world . . . entirely empty" that compels the narrator to "falar a verdade" "speak the truth."

With Freud's notions of the pleasure principle and the death drive, psychoanalysis enounces what is at stake in the confrontation with language's limitations to deal with the drives in the body, as well as in the different modalities (structures) of not having this support and of producing other passageways for the drives. Freud describes the pleasure principle as an unconscious process of lowering excitations to restore the individual's stability. Initially he shows its contrast with the reality principle, which involves acknowledging the external world to some degree, and managing its discrepancy with regard to one's demands by accepting deferred satisfaction. The distinction between subject and object results from the process of deferred satisfaction under the reality principle; prior to it, this distinction is inexistent. Lacan adds that subjectivity is constituted with the acceptance of a loss of jouissance, which denotes the voluptuous, unshared excess of pleasure and pain we have been examining in Clark and in the cited passage by Lispector. In place of this loss comes the signifier, a naming of one's needs in terms coming from outside, from what Lacan calls the Other as the site of signifiers, where subjects seek not only the satisfaction of needs, but also recognition.[63] Yet the correspondence between

63. "Psychoanalysis cannot be indifferent before this opposition that confronts the jouissant body with the desire that goes through the regulation of the signifier and of the law," writes Braunstein (*Goce*, 19). Regarding this law, he insists on the "incompatibility of *jouissance* and the Law which is the Law of language. It Forces one to live by transforming the aspirations to jouissance into the terms of articulated discourse, of the social link. The demand is conditioned by what can be requested" (59).

the subject's body and the Other is imperfect, and the gap, or the residual pieces of the subject that insistently, repeatedly fail to be recognized in language, the censored, in a word, is, for Clark and Lispector, the stuff of a new path for unsymbolizable intensities, without the support of an object and of the signifier, in a revised aesthetic-libidinal operation more radical than sublimation, if the latter is understood as recognition in culture and the artist in a position of mastery.

Lyotard denounced the idea of the artist as "a victorious neurotic"[64] and even claimed that "opposing the work to the symptom like success (reconciliation, peace, victory) is opposed to failure (hostility, dualism), is to accept a position on 'expression' that belongs to academicism," which places art as separate from "life in official alienation."[65] Lyotard's own view on the concept of "expression" opposes it to "signification," which "supposes a common code"[66] and aligns it instead with what he later calls "figural." Expression can occur in plastic and poetic works, even if the latter uses words that can also operate within signification. In this 1969 synthesis of psychoanalytic approaches to literature and art, Lyotard invokes Maurice Blanchot's reading of the myth of Orpheus as artist descending into the hells, in order to stress the operation of exceeding pleasure and confronting what Freud called the death drive. If, to find Eurydice, Orpheus "descends into the night of hell"[67] it is because "the artist is someone in whom the desire to see death at the price of dying is stronger than his desire to create."[68] "Orpheus wants to see in the night, to see the night" rather than to reconcile Eurydice "with the law of daylight, remodeled according to good form and *thingness* (*choséité*)."[69] However, "thingness" in Lyotard's phrase would not concern "the decisive thing," but instead, as Lispector has just put it, the ordinary tendency "to transform the thing into something comparable and then tractable." The survival of the object for Clark, in other words bringing Eurydice safe and sound to daylight, entails, according to the myth, failing to "see the night," that is, the act that results in

64. Jean-François Lyotard, "Principales tendances actuelles de l'étude psychanalytique des expressions artistiques et littéraires," in *Dérive à partir de Freud et Marx* (Paris: Galilée, 1974), 129.

65. Lyotard, 127.

66. Lyotard, 118.

67. Lyotard, 125.

68. Lyotard, 127.

69. Lyotard, 125.

"the dismembered body of Orpheus"[70] or in what we previously saw Clark describe in her personal notes as her body "abandoning" her "or having left her walking." This desire's necessary renunciation of successful shaping and rendering of a valuable object to culture stressed by Lyotard manifests, quite accurately, in the act of cutting along the Möbius strip until it becomes an entanglement of shreds. The remaining mesh would be the trace, but only of the "disseizure" ("le dessaisissement") or "lack in being" that Lyotard considers "a fundamental dimension of the literary and artistic work."[71] Its effect is that of opening up the space[72] (and time) as totality we have been examining. For, "the withdrawal of meaning" ("le retrait du sens") this disseizure brings also opens up an "expanse" ("étendue"), desertic like the sertão Martim appears in, certainly, and in any case "a space deconstructed to the point of distorting the laws of language and perception such that the *formative* operations of the figures of the unconscious and their traces may, in this free field, produce other figures, new figures that will then be poetic or plastic."[73] Thus Lyotard points to a work with the unconscious which is not about simply underlying desires to be unveiled, but about the production of new figures upon renouncing the laws of sense, as well as the wish to bring Eurydice back alive or to compose a beautiful song, in favor of the sole desire of "seeing the night." One recalls here that in Lispector's novel Martim starts walking in the dark, "andava nas trevas," into a darkness, "escuridão," that closes around his body and vision "se mantinha tão colada aos olhos inutilmente abertos" "remained glued to his uselessly open eyes."[74]

"Mute Thought"

Clark took detailed notes of her visions of night, published under the title "On the suppression of the object" in 1975. She knows by then that to suppress the object (Eurydice, for instance) is to pass "from my *I* to the world, perceiving the totality of rhythm, from beach soccer to

70. Lyotard, 125.

71. Lyotard, 132.

72. On "opening up a space," Lyotard follows Milner, under the pseudonym Joana Field.

73. Lyotard, 132.

74. Lispector, *A maçã no escuro*, 16–17.

Mozart."[75] This world is, of course, different from the "life in official alienation" Lyotard decries. But, and in this she takes one step further, it is also different from the confrontation with death exclusively, that even Orpheus as figure of the artist preserves. Instead, Clark records

> o reconhecimento dos espaços percebidos nas últimas proposições em que já não havia nenhum objeto intermediário, como um espaço que reconheço como espaço interior do corpo. Espaço esse ligado *numa noite* com a própria vagina, onde o feto para nascer tem que mergulhar. Espaço abismal, túnel, morte, passagem condutora para a vida. Espaço vivido pelo feto como morte ligando a dualidade vida-morte.[76]

This is not only the space of the body's dismemberment, which Lyotard invokes with Orpheus, and which Nietzsche and Klossowski with Ariadne's thread heading forward to the Minotaur, also invoked in chapter 2. It is total "disseizure"—of death, as Lyotard after Blanchot observes, but also, and perhaps above all, of birth as the site where life and death are linked. By the time Clark writes this text she has been involved in collective propositions where, as she states, "no intermediary object was involved," whereas the previous ones still resorted to materials and objects, to which she will return, revised in the final therapeutic phase of her trajectory, under the previously mentioned name "relational objects." In any case, what she repeatedly names "Pensamento Mudo" "Mute Thought," in this and other texts of hers from the same period (that of her turn to analysis), concerns the sense that there is no adequate object and no word to represent the trauma of disseizure that she sees crucially involved with going into life. Birth appears as that precarious, ongoing rhythmic experience where free drive and not the ego's defenses are in play.

The image of the tunnel or the passage through death leading to life in a female body offers something quite different from the sense of shelter and containment typically linked to the uterine life of the fetus.

75. Clark, "Da suppresão do objeto," in *Lygia* (1998), 265. My emphasis.

76. Clark, 267. "The recognition of spaces perceived in the latest propositions in which there was no longer any intermediary object, like a space that I recognize as space inside the body. A space linked in a night with one's own vagina, where the fetus, to be born, must plunge. Abyssal space, tunnel, death, passage leading to life. Space lived by the fetus like death linking the duality life-death."

A proposition called "Máscara abismo," from 1968, is worn as a mask but not felt like one in that it does not fit snugly against one's face, since it protrudes in a tubular shape that looks, to others, rather like an elephant's trunk. It carries both the word "abyss," in its title, and its experience, for those who decide to put on the mask, whose character of head-on dive into birth the cited text from a few years later brings to light. A later proposition, "Túnel" (1973), also brings a word from this striking text into its title, and has participants crawl through a long, tight, elastic cloth until they emerge at the other end, to offer "new experiences as old as being born, or even before," she explains in a letter to her friend Hélio in 1971.[77] Clark already brings her work to a direct consideration of the specific and in many ways unthinkable process resulting in birth, with the 1968 installation *A casa é o corpo. Penetração, ovulação, germinação, expulsão* ("The House Is the Body. Penetration, Ovulation, Germination, Expulsion" figure 3.4), where participants walk through a huge installed space representing the inside of a woman's body. The cited text on "Pensamento Mudo" focuses more specifically on the critical, decisive passage into life, the letting go and advancing toward the encounter with a heterogeneous element. This is, indeed, Clark's "space," and the newborn's first breath of air inhaled, on which she also reflects, upon reading Groddeck (from whose *Book of the It* [Das Buch vom es], Freud adopts the concept of the *id*):

> When the newborn baby opens its mouth and takes its first breath of air it is the soul which is coming into the body. I see that I am very close to Groddeck because in the *Bicho O dentro é o fora* it is the space of this *Bicho* which I call my lung, an affective space.[78]

In this note from August 22, 1971, Groddeck's image of the soul entering from the first inhalation brings back "the outside that is the inside" from her dream. The trauma of birth is then central to both her production and her clinical practice of the "fantasmatic of the body."[79] Surely this

77. Clark, "Letter to Hélio Oiticia, Paris, May 17, 1971," in *The Abandonment*, 234.

78. Clark, *Lygia* (1998), 282. The passage echoes "the breath is up to you," from the previously cited proposition, and also evokes Clark's *Breathe with Me* (1966).

79. Indeed, Freud saw birth anxiety as prototypical, although he was unsatisfied with understanding subsequent anxiety as a mere automatism. "See Introduction

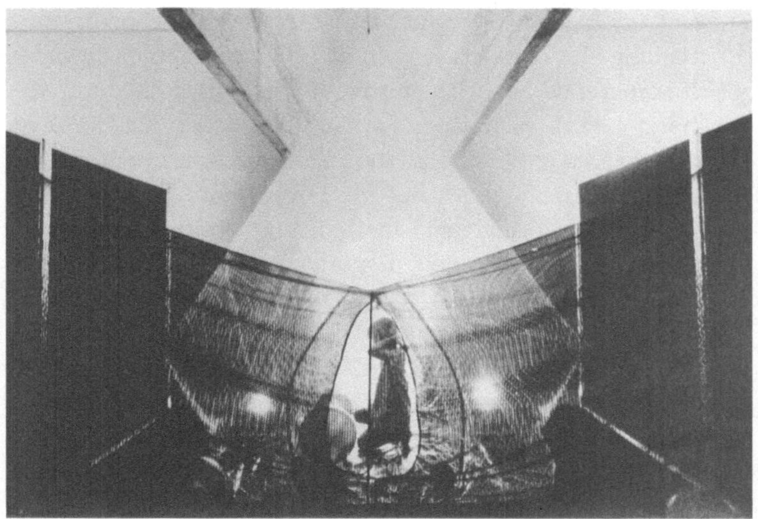

Figure 3.4. Lygia Clark, *A Casa É o Corpo*, 1968. (The House is the Body)—ref. no. 20417A. Courtesy of "The World of Lygia Clark" Cultural Association.

trauma returned in her own birthing experience that gave rise to her creative practice. The development of the "inside is the outside" (figure 3.2) into *Caminhando* (figure 3.3), and onto *A casa é o corpo* (figure 3.4)—whose mesh underscores an inside-out experience, while its shape evokes *O dentro é o fora* in certain positions—insists on the need for participation. While every human begins at this immemorable moment of being cut off from another body of which one was a part, passing thus into life, and while dependence on others during this process is undeniable, no one can stand in for the one undergoing that experience. Likewise, no one can know the other's unique experience of the body; the relational objects, which, Clark stated, "have no identity of their own" outside the experience in the *Estruturação do Self* clinic, concern each body's "mute thought," where the ultimate stakes of "what a body can do" reside.

It was only in the final decade of her life that Clark fully embraced the position of receptivity to the other's irreducibly mute thought, and became concerned with this position as facilitating this mute thought's

to *Inhibitions, Symptoms, and Anxiety*," *SE* XX. Otto Rank's *The Trauma of Birth* encouraged his ambivalence.

way toward finding an expression and a place in the body. In other words, recalling the cited passage from Deleuze's Spinoza, what Clark called *Estruturação do Self* (Structuring of the Self) is an effort to offer the psychotic core of each subject an aesthetic space that turns such a core toward the power of action, "the sole expression of our essence" in Deleuze's reading of Spinoza.[80] But the ethical position of offering just this possibility was already there in Clark's propositions, which is why many of them became materials in the therapeutic work. The idea of a mode of relation that would engage this mute thought, rather than each other's ego, was perhaps most beautifully figured in the 1967 *O eu e o tu* "The Me and the You" (figure 3.1), where two participants wear full-body suits connected at the belly area by a tube as umbilical cord.[81] Participants also wear masks here, and experience against their skin and sense of smell the sensations of a body that they commonly consider "the other sex," while they work on exploring, with their hands, small openings on the other participant's suit, to discover another body. Participants in this proposition are engaged in a blind interaction whose image, as Guy Brett has observed, recalls Francisco de Goya's etching *La confianza* (*Trust*) 1797–98, where two women with head scarves and invisible faces insert keys into little doors' locks on each other's clothing.[82] The notes related to this work held at the Prado Museum indicate that the work is critical of false trust and women's mutual repression, since locked mouths in the literature of the time referred to women's lack of

80. Clark in fact passed on her therapeutic practice to Gina Ferreira and Lula Wanderley. Wanderley to this day practices with Clark's relational objects and other creations of his own, including the public mental health clinic Espaço Aberto ao Tempo, in Rio de Janeiro. He has written about his cases with psychotic subjects and the use of the relational objects in *O dragão posou no espaço* (*The Dragon Landed in Space*) (Rio de Janeiro: Rocco, 2002). See also the recent interview "A restruturação do Selfie" ("The Restructuring of the Selfie") *Concinnitas* 17.2 29 (June 2017): np.

81. There is a resonance between these Clark works and Bracha Ettinger, whose theory is modeled on pregnancy and tied to her experience of artmaking. See, for instance, "Art as the Transport-Station of Trauma" *Bracha Lichtenberg Ettinger: Artworking 1985–1999* (Brussels: Palais des Beaux-arts, Ghent: Ludion), 2000.

82. Brett sees affinities between Clark and Goya in terms of the interest in the body and madness, for instance. He highlights "the sensuality of the exploratory dialogue" between the two figures in Goya's etching. Brett also explores Goya's drawings of mental illness in parallel to Clark's patients. See "Lygia Clark: Séis células" in *Lygia Clark* (1998), 30–32.

judgment or to their sexual subjugation through chastity belts. Indeed, if there were trust between Goya's two female bodies, why would locks and keys be needed?

In Clark's *O eu e o tu* one encounters, again, the hysteric's question of sexual difference ("am I a man or a woman?") as fundamental. A subject, in any structure, is not everything; in this exercise of dwelling in "the other body" things start to turn inside out, as the hands reach out to explore the other body, assumed ordinarily to be "one's own." Visually (for instance to someone observing the photograph of *O eu e o tu* displayed at the Latin American Women Artists exhibit), the participants look not only like Goya's figures but also like astronauts in interconnected suits. The connection, as a two-way umbilical cord, seems vital, like an oxygen tank in outer space. It only makes sense that Clark should have been deeply moved by a human being's physical entry into "outer space" on the first moon landing, two years after *O eu e o tu*, and by the vision of the world "from 'outside'" while she "was 'in' this world" all at once.[83] This work, again, enacts the proposition "the inside is the outside," to the point that there is no longer an impermeable "inside" to return to (and for this reason when she writes about watching the first moon landing on television in Paris, she stresses the moon's beauty and adds that as soon as that flag was raised, it had turned into "a back yard").[84] This is not, then, a merely regressive piece longing for pre-symbolic fusion. The experience is, in fact, also that of the body having "left me—walking" Clark described, regarding *Caminhando*, as cited earlier; "one's own body" loses its imaginary consistency as bodies and space cut through each other endlessly. But perhaps the experience is not entirely "disseizure" either, and a new kind of consistency can emerge between bodies and space passing through each other, as they do here.[85]

One can say trust is in play in Clark's *O eu e o tu* and the other propositions (as it is in being born, or in an analysis)—and not only the participant's trust, in relinquishing the sense of sight, for instance,

83. Clark, "Introject_Incorporate: Appropriation Expropriation," in *The Abandonment*, 242.

84. Clark, 242.

85. Macel suggests that unlike Lacan, who completes the cut of the Möbius strip, Clark emphasizes the continuous moment of an endless cut "never definitive, where the border becomes thin to the point of precariousness yet does not break." "Lygia Clark: At the Borderline," 254.

or trust in the participant's disposition to activate Clark's proposition, although these modes of mutual trust are certainly relevant. At the beginning of this chapter, Deleuze explained Spinoza's insight that "finite modes are born in conditions such that they are cut off in advance from their essence or their degree of power, cut off from that of which they are capable, from their power of action." It is not that the cut that gives rise to a subject at the cost of a lost jouissance should be avoided, since the possibility of desire is concerned with coming to terms with not being everything, not being whole. In the impossible realm of the lost jouissance, Clark investigates that "quelque chose en elle [*la femme*] qui échappe au discours" "something that in her [in the *woman*] escapes discourse."[86] If, as I have stated earlier in this and the previous chapters, woman does not trust the signifier, or if the latter fails to account for something of her jouissance, then the trust at stake in O *eu e o tu* is, especially, in each subject's mute thought, as the each-time-singular site of residence for the "power of action," which was also defined as "the sole affirmation of our power of being affected." And one does not only trust this mute thought's singularity, but also the latter's capacity to become concretely active, that is to say, to exercise the power of being affected. This power may have everything to do with love.

86. Lacan in Bergeron, *Le féminin*, 48.

Part II

Love beyond Pleasure

CHAPTER 4

(Re)Visions of Love

Marguerite Duras

Late in her career as an experimental writer perpetually devoted to the problem of love, Marguerite Duras proposes a provoking definition that tears love away from the common realm of feelings and places it in a sensorial field: "Je ne sais pas si l'amour est un sentiment. Parfois je crois qu'aimer c'est voir"[1] (I don't know if love is a feeling. Sometimes I think that to love is to see). Duras at this point in her work has already gone through a decade devoted to making films, while suspending, during this period, her writing of novels, after the 1971 publication of no other title than *L'amour*. In the latter, an extremely sparse and almost plotless novel, love is indeed nothing like a feeling, not even a recognizably romantic or interpersonal situation.

Before delving into the startling phrases I just cited, and into Duras' notion of love, let me point out that Duras' work not only introduces love as a central concern for the aesthetic clinic; it also invites us to undergo a decidedly scopic sensation, and that, in this exploration, I am placing it just after the plunge into blindness, or into the nonvisual senses Clark's propositions led to, as a way of disrupting the predominantly oppositional subject–object dynamics of social life, including art viewing. In this return to vision, I do not seek, however, to step away from the immediacy of experience Clark strove to give participants access

1. *Emily L* (Paris: Les Éditions de Minuit, 1987), 139.

to. Instead, "seeing" and "love" both become displaced from their usual epistemological and affective implications to reveal differential configurations for thinking relation, as well as different consequences for the subjects that emerge with those configurations.

What is it about love and the scopic drive that so ignited Duras' writing across five decades, and that comes together in a single formula, where they stand for each other in the previously cited passage? In a way, Duras' definition invokes a traditional link in literature, although to call into question love as feeling begins to disrupt that tradition all at once. And this disruption is closely aligned with the injunction and speaker that give Duras' 1969 novel *Détruire, dit elle* (*Destroy, She Said*) its title. For, this "she" who orders destruction, speaking for Duras' oeuvre beyond that novel, is a feminine subject for whom love as a feeling never quite worked, a subject who asks if love can be something other than an ideal of civilization that therefore merely contributes to the repression of unconscious desire, and who is ready to be done with that ideal. Writing for Duras is an experiment in love and vision outside that framework, and thus a wager that these two tenets of civilization hold something beyond repressive and objectifying functions, something radical for desire.

From Duras' first widely read novel from 1950, *Un barrage contre le Pacifique* (*The Sea Wall*), to the late *L'Amant de la Chine du Nord* (*The North China Lover*) in 1991, the work of writing—the same event from her adolescence in the previous two examples, in fact—is not about autobiography, but instead about an unsayable, whose force the event of love makes present for those enduring it, and this includes Duras' readers. After writing *L'Amant* in 1984, Duras tried to collaborate on an adaptation of the film directed by Jean-Jacques Annaud, but she ended up rejecting this project,[2] which was released anyway and surely contributed to making the novel known beyond France. Fundamentally, the problem with this film's approach to a text by Duras is that it misses the crucial point of the unsayable. The certainty that "that's not it" pushes Duras, who by that time had directed several films herself, to rewrite the novel and publish *L'Amant de la Chine du Nord* (with guidelines for its execution as a film or play at the end). This story of rewritings and adaptations may, quite literally, bring to mind Lacan's formulation of love as the displacement

2. See www.marguerite-duras.com/L-amant.php

from contingency to necessity, from "that which stops not being written" to "that which does not stop being written."[3] The crucial point when Lacan makes this statement lies in the negative construction of these formulas, insofar as these negations outline the limits of language and a jouissance to which language is inadequate. Indeed, to Lacan's ear a "ce n'est pas ça" "that's not it" formulates "the cry through which the obtained jouissance is distinguished from the one awaited. It is where (*où*) what can be said in language becomes specified. Negation by all appearances (*a toute semblance de*) comes from there (*là*). But nothing more."[4] These sentences insist on a location (through the French words "où" and "là") that cannot fully be inhabited by language, a breaking point produced by negation's emergence that prompts the final words "nothing more."

As Duras writes on, her orientation is closely related to Lacan's concern for negation and for revealing and upholding the precise location of a gap that Annaud instead misses, seeming to want to cover it up. Lacan famously stated that love "makes up for (*supplée*) the sexual relation insofar as the latter is inexistent."[5] As other readers of this work have already explained,[6] what Lacan means by "no sexual relation" is not that sexual intercourse does not exist, but rather that wholeness, as an absolute correspondence of two bodies, or of the two sexes, for instance, is impossible. The crucial moment in *L'amant* is thus the lovers' mutual confession, once they are together in his bedroom, of a fundamental loneliness: "Il dit qu'il est seul, atrocement seul avec cet amour qu'il a pour elle. Elle lui dit qu'elle aussi elle est seule. Elle ne dit pas avec quoi."[7] ("He says he is alone, atrociously alone with this love he has for her. She says she also is alone. She does not say with what"). This passage, placed just before the couple's first carnal encounter, shows that Duras' writing, in its repetitive character, "no longer refers to a signification,

3. Lacan, *E*, 184.

4. Lacan, 142.

5. Lacan, 59.

6. See, for instance, Bruce Fink, "Knowledge and Jouissance," in *Reading Seminar XX: Lacan's Major Work on Love, Jouissance, and Feminine Sexuality*, ed. Bruce Fink and Suzanne Barnard (Albany, NY: SUNY Press, 2002); and more recently Alenka Zupančič, *What Is Sex?*

7. Duras, *L'amant* (Paris: Les Éditions de Minuit, 1984), 48.

but . . . [is] rather, the means of approximating an inaccessible real."[8] Similarly, if seeing is synonymous with love according to Duras, seeing no longer refers to a spectacle, the one that feeds the illusion of sexual relation. Therefore, the function of the repetition is not to successfully signify the sexual relation.

What is most interesting about Duras' insistence on writing love lies in its very effects on her style, and on the act of reading for which it makes space, both through the novel and cinema. Continuing to write, she reduces the amount of words, the phrases' length, the details of the plot and characters, as though clearing the text to allow the essential elements of love's specificity, an inaccessible real, to emerge. One can describe the transformation across the decades of writing (in different genres and media: novels, theater, screenplays, and films) in terms of a reduction of narrative and content to a minimum, to give full force, instead, to the stage and the gestures related to the love event. This transformation in Duras' writing style through unique procedures of evacuation aims, I find, at nothing less than giving access to a nonimaginary experience of love. Conversely, Annaud's film aims, in his own words, at the spectator's "identifying with the characters" and building excitement about what he calls "la prise de plaisir" "taking of pleasure," that is, the sex scenes, so that pleasure can be shown in the erotic encounters between the story's two lovers.[9] What seems instead relevant about sex in *L'amant* is a man in tears with a young girl who, asking to be treated like any other woman this lover would bring to his bed, discovers a transformation of pain into enjoyment, or a coupling of these two sensations, which prompts an image of formlessness:

> Et pleurant il le fait. D'abord il y a la douleur. Et puis après cette douleur est prise à son tour, elle est changée, lentement arrachée, emportée vers la jouissance, embrassée à elle.
>
> La mer, sans forme, simplement incomparable.[10]

8. Lucie Cantin, "Practices of the Letter, Writing a Space for the Real." *UMBR(a). Writing* (2010), 11–32, 12.

9. Barillaud et al. *Jean-Jacques Annaud Tourne L'amant*. Renn Productions, 1992. www.dailymotion.com/video/xiuvoq

10. Duras, *L'amant*, 50. "And crying he does it. Initially there is pain. And then this pain is taken in turn, it is changed, slowly torn off, swept toward enjoyment, adhered to it. / The sea, formless, simply incomparable."

But why, one might ask, a nonimaginary experience of love (commensurate with her jouissance, evoked here through the formless sea)? Why, of all media, turn to cinema for this? And how does this compulsion to rewrite the same love story, or to repeat what I am calling an evacuation in Duras' creations bear witness to it? As the idiomatic phrase puts it (in English and French, at least), love is something one *makes*—at once due to, and out of the impossibility of sexual relation, or the fundamental solitude of speaking beings. If, as Lacan's statements in Seminar XX indicate, love is a matter of *making*, insofar as the sexual relation fails, it logically follows that any preestablished idea, image, and word of love are inadequate to the task. Marguerite Duras' entire oeuvre develops from her own discovery of this very position. The world's concurrent abundance of platitudes and excellent poetry about love across, for instance, ten centuries of French literature, only confirms language's inadequacy to it. Words are never enough, never just right. Why not? To begin, because, when one is moved to speak, words are already there, ready-made, exchangeable for each other, so they fail to capture love's singularity. The language of speaking beings is necessarily the Other's language, as Lacan insisted, and as Duras is highly aware (and this awareness makes it necessary for Duras to escape platitudes on love in her writing). So how can there be such a thing as love's singularity?

Saint Hommage, Sinthomage

If it is through writing that, as I propose, Duras aims at giving access to a nonimaginary experience of love, the work of literature can have nothing to do with the representation of feelings that would only actually emerge in another plane, commonly called "reality." Deleuze and Guattari insist on the fact that literature and other artforms create something that is nowhere else available and is not there to adapt to reality: "There is no longer a tripartite division between a field of reality (the world) and a field of representation (the book) and a field of subjectivity (the author)."[11] Psychoanalysis, when it understands its work as a creative, experimental endeavor nonadaptive to reality, shares the stakes of the schizoanalysts' rhizomatic work. Instead of dealing with a fixed subject

11. Deleuze and Guattari, *ATP*, 23.

representing the world, rhizomatic writing and analysis relate to "the real" as put by Cantin earlier. This real can never be equivalent to reality. Thus Deleuze and Guattari state: "In short, we think that one cannot write sufficiently in the name of an outside. The outside has no image, no signification, no subjectivity."[12] Love in Duras' writing indeed concerns such an outside, which I will come to shortly. Yet the point is not simply to show that literature, in this case Duras,' makes up feelings, but rather to explore love as an aesthetic effect situated, in Freudian terms, beyond the pleasure principle (determining reality). Duras turns love into a sensation in Deleuze's sense of the term, which, as discussed in chapter 2, underscores the transmission of real intensities, bypassing representation and signification. "Making love, as the locution indicates, is poetry," Lacan states;[13] through this definition, love is removed from the register of pleasure to become a rare, challenging task of embracing the constraints of language for creation.[14]

This "act of love" involves very different things in a man and a woman, as two positions for speaking subjects.[15] The previously cited passage from *L'amant*, where he is alone "with his love" and "she does not say what she is also alone with" reflects this fundamental difference. In Seminar XX Lacan is curious about a love, *amour*, that would be something different from the approach of an object-cause-of-desire (in a woman), or *objet a* as narcissistic support (for a man), for which he proposes the spelling *amûr*—a love where "*a-wall*" is in play. This other, feminine *amour* with its hollow letter "o" restored at the center, as something real that resists the signifier—perhaps ravages it, like the Pacific Ocean that destroys the sea wall built to protect the rice fields in *Un barrage contre le Pacifique*—is what concerns Duras' writing from beginning to end, and again, since the water's destructive erosion only occurs by a force of repetition.

Repetition as a work of sensation becomes something entirely different from the repetition subordinated to representation, discerned in

12. Deleuze and Guattari, 23.

13. Lacan, *E*, 92.

14. On "enabling constraints" see Tracy McNulty, *Wrestling with the Angel*, and "Enabling Constraints: Toward an Aesthetics of Symbolic Life" in *UMBR(a). Writing* (2010), 35–63.

15. Lacan's statements are very nuanced around the formulas of sexuation; "man" and "woman," he repeats, are signifiers and positions in which subjects situate themselves. He considers, for instance, the mystic Saint John of the Cross as feminine. *E*, 97.

a traditionally Oedipal interpretation that turns the man's object into a disguise for an original referent in whose identity his own integrity is founded, the one being replaced in later instances.[16] Deleuze argued that if repetition is usually conceptualized in subordination to identity, it also can and must work in the service of difference, as a repetition that is in itself original, with further-reaching consequences for creation. It is this kind of repetition that Duras' search for genuine love put to work in her writing. Deleuze's argument has psychoanalysis in mind. His protest against "the traditional theory of the compulsion to repeat in psychoanalysis" concerns its subjection "to a principle of identity in the former present and a rule of resemblance in the present one."[17] But the relevance of original repetition, which is never founded in a once-actual present, was certainly noticed by Freud. Deleuze sees his point, that "repetition is necessarily disguised" and "repression takes the form of a consequence in regard to the representation of presents" as something Freud knew, "since he did search for a more profound instance than that of repression, even though he conceived of it in similar terms as a so-called 'primary' repression. We do not repeat because we repress, we repress because we repeat."[18] Repetition is the most powerful device when it is a matter of, as Cantin suggested, "approximating an inaccessible real," where the real's inaccessibility is essential, impossible to signify, and not merely due to a blockage from its supposed true identity. Thus, the feminine, as internal difference or confrontation with the lack of a signifier, can unleash the excessive force of repetition. And writing may give the repetition a unique resonance.

Lacan's late interest in love and letters beyond the signifier, as well as in feminine jouissance must have something to do with his own experience, eight years prior to Seminar XX, of reading Duras, even if he does not mention her in his *Encore*. His omission of her name comes across, in fact, as consistent with Duras' logic of the effaced name, discussed later in this chapter. Lacan was remarkably moved by Duras' 1964 novel *Le ravissement de Lol V. Stein*. His 1965 text on this literary work indicates that it played a significant role in his efforts in the 1970s to develop a notion of love that would break the paradigm

16. Lacan's "unary trait" is not an empirical entity. Colette Soler explains Lacan's trajectory beyond Oedipus in chapter 2 of *Lacan Reading Joyce* (NY: Routledge, 2018).

17. Deleuze, *DR*, 104.

18. Deleuze, 105.

where the other is an object that only reflects self-identity. Considered a "madwoman" in her social circles, the character Lol V. Stein, (whose first name, as Lacan remarks, rhymes with "folle" "crazy") modeled all of Duras' female figures, according to the author. But what is the logic that links "madness" to love, seeing, and a transmission of the unsayable? Lol's madness would have to do with confronting an experience of love that fundamentally does not fit the common ideal.

In *Le ravissement* the reader learns of the rumor around Lol, that she lost her mind at seventeen, on a ball night at the T. Beach casino, where her then-fiancé, Michael Richardson, was stolen away ("ravished") by Anne Marie Stretter, an unknown, older femme-fatale in a black dress with whom he dances the night away. Lol stands by on the margins, quietly fascinated, "ravished" by the vision of the dancing lovers until dawn, when the couple's departure as the music ends, and the arrival of Lol's mother to rescue her result in her painful cry and collapse. But this origin of her madness is called into question, since her childhood friend Tatiana Karl recalls that Lol's heart had never been entirely "there" (là)[19]—in other words, she had been absent from herself. The strange role adopted by the character Jacques Hold, Lol's lover as the text's narrator, although he never witnessed the traumatic scene in her life that organizes the plot, is important to make sense of the logic I wish to interrogate, since the circulating rumor does not quite capture the transmission of the unsayable. Hold, who will only reveal his name and part in Lol's story midway through the novel in which Lol V. Stein is the protagonist, wants to get closer and go beyond the rumor he, too, has heard. So, Hold is moved to give the following hypothetical account of the traumatic scene that marked Lol in her youth:

> Lol ne va pas loin dans l'inconnu sur lequel s'ouvre cet instant. Elle ne dispose d'aucun souvenir même imaginaire, elle n'a aucune idée sur cet inconnu. Mais ce qu'elle croit, c'est qu'elle devait y pénétrer, que c'était ce qu'il lui fallait faire, que ç'aurait été pour toujours, pour sa tête et pour son corps, leur plus grande douleur et leur plus grande joie confondues jusque dans leur définition devenue unique mais innommable faute d'un mot. J'aime à croire, comme je l'aime, que si Lol

19. Duras, *Le ravissement de Lol V. Stein* (Paris: Gallimard, 1964), 13.

> est silencieuse dans la vie c'est qu'elle a cru, l'espace d'un éclair, que ce mot pouvait exister. Faute de son existence, elle se tait. Ç'aurait été un mot-absence, un mot-trou, creusé en son centre d'un trou où tous les autres mots auraient été enterrés. On n'aurait pas pu le dire mais on aurait pu le faire résonner. Immense, sans fin, un gong vide . . .[20]

The "mot-trou" (hole-word) in Duras' novel emerges as its narrator, the man whose words on an event he never witnessed are all we have to read, tries to approach an experience of Lol, who, ten years prior, had witnessed a "ravishing" love scene that disrupted her life profoundly and is beginning to have disruptive consequences in the lives of others, such as Jacques Hold. But what is this scene? Truth is deliberately destabilized to an extreme, on every level of the text—from the event's nature (love itself?) to the man taking on the role of witness (who was not there), to the account's place (within a novel authored by Duras). It is crucial to note that "this instant" at the beginning of the passage is not only something Hold missed, but imagines or hears that Lol saw; rather, it is an instant Lol herself never saw and that would have followed the haunting scene of a ball night at the casino in T. Beach.[21] The crucial matter, again, is not that young Lol's fiancé is "ravished" from her by a femme fatale, but instead what this situation opens up, which the

20. Duras, 47–48. "Lol does not go far in the unknown this instant opens onto. She does not have any memory available, not even imaginary, she has no idea about this unknown. But what she believes, is that she had to penetrate it, that was what she had to do, it would have been forever, for her mind and body, the greatest pain and the greatest joy confounded to their very definition, turned unique but unnamable for lack of a word. I love to believe, like I love her, that if Lol is silent in life it's that she believed, in the space of a lightning bolt, that this word could exist. For lack of its existence, she is silent. It would have been an absence-word, a hole-word, pierced at its center by a hole, of this hole where all the other words would have been buried. It wouldn't have been possible to say it, but it would have been made to resonate. Immense, without end, an empty gong . . ." Serge André quotes from this passage to explain feminine castration in psychoanalysis. See his *Que veut-une femme? (Paris: Navarin, 1986), 186*–187.

21. Catherine Millot has developed a reading of this instant as primal scene. She states that this passage where the "hole-word" appears "calls to mind a sort of primary repression" (69), and she considers Lol's engagement with it as "equivalent to the construction of the fantasy in the psychoanalytic cure" (72). "Why Writers?" in *UMBR(a). Writing* (2010), 65–75.

passage approaches through the hypothetical moment after the band stopped playing and the couple disappeared from Lol's sight. As Hold states in the cited passage, Lol has no memory available for the instant he describes; Duras' point is that no one does, and yet, it sustains "the greatest pain and the greatest joy confounded to their very definition," a very close description of feminine jouissance very close to the later one in *L'amant*. Furthermore, the pain and joy are here "turned unique, but unnamable for lack of a word."

What captivates Lol about the instant Hold describes is not even an imagined love scene featuring the couple in her absence. If "she does not go very far," it is because she confronts something like an impossible vision of the Thing or jouissance itself, unformatted by cultural ideals that, grounded on pleasure, enforce the boundaries she has instead lost. Does the conjunction of madness and love have to do, then, with Freud's description of being in love as the exceptional case in which a mad experience of loss of usual boundaries between ego and object (like the "wall" Lacan invokes) can take place without pathology?[22] Deleuze and Guattari, thinking beyond the Oedipal neurotic model, interestingly propose that courtly love, as field of immanence, requires "that neither the self (*moi*) nor the other (*l'autre*) remain" and this, because this love

> is like the absolute Outside (*Dehors*) that knows no Selves (*les Moi*) because interior and exterior are equally a part of the immanence in which they have fused. "Joi" in courtly love, the exchange of hearts, the test or "assay" (token of love): everything is allowed, as long as it is not external to desire or transcendent to its plane, or else internal to persons.[23]

There is indeed boundlessness in Lol's experience of literally being "beside herself," seeing the dancing couple at the casino, or more precisely, seeing, through that scene, something impossible to see. This writing thus confronts that topological Outside, which is not based on an inside/outside opposition. And years later it allows Lol to extend something of that experience to others, such as Jacques Hold and her old friend Tatiana, who did witness the couple's dance by Lol's side. Crucially, the

22. Freud, *SE* XXI: 66.

23. Deleuze and Guattari, *ATP*, 156.

impossible instant that escapes any conventional means of verification is transmitted as Hold's urge to write Lol's ravishing.

In "Hommage fait à Marguerite Duras, du ravissement de Lol V. Stein," Lacan writes that in paying homage to Duras he is bearing witness to the fact that "the practice of the letter converges with the use of the unconscious."[24] He also recalls Freud's claim that the artist precedes the psychoanalyst and paves the way for the latter, who would be wrong to "play the psychologist" (*faire le psychologue*) in speaking about an artist. These claims from Lacan's text on Duras stand out together, in light of Lacan's development, in the 1970s, of a concept of the letter (of the body) that he sets in contrast with that of the signifier, and in which literature, as "practice of the letter" holds a unique status. Lacan's standpoint in recalling Freud's celebration of Jensen's *Gradiva* is decidedly not as the author's psychoanalyst, but rather as a reader for whom a road as analyst is opened up by the artist's work. Lacan works to foreground the dimension of writing, reading, and the letter at the beginning of his homage, for instance by contemplating different possible readings of the name—or "cipher" as he calls it—"Lol V. Stein," the double genitive in the title, and by interrogating the relationships, not only between characters in the novel, but also between the author and her readers. He explicitly takes the position of reader when he proposes that Duras ravishes "us" with her text.[25]

This position invites a question: what, indeed, are the effects of Duras' ravishing on Lacan's work on the letter? One might say an effect appears as the homage itself. "Hommage" is a notable name for this text of Lacan's, especially regarding Duras' *Ravissement*. The *Trésor de la langue française* states that "hommage" has medieval origins, and calls up the devotion owed by a vassal to a lord. In a homage, the entry adds, the gesture of acknowledgment is also an offering that elevates its addressee. While the etymology of "hommage" is simply "homme" (man), to which the suffix *-age* is added, and the first "hommage" is addressed to a man "seigneur," the second instance from 1165 intends "a mark of courtesy addressed to a

24. Lacan, *AE*, 193. In Lacan's writing and teaching "the letter" repeatedly features a link of the unconscious to literature (for example, Poe, Provençal courtly poetry, Duras, Joyce, Beckett).

25. Lacan, 191. Millot explores the ternary structures at work in Lacan's homage to Duras.

woman,"[26] so "hommage" leads straight into the tradition of the practice of the letter that, through the troubadour's cult of the Lady in courtly love, also favored Lacan's approach to sublimation as a matter of "elevating the object to the dignity of the Thing."[27] This background of the word "hommage" chosen by Lacan in relation to Duras, and specifically to *Le ravissement* underscores the following: first, that the novel's crucial point lies in the cited passage that pinpoints the "mot-trou," the hole-word that, like the Thing to which the homage is payed, escapes representation and is unsayable, though it could be made to resonate. If the "mot-trou" could be written in one letter, it would have to be the "o" at the center of the palindrome "Lol," in "Hold," the narrator's last name resonant with both "Lol" and the English "hole," and also stressed in the word "homage." If it could be made to resonate, it would resemble French's apostrophic cry "ô," which applies "to the greatest pain and the greatest joy" Hold invokes in the passage. Second, by setting up the feminine unsayable through a web of figures across genders, and by the introduction of a male narrator-lover engaged with the hole-word that captured the silent Lol, a kind of "hommage" takes place in the novel, literally, as it should be taken: "homme-age" is a man-making. But we have yet to discuss the kind of man made here, made receptive, that is, to the unsayable, since this receptor holds the conditions for the analyst's position according to Lacan, and for being a viewer of Duras' cinema. That courtly "joi" is much more than a word for the feeling of joy, that it is also not simply "jouissance" in the sense of orgasm, but instead a unique aesthetic process or "a joy immanent to desire"[28] suggests the required conditions.

A temporal lag is part of the logic of writing and the letter, between the time of the inscription and the time of reading. What becomes inscribed can remain dormant for a long time. The specific effects on Lacan of the hole-word in *Le ravissement de Lol V. Stein*, I find, begin to be confirmed almost ten years later, in the striking resonance between the cited passage from Duras' 1964 novel, where "for lack of [this word's] existence, [Lol] is silent" and Lacan's stress, in 1973, on "mot" "word" as the negation of words, "*motus*" ("not a word"), that is to say, on word as silence, or uncanny word that names its absence: hole-word. Furthermore, this aspect of "mot"

26. In Benoît de Sainte-Maure, *Roman de Troie*. A plausible addressee of the homage is the patroness of poets Elienor d'Aquitaine.

27. Lacan, *Éthique*, 133.

28. Deleuze and Guattari, *ATP*, 192.

comes up in the seminar when Lacan speaks of feminine *jouissance*, about which, to the psychoanalyst's frustration, women who may experience it remain silent: "not a word! We've never been able to get anything out of them."[29] The subsequent seminar session specifies the place of this "no answer, not a word" (*pas de réponse, motus*)[30] as marking the limit and failure of meaning, remarkably close to the "empty gong" Jacques Hold (Jacques Lacan's uncanny namesake[31]) proposes to think the hole-word.

Although Lacan linked "homme" and the symptom in his later work with James Joyce, showing, exactly, how the symptom can make the man (as his 1975 title "Joyce le symptôme" indicates), he did not return to the operation already present in the word "hommage," chosen to celebrate Duras. In Seminar XXIII he proposes *sinthome*, a forgotten writing of "symptom" in French, *symptôme*, in order to go beyond interpretation, metaphor, and the endless substitution of signifiers in approaching the symptom, to the knotting of jouissance and an act of saying.[32] The spelling practiced by medical doctor and man of letters François Rabelais in the sixteenth century, *sinthome*, allows Lacan to

29. Lacan, *E*, 96.

30. Lacan, 79.

31. Lacan reads proper names as a writing of the subject's fate where the real can come forth. In "L'instance de la lettre dans l'inconscient," he states that the subject "if he can seem to be a servant to language, is more so the servant of a discourse, in whose universal moment his place is already inscribed at birth, if only under the form of his proper name." *Ecrits I* (Paris: Seuil, 1999), 492. Lacan developed wordplay on his own name, exploring the unconscious work of these meanings on his life. Dany Nobus in a lecture on psychoanalysis as poetry remarked on a poem by Lacan, where the signature "Lacan" becomes "là . . . quand?" ("there . . . when?") and observed that "meaning is balanced against a hole/gap." ("The Poetic Wisdom of Psychoanalysis: On the Trail of Lacan's New Signifier." Lecture for the Center for the Study of Psychoanalysis and Culture, SUNY at Buffalo, 3/1/17). Millot suggests that one of the text's ternaries is "composed of Jacques Lacan (provoked, in a way, by the Jacques of Jacques Hold)" (70). In his analysis of Lacan's response to Duras' novel, Jean-Michel Rabaté sees the name "Lol V. Stein" as a kind of "anagram of LOVe." *Jacques Lacan: Psychoanalysis and the Subject of Literature* (New York: Palgrave, 2001), 134.

32. On this, see Geneviève Morel "A Young Man without an Ego: A Study on James Joyce and the Mirror Stage" and Franz Kaltenbeck "Sublimation and Symptom" in *Art: Sublimation or Symptom*. Edited by Parveen Adams (London: Karnac, 2003). See also Colette Soler in *Lacan Reading Joyce*, and Raul Moncayo, *Lalangue, Sinthome, Jouissance, and Nomination: A Reading Companion to Lacan's Seminar XXIII* (London: Karnac, 2017).

follow the homophonies of "saint homme" ("holy man") and "Saint Thomas (d'Aquin)" (Aquinas). These support an exploration of Joyce as a psychotic structure where writing makes up for the foreclosure of the subject's symbolic grounding through what Lacan had called earlier the Name-of-the-Father (*Nom-du-Père*), whose "no" (*non*) function places a limit on jouissance. Lacan's "Hommage à Duras" does not suggest anything about the author's structure; only the character Lol is "mad" here, and the passage I have cited from the novel offers the cause of this madness, which is the absence of a word for an experienced jouissance. In both the Joyce seminar and in the homage to Duras, Lacan focuses on a shedding or being undressed of a top layer that holds an ego together in (the misrecognition of) a unified body. He is intrigued by Joyce's expression about his body peeling off "like a fruit skin,"[33] and he states that the crucial moment in *Le ravissement*, where the hole-word emerges, is about "removing the dress" (*dérober/enlever la robe*) of the narcissistic image: "au moment où son amant eût enlevé la robe, la robe noire de la femme et dévoilé sa nudité. Ceci va-t-il plus loin? Oui, à *l'indicible de cette nudité* qui s'insinue à remplacer son propre corps. Là tout s'arrête."[34]

The sinthomage is there. Both the young Joyce, through the character Stephen, and the character Lol experience this symptom like an inscription in the body beneath the ego image, and it unleashes a writing beyond the signifier that remains subject to interpretation and substitution.[35]

33. "comme une pelure." *Le séminaire Livre XXIII: Le sinthome* (Paris: Seuil, 2005), 149.

34. Lacan, *AE*, 193. "In the moment when her lover would have taken off the dress, the woman's black dress, and unveiled her nakedness. Does this go further? Yes, to *the unsayable of this nakedness* that suggests itself to replace her own body. Everything stops there." My emphasis.

35. While this "undressing" applies to both psychosis and the feminine, given their experience of the cultural ideal's failure, they are not simply exchangeable. Each has its distinct relation to the Other's jouissance. The psychotic's delusion indicates their sacrificial position with regard to the lack in the Other. Joyce would have resolved this by introducing writing in the place of the psychotic redeeming mission. The feminine link to the other without a signifier, or S(Ⱥ) in the diagram below the formulas of sexuation in Seminar XX, is not about repairing that lack by placing themselves as the Other's missing object in the fantasy (hysteria), but instead of bearing that encountered lack as such.

The Royal Road to a Knowledge of the Unconscious

If the letter brings Lacan close to literature *qua* practice of the letter, it also plays a crucial role in the clinical context, where the analysand's speech is the sole resource.[36] Literature gives Lacan access to a unique approach to love, which in fact reveals the central role of letters and reading in analytic work. An important change takes place at once in the notion of love and the position of the analyst, which distinguishes itself from those of doctor, master, and ordinary other. To consider this displacement, let us briefly read a crucial moment in *The Interpretation of Dreams*.

The "navel of the dream" first appears in a footnote to Freud's analysis of a part of his own dream of examining Irma's throat, where he acknowledges that his replacement, in the dream, of his patient Irma, who he had been unable to fully cure, for her friend, contains the idea that this friend "would have *opened her mouth properly*, and have told [him] more than Irma."[37] In the footnote to this phrase, considering that his analysis of this part of the dream remains incomplete, Freud makes this decisive statement for the practice of psychoanalysis: "There is at least one spot in every dream at which it is unplumbable—a navel, as it were, that is its point of contact with the unknown."[38] The open mouth revealing the oral cavity in Freud's dream provides not an answer to Irma's symptoms, but the uninterpretable navel of every dream that knots the dream together, connects with the unknown, and makes the interpretation of dreams "the royal road to a knowledge of the unconscious."[39] This well-known expression, with the navel as departure point and its double genitive reorients the relationship to knowledge, where it is no longer

---

36. Soler highlights the fact that psychoanalysis is "a practice that has no other instrument than speech," so interrogates Lacan's insistent claim that through "analytic saying, something writes itself." *Lacan: The Unconscious Reinvented*, trans. Esther Faye and Susan Schwartz (London: Karnak, 2014), 19.

37. Freud, *SE* IV: 111. Emphasis in original.

38. Freud, 111.

39. Freud, *SE* XI: 33. The École Freudienne du Québec highlights the navel of the dream as its crucial element in the clinic. Annual Training Seminar on *The Clinic of the Dream*, 2017.

only a matter of the researcher conquering and making everything known to consciousness through interpretation, but rather of the researcher undergoing a transformation in the approach of a knowledge proper to the unconscious, or unconscious *savoir* that cannot be interpreted. Lacan speaks to this very displacement of knowledge and of the work of the analyst in the 1970 interview "Radiophonie," responding to a question on the "discovery of the unconscious" and its effects on epistemology. He states: "The unconscious, one sees [*on le voit*], is only a metaphorical term to designate the knowledge [*savoir*] that can only support itself by presenting itself as impossible, so that from there/it [*de ça*], it confirms itself to be real (hear real discourse) [*entendez discours réel*]."[40] Thus, the unconscious is unlike any other place to which a path or "royal road" may lead, and so the "navel" is that impossible, crucial point of support of the unconscious as a knowledge of its own. The analyst taking this royal road is then confronted by something impossible to interpret or bring into signifiers; still, this confrontation is not merely an obstacle to this road's destination, insofar as it supposes a work of approaching what defies signifiers as something precise that can be confirmed or verified without being betrayed (thus missed) by an interpretation. The context of Lacan's sentence, a radio interview that takes the title "Radiophonie," prompts one to notice in the cited phrase Lacan's emphasis on seeing and hearing (and his final parenthesis even instructs the reader to "hear/understand" "*entendez*"): he punctuates his definition of the unconscious by the parenthetical interjection "on le voit," which fits in as an idiomatic, rhetorical "one can see." But, taken literally, the beginning of this phrase reads "the unconscious, one sees it." If one is to see (although in radio, precisely, one does not see) and also hear, two homophonies of "voit" also become audible, namely, "voix" and "voie," which would invite one to consider that the resonances of "voice" (*voix*—a partial object or mode of *objet a*) and "road" (*voie*—for instance "la voie royale vers l'inconscient" "the royal road to the unconscious" or the radio as a kind of medicine administered by "voie auriculaire" "otic route") indirectly tell us more about how one might "see" this unconscious. And this would be the difference between the unconscious merely not appearing or being irrelevant to knowledge, and, quite differently, as these displacements help us "see," its distinct presentation as impossible,

40. Lacan, *AE*, 425.

in the precise location of "ça." In "de ça il se confirme d'être réel," the pronoun *ça* grammatically refers to the unconscious knowledge presenting itself as impossible (previously stated in the sentence), and this location is "*deçà*" "below," and also simply *ça*, the *id*.[41]

The idea of a "navel of every dream" emerges in the context of Freud's efforts to demonstrate the technique of dream interpretation, and of his wish to establish the validity of psychoanalysis in the medical field at the time of Irma's treatment, which the dream of finding something in Irma's throat reveals. Yet, as psychoanalysis implies, and as explicitly stated in Freud's chapter on his dream of Irma, the clinical context that concerns Freud certainly places sexuality and desire at its center. Moreover, Freud is dealing with dreams, in other words, with accounts of events that only "happen" to the dreamer, or the most private and least empirically verifiable of stories. Just as Jacques Hold is only trying to approach something unknown but distinctly present in Lol, Freud does not know what makes Irma suffer (even if he supposes that Irma's being a young widow plays an important part), as he can acknowledge when analyzing the dream in his book, that is, after the treatment, which, he admits, occurred at a time when he was worried about his reputation. As both men, moved by a desire to know about the other's (a woman's) unconscious desire, interrogate the cause of a rebellious jouissance in these women's bodies, they approach a mysterious unknown, a "cavity" that transforms their own search and even, one might say, their own being. Freud leaves the position of wanting success and his peer's recognition to embrace his commitment to the unconscious, which is indifferent to ideals of success. For his part, Hold—one might also write "Holed" and even "Loled"—follows Lol back to the stage and staging of this primal scene, losing any sense of mastery along the way.[42]

Since "it wouldn't have been possible to say" this "hole-word," and the "spot" discerned by Freud in every dream is "unplumbable" or uninterpretable, "hole" and "navel" indicate the necessity of a different

41. In a related gesture, Lacan refers to the Provençal *Gai sçavoir* poetry contests to bring forth the approach of the letter as a *ça voir*, a knowledge that is an "id-seeing" in *Télévision* (Paris: Seuil, 1973), 40.

42. In his reading of *Le ravissement de Lol V. Stein*, Dominiek Hoens convincingly proposes the novel as tragic, and wonders whether its tragic figure is Hold, rather than Lol. "When Love is the Law: On *the Ravishing of Lol V. Stein*" *UMBR(a)* (2005), 105–116, 106. On the primal scene, see my chapter 2.

speech, an act of saying. Furthermore, there is also something endless about these figures, since, "pierced at its center by a hole," the "word-hole" discloses a mise-en-abyme, which is why its gong-like resonance would be "immense, without end," and since the "navel" Irma's oral cavity reveals is not simply an opaque spot, but instead an opening onto "the unknown" both texts underscore, as the limit of interpretation and representation Deleuze had critiqued, where something limitless begins. The navel or hole-word thus shows and exceeds the limits of the signifier, there where the drives attest to the "Other," nonphallic jouissance Lacan discusses in the seminar for which he chose the title *Encore*, a word to suggest exactly this infinite excess beyond meaning ("still," "again," "more"). Duras and Freud underscore here a feminine force of the unsayable, resistant to any translation and resonating *ad infinitum*.

Freud writes his dream of Irma's throat, in order to read it word by word. This technical detail, of following the dream "to the letter," is crucial. For, if dream interpretation is "the royal road to a knowledge of the unconscious," the treatment of the dream as an original writing to be read, a writing organized around an uninterpretable navel that connects to the unknown, is fundamental to the position of the analyst. Indeed, Lacan in Seminar XX presents the analyst's task before speaking beings as one of reading. Specifically, the analyst reads "the troubling effects of a saying (*dire*)."[43] This certainly includes the dreams analysands bring to their analysis, along with symptoms, slips of the tongue, dreams, and actings-out. He also points out that something speaking beings make from this troubling saying is "this feeling called/said (*dit*) of love," and that, while cultivating this feeling—or "making it last" ("que ça dure encore") in the body ("en corps")—is known to result in "the reproduction of bodies," it may also produce a different effect, and that is writing (*l'écrit*).[44] Duras, it seems, would exemplify the latter road beyond the clinical frame of psychoanalysis (although its relevance is clinical and aesthetic at once). Lacan suggests that the analyst is a reader to this writing; in another part of the seminar Lacan states that what calls to be read is "the letter" (*Encore* 37–38). Thus, the letter can be considered a troubling effect of a saying, insofar as it inscribes itself in the body, speech, and life of the subject. The analyst's reading of these letters in an other's saying entails

43. Lacan, *E*, 60.

44. Lacan, 60.

that the analysand enduring these letters inscribed in him/her addresses them to his/her partner (where they may result in the reproduction of bodies) and/or to the analyst, where the consequences are very different. Insofar as the work with the letters of the body is here put through the constraints of speech, the analyst's reception of these letters takes into account this excess, beyond the semblance where Lacan situates meaning (underscored by Lacan in the expression "this feeling said of/called love" that suggests the clichés and ready-made feelings to which love is susceptible). In the clinical context, writing as another possible result of love would be about finding a nonimaginary way with these letters, a formula aimed at the construction of a nonimaginary *objet a*, at the end of an analysis.[45] That this work of isolating and transmitting the letters and space of love beyond imaginary formations is also central to Duras' writing of love is relevant to the aesthetic clinic.

Echoing "Genesis," Lacan stated that "in the beginning of the psychoanalytic experience, let us remember it, there was love."[46] This is consistent with the later invocation in Seminar XX of transference with the formula for the analyst that marks their separation from a master position: "I believed I had to support the transference, insofar as it does not distinguish itself from love, with the formula *the subject supposed to know*."[47] The analyst cannot know, but the analysand's demand to the analyst as "subject supposed to know," combined with the analyst's desire which supposes a *savoir* to the analysand's unconscious, is the condition to initiate an analysis and what sustains its work of deciphering and construction. All this enables the analyst to slip out of the position of frustration at the lack of a word from the hysteric's mouth, interpreted as resistance, in order to embrace the emergence of the uninterpretable hole-word, as Duras' Jacques Hold does.[48] Love, as the address of something unsayable to someone supposed to know what this Thing is about, along with the analyst's love of the unsayable Thing, can then be a cornerstone of the analytic experience.

45. See Cantin "The Drive," 43.

46. *Le Séminaire VIII (1960–1961): Le transfert* (Paris: Seuil, 2001), 11.

47. Lacan, *E*, 87.

48. Bracha L. Ettinger's reads Hold's position as an ethical act of impossible witnessing with Lol. See "Fascinance and the Girl-to-m/Other Matrixial Feminine Difference," in *Psychoanalysis and the Image*, ed. Griselda Pollock (Oxford, UK: Blackwell, 2006), 60–92.

Losing the Name, Clearing the Stage

A love of the unsayable thing—which as I have said, implies its transmission to an other—is also the cornerstone of the aesthetic experience in Duras. Titles such as *Hiroshima mon amour* (1959), *L'amour* (1971), and *L'amant* (1984) may well convey the importance of love in Duras' work to any reader, before even entering into what love might involve. Yet the repetition of places in the world as part of the title—Hiroshima, North China, India, Venice, and Caesarea, for example[49]—is no minor detail: beyond providing contexts for love's emergence, in Duras' writing these proper names linked to specific political regimes undergo a literary operation that confronts the symbolic from a distinctly feminine perspective. The evacuations of name and place through which Duras offers an encounter of this rare experience of love begin before the unsayable hole-word at the center of the paradigmatic *Ravissement*, and remain a consistent, crucial feature of the author's proposition of love as aesthetic experience, which the beginning of this chapter has underscored in the equation between "love and seeing."

Let us consider Duras' screenplay for the film *Hiroshima mon amour*, directed by Alain Resnais and released in 1960, before Duras' turn to film direction. Its initial synopsis brings a woman into focus as the protagonist of a story taking place in Hiroshima in 1957, whereas in the film our first impression is of a dialogue taking place between a woman and a man whose faces we do not immediately see. In the script's synopsis, it is immediately stated that the woman is French, an actress abroad, participating in a film about peace after the Hiroshima bomb, and, importantly, that the woman will never be named in the film: "C'est la veille de son retour en France que cette Française, qui ne sera jamais nommée dans le film—cette femme anonyme—rencontrera un Japonais (ingénieur, ou architecte), et qu'ils auront ensemble une histoire d'amour très courte."[50]

The only capitalized names the original French text grants to these characters in the synopsis, then, are "Frenchwoman" and "Japanese (man),"

49. Two Duras films are titled *India Song* and *Son nom de Vénise à Calcutta désert*.

50. Duras, *Hiroshima mon amour* (Paris: Gallimard, 1959), 9. "It is on the day before her return from France that this Frenchwoman, who will never be named in the film—this anonymous woman—will meet a Japanese man (engineer, or architect), and that they will have together a very short love story."

cast in an anonymous light related to the fact that in the plot they are strangers to one another and can logically only remain thus, given the tight time constraints of her stay in Hiroshima for the making of the film. The woman's profession, "actress," and condition in the site of the events, "foreigner," only contribute to the anonymity Duras in the script highlights in the woman, although he is not named either. While she performs as someone else, he designs the buildings of civilized human life.

The specification of anonymity and the indication that the woman never be named in the film go much further, both in terms of their significance and of Duras' writing strategies beyond this particular screenplay. For example, *Le ravissement* inaugurates Duras' "India Cycle," where Lol, like the other characters, certainly has a full name, but the next novel, *Le viceconsul* (1966), features Anne Marie Stretter and Lol's former fiancé in Calcutta, in Lol's absence. Importantly, the song of a mad female beggar (*la mendiante*) haunts the characters in Calcutta. The contrast between these resonant, full names that are repeated quite frequently in the novels, and a nameless woman casts an interesting effect on the names. They become, indeed, "ciphers," as Lacan's "Hommage" suggests, or "hole-words"—letters rather than metaphors. *L'amour* (1971), the last novel before Duras' shift into a period of film, continues this process of evacuation by presenting three unnamed characters wandering aimlessly on the beach: a woman, who can be recognized as Lol by readers of the former novels, due to her speech about the ball night at the Casino, and two men. In line with this process, the film *La femme du Gange* (1974) (*The Woman of the Ganges*) places an unnamed woman, or a woman only named through a river, in the title. Next is the better known film *India Song* (1975), which returns to the plot of the novel *Le viceconsul* in a complex experiment where image and sound are out of joint. This film's soundtrack is reused in *Son nom de Venise à Calcutta déserte* (*Her Venice Name in Deserted Calcutta*; 1976). Here the actors disappear, and the images from *India Song* are replaced by close scans of an empty French chateau in ruins.

Such a consistent logic is present within the *Hiroshima mon amour* screenplay. The woman and man in the synopsis are "the Frenchwoman" and "the Japanese (man)," but once the script's dialogues begin, the characters' speech is only distinguished by the gendered pronouns "elle" "her" and "lui" "him." This is already a reduction from proper names to anonymity and two pronouns marking sexual difference between speakers. What, then, is the purpose of losing the name and clearing the stage? While the couple are strangers to one another, she is the stranger in Hiroshima, and as it turns out, a stranger to herself as well. Paradoxically, and this is crucial to the implications of love and writing for Duras, the two strangers do not merely engage in a carnal form of shared intimacy, but also in another intimacy, of a traumatic sort. The Frenchwoman reveals to her Japanese lover that, fourteen years before their meeting she experienced madness, upon the death of her German boyfriend, a soldier in Nevers, her hometown, during the Occupation. This relationship, she recalls, led to public shaming—her head was shaved in public as punishment[51]—and to a period of solitary confinement, a suspension from the social order which she and the Japanese man identify as "eternity" (*l'étérnité*).[52] Hiroshima, the city where the casual encounter takes place, the man's hometown, has, in turn, been destroyed by the atomic bomb in the same war. Duras knows exactly what she is doing when she decides to tell a brief, adulterous love story against the backdrop of Second World War catastrophes, instead of working on a commissioned documentary about the Hiroshima horrors. Duras clearly states that the point, for her, is

> en finir avec la description de l'horreur par l'horreur . . . mais faire renaître cette horreur de ces cendres en la faisant s'inscrire en un amour qui sera forcément particulier et "émerveillant." Et auquel on croira davantage que s'il était produit partout ailleurs dans le monde, dans un endroit que la mort n'a pas *conservé*.[53]

The passage moves from general "horror" (*l'horreur*) to "this horror" (*cette horreur*) that becomes inscribed, in an also specific love "un amour" with the implication that this inscription of horror, or the trauma, is key to its "dazzling" kind of beauty. This set of precisions, through definite

51. Duras chooses to include this sexualized and gendered practice of marking bodies that was common in France during the Liberation. Historian Fabrice Virgili studied this phenomenon in *La France "virile": Des femmes tondues à la Libération* (Paris: Payot, 2000).

52. Duras, *Hiroshima*, 94, 97.

53. Duras, 11. "To be done with the description of horror by horror . . . but to reawaken this horror from these ashes by making it inscribe itself in a love that will be necessarily particular and "dazzling." And in which one will believe more than if it were produced anywhere else in the world, in a place that death did not *preserve*."

and indefinite articles for horror and love, consistent with a register of anonymity, is immediately followed by a consideration on the conditions for believing in love, after the Second World War's unthinkable destruction of humanity and the social order, of course, but also after a certain awareness of illusion, of "make-believe" things, and the problem this awareness raises when it comes to love. Had the plot's love affair taken place anywhere else, far away from the site of these traumas, the affair would easily fall into the old ideals of completion, unity, harmony of two bodies finding their other half.[54]

The synopsis instead prepares us to face the dialogue with a final note, which is that the encounter leads the characters to an impasse that silences them ("Il s'agit bien d'amour. Ils ne peuvent plus que se taire"[55]), and, paradoxically, that the lovers' final exchanges are reduced to still calling each other:

> Pas d'aveux échangés. Plus un geste.
>
> Simplement, ils s'appelleront encore. Quoi? NEVERS, HIROSHIMA. Ils ne sont en effet personne à leurs yeux respectifs. Ils sont des noms de lieu, des noms qui n'en sont pas. C'est, comme si le désastre d'une femme tondue à NEVERS et le désastre de HIROSHIMA se répondaient EXACTEMENT.
>
> Elle lui dira: "Hiroshima, c'est ton nom."[56]

---

54. MacCannell's reading suggests that the woman is unable to break out of the confines of territoriality that have been laid out for her gender within the paradigm of the nation-state, and that the thought of staying in Hiroshima with the man has to do with not overcoming this model that in fact prevents love and makes the city into a representation of the ego's isolation. See *The Regime of the Brother* (London & New York: Routledge, 1991), 116–123. My reading focuses instead on the way in which Duras' writing re-marks the empty space this love affair creates as a space of love, where an encounter on the level of the unconscious can take place. Trauma here is not metaphorized, but instead given a letter that gives rise to a sinthome.

55. Duras, *Hiroshima*, 17. "It is in fact love. They can no longer but be silent."

56. Duras, 17. "No more exchanged confessions, not another gesture. / Simply, they will still call each other. What? NEVERS, HIROSHIMA. They are in fact no one to each other's eyes. They are names of place, names that are not names. It is as if the disaster of a woman whose head was shaved in NEVERS and the disaster of HIROSHIMA corresponded EXACTLY. / She will say to him: "Hiroshima, that's your name."

The exhaustion of dialogue enacts this love's tragic endpoint. In the deliberately strange title *Hiroshima mon amour*, the fusion of love and a toponym indicates the crucial point of the story it tells. To Duras, this particular fusion expresses the essence of tragedy. The phrase suggests an equation between "Hiroshima" and "my love," as if Hiroshima were the name of a speaker's love, or beloved, which, given the first affirmations in the synopsis, indicates that this first person speaking in the title would have to be the nameless Frenchwoman.[57] Would she say "Hiroshima my love" like Lacan said "Joyce the Symptom," to point out the indissociable character of the symptom from the name that would otherwise slip away, as it were? Duras' title is complicated by the fact that "Hiroshima" is already a metonym for the first nuclear bombing in history, so it cannot help calling up destruction and annihilation in a continuum and on equal footing with what a speaking being can call "my love." What blatantly disappears in the title's odd locution, then, is the common "a-mur" in which the addressee of the designation "my love" has the role of an object propping up the ego's specular image, in a relation Lacan identified on the male side of his formulas of sexuation. If the feminine side of sexuation concerns a link to the lack in the Other, the love she, who says "Hiroshima mon amour" names, is just this lack; it cannot possibly signify a cultural ideal, and can only be marked as an irreplaceable name with its tinge of nonsense or "outside-sense."[58]

The Name of the Place

The stakes of Duras' insistence on the woman's namelessness in conjunction with a toponym are best grasped through the text of her lesser known *Césarée*, a 1979 short film that receives its title from the

57. On "Hiroshima" as a name of love see Ettinger and Gardiner, "Affectuous Encounters: Feminine Matrixial Encounters in Duras/Resnais' *Hiroshima mon amour*," *PostGender: Gender, Sexuality and Performativity in Japanese Culture*, ed. Ayelet Zohar (Newcastle-upon-Tyne: Cambridge Scholars, 2009), 251–274.

58. If Deleuze and Guattari wrote of the need to write beyond signification with regard to an "outside," (*dehors*), and Deleuze's concept of "sense" (*sens*) emerges through nonsense (non-sens), Lacan's in his later period arrives at the symptom as jouissance outside-meaning (*hors-sens*).

Palestine city of Caesarea, and through the end of Jean Racine's 1670 tragedy, the controversial *Bérénice*. *Bérénice* tells the love story between two historical figures, Berenice, Palestinian queen of Caesarea, and Titus, heir to the Roman Empire. The play evokes the beginning of this love relationship during Titus' excursion in Jerusalem, in 70 ACE, where he met and fell in love with Bérénice. After five years of enjoying their love in Rome, the death of Vespasian comes between Titus and Bérénice, since Roman law forbids the marriage of an emperor to a foreigner. Titus must say to Bérénice that he cannot marry her because of Rome, and Bérénice resists hearing this until it becomes unavoidable. Duras' film importantly recalls the violence involved in the historical event of the lovers' encounter, by referring to him only as "Lui. Le criminel, / Celui qui avait détruit le Temple de Jérusalem."[59] This phrase and the title are the only references that confirm that the whole text speaks in the wake of *Bérénice's* ending, in which she accepts that she must leave Titus to Rome and go alone, even if she could have accepted Antiochus, a friend of Titus and Roman soldier who has always been silently in love with Bérénice and saw her follow Titus to Rome. If, in Bérénice's voice at the brink of disappearing from both men's view, Racine writes "Adieu, servons tous trois d'exemple à l'Univers / De l'amour la plus tendre, et la plus malheureuse / Dont il puisse garder l'histoire douloureuse."[60] Duras meets Bérénice at the site of this pain, which she invokes in *Césarée* as "la douleur de leur séparation" (the pain of their separation). If *Césarée* responds to Bérénice's hope by remembering, indeed, the painful story, it does so from the perspective of the reduction or evacuation I have been outlining, as Duras' reciting voice in the film states: "*Il n'en reste que la mémoire de l'histoire/ et ce seul mot pour la nommer/ Césarée/ La totalité./ Rien que l'endroit/ Et le mot.*"[61]

59. Duras, *Le Navire night; Césarée; Les mains négatives* (Paris: Mercure de France, 2001), 97. "Him. The criminal, / The one who had destroyed the Temple of Jerusalem."

60. *Oeuvres complètes 1* (Paris: La Pléiade, 1950), Act V, final scene. "Berenice." *Andromache and Other Plays*, trans. John Cairncross (London: Penguin Classics, 1967). "Farewell, let us, all three, exemplify / The most devoted, tender, ill-starred love/ Whose grievous history time will e'er record."

61. Duras, *Césarée*, 95. "What is left of it is but the memory of the story / and this single word to name her / Césarée / The totality / Nothing but the place / And the word."

Duras' film title has a metonymical function, but why, one might ask, does she replace Bérénice's name with that of her destroyed city, which plays a very minor role in Racine's tragedy, as does the important historical fact that Titus destroyed the Second Temple? Destroy, she said. In *Césarée*'s poetic text, as in *Hiroshima mon amour*, this foreign woman is never named, so that the unsayable may emerge with the specificity of a vacant place, vacant from a signifier that would keep love within the confines of Roman law.[62]

The name of Bérénice's abandoned city initiates Duras' account and is repeated intermittently across the whole text in French and Latin. "Césarée, Césaréa" is the refrain Duras recites emphatically, with a strongly marked silence between the name's French and Greco-Latin versions. As an inevitable endpoint to anything the voice starts describing, the refrain's function is to introduce a cut, a fall into silence.[63] Exemplary of Duras' writing, her punctuation of the great tragedy *Bérenice* aims exactly at what MacCannell has discerned on the importance of emptiness with regard to creation for Lacan:

> Marking the emptiness left by the untouchability of the Thing is, for Lacan, the essence of all art, all making. Re-marking this emptiness, *noticing* that it has constantly to be renewed because it always tends to come under the sway of the signifier and lose its value as sign, is a marking-out of another foundation, a different set of directions, paths, limits, coordinates for the subject and its drives.[64]

Together with the intermittent repetitions of "Césarée," Duras' strategy of never naming Berenice in a work that would situate itself after the

62. The "forbidden" love Duras and Resnais stage in the film is there to remind its viewers that the death drive, at work both in the lovers and the world disaster, is beyond pleasure and the law, if by the latter we understand submission to the rules of an authority. See McNulty's distinction between the imaginary law and the experimental symbolic in "Enabling Constraints."

63. This operation brings to mind the phonetically close "caesura," the Latin word for "cut," also related to "fall," which in music serves as a pause, a spacing of the melody's sounds. In the French verse of the seventeenth century practiced by Racine in his tragedies, the caesura articulates the alexandrine verse's hemistiches.

64. MacCannell, *The Hysteric's Guide*, 251.

end of the tragedy (where, as Racine himself and his critics were well aware, no one dies and nothing happens,[65]) aims at making evident the creation of this gap, one that cannot be filled by any person's name. The name of the place in Racine's text evokes emptiness, when Antiochus says, confessing his love to Bérénice:

> Rome vous vit, Madame, arriver avec lui.
> Dans l'Orient désert quel devint mon ennui!
> Je demeurai longtemps errant dans Césarée,
> Lieux charmants où mon cœur vous avait adorée.[66]

This empty place is described by Duras' text as also completely destroyed, its columns by the sea fallen, so it recalls the ravages of the Roman intervention, whose highlight is the Temple's destruction that set the Jews adrift; she thus stresses this "adrift," listless condition in which separation from their beloved leaves the three characters, with Bérénice's loss of her proper name or the name her lover would have called her, replaced by a name that evokes ruins, as proof of the ravages of love and the very pain of separation.[67]

Such a production of the gap is also at stake in the title *Hiroshima mon amour*, a title that constructs a strange phrase suggesting an equation between "Hiroshima" and "my love," as if Hiroshima were the name of a speaker's love, or beloved, which, given the first affirmations in the synopsis, indicates that this first person speaking in the title would have to be the nameless Frenchwoman. But "Hiroshima" is already a metonym for the first nuclear bombing in history, so it cannot help calling up destruction and annihilation in a continuum and on equal footing with what a speaking being can call "my love." Becoming "the name of a

65. See Racine's preface to *Bérénice*. This absence of death is what the seventeenth-century critics find controversial for Classicist theater. The only catastrophe here is the separation of the play's three main characters, who must continue to love alone, when Bérénice decides to leave Rome.

66. (Act I, scene IV) Rome saw you, Madam, arrive with him. / In the deserted Orient how great my ennui grew! / For a long time I remained drifting in Caesarea, / The charming whereabouts where my heart had adored you.

67. Véronique Voruz recalls Lacan's mention of the "ravages of love" in relation to women. "Psychoanalysis at the Time of the Post-human: Insisting on the Outside-Sense." *Paragraph* 33.3 (2010): 423–443, n18. See also Voruz and Wolf, *The Later Lacan*, xv.

place," as both *Hiroshima* and *Césarée* indicate, entails the evacuation of an imaginary identity, and the exposure of a fundamental wound. Instead of the dream of a man and a woman matching each other perfectly, the place names are letters of wounds that "correspond exactly" without covering each other up.[68] The dazzling beauty of this love resides in this revelation, and in a different way of seeing that emerges at the end of the love affair, which also casts a different light on the regimes those places ordinarily name. In love's beauty, a glimpse at their unassimilable core, or horror, becomes possible. Why, one might ask, would this horror be at the core of Hiroshima, and of any other city? Because the bomb and event are privileged, unsettling manifestations of what is inherent, though denied, to the very project of civilization, namely, the death drive in its most annihilating power.

In bringing passion between a man and a woman and historical trauma together in this screenplay, Duras' text supports itself on the fact that, beyond the context it engages with in this story, the relation between the carnal and traumatic modes of intimacy is no accident, even if the dimension of trauma does not always make its way to the surface in the form of word exchanges between lovers carried to the point of exhaustion, as it does in *Hiroshima mon amour* and *Césarée*. What, after all, makes carnal intimacy possible in a human being, if not that its organism has suffered the intrusion of something impossible yet real, which takes hold of the drives and pushes them beyond the pleasure principle as the one responsible for homeostasis? This structural trauma that carves out a body in the psychoanalytic sense, and that logically precedes the being's entrance into language is evoked (and disguised) by the unconscious primal fantasy that supposes an encounter with the Other's jouissance. This trauma's impossibility, its being "a pure mental representation, a power of thought" whose distinctive mark is "the capacity to represent to oneself that which has never taken place and does not exist"[69] sets in motion another kind of sensibility in the body, at odds with that strictly related to organic functions. Since there's no original in empirical reality versus its copy in the imagination here, one

68. In this light, the shorn Frenchwoman presents a well-known image of castration.

69. Willy Apollon, "The Originary Fantasy" schema presented at GIFRIC Training Seminar, *The Clinic of the Fantasy*, 2018.

might say, in more Deleuzian terms, that a creative capacity beyond representation is in play.[70]

The Letters of the Landscape

If speaking is the effect of a fundamental trauma in a human being, the letters of the body address this sensibility—beyond the organism and always inadequate to language—to a partner. This is what is at stake in the intimacy between "elle" and "lui" in *Hiroshima mon amour*, and also between "elle" and her German lover in Nevers. In fact, the point of Duras' inclusion of a previous story of the woman's "first love" in the love affair with the Japanese man, more than a decade later, is to punctuate the specificity of the trauma in the woman's body, that is to say, that the inscription it makes, giving rise to that body's sensibility beyond instinct and pleasure, does not reside in this Japanese man or that German one, but rather in a real whose correspondence in the world is strictly impossible.[71] Furthermore, the woman in Hiroshima confronts this quite directly, which is why telling her youth's tragic love story to this man for the first time results in a state of solitary errancy in the void, reminiscent of Antiochus' errancy in *Césarée*.

Duras' screenplay for *Hiroshima* evokes this through descriptions of the night in Hiroshima, especially the image of the river that follows the woman's account of her first love. The subsequent scene begins with an image of the river in Hiroshima filling up and emptying itself out at different hours, the different possible views of this body of water, and of the river's mouth: "C'est là que finit Hiroshima et commence le Pacifique."[72] This image of emptiness, of the city without its lovers, of literal emptying out and filling up of the river, and of the shore that outlines the difference between city and sea becomes paradigmatic of

70. *Hiroshima mon amour* invokes this logic in the initial dialogues between "lui" and "elle," where they argue, while making love, about her visions of the destruction of Hiroshima, which he insists she could not have possibly seen.

71. On the problem of loving and "first love" with regard to the primal fantasy, see Sigi Jottkandt's "Signifier and Letter in Kierkegaard and Lacan" in *UMBR(a). Writing* (2010), 105 and 105 n5.

72. Duras, *Hiroshima*, 85. "It is there that Hiroshima ends and the Pacific begins."

Duras' writing.[73] Such an image evokes, in turn, Lacan's bird's-eye view on the desolate Siberian plane with the river coursing through it in his 1970 "Lituraterre," written on a flight returning to France from Japan, in fact. This unusual view allows him to consider the rain runoff (*ruissellement*) on the surface, which prompts a meditation on the constitution of the subject from the conjunction of "the first trait and what erases it."[74] Writing, at stake in this process that calls for a trait that bars the subject, allows the separation or shore (*littoral*) "in between center and absence, between *savoir* and jouissance . . . [to] turn toward the literal,"[75] that is, to somehow leave a trace. While all subjects are barred, writing as the work of the letter is defined as "that which in the real presents itself as an erosion (*ravinement*)"[76] of the body and of meaning by *jouissance*. Literature, with the work of analytic reading and the shifts it seeks in the subject also in mind, consists in an original bringing forth of this erosion. Duras' insertion of these views of the river's mouth and the shore between the city and the Pacific has to do with bringing forth the real of love, beyond all memory.

The fall of the "a-wall" separating the subject from *das Ding* creates an empty space, then. Much like Racine's Bérénice, *Hiroshima*'s "elle" loves and addresses the lack in the Other, the unrepresentable gap in the symbolic, just as he (*lui*) loves, without mastery, the letters that have shaped her body.[77] Thus if Lol is the paradigmatic woman in Duras' work, there is also something of Bérénice's destiny in Lol. In this case, the Japanese man who listens to her story would be the paradigmatic reader/lover Duras constructs, reiterated, as already discussed, by Jacques Hold, and finally by the reader, especially the specific reader/viewer in Duras' cinema.

---

73. For instance, in the India Cycle, Duras returns to this demarcation of limits between shore and water, in the novel *L'amour*, *La femme du Gange*, and in *India Song* and *Son nom de Vénise*.

74. Lacan, *AE*, 16.

75. Lacan, 16.

76. Lacan, 17.

77. I have examined Bérénice's speech about love of nothing in "Duras' *Césarée* and the Subject of Love," *CR: The New Centennial Review* 15.3 (2015): 167–199. While in Bérénice the love of the objectless Thing can be discerned in Racine already, the Japanese man's position with regard to her love is an innovation of Duras'.

Encore: To Love Is to See

Having examined the questions of the unsayable, of love as devastating separation at the encounter of the lack in the Other, correlated to the reduction to a toponym, and of a reader of the letters of the body, we can return to the proposition "to love is to see" in Duras' work with the camera. How does film function when the operation of presenting something to the senses must relate to love according to Duras? This love complicates the stakes of seeing since the object dynamics to cover up lack do not apply here. Clearly, to Duras, the camera engages in repetitions that, rather than the scene featuring lovers in a moment of pleasure, come to show the empty stage. This work is time as a force of erosion itself. It should reveal not only the erosion but the singularity of a shape and texture that are its result. I have mentioned the reduction on the screen from *India Song* to *Son nom de Vénise*, from actors to an empty chateau in ruins.[78] But in *Césarée* (1978), whose backstory we have examined alongside key phrases pronounced by Duras, a different assemblage with the camera shooting outdoors occurs, since it films, in Paris, sculptures by Aristide Maillol with names of natural phenomena such as *Montagne* (Mountain), *Rivière* (River), and *Air*, statues by Caillouette named after other French cities, the Obelisk, and the surface of the River Seine.

Césarée begins with a black screen and a violin's brief ritornello scaling up in minimal variations only to fall back to a very low grounding note. After thirty seconds, the screen abruptly opens with a traveling shot of Maillol's 1937 sculpture *Montagne* (Mountain) (figure 4.1), surrounded by the Tuileries gardens, where a few people sporadically pass by in the background. The camera sweeps along the surface of this lead mass shaped as a seated female body, reclining on one hand and bending one leg up to form a triangular figure that indeed suggests a mountain—or a wave, which is what in *Césarée* the musical structure describes with its repetitive rising and falling notes. While the camera sweeps over this sculpture, Duras' voice begins to recite her text over the music. The camera, through rhythmic rises and falls of its own continues beyond

78. It is also present within *La femme du Ganges*, which precedes them, in the large empty surfaces of beach and sea, outdoors, and of corridors and salon floors, inside the beach hotel, interrupted sporadically by one or two human figures walking silently across them.

the sculpture, along the Tuileries grass to others, and back. A similar trajectory occurs for some of the other sculptures. The viewer might recognize Paris, but it clearly does not correspond to the place verbally evoked. The hazy white light and the absence of city sounds, replaced by this hypnotic violin tune and Duras' quiet, broken phrases that, without corresponding, accompany this contemplation of blind bodies of lead instead of human ones of flesh and bone (figure 4.1), introduce a sense of withdrawal from everyday reality in Paris, all while it visibly continues in the background (the façades of the Louvre and the casual cars, passersby, pigeons fluttering about).

These effects draw attention to one's likely physical motionlessness (resembling that of the sculpture) as a viewer, except, of course, for the eyes, scanning under the constraints of the screen's time-space, the camera's movement, and the soundtrack with Duras' reciting voice over the violin. Disjunction of sound and moving image, a much-discussed strategy Duras developed since the early 1970s films, prevent the viewer from assembling the multiple stimuli so as to become immersed in the illusions of a cohesive narrative[79] and of specular dominance over what is shown. Deleuze observes this strategy in *India Song* as a "resistance drawn from the collapse of the sensorimotor schema, which separates the visual and sound image, yet places them all the more in a non-totalizable relation."[80] As the camera insistently scans these massive lead female bodies around which it turns several times, the viewer is less and less in a position of accumulating information, or of traditional spectatorship. The proposed role is closer to that of a reader before a text, a role of deciphering.[81]

However, as this chapter's previous sections have observed, deciphering in Duras' work is nothing like figuring out a hidden meaning. Deciphering as a process confronting a hole-word rather than significa-

79. Duras' dissociative strategy has mostly been discussed through the full-length features *India Song* and *Son nom de Venise à Calcutta déserte*, which share a dialogue that runs along each whole film between two voices, relating the love tragedies that took place at the French embassy in Calcutta. The first film displays human figures portraying the characters in question, but they never speak; their intervention is visual and kinesthetic. See Duras' interview on this film with Dominique Noguez. *La couleur des mots* (Paris: Benoît Jacob, 2001), 61–101.

80. Deleuze, *Cinéma 2: L'image-temps* (Paris: Les Éditions de Minuit, 1985), 334 (hereafter cited as *Cinéma 2*).

81. Julie Beaulieu also suggests this in *In the Dark Room: Marguerite Duras and Cinema*, ed. Rosanna Maule and Julie Beaulieu (Oxford: Peter Lang, 2009), 142.

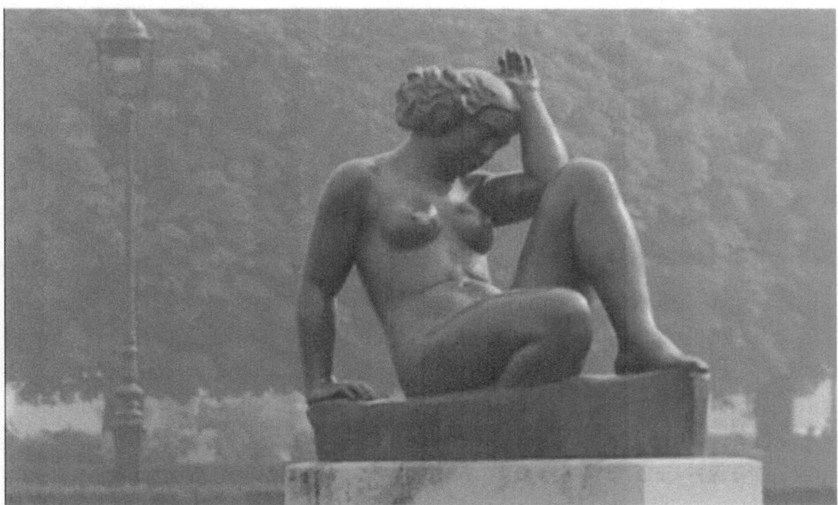

Figure 4.1. Marguerite Duras, Still from *Cesarée*, 1979 (Aristide Maillol, *Montagne*, 1937).

tion transforms the reader along the way. The images' instability on the screen matters to this deciphering process; the disappearance of images, sounds, and words is not only structural to the medium's production of meaning in what continues to appear onscreen. Duras uses this feature of the moving image to showcase repetitive scans over Maillol's multiple sculptures of female nudes and the camera's return to certain ones that have already been shown, now from a different direction and side. What becomes visible is the fact that the spatial continuity of the empty garden is interrupted by these bodies that result from a process of molding into distinct shapes, and that they are both the result and an element of insistent repetition, like Duras' own works. To love is to see, Duras writes, and to see, *Césarée* shows, is to repeat, creatively. But with Deleuze we had noticed that, as long as repetition is subordinated to identity, the creative repetition is missed. As long as there is a fixed subject, there is only the fantasy of the primal scene, covering up the hole-word.

A work against capture by fantasy fuels the film's discordances between visual and verbal images that upset the synthesis of stimuli grounding an individual's perception, enabling the nontotalizable relation Deleuze noticed. We had mentioned Duras' claim that all the women in her books "derive from Lol V. Stein." To this statement she immediately adds, "That is to say, from a certain self-oblivion."[82] This self-oblivion, exactly, becomes an experience for the viewer of *Césarée*, which suggests its unavoidability in the transmission of love as a sensation.

Consequently, one of the difficulties is to know whose point of view the camera discloses. If the speaking voice were in the first person, one would suppose a character, even without its visual appearance on the screen, but the voice is not self-referential, impersonal, and not subjected to the visual image. The sculptures of female bodies in turn stand, paradoxically, as compact absences. With the term "irrational cut," Deleuze saw the relevance of this gap between sonorous and visual images in Duras' cinema in terms of "an interstice, an irrational cut between them."[83] Its interesting effect is "the invention of a point of view that disconnects the sides or introduces a void between them, extracting a pure space, a space of sorts, space given in the objects."[84] Sculpture in *Césarée*'s visual images serves to ground this specific effect beyond the dominance of an individual viewpoint. In the new conception of the irrational cut Deleuze finds in Duras' cinema, the sound image "becomes pure speech act," which in Duras is "total love or absolute desire," while the visual image becomes "readable or stratigraphic."[85] The clinical relevance of the speech act, that is, a "saying" in the sense of the sinthome, can only be grasped with what this chapter has examined: Duras' own notion of the gap as site of nonimaginary love, and the viewer/reader's involvement in such love. Since the irrational cut upsets attempts at establishing meaning, to engage with the film the reader must seek a different mode of deciphering, taking on a creative role. Because *Césarée* thwarts the synthetic process of perception, the prompt to reinvent reading cannot seek to fill in the gaps by supplying more meaningful or signifying virtual images.[86] More radically, the viewer falls from the privileged position where s/he could follow the situation logically. This "fall," for Duras, is falling in love according to her unique take on the operation.

---

82. Duras, *La vie matérielle* (Paris: Folio, 1987), 36.

83. Deleuze, *Cinéma 2*, 327.

84. Deleuze, 328.

85. Deleuze, 337.

86. Beaulieu instead thinks Duras' intention is "to give back the spectator's capacity to fantasize, to imagine; that is to create for him or herself what is not shown on the screen, in order to read the film as if appreciating a moving poem" (152).

The knot between love and seeing, and its effects upon desire recalls courtly love, where a very specific process between lover/troubadour and desired Lady, feminine "Thing" of the troubadour's poem or homage, is essential. The network of signifiers that in courtly love—as in *Césarée*—turn upon a center impossible to represent, situate desire beyond a realm where objects lie within the subject's reach.[87] Love here requires an encounter between the lover's eyes and those of the beloved, forbidden *Domna*, without leading to love's consummation. In the mind of the troubadours, the heart of the Lady emanates *joi*, a fluid substance that is communicated when her eyes meet the man's.[88] His infatuation begins when the substance descends into his heart. Indeed, the *joi* Deleuze and Guattari invoked earlier engages man and Lady in this subtly physical way, without any carnal pleasure; it is a sensation the lover experiences but also an ethereal characteristic of the Lady, tied to her dazzling beauty. What binds them intimately, her essence, also preserves their separation: an ungraspable nothing flowing between the two.

Duras offers a modern take on this scopic transmission. The rhythmic scans of Maillols repeating the erosion that would have caused each body's unique shape alternate with another kind of sequence. In contrast with the sweeping motions scanning the bronze and lead bodies, in this second kind of sequence the camera is still, looking up from various low-angle perspectives, through jump-cuts, at scaffolds surrounding a monumental grayish sculpture of a seated woman—appropriately, as its title indicates, an allegory of a city (Bordeaux/Nantes).[89]

---

87. Lacan, like the schizoanalysts, cited earlier, noted how this writing treated language in a non-representative manner, and how this style was intrinsic to the particular functioning of desire. Instead of making a common image of the beloved woman, the troubadours, addressing an unreachable, prohibited Lady, wrote by spinning a web of signifiers such that "the absence at its heart is included" (MacCannell, *The Hysteric's Guide*, 28). For examples of this strategy in such poems, see Sarah Kay "Desire and Subjectivity" in *The Troubadours: An Introduction*.

88. René Neilli, *L'érotique des troubadours classiques* (Paris: Bibliothèque Méridionale, 1963), 164–174.

89. The shots were created by combining *Nantes* and *Bordeaux*, two of the eight sculptures by Louis-Denis Caillouette (1790–1868) that sit at each of the Place de la Concorde's corners, in restoration when Duras shot the film. The sculptures' representation of French cities corresponds with Duras' allusion to the tragic woman in Racine's play through the name of her city.

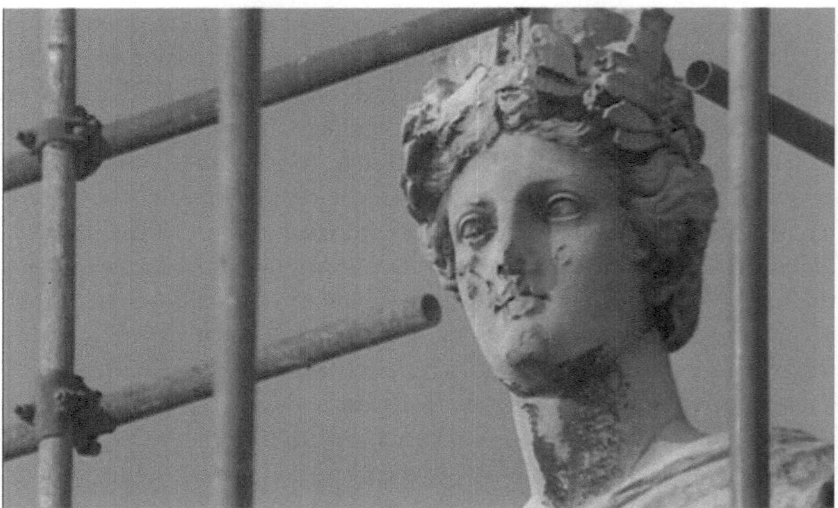

Figure 4.2. Marguerite Duras, Still from *Cesarée*, 1979. (Louis-Denis Caillouette, *Bordeaux*, 1835–38).

The scaffolding's metal pipes striate the screen, turning it into a complicated grid, tilted by the camera's angle. None of the camera's perspectives can get beyond the obstructive metal pipes (figure 4.2). Besides placing the sculpture of the woman as off-limits, this composition's striation of the sculpted body disrupts the typical reinforcement of woman as pleasurable object filmic images execute. Through the scaffolds, she becomes at once unavailable and fragmented. Her fragmentation corresponds with that of the viewer, deprived from sensorial synthesis. In thwarting the attempt to admire the woman's body, this composition stresses that love between two has nothing to do with overcoming the distance separating them. These two, like their speech, would both be in pieces, rather than whole.[90] Why, then, one might ask, alternate these images with closeups of the Maillol bodies that stand on the public garden unprotected, at anyone's reach? Anyone can touch the Maillols at the Tuileries Garden, which is not the case with the sculptures in the Louvre, nearby. The camera's caressing movement indeed suggests as

90. Roland Barthes accurately observed that *Bérénice* was Racine's "tragedy of aphasia." *Sur Racine* (Paris: Seuil, 1963), 97. True love speech would necessarily be fragmentary, like the text Duras recites in *Césarée*, and as Barthes' title *Fragments d'un discours amoureux* suggests.

much. But perhaps in putting sculpture through cinema, *Césarée* dismantles a "realist" illusion of both perception and film, where the limit to satisfaction is external, imposed by the Other. So the viewer of *Césarée* cannot reach out and touch the Maillols, but the passerby in the garden who could, still cannot take possession of the Thing, or even be in its vicinity in this way. This surges forth by the process of making visible these sculptures in downtown Paris differently, onscreen. What makes the barred Caillouettes unavailable is bare, ordinary scaffolding, after all, as opposed to a frame, which would ornament and exalt the object.

Montage, employed in the Caillouette sequences, tears the illusion of ongoing time as a smooth continuum, and conveys the drive's pulse. Within the sequences showing the statue behind four walls of scaffolding, the still shots switch between its planes through jump-cuts, in a tempo dramatically different from the one used for the Tuileries Garden sequences. Neither technique is more realistic than the other. Instead of offering an ordinary experience of duration, the cuts' subtle violence suggest an irregular state of consciousness that gives way to an uncanny, discontinuous view of what would otherwise be an unremarkable statue under the process of restoration, through which the statue can reappear as unharmed by time and exposure to the environment. The scaffolds striating the screen participate in this tearing of continuity. While restoration serves to preserve monuments from decay, to conceal time as a ravaging force from one's eye, the scaffolds on the screen expose the artifice, employed to reassure inhabitants of the city's continuous, meaningful unfolding in time up to the present, of sheltering them, and also, since these sculptures represent other French cities, of uniting Paris to other symbolic spaces of France.

The Maillol sculptures in *Césarée*—viewed according to the tempo of the camera's scanning motion and the violin's rising and falling scales—give a sense of floating adrift because the destination of the camera's own course is inscrutable or non-existent. One sees the sculptures in the garden as from a ship adrift, then, perhaps in the perspective of Bérénice (in self-oblivion) after her ship sails away from Rome on the Mediterranean.[91] Indeed, with Maillol's lustrous, rounded, winding bodies the film composes

91. It is no accident that the shots Duras used to make this short film were left over from another film on love called *Le Navire Night* (*The Ship* Night). This is also the case with the shots in *Les mains negatives*, released simultaneously. *Césarée* features day scenes, whereas in *Les mains* the scenes were shot before dawn. See Duras, *La couleur des mots*, 169–170.

liquid shots of Paris, which contribute to destabilizing perception and unmooring love from meaning and action. Deleuze also considered this feature in Duras' filmic trajectory: "a liquid quality which increasingly marks the visual image."[92] Moving back and forth between Maillols and Caillouettes, *Césarée* arrives at a scene from the actual viewpoint of the river Seine flowing from right to left. Instead of looking up at the city from this angle (as would tourists on a bateau-mouche) the gaze rests on the water surface reflecting Right Bank façades. Through the traveling shot, the place passing before one's eyes conveys impermanence; the cityscape reflected on a liquid, wavering surface exacerbates the sensation of evanescence.[93] This example of cinema's visual singularity as a writing medium expresses the logic that led Duras from novels to cinema in a moment when her writing reached a limit with words, while a space for desire to emerge remained necessary. Liquid "floods" the permanence of a monumental city such as Paris. It dissolves the signifier, transmitting the time of separation.

In *Césarée*, the camera also intently scans the surface of "Cleopatra's Needle,"[94] the obelisk at the Place de la Concorde whose hieroglyphs' meaning is unavailable to most. In an exceptional coinciding moment of image and voice, the latter speaks of reading an ancient past through its cryptic remainders: "on lit encore la pensée des gens de Césarée" (one still reads the thought of the people of Caesarea). On the obelisk's surface one still reads the thought of the still more ancient people of

92. Deleuze, *Cinéma 2*, 337. Deleuze recognizes a shift in Duras' cinema work, from the house, as privileged space to stage the idea that "passions 'inhabit' women," to the beach-sea, for "a story that no longer has a place (sound image) for places that no longer have a history [*histoire*] (visual image)" (336; 335 n60).

93. The shot closely evokes Du Bellay's *Antiquités de Rome* III: "Le Tibre seul, qui vers la mer s'enfuit, / Reste de Rome. Ô mondaine inconstance! / Ce qui est ferme est par le temps détruit, / Et ce qui fuit au temps fait résistance." *Les regrets*, ed. Samuel S. de Sacy (Paris: Gallimard, 1975).

94. Through its name, the Paris obelisk alludes to the love tragedy between Cleopatra and Mark Antony, Titus's predecessor. It repeats the themes of the foreign woman as a threat to the Roman power structure and the maritime voyage/exile. The story of "Cleopatra's Needle" in Paris itself parallels the tragic separation of lovers: in 1829 the government of Egypt had offered two twin obelisks from the Luxor Temple in Egypt, and the first was sent in a ship that arrived via the Seine. Its twin was left behind in Egypt, and officially returned by Mitterrand in the 1980s.

Egypt in the thirteenth century BCE. Except one cannot hope to translate their thoughts carved onto the surface. The traveling shot preserves the illegible drawings of an ancient writing. If the film transmits the memory Bérénice hoped to preserve at the end of Racine's tragedy, then its act is itself beyond signification.

This moment stresses the illegibility of the traces in this and every signifier in the film. And yet these traces, scanned, retraced, and spoken time and again like the violin's refrain, insist upon a certain feminine "joi" in the useless repetitions. A memory procedure unable to seize the traces' meaning suggests an important gap between the mind contemporary to the act of tracing and that trying to remember. In other words, it is not the same "I" in each of the two moments, so the production of this difference implies a destruction or radical disappearance of the past "I" to whom the traces were legible. It is in this sense that repetition, for instance of the mantra "Césarée," can be radically creative. A space of genuine creation is possible with a reader/viewer who can hear, beyond the imaginary "I," the "hole-word" reverberate. To love is to see *and* hear the unknown.

CHAPTER 5

Developing *Douleur exquise*

Sophie Calle et al.

The previous chapter's meditation on relation beyond self and social identities introduced the idea that reading the letters of the body takes time, just as it takes time to verify the effects of this work of reading. This chapter continues to investigate the emergence, in aesthetic experience, of this *other* mode of relation, and it also probes into the conjunction of untimeliness and pain—an unequivocal sign of the letter as intractable element that commands a repetition in its singularity. How does pain enter into the aesthetic clinic? Aside from the work of reading as an act of love that Duras' cinema requests, in what other ways can an artwork stir an act of love that speaks to the intractable in others? Sophie Calle's answer takes us to a scenario we have visited before, in Louise Bourgeois' *Precious Liquids*. It is the "bedside-art" scenario, in red, this time, where a space to welcome the unconscious opens up in aesthetic experience.

It took almost nineteen years for Calle's *Douleur exquise* to *develop*, like an extremely resistant strip of photographic film. The piece's slow gestation and the slow reading process it demands from the viewer stand out together. By 2003, when the work was finally completed, the end of the world had occurred in more than one way: the USSR had fallen in 1991 (some consider the twentieth century to end with this dissolution of sociopolitical worlds, after all), and analogue photography had begun its decline as digital technology replaced it. Both ends inform *Douleur exquise*, which consists of a photo-textual-installation narrative in three stages. First is "Avant la douleur," a travel narrative beginning in 1984 with an Eastward-bound train departure from Paris' Gare du Nord that takes its protagonist, Sophie, through communist Russia and China, before her arrival to Tokyo for a three-month stay under an art grant, followed by a brief stop, before returning home, in New Delhi, which serves as the travel narrative's endpoint and plays host to another, private kind of end of the world for the protagonist. This dead end constitutes the second part and center of the tale, "Le lieu de la douleur," the vacant scene of a moment of pain that gives the entire piece its title, reconstructed in both an installation and a photograph. Part three, "Après la douleur" returns to a practice of daily phototextual inscriptions, for ninety-nine days of dealing with the rupture, adding to the photograph of pain the technique of sewing the letters onto a linen canvas to tell its story, and also the strategy of pairing this story with those of ninety-nine other people.

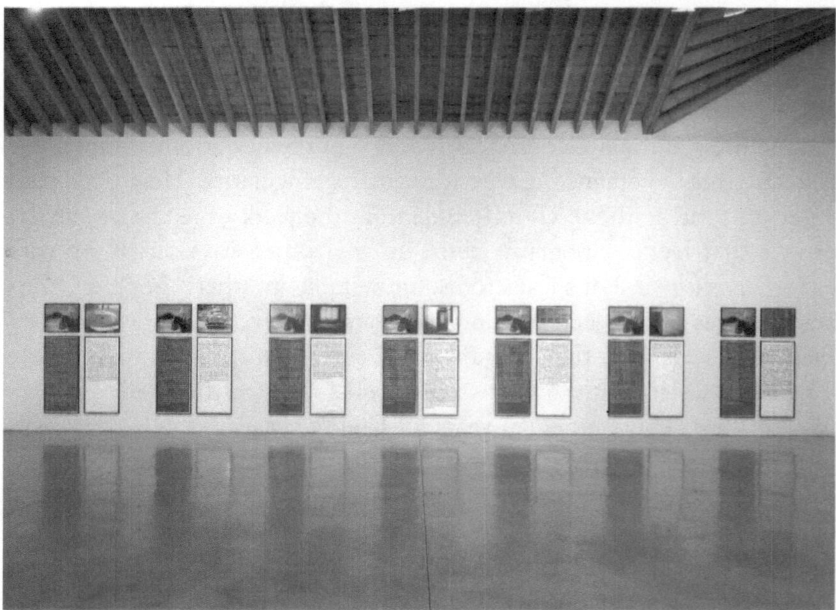

Figure 5.1. Sophie Calle, *Exquisite Pain*, 1984–2003. Installation view of "After the Pain." 36 quadriptychs each containing two elements of 120 × 60 cm, two elements of 48 × 60 cm. © 2019 Artists Rights Society (ARS), New York/ ADAGP, Paris.

The much longer story of "revealing" the work (and this verb in French, *révéler*, is used in the context of photography to indicate the appearance of a latent image on a plate, film or paper, in other words in the way English uses "to develop") interacts with its plot, which reflects on the time it takes for the components of a given actuality (in perception and consciousness) to fade, as others replace them in what we call "the present," and the number of takes (of time) jouissance, like a virtual grueling film director of sorts, requires of a subject of the drive before bringing the strange logic of its writing to the light. And this process of revealing/developing is also the logical step after hearing and collecting the stories of others' unique pain. Can a sensation be transmitted in telling someone else's *exquisite pain*? This is the experiment.[1]

Douleur Exquise was first displayed in its final form at a major retrospective exhibit of Calle's work called *M'as tu vue?* (*Have you seen me?*) in November 2003 at the Centre Georges Pompidou in Paris. This was also my first encounter with it and Calle's work. A book version was also published then by the press Actes Sud. Calle's approach to love, which repeatedly showcases the banality of most romantic relations where she is the protagonist,[2] may initially seem pessimistic about love's potential to be anything else than the reproduction of the stale and failed modes of relation (especially after the tragic beauty of Duras' writing on love, in the previous chapter). But another dimension can be glimpsed, between Calle's words and images. Joan Copjec's analysis of Cindy Sherman's *Untitled (Film Stills)* photographs compellingly observes that narcissism involves, much more than self-obsession, the impossibility of directly apprehending the "I," and this is in play in Sherman's "self-portraits," where she poses as different female characters in cinematic situations. She also suggests that the *Untitled Film Stills* may be, above all, about a

1. The analytic process of the pass Lacan introduced at the end of analysis, to determine, in the context of a school of psychoanalysis, whether an analysand has shifted to the position of analyst, involves someone outside the analysand-analyst relation. Two analysands nearing the end of their own analysis takes the role of *passeur* by independently listening to the *passant* and later bringing the unconscious object to a group of analysts of the school, who then conclude whether an object has been transmitted, in which case the pass has taken place. The telling of someone else's exquisite pain in Calle's work seems to me relatable to the *passeur*'s role.

2. See, for instance, the 1992 film *No Sex Last Night* and the more recent *Prenez soin de vous* "Take Care of Yourself" (2007).

love for cinema, as a nonidentical object.[3] The presence in Calle's work of blurry boundaries between author, narrator, and protagonist, alongside the emphasis on the dissolution of an era and the passage of time made felt to the reader in the large and detailed *Douleur Exquise* may instead be about a love of literature. For, they strongly recall Marcel Proust's *A la recherche du temps perdu*.[4] Proust's novel and *Douleur Exquise* share more, even, than the complicated relationship between the time of living and the time of writing what has been lived.

Importantly, both insist on the work's own opaque speech and uncanny power to destabilize reality. Proust examines and fights the anesthetic effect of "Habit," carefully noting its disruption by uncanny aesthetic powers. Calle seems concerned with enabling this uncanny amidst the everyday, so as to inhabit it and allow others to do so too. (After all, Freud, reading Schelling, discerns the uncanny as a distinct power of the aesthetic.) This motor of Calle's research projects brings her very close to the kind of experience Proust's narrator is most concerned with encountering and articulating as well, as the famous *madeleine* scene and others even more so prove.

In this light, the distinction between modern and postmodern commonly applied to Proust and Calle appears insufficient to seize the function of the aesthetic, in its connection with the problematic of the fundamentally untimely desiring subject, which links *Douleur exquise* and the *Recherche* to Freud's own early twentieth-century investigation too. Pawel Leszkowicz has suggested that "at the beginning of [the] modernity" that "discovered, affirmed, and ultimately extinguished the unconscious,"

> there are Sigmund Freud and Marcel Proust—at its end there is Louise Bourgeois. At the beginning there are men, at the end there is a woman. They all worked in the realm of secrets and traps of inner life. That inner life was the foundation of

3. See Copjec, "Narcissism Approached Obliquely," *Imagine There's No Woman: Ethics and Sublimation* (Cambridge, MA: MIT Press, 2002).

4. Sophie Calle herself has explicitly, though briefly, referred to Proust in projects such as the 1980 *Suite vénitienne* and *Pas pu saisir la mort* in 2007. The latter, exhibited in the Venice Biennale that year, was a video shooting of her mother in her deathbed, which allowed Calle to fulfill her mother's wish to be present in the Biennale. Another late wish of her mother's she fulfilled was visiting Proust's "Balbec" together.

> subjectivity—one they all tried to reach through psychoanalysis, the language of literature, or a visual form.[5]

Indeed, Bourgeois (as seen in chapters 1 and 2) is a consistent artist of the unconscious, and there is something specific to modern subjectivity, which Freud and Proust brought to different writing forms and reading practices. Yet, as Calle's work suggests, the unconscious cannot be simply extinguished by a culture, and at the turn of the twenty-first century there is not only "a woman," but several women consistently engaged with approaching that unconscious, with consequences for culture and theories of subjectivity.[6] The fact that both artists have exhibited their work at the Freud Museum in London in the 2000s speaks to this.

Signaling what does not work, the perspective of the symptom enables an approach to what remains when, for instance, a social order replaces another that has either been wiped out or left behind. Such a remainder calls to be read, and thus invokes a reader who may come to decipher it in spite of a missing world or a people to make it intelligible.[7] In fact, without this work of deciphering, the symptom only features, to quote Proust, "lost time," that is, gone and wasted at once. Deciphering, a mode of reading that allows the encryption to lead the process, is a labor integral to the artwork's being, and it is what creates the perspective of "time regained." Thus *Douleur exquise* incorporates this need for a reader and even presents the stakes of such a role, especially in its third and final part. In *Douleur exquise* photography–text juxtapositions and installation are the forms where the symptom materializes in this condition of ciphered remainder, so in my argument I will consider the installation version of the work, while also reading the texts closely.[8]

At the installation's entrance and the book's first page, the title, *Douleur exquise*, includes a footnote that clarifies this is a medical term of modern use, whose definition is: "Douleur vive et nettement localisée"—"acutely

5. "In search of Lost Space. A la recherche de l'espace perdu" in *Louise Bourgeois. Geometry of Desire* (Warsaw: National Gallery of Art Zachęta, 2003), 249.

6. Griselda Pollock considers Leszkowicz' affirmation too, and adds a list of twentieth-century women writers and painters (*After-affects*, 88–89).

7. Deleuze and Guattari suggest this in *ATP*, 337.

8. Citations are from *Douleur exquise* (Arles: Actes Sud, 2003); *Exquisite Pain* (New York: Hudson & Thames, 2005). Pagination is the same in both versions. Hereafter cited as *Douleur*.

felt, pin-point suffering," reads the English translation. Without revealing what kind of pain or suffering is at stake, this initial gesture with regard to the title draws attention to the lexical field its words pull us into, and it gives the artwork or text about to be read the status of a very specific symptom. Why, how should, of all things, an artwork appear as or address a symptom? One notices that the definition of *douleur exquise*, complete with its ungraspable side (the *douleur* is "vive" and "nettement localisée," but where, and what, does it indicate?) strongly resonates with a jouissance at stake in the symptom for clinical psychoanalysis. After all, the adjective "exquis" is also about the most delicate enjoyment.

Willy Apollon defines the symptom in the psychoanalytic clinic as a two-dimensional "writing of a jouissance." First, the signifying dimension of the symptom, insofar as it is a writing, acts by "inscribing the signifier in order to close in on its failing," which at once "fuels the patient's complaint and [what] unconsciously dictates the patient's demand to the analyst upon deciding to undergo treatment."[9] In other words, a symptom in the patient's body that refuses to be resolved by medical explanation/treatment drives her to seek an analyst who might make sense of it, just as this bodily inscription indicates that the signifier has failed to process this jouissance and represent it. The symptom implies, then, not only a solution but also a call for a new mode of relation that may address this writing, as explored in the previous chapter. Also at stake is another jouissance, detached from the signifier and the phallus, in the symptom's other, "real dimension": "a jouissance which escapes the action of the letter of the symptom, returns with insistence, and thereby determines the repetition of the symptom." The analyst's task here is a "maneuvering [that] can disengage the fantasy" from this real dimension that only appears as a-signifying repetition, since "the scenario of the fantasy reveals the subject's relation to a singular jouissance."[10] This jouissance appears as a stubborn, senseless repetition and by extracting the fantasy it becomes possible to examine the singularity of this jouissance for its subject. The fantasy, then, gives insight to what has positioned and shaped the subject in a relation to the Other; because the analyst does not merely repeat this role, it is possible for them to "disengage the fantasy" that occludes the real.

Douleur exquise, we will see, suggests that the necessity of the work of art emerges with an impetus to articulate a real that, however inti-

9. Apollon, *After Lacan*, 122.

10. Apollon, 122.

mately tied to one's life, is missing from ordinary modes of language and of interacting in the world, and from any given reality or vocabulary, simply. In the terms of the *Recherche*:

> La grandeur de l'art véritable, au contraire de celui que M. de Norpois eût appelé un jeu de dilettante, c'était de retrouver, de ressaisir, de nous faire connaître cette réalité loin de laquelle nous vivons, de laquelle nous nous écartons de plus en plus au fur et à mesure que prend plus d'épaisseur et d'imperméabilité la connaissance conventionnelle que nous lui substituons, cette réalité que nous risquerions fort de mourir sans avoir connue, et qui est tout simplement notre vie.[11]

True art is not what someone can call a dilettante's pastime, writes Proust, making one wonder about the implications of the word "dilettante," since he opposes it to the true, and to the possibility of accessing a research object ("a reality") that is not readily available.[12] "Dilettante" is used with negative connotations, to signal a lack of commitment to knowledge and research, which this passage stresses in its choice of verbs ("retrouver," "ressaisir," "faire connaître") and in the very opposition of this true art to a "conventional knowledge;" in its etymology, nonetheless, "dilettante" also contains a key to the mark of true art. From "*delectare*," to delight, what drives both the dilettante and the true researcher is, one might say, a unique quest for delight (or a unique relation to jouissance). However, only the researcher is willing to step outside the dense layer of conventions for this delight, to take it seriously, in other words, through an experimental kind of knowledge.

Calle seeks this uncommon reality by approaching the work of art as a clinical site, where a symptom such as "douleur exquise" may be

11. *Le Temps retrouvé* (Paris: Gallimard, 1990), 289–290. "The greatness of true art, unlike the one M. de Norpois would have called a dilettante's pastime, was to rediscover (retrouver), to reapprehend, to make ourselves fully aware of that reality, remote from our daily preoccupations, from which we separate ourselves by an even greater gulf, as the conventional knowledge which we substitute for it grows thicker and more impermeable, that reality which it is very easy for us to die without ever having known and which is, quite simply, our life" (Marcel Proust, *Time Regained*, trans. C.K. Scott [London: Vintage, 2000], 298). Translation modified.

12. Deleuze rightly argues that the title *Á la recherche du temps perdu* should be taken literally, in the rigorous sense of research, a research for truth that must exceed common knowledge. *Proust et les signes* (Paris: PUF, 2003), 23.

the point of departure. What does the clinical entail in *Douleur exquise*? The work of accessing experimental knowledge of a real at the cost of renouncing familiarity is an important part of it. Furthermore, to be such a site, the work involves the effort to enable modes of relation and of being in the world different from those available through conventional knowledge. The clinic is therefore not an apparatus for the individual, but rather an experiment of two, at a minimum, and this attempt at exploring the subject beyond both the individual and the group (which also strives for unity) already begins the difficult task of forging a path of uncommon reality. The artwork's clinical space offers to those involved with it, here the artist and participants, a way of approaching that mostly unexplored reality of what is paradoxically called by Proust's narrator "one's own" life. This clinical endeavor thus precedes any readily formulated theory, aiming at a knowledge both experimental and experiential, two conditions the French word *expérience* captures at once.[13]

"Bedside art" translates the Greek etymology of "clinic" (*kliniké techné*). Through both a long series of photographs and an installation, *Douleur exquise* places its viewing participants exactly at a bedside that is the locus of the exquisite pain that gives the artwork its title. The distinction between a detached, "critical" viewer and, instead, a participant who is vital to the transformative *expérience* a work can offer has been discussed in the vision of the artwork Lygia Clark set forth, by eliminating any bystanders and reducing the visual support of the work in favor of a plasticity encountered spatially and through other senses. Participation was also examined in Louise Bourgeois' use of sculpture and installation art forms that implicate their viewer in the logic of hysteria. Similarly, the viewers and participants of Calle's photographs and installation are invited to witness the uncanny scenario presented by these art forms as their subject, somehow; thus, their position is not that of the doctor located at the bedside to observe the patient closely without getting caught up in

13. I have mentioned this in Deleuze's *Difference and Repetition* in chapter 2, in the section "Challenges of Extimate Knowledge." Johnnie Gratton elegantly formulates Calle's open-ended experimental tactics as a way "to see what happens" "Experiment and Experience in the Phototextual Projects of Sophie Calle," *Women's Writing in Contemporary France: New Writers, New Literatures in the 1990s*, ed. G. Rye and M. Worton (Manchester & New York: Manchester University Press, 2002), 158. My analysis differs from Gratton's, however, insofar as it finds the core of the experiment in an aesthetic clinic confronting the cause of desire, as a process that may enable new modes of relation, rather than in producing "techniques of the self in new ways," as he states in quoting Celia Lury (158).

her trouble. Yet the participants' experience cannot be understood as a matter of plain emotional identification with the narrative's protagonist. This mechanism, within the realm of what Proust called "conventional knowledge," is disrupted from the outset, since what is read and observed of the work does not correspond to the reader's personal story. And this is also true of Proust's novel, where the time of reading fosters an experience of intimacy with the narrator and of familiarity with his different "worlds," which are nonetheless separate from one's life. The aesthetic register Calle's and Proust's experiments awaken exceeds the domain of identity and the personal. In Duras we saw that reading had to do with welcoming love in its tie to the scopic drive, a love closer to the analyst's position of desire of the unconscious that removes it from a will to mastery, than to the love of the other that sustains one's sense of self. Specifically, what facilitates access to the aesthetic in Calle is a series of oblique eruptions of the uncanny amidst the ordinary, and a gesture of hospitality toward that uncanny dimension in others.

Uncanny Narcissism

How exactly is pain dealt with in this clinic or bedside art? To answer this, one must consider that beds are in fact crucial, erotically charged devices across Sophie Calle's works, just as they are in Proust's *Recherche*; in fact, Calle's attention to beds as privileged sites for her experiments resembles that of Proust, whose novel begins, indeed, by bringing the reader to the narrator's bedside.[14] The issues and situations that the bed prompts in Calle's projects often recall several detailed accounts that demonstrate the same signifier's complexity in the *Recherche*. For instance, as early as 1979, her project *Les dormeurs* consisted in lending her own bed to friends, neighbors, and, perhaps most interestingly, strangers who took turns sleeping in it for eight-hour periods to cover a week, while Calle, decidedly in a clinician's role, observed them, taking notes and photographing them. From experiments such as this one, what Calle presents to viewers are these documents, introduced by personal accounts of the situations she became involved in, usually exhibited on walls as framed printed texts juxtaposed with the photographs.

14. Thus *Recherche*, whose first sentence is "Longtemps, je me suis couché de bonne heure" (For a long time, I would go to bed early), undertakes in itself a literal investigation of clinical aesthetics.

Les dormeurs places Calle the photographer/researcher/clinician literally at the bedside; the viewers of the artwork are therefore offered that perspective too, through photography. The viewers seem therefore to be kept out of the experiment, since to participate in it means to sleep rather than look. But perhaps looking is another mode of participating, and of getting close to the liminal situation the experiment's bedside perspective highlights, for even if the sleepers themselves can look at the resulting photographs, they must wake to do so; the experiment in this way stresses a necessary division between sleeping and waking up to look and see. The double mode of presentation to which Calle resorts for these projects parallels this irreducible split, since the book format, on the one hand, implies the texts and images' horizontality as they are held in the reader's hands, whereas the installations presuppose a different physical relation to the texts and images propped on the walls. In both formats, moreover, the reader's perspective is never all-seeing, and the very juxtaposition of text and image sustains an intermittence between reading and looking.

We are reminded by this question of spectatorship versus participation that, in chapter 3, Clark's propositions sought to abolish any space or time that transcends the moment of the artwork's execution with the participant, in order to inhabit a pure present. Calle, however, doesn't simply grant one of the parties involved with the artwork a privileged view over another, subjected party. Rather, her bedside art strives to explore the space between perception and consciousness, that is to say, the unconscious according to Lacan. Leo Bersani has argued for this very approach to the unconscious as: "the start of a reconstruction of subjectivity . . . on which all effective political reconstructions ultimately depend."[15] This reconstruction of subjectivity and relationality grounded on an interstitial unconscious brings into focus exactly what the artwork in *Douleur exquise* seeks—between perception and consciousness, photography and its referent, image and text.

15. Bersani, *Is The Rectum a Grave?* (Chicago: University of Chicago Press, 2009), 138. Bersani's main concern is thinking "new relational modes," a problem that leads him to a critical reading of psychoanalysis in dialogue with Foucault. Bersani considers the affirmation of identities, a "gay subjectivity," for instance, insufficient, and, in turn, the conception of desire as lack, inaccurate, as it preserves antagonism between subject and world. My interest in the feminine in aesthetics explores a way of overcoming this antagonism with psychoanalysis.

So, while in *Les dormeurs* the sleeper agrees to surrender under the photographer's gaze and the researcher's interrogation,[16] this does not guarantee a dominant position to the viewers or even to Sophie, who lends her bed to strangers. Rather, intimacy between strangers is the main force guiding the experiment. The premise of the early *Dormeurs* piece indicates more than Calle's sense of humor and irrepressible taste for prying. In *La prisonnière*, where Proust's narrator describes his observations of Albertine while she sleeps, precisely, he insists that his pleasure in observing his lover in this state of unawareness is tied to the feeling of possessing her:

> En fermant les yeux, en perdant la conscience, Albertine avait dépouillé, l'un après l'autre, ses différents caractères d'humanité qui m'avaient déçu depuis le jour où j'avais fait sa connaissance. Elle n'était plus animée que de la vie inconsciente des végétaux, des arbres, vie plus différente de la mienne, plus étrange, et qui cependant m'appartenait davantage. Son moi ne s'échappait pas à tous moments, comme quand nous causions, par les issues de la pensée inavouée et du regard. Elle avait rappelé à soi tout ce qui d'elle était au dehors; elle s'était réfugiée, enclose, résumée, dans son corps. En le tenant sous mon regard, dans mes mains, j'avais cette impression de la posséder tout entière que je n'avais pas quand elle était réveillée.[17]

16. There is a long visual tradition of this dynamic not only in medicine, as noted in chapter 1, but also in the history of French painting, of course, specifically concerning the theme of "the sleeper." Consider, for instance, Ingres, Poussin, Courbet, or Eva Gonzalès. The latter in *Le réveil* (1877–78) interestingly directs the female figure's gaze outside the right frame of the canvas, while the body and hands press against the pillow, as though attached to something invisible, the dream from which she has just awoken. The canvas indeed opens up through the painted body's opposing attachments that space "between perception and consciousness."

17. Proust, *A la recherche du temps perdu* 3 (Paris: Pléiade, 1954), 578. "By shutting her eyes, by losing consciousness, Albertine had stripped off, one after another, the different human personalities with which she had deceived me ever since the day I had first made her acquaintance. She was animated now only by the unconscious life of plants, of trees, a life more different from my own, more alien, and yet one that belonged more to me. Her personality was not constantly escaping, as when we talked, by the outlets of her unacknowledged thoughts and eyes. She had called back into herself everything that lay outside, had withdrawn, enclosed, reabsorbed

Calle's experiment, a genuine *recherche*, surely involves the thrill of strangers surrendering and exposing themselves in the most vulnerable way possible, as "vie inconsciente" before her eyes. Yet it invites us to read Marcel's account against the grain. If, in the passage, Proust's narrator insists on the pleasurable "impression de la posséder tout entière" when Albertine does not "escape" through "her unspoken thoughts and looking eyes," he cannot avoid conveying the sense that having "dépouillé, l'un après l'autre, ses différents caratères d'humanité," she remains, and is perhaps more than ever, a stranger. The alterity of this body's life surfaces, "vie plus différente de la mienne, plus étrange," and perhaps this is what maintains the observer's curiosity—and anxiety. Freud's 1914 "On Narcissism" remarked upon such a withdrawal from the world, in the sick man and the sleeper: "The condition of sleep, too, resembles illness in implying a narcissistic withdrawal of the position of the libido onto the subject's own self, or, more precisely, on to the single wish to sleep."[18] Freud is examining ego-attachment and object-attachment here, two different positions for the subject that tell us something about love and its power of exposing us to "loss of reality," or the experience of "the end of the world" when it is experienced as unrequited. While sleep implies libidinal withdrawal, it complicates the common idea that narcissism is simply egoism or self-absorption, since the sleeper is in many ways inaccessible to herself in this act too.[19] In his essay, Freud finds the best examples of narcissism in a certain kind of woman.[20] In the previously cited passage by Proust, Albertine exemplifies not only the withdrawal inherent to sleep, but, to Marcel's mind, the inaccessible narcissistic woman. Freud writes:

herself into her body. In keeping her in front of my eyes, in my hands, I had an impression of possessing her entirely which I never had when she was awake." *The Captive*, trans. C.K. Scott (London: Vintage, 2001), 84–85.

18. Freud, *SE* XIV: 83.

19. Recall Proust's accounts of the dissolved self during sleep. In *Combray*, already, the experience of sleep involves losing human form and also a sense of orientation in time.

20. "The importance of this type of woman for the erotic life of mankind is to be rated very high," Freud writes (89). His phrase recalls the Domna or Lady in courtly love. From Petrarch to Proust and beyond, this inaccessible Lady insistently returns across the ages in Western literature (a site to consider closely to understand the erotic life of humankind). The question of desire, love, and approach of the nonrepresentable das Ding from a feminine subject position is complicated by her elusiveness and detachment from an object of love.

> It is indeed as if we envied [narcissists] for maintaining a blissful state of mind—an unassailable libidinal position which we ourselves have since abandoned. The great charm of narcissistic women has, however, its reverse side; a large part of the lover's dissatisfaction, of his doubts of the woman's love, of his complaints of her enigmatic nature, has its root in this incongruity between the types of object-choice.[21]

The position of the lover captivated by the narcissistic type presupposes that he has given up his own "blissful state of mind" or primary narcissism, of which she reminds him (and in this "reverse side," of its loss).[22] We know Marcel's jealousy triggered his urge to possess and imprison his lover, along with its tragic consequences. Regarding this simultaneous vulnerability and alterity that the observed sleeper discloses, where does Sophie stand, and where does *Douleur exquise* ask us, its viewers and readers, to stand (or sit, or lie) regarding the other?

Les dormeurs already features some of the overarching elements in Calle's artistic research projects. First, there is acting on her intense curiosity for the other, who is importantly set forth as a stranger or personification of the unknown (Calle notes down how the sleeper came into the project, what his or her habits are, and how they interact with the other sleepers when they meet during a change of shift). Second, this decision to act on her curiosity implies the disruption of conventional boundaries between public and private life, muddling also art and everyday life (using her own and others' life for this). Third, and most importantly, is revealing or outlining, often through the media of photography and writing, the impasse that this curiosity for the other must face. In contrast, then, to Marcel's dream of possessing Albertine while watching her sleep, Calle's documents indicate no interest in serving as proof of a supposed conquest; rather, as sensual as the idea of inviting a procession of individuals into one's bed may initially seem, the photographs and texts set forth the other's irreducible otherness,

21. Freud, 89.

22. For a compelling commentary of this passage, see Aaron Schuster, *The Trouble with Pleasure. Deleuze and Psychoanalysis* (Cambridge, MA: MIT Press, 2016). One of his examples of the narcissim of the drive comes from a Klossowski's scene of the Louvre at night, when the artworks "enjoy themselves" without the spectators (129).

without concealing or mitigating the anxiety this entails. We are faced, then, with a different desire than the one shaping a subject who relates to itself and to the world in imaginary terms of appropriation.[23]

In the situation *Douleur exquise* describes, where Sophie ends up abandoned by her lover M (after she deliberately left Paris to undertake her research project abroad), this distinction between imaginary and what one might call nonimaginary desire, means that the *crucial aim* of the work that stages and narrates this event is *not* to heal the narcissistic wound this rejection inflicts upon its protagonist, Sophie, just as it does not reassure its viewers of themselves.[24] *Douleur exquise*'s personal narrative does introduce an imaginary dimension, but the work's crucial aim, where my focus is directed, lies elsewhere. This elsewhere is indeed the site of the strange, unfathomable *Thing* without a signifier, or a void. Consonant with Calle's interest in strangers, or even revealing the stakes of such an interest, this Thing, Lacan states, is "a stranger to me although it is at the heart of this 'me.'"[25] Thus, instead of mirroring or endorsing the viewer's self-mastery, for instance in his or her capacity as a distant art critic, or as some kind of heroic participant in *Douleur exquise*'s plot, who would step into the installation to eradicate pain and reestablish well-being, instead of a pleasing self-reflection, then, what the vacant bedroom and its related photographs expose the viewer to is an intractable[26] image of this foreign Thing. This image, which stubbornly returns, does not represent something else and refuses to be reduced by words to meaning. Beds in Calle's art, then, are the special sites of

---

23. Bersani remarks that the mode of relation that the civilization in which psychoanalysis was born has privileged "assumes a secure and fundamentally antagonistic distinction between subject and object." *Is the Rectum a Grave?*, 106.

24. The work's interest in relationality is not compatible with the approach Nicolas Bourriaud set forth in his *Relational Aesthetics*, mentioned in chapter 3.

25. Lacan, *Éthique*, 71.

26. "Intraitable" is an important word for Roland Barthes. He uses it in his book on photography, which we will consider shortly, and beyond (for instance in *Fragments d'un discours amoureux*). By "intractable," he points to something constitutive in the subject that refuses to be translated, interpreted, or removed. In psychoanalysis, Apollon discusses Freud's "negative therapeutic reaction" in terms of "l'intraitable" precisely, translated as "the untreatable" (which highlights the clinical context where Barthes' word emerges). See my Introduction.

operations that enable an encounter of the order of the symptom, with the other's opacity and with the various sensations that this unsettling encounter stirs up.

Furthermore, what the work's own symptom enables is a trans-subjective encounter, as the third part of *Douleur exquise* emphasizes. If this encounter matters it is because, through it, the work of art foregrounds and upholds a new possibility for desire to flow across bodies. And this is the clinical labor of the artwork beyond pleasure, for instance in the unique site of an exquisite pain.[27] Confronting this irreducible opacity can be a liberating experience, where a connection occurs, between the other's alterity and what is alien in one's self, as an aesthetic transmission of "strange Things" within the artwork's constraints. So let us enter into this framework and explore its effects.

Chronology Disrupted

In exhibiting *Douleur exquise*, Calle carefully organized two long photo-textual narratives, "Avant la douleur" ("Before the Pain") and "Après la douleur" ("After the Pain"), around the installation "Le lieu de la douleur" ("The Site of Pain"). The latter recreates a hotel bedroom in New Delhi that Sophie entered on January 24, 1985, expecting to reunite with her lover after her three-month trip to Japan, charted in "Avant la douleur," to benefit from an art grant. In its simplest sense, the vacant bedroom with two twin beds and a red analogue telephone sitting on one of them is "The site of Douleur" because it stages the drama of her lover's failure to show up for the reunion. This is due to an accident in Paris, according to a written message she receives at the airport, which turns out to be a ludicrous excuse. The truth, as the third part of the work begins to tell the reader, is that the lover—designated

27. Lacan's words on the distinction between the (Platonic) true and the real with regard to pleasure and pain are worth recalling here. Unlike the true, "Le réel, ça ne fait pas plaisir [. . .] il est clair que la jouissance du réel comporte le masochisme, ce dont Freud s'est aperçu. Le masochisme est le majeur de la jouissance que donne le réel." (*Le Seminaire XXIII*, 78). "The real does not give pleasure [. . .] it's clear that the jouissance of the real involves masochism, which Freud noticed. Masochism is the major term of the jouissance given by the real."

as "M"—stopped by the hospital to treat a perhaps painful but in any case trivial blister on his finger, and his real motivation for missing the flight to Delhi, as she learns in a short conversation with him over the telephone, is to end the relationship, since he has found a new partner. This, then, is the situation from which *Douleur exquise* originates, unfolding in a process that eighteen years later emerges as a work of art. M's care for an insignificant physical pain foretells Sophie's exquisite pain, which she will also have to take care of.[28] Such pain, and the time it takes to reemerge as an artwork in a different era and world to that of its inception, far exceeds the fact of this breakup of a brief relationship after a three-month separation.

A specific moment in the protagonist's life, the missed encounter alters and even undermines the meaning of her life story before and after this moment—before and after pain. The viewers' journey through the artwork follows a chronological order, showing, however, how pain has altered time or introduced a nonlinear dimension. In "Avant la douleur," Sophie's story is presented in a long sequence of framed photographs, texts, and ephemera that document the three-week train trip to Japan and stay in this country day by day, where the texts (made up of letters between Sophie and M, mainly her letters to him) state quite clearly that for Sophie, at the time of the travel experience, this record-keeping made sense as a countdown to reunite with M, whom she constantly longs for. "Je suis partie le 25 octobre," we read in the work's introductory text, "sans savoir que cette date marquait le début d'un compte à rebours de quatre-vingt-douze jours qui allait aboutir à une rupture."[29] The photographic sequence of days simultaneously indicates to the reader the complete disruption of its original sense, by means of a red stamp impressed in looking back over each day's document, whose descending numbers indicate how many days are left before arriving at the day of pain (figures 5.2, 5.3, 5.4, and 5.5).

28. *Prenez soin de vous* (*Take Care of Yourself*; 2007) is the title of a later piece in which Calle returns to the breakup as prompt for an artwork. This phrase that gives the work its title is the sendoff line her lover writes to break up with her in an email. Her way of following this advice is to ask 107 women of different professions, social roles, and ages to interpret the letter for her.

29. "I left on October 25th without knowing this date marked the beginning of a ninety-two-day countdown that would lead to a breakup" (Calle, *Douleur*, 13).

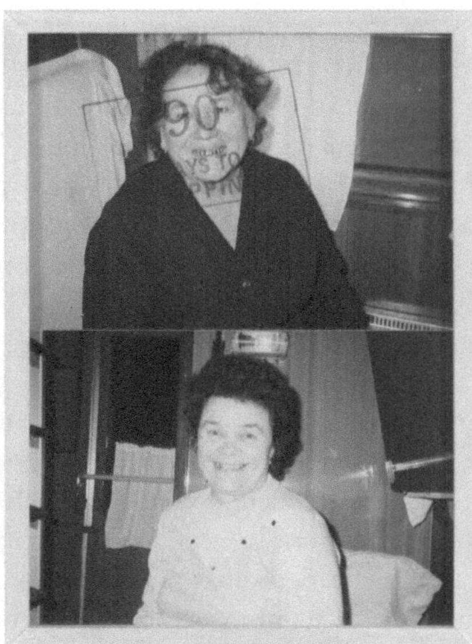

Figure 5.2. Sophie Calle, "90 Days to Unhappiness." *Exquisite Pain*, 1984–2003. 92 framed elements of variable dimensions: 21 × 16 cm (minimum) 82 × 124 cm (maximum) Courtesy of the Paula Cooper Gallery © 2019 Artists Rights Society (ARS), New York/ADAGP, Paris.

The textual narratives and the stamp introduce, then, a double lens on the photographs' affective register.[30] If Sophie was feeling some degree of discomfort at the fact of leaving her new lover (she writes, "après la douleur," that she was awarded the grant one day after the relationship with M began), the sort and intensity of this pain do not hinder friendly encounters with fellow travelers. This is first demonstrated by a pair of portraits of jolly, smiling women, her companions in the first train compartment she sleeps in (figure 5.2). But the portraits do not simply convey joy, as they are traversed at once by very different intensities and temporalities. The sense of well-being in their broad, flashy smiles is

30. Shirley Ann Jordan's analysis of *Douleur Exquise* reflects on its effect of introducing absence just as presence is recorded (200). "Exhibiting Pain: Sophie Calle's *Douleur Exquise*," *French Studies: A Quarterly Review* 61.2 (April 2007): 196–208.

not only met with some degree of nostalgia on the part of Sophie who, on the train, is drifting apart from her lover (geographically at the very least), but additionally clouded by the red stamp announcing the arrival of "Unhappiness" or "Douleur-J." By way of a homophony between the French name of the letter *J* and the French word "gît," the stamp in the French version calls to be read as ci-gît *Douleur*, herein, latent in the photograph, lies pain, from the verb *gésir*, meaning lying down still, due to illness, wounding, or death.

This sequence of voided photographs suggests that Douleur-J's unexpected irruption into Sophie's life disrupts the meaning of its spatio-temporal continuum. Moreover, in such a disruption an original meaning is not merely replaced by an equivalent or compensatory one; pain in the narrative introduces an irreducible void, as the third part, "Après la douleur," will show. It is this unexpected and unsymbolizable character of Douleur-J that gives it the rigorous status of an event, in contrast to the long-awaited moment of reunion, which would have left the order of time intact. Since the love letters to M are juxtaposed with these voided photos and thus inscribed in the countdown, the stories of the lived moment they relate also suffer Douleur-J's *Nachträglichkeit* effects, to borrow a term Freud uses to designate the operation of unconscious psychical traces inscribed at an earlier moment and detected through their effects at a later one. Specifically, Freud speaks of sexual experiences of childhood which, due to the state of childhood, are neither fully experienced nor understood until after the time of their occurrence. Their meaning and effect are felt only retroactively.[31] In the case of Sophie's love letters, they discuss the pain of distance and absence without, at the time, knowing the imminent rupture these conditions prepare. The stamp that voids hope also retroactively certifies the pain in them; furthermore, it helps to show something in fact already intrinsic to photography but rarely realized in looking at photos, and that, as Roland Barthes has shown us in *La chambre claire*, is a catastrophe of time, producing "ce vertige du Temps écrasé" "this vertigo of crushed Time";[32] between the instant the photo is shot, seizing its referent, that is, something of the material reality of that moment, and its incongruous insertion into

31. See, for instance, Lecture XXIII, "The Paths to the Formation of Symptoms," in *SE* XVI.

32. Barthes, *La chambre claire. Note sur la photographie* (Paris: Gallimard, Le Seuil, 1980), 151.

another present, the moment captured in the photo presents itself as all at once alive *and* dead or erased by a new present.[33] As a primary medium in Calle's artwork, photography itself figures an important effect of the experienced exquisite pain. As we, the readers-viewers, follow this day-by-day sequence, we become involved in the experience of disrupted time the photographs present. Calle's phototextual, retrospective strategy allows in this way an uncanny dimension of the lived and told stories to emerge for the readers-viewers. Take, for instance, the humorous account that accompanies the two smiling women:

> Mon amour, Elles sont montées dans le train à trois heures du matin. Elles m'ont forcée à partager leur poulet froid et un kilo de tomates. Celle qui a les dents de devant en or m'a caressé la cuisse. Elles ont décidé que j'étais le mâle du compartiment: elles me nourrissent et, en échange, je descends et remonte continuellement leurs neuf valises. Celle qui porte une robe de chambre rose et des savates vertes m'a fait comprendre par signes qu'elle me trouvait jolie, alors, pourquoi seule?[34]

While this letter indicates that the photographs are addressed by Sophie to the missing partner, her neighbor's innocent question retroactively foreshadows the breakup; the comment on her solitary travels becomes unhinged from that context (where it is only temporary for Sophie) and heralds the event prompting the work of art it reappears in. Also, if the letter states that among these women she takes the role of the male in the compartment, what also becomes audible in retrospect is that she is assigned not just the male, "le mâle," but also "le mal," the latent pain in the compartment. From the situations she tracks down to the display strategies in both the installation and book forms, Calle's projects, I argue, are all about producing a slanted viewpoint on reality, one that

33. Barthes's study is a predigital one, and the process of developing photographs implicates this materiality in a way that digital photography does not. Calle's project uses this analog process.

34. "They got on the train at three in the morning. They forced me to share their cold chicken and a kilo of tomatoes. The one with the gold front teeth stroked my thigh. They decided that I was the male of the compartment: they fed me and, in exchange, I was to keep getting down and putting back their nine suitcases. The one wearing a pink dressing gown and worn out green slippers made signs saying I was pretty, so how come I was alone?" Calle, *Douleur*, 18.

opens up the dimension of the unconscious, that becomes accessible to the readers-viewers. What loses its consistency in this narrative strategy is what Lacan defined in terms of a link between the symbolic and the imaginary, in other words, the certainty that civilization is able to support, contain, and channel the drive, or, to put this in Hippocrates's clinical terms, "to keep the womb from wandering,"[35] so let us bring this important maneuver into focus.

I have pointed out that Douleur-J, the event that generates the artwork and restructures time as a Before and After Douleur, importantly implies the dismantling of meaning for the subject who experiences that moment—in other words, a void that makes the photographed and scripturally recorded past return hauntingly, having lost their unambiguous "innocence," as *unheimlich*. The unhomely feeling is in fact brought to the fore in the form of a bedroom within a moving train, which Calle photographs repeatedly throughout the piece. The brief account of Sophie's exchange with the two women who speak Russian also betrays Sophie's perspective as interpreter of social interactions; attuned to sexuality, gender roles, intimacy, and sharing, this perspective comes effortlessly to the foreground when gestures take over as verbal communication recedes for lack of a common language. What indeed, is she doing alone, traveling across Siberia and China to get to Japan in a little compartment, spending her nights with a parade of strangers? Calle the artist, beneficiary of a grant, could have gone anywhere, as she tells us, but instead of going somewhere she loves and feels at home, like New York City, she goes to Japan, where she cannot read, speak, or understand the language. Not only this: as she explains in a text juxtaposed with the train reservation slip, she could have taken a plane to Japan and arrived there just two days later, but she worried that it was a long time: "c'est long, trois mois. Afin d'écourter mon séjour sur place, j'ai opté pour un voyage lent. En train."[36]

What she doesn't explain, choosing instead to present it in the selection of photographs and stories, is that the train involves a more sustained

35. Hysteria, the trouble of "the wandering womb," is exemplary in producing the shift out of the ego square or sphere and toward the id, insofar as this structure presents the "incomplete" subject assailed by the symptom that bears witness to the logic of the drive derailing the organism and overwriting the body with the unconscious. See Part I of this book.

36. "three months is a long time. I therefore chose to shorten my stay by lengthening my journey. The appropriate mode of transportation was the train" (Calle, 16).

experience of displacement and of intimate engagement with strangers than a flight. Exposing herself to the stranger, she minimizes the months, "les mois," but also the me, "le moi," the self, inviting something that destabilizes the unity of *moi* to take over. Her companions seem to sense this unhinging from "moi" in Sophie when they decide she is "le mâle."

MacCannell's analysis of Calle's 1980 project *Suite Vénitienne* sheds light on what this seeming incongruence is about:

> The reason Calle can submit herself to Venice has to do with *the city itself*. [. . .] In Venice, you walk or slow down to the tempo of water transport; you forgo the torque and acceleration of vehicular land transit; you dispense with motorized, wheeled, high velocity conveyances. Venice audaciously deprives you of the illusion that you (and by analogy) your civilization have *drive* under control. Venice's canals could never properly represent the traffic-controlling of desire (nor its patriarchal shaping of male/female positions) as urban arteries elsewhere do.[37]

In "Avant la douleur," too, Calle slows down and drifts off to welcome the drive's disruptions into her life. "Drive disrupts the familiar itineraries of narrative and of desire."[38] Calle's choice to put herself in a situation where the power of verbal exchanges becomes as weak as possible while the intimate sharing of space is intensified, is a key strategy to unsettle the discursive connection to other social, speaking beings, and in this way make the unthought of those interactions come uncannily to the fore. A gap between the conscious, recognized account of her actions and decisions, on the one hand, and the defamiliarization of reality to which she exposes herself, on the other, becomes visible to readers-viewers in the process of following this spatiotemporal composition of texts, photos and objects. "C'est long, trois mois," she wrote, in a hardly veiled confession of at least three me's, since the unity of "me" is what this voyage is displacing and disrupting. As she slowly drifts away from home on the train, a different force than the one in charge of preserving the self begins to take over, beyond the pleasure principle.

37. MacCannell, "Death Drive in Venice Sophie Calle as Guide to the Future of Cities," *a: A Journal of Culture and the Unconscious* 11.1 (2002): 55–78, 63.

38. MacCannell, 64.

"Me," then, is a masquerade, and *Douleur exquise* reveals this in Sophie's way of playing with masks of femininity. Sophie shows interest in the gendered roles she plays, not only in the compartment as the male lifting the two women's suitcases, but with many other strangers and friends along this voyage, and also in her relationship to M, from whom she receives a letter on day 42 before Douleur with the words "Ma petite femme chérie" ("My darling little wife").[39] We learn further along through the artwork that this is a reference to their first night together: "Pour notre première nuit" ("On our first night"), the first text written "after pain," recalls, "je me suis glissée dans le lit dans une robe de mariée" (figure 5.6) This game of "slipping into bed in a wedding dress" without having the wedding (discussed in more detail in this book's introduction) exposes her unhinged position in the social order. As easily as she can "slip" into bed, she can slip in and out of the dress that turns her into someone's "petite femme chérie." But her skepticism, the fact that she is not completely immersed in the roles she plays with others, is not in the service of proving to M, or to the jealous Marcel, or to male subjects in general, that she is free and unconquerable, no matter how docile she may seem in the bed. Rather, this playfulness expresses her dissatisfaction with what Proust had called "conventional knowledge," which seemed to steadily gain more and more "thickness and impermeability" ("plus d'épaisseur et d'imperméabilité") by the force of habit, unless we have "l'art véritable," and I would say, with Deleuze, "la clinique véritable" to break us out of it. Calle's masquerade points out that these social conventions that organize human bodies, perception, and modes of relation, are indeed like a thick layer, blanket, or dress covering a void that can nonetheless be slipped or peeled off,[40] and that, as painful as it may sound, this process is key to the crucial function of "transmuting pain into joy" in the aesthetic clinic.

Interspersed with the many photos of temporary companions on the train and in Japan in "Avant la douleur" is a series of images that keep track of banal and unusual things, scenes, and people seen by the traveler, several of the images falling under the theme of superstition,

39. Calle, *Douleur*, 115.

40. This gesture of slipping out of a dress or a skin as of a self was discussed with Duras, Lacan, and Joyce in chapter 4. Calle's "Avant la douleur" contains a series of photographs of Sophie's outfits laid out on a surface, which also stresses the disjunction between unified body image and subject. See also my Introduction on this gesture.

whether consulting fortune-tellers, or participating in Buddhist and Shinto wish-making practices. The latter, a photograph states, has a curative aim: "your troubles will be cleared up," a sign in English promises to tourists. These sets of photos and their correlative texts presenting the protagonist's efforts to discover and sometimes control her destiny reveal, all at once, that these activities mostly take place in a language Sophie does not understand. The comical paradox emphasizes the anxiety of drifting in this foreign territory where she experiences loss of control over her life, and it also reminds us that what unconsciously drives her research, concerns a message or cryptic letter that resists decoding.[41]

In addition to that category of images there is the recurrent appearance of beds she sleeps in, sometimes unmade.

Particularly striking are the portraits of beds shot at a slightly high angle from the foot and exceeding the frame on both sides. The pillows, piled up for a single head, appear centered and in focus, then voided by the red countdown stamp, which appears aligned with the pillows' rectangular shape. The insistent return of the camera to single out this view indicates its importance, first, within the context of the journey taking place, where the protagonist is a photographer using her travel grant and missing her lover, and second, in the previously discussed retrospective of Douleur-J, as the most literal premonition of the event of M's absence in the New Delhi hotel bedroom. But beyond these functions lies a third relevant matter. The bed's cropped contours establish a blind field that, together with the point of view shot, has a subjectifying effect. As Iversen explains about works of art that involve a blind field, here the viewer recognizes "the implicit presence of a spectator or an 'actor' of some kind in the spectator's space,"[42] a presence of the camera's or the photographer's "eye" that is structurally necessary to photography. Above all, the implication of Sophie's viewpoint exactly where I, as viewer, stand shatters any objective distance to the sight before me. It is as if the scene somehow corresponded to me directly, and where what I sense about the blind field that exposes me is, paradoxically, the implicit spectator's absence. This strategy constrains viewing to an experience of the sort one has in dreams insofar as the intense and repeated focus on

41. Calle points to a French fascination with Kanji and Chinese calligraphy in the twentieth century, evident in authors such as Roland Barthes, Jacques Lacan, and Henri Michaux.

42. Iversen, *Beyond Pleasure*, 33.

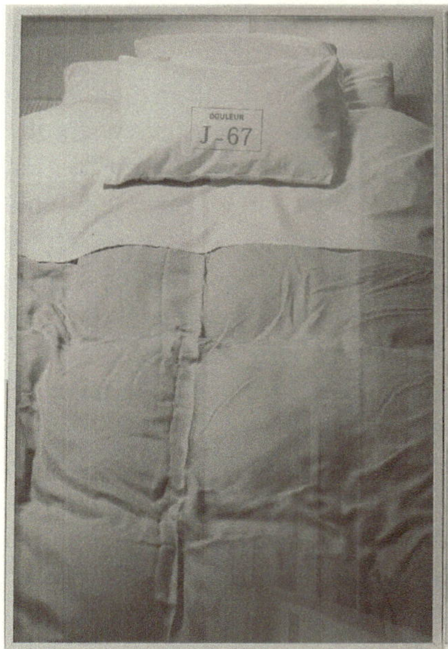

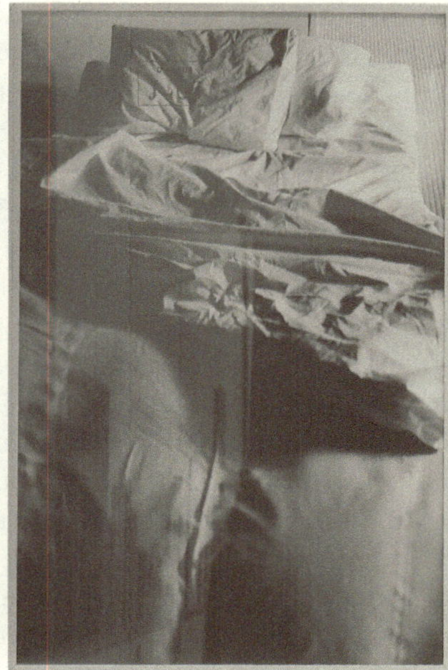

Figure 5.3. (Left) Sophie Calle, "J-67." *Douleur Exquise*, 1984–2003. Courtesy of the Paula Cooper Gallery. © 2019 Artists Rights Society (ARS), New York/ADAGP, Paris.

Figure 5.4. (Right) Sophie Calle, "J-66." *Douleur Exquise*, 1984–2003. Courtesy of the Paula Cooper Gallery. © 2019 Artists Rights Society (ARS), New York/ADAGP, Paris.

this object is not commensurate with its established meaning for me; the image is only of a banal object of everyday life, and it is empty, so why do I keep encountering it? The made beds where the covers and pillow are smoothed out give the impression of an incongruous blank, while the slept-in beds, unmade, sheets full of wrinkles, exhibit their vacancy as well. These objects render a distinct image—a horizontal plane of still, suspended silence—not only of the disheveling of the social fabric in which speaking beings function and interact, but also of a related unsymbolizable void I have been stressing, in stating that the trajectory of *Douleur exquise*, like that of Sophie in Japan, is one of approaching the sight/site[43] where a strange, usually repressed, reality comes to surface.

43. Bersani highlights this homophony in *Is The Rectum a Grave?*, 104.

The bed photos are presented as Sophie's sleeping locations, where the traveler's body lays down to rest when she is not photographing, writing, or interacting with others. Their interest lies (pun intended) in their enactment of a paradox of photography: the impossibility of being simultaneously present as the eye, with a unique focus the camera helps to capture, and the target of the lens that will appear within the frame. And this brings us back to the problem of primary narcissism. The beds are then anamorphic self-portraits, evoking the limit of self-consciousness and self-possession, the impasse of the split subject. Because I, as viewer, am in the position of the subject observing her bed, I, too endure the experience of a split between my "self" and something that corresponds and stares at me with its inhuman gaze. Iversen writes:

> If the reflection in the mirror is the prototype of all images of the ego, then this contradictory, ungraspable, fleeting object [the objet cause of desire] is the prototype for images of the castrated, barred, split—in short, anamorphic—subject. This subject, called punningly by Lacan *le sujet troué* (the subject full of holes), uses an *objet trouvé* (a found object) to figure both the hole and the missing bit.[44]

In this light, the unmade bed emerges as the peeled-off skin or blanket of conventional perception, as an eroded imaginary-symbolic shell supposed to preserve the self; what the pulled-away sheets reveal the next morning is an anamorphic network of creases—they are the writing left behind by the sleeper's body, but it is illegible.[45]

This "peeling away" of the unified body image is a crucial condition for sublimation. It opens onto the fundamental lack, which, Franz Kaltenbeck states, "can never be absorbed by creative work, for the creation

44. Iversen, *Beyond Pleasure*, 66.

45. Anamorphoses gained attention in the Baroque, a decadent period that confronted the fragility of its symbolic structures, or its feeling of an imminent end of the world, directly, and also in acts of sublimation that emerge in decentered, elliptical, groundless play with form in architecture, painting, and music. See Christine Buci-Glucksman's *La folie du voir. Une esthétique du virtuel* (Paris: Galilée, 2002). It is tempting to transpose the conditions of the Baroque to Calle's piece, and to the end of the twentieth century it presents.

will reproduce it."[46] The sequence of days "67" and "66," represented by a made and then unmade bed, implying the night's sleep that has gone by, is followed by an image that could initially seem unrelated to the beds.

The cultural reference in this photo—the *studium*, to adopt Barthes's term—is the famous Tsukiji Wholesale Market in Tokyo, an icon of the national commercial life and a tourist attraction famous for its tuna auctions. The fishtails are chopped off to leave the meat exposed, allowing auction participants to appraise and compare the quality of the numbered fish before bidding. Calle's photo offers a close shot of four fragmented tuna fish, probably aligned with others in a row, as the objects cropped by the frame's sides suggest. However, placed within the sequence of beds, the image discloses itself as a mise-en-abyme. The incomplete bodies fragmented by a cut reproduce the frame's cut of the image from a broader unseen space; meanwhile, the resting disposition of the dead fish with their heads furthest away from us evoke the bed photographs, with the peeled-off bits of skin reminding us of the opened sheets, just as the skins numbered in red replicate the red numbering Calle applies to each of the photographs that are also set in a row. In this way the numbers eleven, twelve, thirteen also leave the trace of another, invisible standpoint, behind the fish in the darkness, imposing an order to Sophie's and our visual and reading experience, which propels us forward, to "14" or Douleur J-64, each time closer to meeting "Douleur en personne." This reading becomes possible not just by getting into the banal drama of temporary separation that leads to a breakup, but upon continuing to look and move closer to pain, by undergoing the empty beds' uncanny, inhuman gaze staring at me, the viewer. In other words, with its narrative and nonnarrative elements, particularly through the installation medium that makes us move forward and slow down, to read and observe the photographs, repetition, and subjective shots and closeups, the artwork produces an aesthetic experience that makes us sensitive to the photos' affective potency, or again in Barthes's word, their *punctum*, the details in them that can puncture and wound the viewer. One can therefore be struck by the bed image of illegible writing, and by this still life that places in the foreground a figure of castration, the chopped off fishtails revealing fleshy, open wounds appearing closest to the eye along the bottom frame.

46. Kaltenbeck, "Sublimation and Symptom," 113.

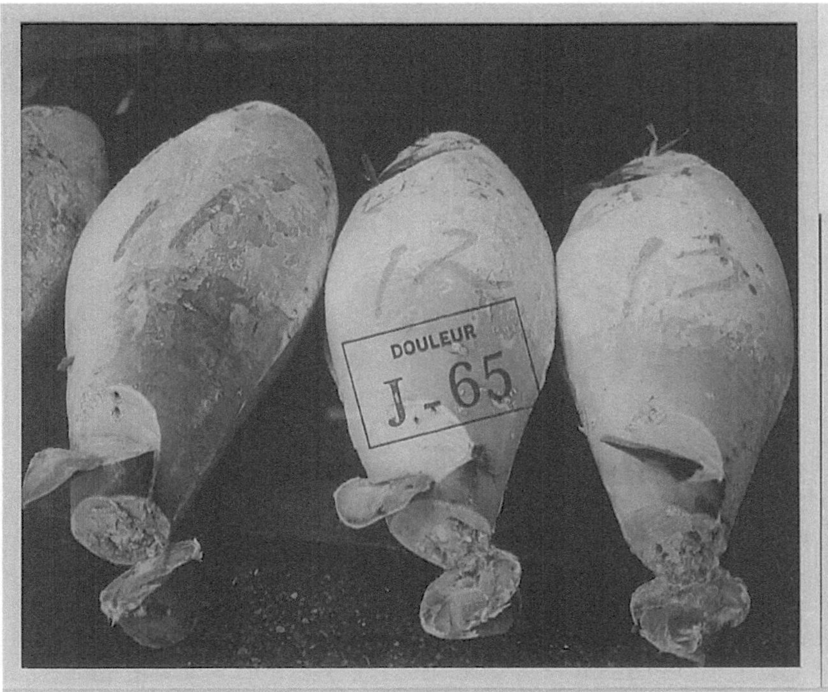

Figure 5.5. Sophie Calle, "Douleur J-65." *Douleur Exquise*, 1984–2003. © 2019 Artists Rights Society (ARS), New York/ADAGP, Paris.

Douleur without Borders

Just before the travel narrative stops, we find a snapshot of a smiling Sophie, whose symmetrical placement in "Avant la douleur" evokes the two smiles of her compartment companions at the start of the trip. "Plus qu'un seul jour. Je n'ai jamais été aussi heureuse. Tu m'as attendue."[47] The exaggerated and deluded phrases placed here read as if happiness needed to be imagined at its peak, in order to make the intensity of the pain that follows *exquisitely* felt. After this image, we read the message delivered to Sophie at the airport stating that her lover, M, will not arrive in Delhi, and then the mediations of writing and photography

47. "Only one more day. I have never been happier. You waited for me." Calle, *Douleur*, 194.

fall away, leaving us face to face with the installation: a half-open door displaying the number 261, a pair of twin beds, reminding one that the isolation throughout the trip has extended its reach to this room that was supposed to host a romantic reunion, a red analogue telephone close to the left bed's pillows, a bedside table.[48] We, in Sophie's place, find ourselves situated in Douleur-J itself, "25 janvier 1985, chambre 261, hôtel Imperial, New Delhi." The moment of reaching the *Douleur* installation accomplishes the aesthetic undermining of our already dimmed sense of exteriority and independence from the narrative. Specifically, by the time we get to "Le lieu de la Douleur," we are constrained by the order of time that "Avant la douleur" has made us follow, day by day, closing in on the core, cause, and Chose (Thing) of exquisite pain.

Iversen argues that in *La chambre claire* Barthes, influenced by Lacan on the scopic drive, restitutes the real to photography, there where postmodernism has misunderstood it in terms of the *simulacrum*. Barthes's *punctum* is a detail that exceeds the internal coherence of the image: "The punctum breaks up that coherence, bursting through the frame and plane."[49] If the previously examined cropped images introduce the sense of nonmastery in a restricted, subjective viewpoint, and with it, the uncanny sense of a gaze, the effect of full physical immersion within a moment anticipated by the photographs, an immersion into a vacant intimate dwelling space in particular, turns the dynamic of seeing around, exposing me as a contingent visible body, caught within the light, as Lacan suggests in Seminar XI. "I may see objects," writes Iversen showing the tight link between Barthes's and Lacan's notion of the gaze, "but I am also enveloped by a light or a gaze that unsettles the position that I want to occupy as the source of the coordinates of

48. My analysis differs from Jordan's on this point; she devotes only a short paragraph to the "Lieu de la douleur" marked by the installation of the hotel bedroom, admitting that "its logic is to take us as close as possible to the experiential quality of Calle's suffering at its height" but considering that "it has less emotive charge than the rest of the work, being above all a space of transition" ("Exhibiting," 203). Martine Delvaux highlights the central question of the failed sexual encounter in Calle's works, noting its connection to the failure of representation, while considering "psychoanalytic discourse . . . impotent as a critical tool" for Calle's works (427). I clearly differ. "Sophie Calle: No Sex." *Contemporary French and Francophone Studies* 10.4 (December 2006): 425–435.

49. Iversen, *Beyond Pleasure*, 120.

sight."[50] The reincarnation of a critical moment "Douleur" performs is possible since Calle photographed the scene after hanging up with M, who explains, still in Paris, that he has moved on to a new relationship. We know the story, and the fact that this scene was photographed, from the writing that begins to retell this story every day from that moment on, and this writing is part of "Après la douleur." The other constant and strictly unchanging element in each day after "Douleur" is, in fact, that photograph of the telephone on the bed. Why also recreate this room, in addition to its dizzying photographic repetition ninety-nine days "Après la douleur"? Because the artwork is not only about reporting an incident; in this piece it is very close to Lacan's description of what is at stake in a successful work of sublimation: "only by reworking lack in an infinitely repeated way is the limit that gives the work its measure reached."[51] *Douleur exquise* presents this logic and suggests, additionally, that the work aims at transmitting an experience. In the aesthetic clinic, then, this singular transmission treats the anesthesia, deplored by Proust, of conventional knowledge.

In Barthes's *La chambre claire*, the mourning narrator "à la recherche," through photographs, of what he names the "essence of Photography" stresses the difficulties of encountering both a photograph's *punctum* at its profound affective level *and* a true portrait, one that captures the living singularity of the photographed, loved being. Iversen convincingly argues that the Surrealist *trouvaille* (found object) crosses paths with Lacan in aesthetically relevant formulations of the object cause of desire as *trouvé* (found) and, spun in this way, such *trouvaille* sweeps through Barthes's analysis of Photography, where the *punctum*, which can only be *trouvé* by accident pierces or punctures the spectator, making a *trou* (a hole). I would add that the distinct notion Proust elaborates of "temps *retrouvé*" (found again, recovered) with its involuntary, destabilizing, and even painful conditions, participates in this circuit refueled by Calle's *retrouvailles manquées*, this missed reencounter that highlights the problem of "no sexual relation."

When Barthes's narrator finds his deceased mother's portait as a child, he writes: "Pour une fois, la photographie me donnait un sentiment

50. Iversen, 127.

51. *La logique du fantasme*, session 14, March 8, 1967 (unpublished). Lacan here stresses that sublimation is not restricted to artworks, illustrating the point of sublimation through the golden ratio in mathematics.

aussi sûr que le souvenir, tel que l'éprouva Proust, lorsque se baissant un jour pour se déchausser il aperçut brusquement dans sa mémoire le visage de sa grand-mère véritable."[52] This is all Barthes makes explicit about that scene from "Les intérmittences du coeur," although his own search is (theoretically and affectively) traversed by Proust's *Recherche*. In the evoked passage, Marcel states: "je venais d'apercevoir, dans ma mémoire, penché sur ma fatigue [. . .] le visage de ma grand-mère véritable dont [. . .] je retrouvais dans un souvenir involontaire et complet la réalité vivante."[53] This involuntary memory is more than a memory, since it contains "the living reality" of his grandmother's face. Interestingly, this fortuitous encounter in Proust's *Recherche* is simultaneous with the realization of her death, which had occurred a year before this moment. Not only does the narrator reflect on the temporal delay between facts and experience (which highlights the deferred action of photography and of Calle bringing together her experience in the artwork *Douleur exquise* eighteen years later), Marcel also states that this involuntary memory causes a "bouleversement de toute ma personne"[54] ("an upturning of my entire self")—that is to say, the kind of experience we noticed in Sophie as well. This upturning of the self makes way for a strange and dazzling reality. It is conveyed in Proust's text through the description of the painful awakening to the bright light the following morning, in the hotel room Marcel used to share with his grandmother in Balbec:

> J'avais oublié de fermer les volets et sans doute le grand jour m'avait éveillé. Mais je ne pus supporter d'avoir sous les yeux ces flots de la mer que ma grand-mère pouvait autrefois contempler pendant des heures; l'image nouvelle de leur beauté indifférente se complétait aussitôt par l'idée qu'elle ne

52. Barthes, *La chambre claire* (Paris: Gallimard, Le Seuil, 1980), 109. "For once, photography gave me a feeling as certain as remembrance, as Proust experienced it one day when, leaning over to take off his boots, there suddenly came to him his grandmother's true face." *Camera Lucida*, trans. Geoff Dyer (New York: Hill & Wang, 2010), 70.

53. Proust, *A la recherche du temps perdu* 2, 755–756. "I had just perceived, in my memory, leaning over my exhaustion . . . my grandmother's true face whose . . . living reality I found again in a complete and involuntary memory." *Remembrance of Things Past* 2, trans. Moncrieff and Kilmartin (New York: Vintage, 1982), 783 (hereafter cited as *Remembrance 2*).

54. Proust, 755.

> les voyait pas; j'aurais voulu boucher mes oreilles à leur bruit, car maintenant la plénitude lumineuse de la plage creusait un vide dans mon coeur; tout semblait me dire comme ces allées et ces pelouses d'un jardin public où je l'avais autrefois perdue, quand j'étais tout enfant: "Nous ne l'avons pas vue," et sous la rotondité du ciel pâle et divin je me sentais oppressé comme sous une immense cloche bleuâtre fermant un horizon où ma grand-mère n'était pas.[55]

The visible and audible objects around Marcel in his bed acquire a new force when he is shaken from numbness by the image of his grandmother the previous night, and by this accident of "forgetting to close the shutters" that expresses this sensorial reality's beauty, a photographic one, indeed, as experienced when the protective shell of "self" disappears, upon the Other's disappearance. Pain comes to Marcel not only from knowing as a fact that his grandmother has died, disappeared, since he has known this for an entire year since it occurred, but instead from suddenly entering into the intimate experience of this loss, which upturns his very way of being in the world. Bed offers no safe harbor. Through the torrent of sensations traversing the protagonist, "hollowing out a void in his heart," he discovers that she is nowhere to be found in the full, vast, luminous world whose horizon closes without her. The passage (which gives Barthes the title "la chambre claire"—the bright room, literally) suggests that the room and view flood him unbearably in their light and sound that reinstate an absolute absence. The split we have mentioned, between perception and consciousness that defines the unconscious, here seems to cease to shelter the self, as they come dangerously close, exposing the senselessness of existence without an indispensable Other's (loving) gaze. Calle

55. Proust, 762. "I had forgotten to close the shutters, so probably the broad daylight had awakened me. But I could not bear to have before my eyes those sea vistas which my grandmother used to contemplate for hours on end; the fresh image of their heedless beauty was at once supplemented by the thought that she could not see them; I should have liked to stop my ears against their sound, for now the luminous plenitude of the beach carved out an emptiness in my heart; everything seemed to be saying to me, like the paths and the lawns of a public garden in which I had once lost her, long ago, when I was a little child, 'We haven't seen her,' and beneath the roundness of the pale vault of heaven I felt crushed as though beneath a huge bell of bluish glass forming a horizon from which my grandmother was excluded" (*Remembrance 2*, 789–790).

in "The site of Douleur" is concerned with transmitting to the viewer an experience close to this Proustian account of the uncanny, where what was once familiar returns, suddenly and disturbingly unfamiliar, as Freud describes. Instead of only narrating her rude awakening from the dream of *retrouvailles*, of lovers meeting, Calle opens up a space in the gallery and in the middle of her book for the irruption of the radical absence of the Other with regard to whom our self finds its position.[56] This space, in *Douleur exquise*, is encountered as perception in absence of any narrative to relativize the blow of the empty hotel room; it brings the frozen moment's nonmetaphoric insertion in another present, a radical experience to Marcel, too, awakening in the Balbec Hotel.

Sublimation with Symptom

Without a spatial experience of *Douleur* as the room where pain found Sophie and as the very scene of pain, no direct sense of pain, embodied by each material component, would adhere to the viewer. Consequently, without the installation experience, the insistent photograph in "Après la douleur" could not convey pain directly. Its power would be exclusive to Sophie's sight, in the way that "la Photo du Jardin d'hiver" (The Winter Garden Photo) was impossible to see by anyone besides Barthes.[57] Yet

56. Deleuze reflects on the absence of the Other in the structure of perversion, in "Michel Tournier and The World without Others (*Autrui*)" in *Logic of Sense*, trans. Mark Lester (New York: Columbia University Press, 1990). Iversen's article "The World Without a Self: Edward Hopper and Chantal Ackermann," *Art History* (September 2018): 742–760, is highly relevant to think of impersonal space and the proximity of banal scenarios and sites of trauma in visual terms.

57. Barthes writes the following in parentheses: "(Je ne puis montrer la Photo du Jardin d'Hiver. Elle n'existe que pour moi. Pour vous, elle ne serait rien d'autre qu'une photo indifférente, l'une des mille manifestations du 'quelconque'; elle ne peut en rien constituer l'objet visible d'une science; elle ne peut fonder une objectivité, au sens positif du terme; tout au plus intéresserait-elle votre *studium*: époque, vêtements, photogénie, mais en elle, pour vous, aucune blessure)," *La chambre*, 114–115. "(I cannot reproduce the Winter Garden Photograph. It exists only for me. For you, it would be nothing but an indifferent picture, one of the thousand manifestations of the 'ordinary'; it cannot in any way constitute the visible object of a science; it cannot establish an objectivity, in the positive sense of the term; at most it would interest your *studium*: period, clothes, photogeny; but in it, for you, no wound)," *Camera Lucida*, 73.

the special kind of aesthetic-affective short-circuit or wounding "The site of Douleur" enables is the center, and not the final gesture, in *Douleur exquise*. If "Le lieu de la Douleur" indicates the most exquisite pain of losing the Other, "Après la douleur" finds a way to reactivate the connection to the stranger we briefly considered "Avant la douleur," on the trip to Tokyo. It is a way to follow, beyond the imaginary possession of the familiar object, the command in the letter "M" that represented the beloved in this story: "M," *aime*, "love." Pain might enable an embrace of "the stranger at the very heart of (each) me" as sublimation.

> J'ai demandé à mes interlocuteurs, amis ou rencontres de fortune: "Quand avez-vous le plus souffert?" Cet échange cesserait quand j'aurais épuisé ma propre histoire à force de la raconter ou bien relativisé ma peine face à celle des autres. La méthode a été radicale: en trois mois j'étais guérie. L'exorcisme réussi, dans la crainte d'une rechute, j'ai délaissé mon projet. Pour l'exhumer quinze ans plus tard.[58]

The narrator of *Douleur exquise* insists in this key moment on the lexical field of pain and clinical practice: after her practice of talking her way through the pain and inviting others to do the same, "I was cured," she states, but she was afraid of "la rechute," "a relapse." "Après la douleur" is described as a three-month therapeutic treatment (figure 5.1). While it appears to be all about being cured and exhausting or relativizing the pain, its specific materialization, after the artist decides to "exhume" it, to bring its buried remainders back into the light, that is, reveals that this treatment remains, to the very end, attuned to the kind of clinical rigor we have been discussing in her photographs and texts, in the Balbec Hotel scene, and in Barthes's *punctum*.

As I mentioned, this third part includes the photograph of the hotel bed and the glaring red telephone, as a heading to her story of the breakup, to constitute the left side of each day's quadriptych after

58. "I started asking both friends and chance encounters: 'When did you suffer most?' I decided to continue such exchanges until I had got over my pain by comparing it with other people's, or had worn out my own story through sheer repetition. The method proved radically effective. In three months I had cured myself. Yet, while the exorcism had worked, I still feared a possible relapse, and so I decided not to exploit this experiment artistically. By the time I returned to it, fifteen years had passed." Calle, *Douleur*, 202–203.

pain (figure 5.6 offers a closeup of a quadriptych). The words, sewn on vertical black linen rectangles that have their own frame, are a gesture to the tragic courtly love tales Marie de France narrates in her *Lais*, where lovers monumentalize their loss by painstakingly carving or embroidering their story.[59] This elaborate writing gesture also insists on the tremendous expense of time on this pain, an excess that makes visible a certain enjoyment in the process of telling the story. For each day, this composition of Sophie's story is paired, on the right, with a different individual's story of pain (they range from breakup stories to tragic deaths of loved ones to an experience of going blind), which is contrastingly sewn with black thread onto white linen. Calle stages the slow but steady fading of pain by retelling her own tragic story every day with new details, but each time producing a shorter text than the previous one. She also transitions from white thread on black linen to pale gray that eventually is almost indistinguishable from the linen. The passage of time, explicitly noted at the start of each narrative (for instance, "Il y a 90 jours, l'homme que j'aime m'a quitté" ["90 days ago the man I love left me"]) is sharply opposed by the photographic image that remains as clear and distinct as the first day. Here, in what Yve-Alain Bois calls "the Catastrophe photograph,"[60] is an affirmation of *Douleur* remaining unassimilable by the work of the signifier, *intractable*.

On the side of the others' stories, Calle supplements each of the accounts with a photograph of what they describe, producing in this way a photographic image for a memory she never experienced in first person.[61] This gesture does more than put Sophie's pain into perspective by comparing it to that of others, if by this we understand that she will feel relieved when she hears how others have had it worse. The gesture

59. In *Le rossignol* (*The Nightingale*), the Lady embroiders the story of her husband ruining the lovers' meetings at the window by killing the nightingale designated as the cause of her sleepless nights, and wraps the dead bird in this cloth to send to her lover. In *Le chèvrefeuille*, Tristan carves words of eternal love onto a piece of wood for Isolde to see. Marie de France, *Lais*, trans. Philippe Walter (Paris: Gallimard, 2000).

60. Yve-Alain Bois, "Paper Tigress," *October* 116 (Spring 2006): 35–54, 51.

61. An interesting effect that my first viewing of *Douleur Exquise* had was not on me, but rather on someone else, a close friend, who had not seen the work. Upon my return from the trip to Paris where I had seen the piece, my narrative, to a close friend, of what I remembered about *Douleur exquise*, unexpectedly brought tears to her eyes, as if, between my words, I had involuntarily transmitted something of the work's pain.

invents a mode of relation from the perspective of the intractable in each one's life, of its expression in an encounter with the alterity of pain, reiterating at once this gesture in the viewer's patient process of reading Sophie's story of pain, and now the others'. This construction of a sequence made from four panels each time, with a different "other" on the right side for each day, reveals another technique echoed in the title *Douleur exquise*. The surrealist *cadavre exquis*—exquisite corpse—is a parlor game where a text or image is collectively assembled by each player introducing a fragment. In the image version of the game, the body is typically divided into three sections—head, torso and upper extremities, and legs. Calle's piece includes processual features from this surrealist variation on the triptych form, given its own tripartite division (Avant, Le lieu, and Après). Exquisite corpses are developed among several participants who are unable to see what the others have previously inscribed or drawn. In "Après la douleur," Calle is blindly placing an image for something she has never seen before, for a pain that no one, except its narrator, has ever experienced. As a "heading" for the text where this experience is narrated, the photograph's irreducible heterogeneity to the text, in the place of a long vertical rectangular body, is prominent. In the combination "Après la douleur" presents, the process of viewing, narrating, and reading lead to a reader's experience of nonsynchronicity between text and image, as a way of presenting what is at stake in this combination, namely, a limit to total processing, or in this case, to the dissolution of pain. This is central to the work of the symptom in the aesthetic clinic.

Words in Sophie's repeated "Tale of Betrayal"[62] land just below the image, never exactly on the wordless target the snapshot hits.[63] A guest in the "Douleur" hotel room will have acquired an intimate sense of this residue that nonetheless leaves her searching for the sense of this pain, beyond its futile circumstances. While, on the left side, words never zero in on the untranslatable "thisness" of the hotel bedroom image, on the

62. Bois, 51.

63. "In order to designate reality, Buddhism says *sunya*, the void; but better still, *tathata*, the fact of being this, of being thus, of being so; *tat* means *that* in Sanskrit and suggests the gesture of a child pointing his finger at something and saying *Ta, Da, Ça!* A photograph is always located at the edge of this gesture; it says *that, there it is, lo!* But says nothing else; a photograph cannot be transformed (spoken) philosophically, it is wholly ballasted by the contingency of which it is the weightless, transparent envelope" (*Camera Lucida*, 4–5. Translation modified to include a missing sentence from the original French text).

right side it is the photo that strives to approach the tale, to lend an image to a solitary experience and raise its aesthetic singularity to the status of art.[64] What exactly does raising pain's singularity to the status of art mean, and how does it relate to the supposed cure from pain the narrator of exquisite pain is undertaking in "Après la douleur"?

The fifth in the series of others' stories sheds light upon this question (figure 5.6). The white sink placed as the story's heading stands in for a breakup letter left one morning in the basin of the female narrator's bathroom. It is a scene in which a certain "Jean" has abruptly left her, deciding privately that their passionate relationship should not continue. Her experience after this letter and his absence is described specifically: "En moi un vide, un blanc total, comme on dit une voix blanche, une peur blanche" (Inside me a void, a total blank, as they say blank voice, a blank fear).[65] Her sensations involve not only a feeling, but also a distinct color. White is the color of the void. To fill the void she feels in her empty hands, she asks to borrow a book from her psychoanalyst, and in her account she remembers the book cover's red leather. The terrible whiteness reemerges further on in the narrative, as the letter's feature: "La brutalité féroce de la lettre blanche sur le lavabo" (The ferocious brutality of the white letter on the sink). As in the Tale of Betrayal, an altered sense of time forms part of this white pain; the mourning process involves withdrawing from the world for months, and this striking detail:

64. Jean-Michel Rabaté examines this gesture in Calle's controversial *Pas pu saisir la mort* (2007). In his palinode to a previous judgment against this video installation featuring Calle's dying mother in her deathbed while listening to Mozart's *Clarinet Concerto in A Major* (K622), Rabaté compares Calle's gesture—of finding a way for her mother to be present at the Venice Biennale since this was one of her wishes (others included listening to Mozart in her deathbed, visiting Proust's "Balbec" with Sophie before dying)—to that of Sophocles's *Antigone* as interpreted by Lacan in his *Ethics* seminar. He explains that *Antigone* does not counter Creon's order against burying Polynices based on another universal "categorical imperative," but rather on the grounds of desire as a figure of absolute singularity. In the Greek tragedy, this desire's visibility is "blinding," difficult to behold, much in the way that it was difficult for Rabaté to bear the sight of this video for more than a moment, and especially in the way that the moment of death Calle wanted to capture with either her own eyes or the camera that rolled for eighty hours nonstop for this purpose, remains ungrasped. "Kallos Anti-Bathos? (From Calle to Freud, Lacan, and Back)," *On Bathos. Literature, Art, Music*, ed. Sara Crangle & Peter Nicholls (London/NY: Continuum, 2010), 179.

65. *Douleur*, 205, my English translation. "Voix blanche," a toneless voice, literally means "a white voice."

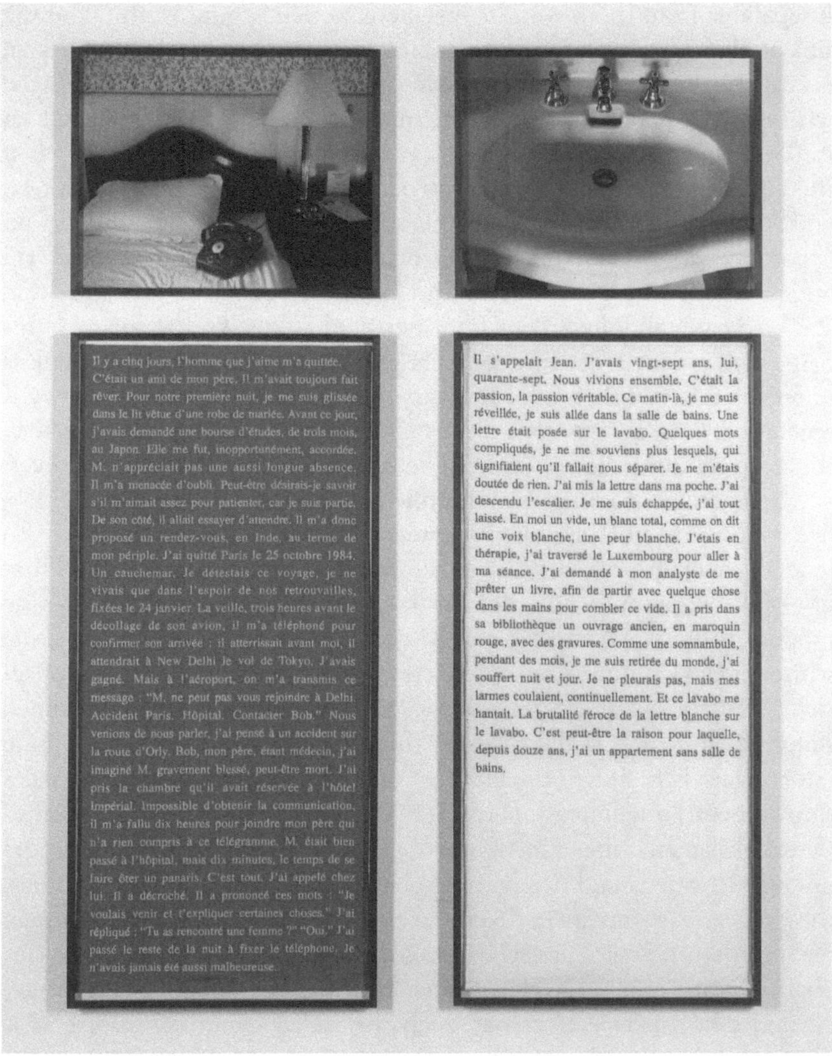

Figure 5.6. "5 Days after the Pain," Sophie Calle, *Exquisite Pain*, 1984–2003. © 2019 Artists Rights Society (ARS), New York/ADAGP, Paris.

"Je ne pleurais pas, mais mes larmes coulaient, continuellement. Et ce lavabo me hantait." (I didn't cry, but tears were constantly streaming from my eyes. And this washbasin haunted me). This sink is haunting insofar as it refers to the memory of its holding the awful letter; it is present in the moment of her loss. But as Proust's scene in the Balbec Hotel and Calle's *Douleur* have shown, in pain the referent adheres, becoming inseparable from the loss in its specific materiality. And in this case the sink itself, as a device to wash one's hands, quite accurately becomes an unreadable letter, and a ghost sucking down the drain and into the void whatever her hands hold, from the moment they hold the letter left on it. This void in her starts a leak, an unstoppable stream of tears, as if the sink's hole with its ghostly gravity were drawing them. To put an end to being haunted, she finds this solution: "depuis douze ans, j'ai un appartement sans salle de bains" (for the last twelve years I have had an apartment with no bathroom, no basin). To definitely stop the leak, she eradicates the washroom from her home. Outside the logic of this pain, such a drastic measure seems absurd, and a photograph of a sink is unremarkable. While humor is obviously present in the way the story is recounted, as in the ghostly sink's eerie reappearance above the narrative, this comical dimension is far from belittling the pain the story involves.

According to this tale, borrowing something, like a red book, derives directly from a white experience of the void, as its antidote. To lend an image to this story, Calle reintroduces no other image than that of a sink, in painful white, demonstrating that the point of this sharing process in the work of art is not to cork up the void and its liquefying white force. Coming from a concrete, lived moment, the stories all involve some detail on sensations and perceptions that accompanied suffering, and such is the focus of the photographs. They do not hide but conversely highlight the fact that once the moment of suffering fades into the past, a memory replaces it.[66] Giving an image to this narrativized replacement, then, insists on the loss and attunes viewing to the unique alterations and heightening of sensation pain introduces.[67] Thus, the clinical experiment in "Après la douleur" gives access to the joy of reading the unsymbolizable bits of each other's lives and of seeing this chain of intractables develop a link from the standpoint of *expérience*, beyond self, a perspective that might be called feminine, insofar as it ultimately escapes the sayable, while insisting on its transmission.

66. In many cases the photographs feature empty, monochromatic scenes that convey the irrevocable disappearance of that moment, a "remembrance of things past."

67. The importance of blindness for Calle, who dedicated other projects to beauty and color according to the blind (*Les aveugles*, 1986; *La couleur aveugle*, 1991), is included in this sequence of others' stories and lent images, in a tragic story of going blind, described as suddenly seeing only the color red. *La dernière image* (2010) and *Voir la mer* (2011) continue to investigate vision and lack.

Part III

For an Uncanny Ethics of Care

CHAPTER 6

Water, Weather, Words

Le Temps with Roni Horn and Clarice Lispector

Literature has emerged throughout *The Aesthetic Clinic* as an approach to words that retains the dimension of jouissance beyond meaning. In the 1970s Lacan spoke of this dimension of language with the term "lalangue," whose onomatopoeic effect evokes an infant's playful, singsong vocal repetitions. But *lalangue* continues to work after the child speaks, as irruptions of jouissance within language, through which a speaking being's singularity emerges.[1] Writing can be a field of exploration for this joyful dimension beyond meaning. The register disclosed by this approach concerns the aesthetic clinic insofar as it has to do with the subject beyond personal will and agency over itself or its surroundings, a subject of the real unconscious, which is crucial to rethinking sublimation with the feminine. In this book's Part I, Baudelaire partnered with Bourgeois, and Lispector with Clark. Part II hosted the beginning of a fuller turn to literature, with the questions of love and separation Marguerite Duras raised across her body of work, in chapter 4. The force of her writing derives from a treatment of words that makes silence

1. Lacan's work on James Joyce rests on this thesis, and in the first session of his Seminar XXIII, *Le sinthome*, he cites Phillipe Sollers's statement that Joyce wrote in English "in such a way that the English language does not exist anymore." *Le séminaire XXIII*, 11. This is also Deleuze's understanding of literature, and Sollers's statement closely recalls what Deleuze and Guattari develop in *Kafka: Pour une littérature mineure* (Paris: Les Éditions de Minuit, 1975).

and the music of words beyond meaning resonate. In chapter 5, the analysis of the complex work of photography, writing, and installation that Sophie Calle's *Douleur exquise* sets forth, also led to literature. A link to Marcel Proust's *A la recherche du temps perdu* was distinguished, due to the extended temporality and the experience of loss both works engage. It is from the locus of loss that the possibility of enabling an aesthetic encounter between unconscious subjects emerges, as a result of the discovery that interpersonal relations are flawed, and mostly miss the part of a speaking being where its singularity or difference resides. Literature can be a superbly suited form to such an encounter, although—or perhaps because—its demands over a reader's attention and time are arguably much higher than other forms explored throughout this book.

What about the unconscious subject's encounter with what Deleuze and Guattari call "Cosmos"? Can literature foster this? The interest Paul Klee declared in painting "cosmic things" highlighted "cosmos" for the schizoanalysts, as a matter of imperceptible forces that can be rendered sensible, through specific processes. The encounter with the Cosmos implies, then, a composition from disparate materials, worlds, and orders of things through which a cosmic, unthinkable "outside" breaks in, or through which the Earth, as a name for whatever finds itself "inside" finds a true outlet ("une échappée").[2] It decompletes the Earth. In literature, this process surges forth precisely through a treatment of language that bears the mark of jouissance as a real outside, and that carries language off to an uncharted space. The Cosmos is no preestablished home for the harmony of the spheres, species, and elements, but rather a burgeoning site of intensities that continually makes dwelling strange, or extimate. How does a subject "connect" and act on this cosmic level? This is the question I wish to address in this part of *The Aesthetic Clinic*.

Throughout this book, I have insisted that an artwork establishes its own reading conditions and constraints; in order to welcome its transmission of sensation, one must learn, each time, how to read beyond the effort at retrieving meaning, according to the work's singularity. In this final chapter I engage with two experimental works by way of an experiment of my own, which consists in bringing Clarice Lispector's 1973 novel *Água Viva* into Roni Horn's 2007 installation *Vatnasafn/ Library of Water* (figures 6.1–6.4). Horn herself, in other projects, has

2. Deleuze and Guattari, *ATP*, 337.

engaged with modernist literature, including, exactly, *Água Viva* (in *Rings of Clarice Lispector*, 2004, and *Agua Viva: Seventeen Paradoxes*, 2004). While bringing a book into a library may seem like a conventional action, at least far from cosmic revolution, its experimental quality has to do with the fact that the installation into which I introduce the work of Brazilian literature is an actual library in Iceland, with a collection of Icelandic glacial waters, a collection of adjectives descriptive of weather and mood in Icelandic and English, and a collection of testimonies by local people about the weather. The displacement of bodies of water and words from two languages contribute to a strange experience of dwelling in a fluctuating site of atmospheric changes at diverse speeds. A quasi-plotless work whose personages are the writing first-person voice and its addressed second-person reader, *Água Viva* makes explicit the search for an encounter of subjects in the act of writing and reading. The text is catalyzed by the strategy of bringing words to overflow the sayable, and by the fiction of a "me" and "you" who inhabit, impersonally, cosmically, the "instant-now," which can be seen as the novel's true protagonist. This mode of operation I detect in *Água Viva* reveals the more uncanny possibility for dwelling that *Vatnasafn/Library of Water* also welcomes. The effect of this experiment will have to do with the aesthetic process of making time sensible, as the basis of an uncanny ethics of care on the impersonal level of *it*. In order to see this subtle dimension, before the full immersion in the library of water which brings this book to its conclusion, the chapter's first sections will discuss the implications of making time sensible "in itself" by reflecting on the question of aesthetic contemplation for Horn and Lispector, and by introducing Paul Cézanne and Stéphane Mallarmé as key explorers of a scintillating, silent "instant of the world" and "of the word" without a self.

Water Contemplation

Water and Iceland play prominent roles in the artworks of Roni Horn. She speaks of Iceland as "an open-air studio of unlimited scale and newness," which had hosted several projects for three decades already when *Vatnasafn/Library of Water* was conceived.[3] Horn photographs water,

3. In James Lingwood, "Journey to the LIBRARY OF WATER." *Vatnasafn/Library of Water* (London/Göttingen: Artangel/Steidl, 2009), 15.

collects words about it, evokes it in her sculpture, and even incorporates it as an element of her installation *Vatnasafn/Library of Water* (2007). *You Are the Weather* (1994–95), photographed in Iceland, explores variation through a sequence of one hundred portraits of a girl surrounded by water from different pools under different kinds of light, where modulations of mood and light appear inextricably and spontaneously. As one continues to look at the sequence of portraits, the fairly neutral expression of the face gives way to striking changes in mood. The camera's insistence in revealing these from one second to the next recalls the obsession with which Charcot and his peers recorded hysterical attacks of female patients, with an important revision, however. Horn envisioned a four-wall installation of the headshots, and it wraps around the viewers' space, as the girl's eyes intently look back at us.[4] This work of revealing the singularity of the instant under a certain light and water, here carried out by the portrait's proliferation, will return in *Vatnasafn/Library of Water*, in other forms and media.

Horn and Lispector rethink the stakes of contemplation in their work with water. In an essay on *Vatnasafn/Library of Water*, the word "contemplative" comes to Briony Fer's mind, as she considers the space that "bears the imprint of the life of books of several generations" and "seems to resonate with all that silent thought."[5] But she soon withdraws this statement, because the word in her field evokes "transcendentalist rhetoric" that does not express the "kind of inwardness" she encounters in this library. Fer, I find, is right that the stakes are different. A very different understanding of contemplative, then, can be retrieved from Horn and Lispector, and yet others (Tournier, Deleuze, Guattari, and other "several generations" old books).

A series of projects around water resulted from photographing close shots of the surface of the river Thames. The fifteen large-format photo-lithographs in *Still Water (The River Thames, for Example)* (1999) are widely diverse in color, texture, and mood, sprinkled with tiny, white superscript numbers corresponding to footnotes along the bottom edge of the images. The back-and-forth between number-specks in the image and

4. In a way, Horn also literalizes one sense of Ernst's "femme 100 têtes," discussed in chapter 1 with Bourgeois' *Arch*.

5. "Storm of the Eye," in *Vatnasafn/Library of Water* (London/Göttingen: Artangel/Steidl, 2009), 23.

sentences along the bottom introduce the reader into a contemplative exercise, on life, death, solubility, and the unknown. At Tate Modern in 2009, the major retrospective exhibit dedicated to her work placed this work in a room whose large windows face the River Thames, intensifying the sense of contemplation along the bank, and the vertigo of standing on the edge of language, in the face of something ungraspable, even by the most zealous academic. Horn insisted on the interplay of water and words in a scholarly format by bringing Thames photographs into the books *Another Water* (2000), with a strip of footnotes along the book's bottom edge, from cover to cover, and a wordless *Dictionary of Water* (2001). In *Some Thames* (2000), Horn permanently installed eighty large photo-lithographs of the Thames at the University of Akureyri, Iceland, to flow across one of the buildings' halls and rooms. It is as if the images opened pockets of ineffability along the institution's walls, by making the familiar again strange, with this foreign flow through the building. The strategy is similar to the disruptions found in *Another Water*, where the image sequence is sporadically interrupted to present suicide accounts for cadavers found in the Thames in Central London. The morbid topic, while presented through impersonal reports with objective details on the events, shatters the book's scholarly style. Both the photo-lithographs and the suicide reports irrupting, respectively, in the spaces of the university and the book include an uncanny, vital and deadly force, in the water contemplation they invite. This force has been discussed in terms of the drive's excess in *The Aesthetic Clinic*, and its watery appearance in Roni Horn's art proposes awareness about the aesthetic as an experience of boundlessness. But the contemplation is simultaneously connection, a bind of sorts that, perhaps, does not turn away from unbinding. These operations are also active in *Vatnasafn/Library of Water* (2007), although here it is in contemplative dwelling that uncanny boundlessness emerges—at the intersection of water, weather, and words that "make time sensible," as this chapter will show.

Let me now turn to Clarice Lispector, not just on the theme of water, which occupied her thoughts in writing *Água Viva*, but also on contemplation as an aesthetic practice. Lispector returns across her writings in different genres to a set of gestures specific to an aesthetic mode of attention that invites us to a subtle, transversal attitude, attuned to what the author calls "life." She conveys this especially through the Portuguese verb "captar," which can be translated as to "catch," "receive," "perceive," and "understand" something. This operation is essential to the ethics of care I wish to articulate with Lispector and Horn. While *captar* is often translated in Lispector's texts as "capture," the possessive gesture of apprehension is inaccurate to convey the ethical stakes of *captar*. One might say that *captar* functions like antennae, where to receive the signal is to transmit it. Or like a mirror that holds an image only as long as it poses itself in its reflecting surface. The emphasis shifts from the recording or retention of a trace to an ongoing, live transmission. What, then, does photographing water entail in this regard? "When you photograph water you strip it of its form: of its restless, liquid reality," Horn writes.[6] But the exercise in repetition and contemplation that she develops from the photographically deformed water restarts its flow and the reader/viewer's, through a process one can accurately call *captar*, too.

The *I* who speaks and writes in *Água Viva* describes her[7] activity as an intense, constant caring contemplation: "Tomo conta do mundo" (I look after the world).[8] Her contemplation, involves a purposeless looking, writing, painting, and playing the music of each living thing and moment, while inviting her reader to join her. It can be seen in terms of Deleuze's thoughts about contemplation as not merely passive, when he examines Leibniz's, Plotinus's, and Whitehead's ontologies.[9] Deleuze sees in "contemplation" a key operation in the world's reality-in-creation. Reality occurs as an exercise of multiple contemplations that involve the contraction of something else, in each case according to the specificities of what is contracting and contracted. Thus, there is a receptive gesture that requires force and vulnerability at once. When *Água Viva*'s voice summons her reader: "pay attention and as a favor: I am inviting you to move to a new kingdom,"[10] she turns to the contemplation of a variety of flowers for several paragraphs. The descriptions themselves enact attention to each one's peculiar expressivity, and if contemplating is contracting, then both the sentences and its reader contract each floral mode in the sequence, which is autonomous in the text rather than serving the development of

---

6. Roni Horn, *Another Water* (Zurich: Scalo, 2000), n125.

7. The narrator declines its statements in the feminine in Portuguese.

8. Clarice Lispector, *Água Viva* (Rio de Janeiro: Rocco, 1973), 55 (hereafter cited as *AV*).

9. I have more fully compared Lispector and Deleuze in "Approaching Impersonal Life with Clarice Lispector," *Humanities* 7.55 (2018): doi:10.3390/h7020055

10. Lispector, 50.

a plot or the décor for a scene.[11] The only plot and scene are the passing instants and the acts of writing and reading. Meanwhile, the example Deleuze provides for contemplation is "the lily and the flowers sing the glory of God."[12] His point, in evoking Matthew 6:28, is that the lily is a specific and sensorially distinct contraction of infinity. One can see that contemplation, and, therefore, the logic of becoming occurs as a set of contagious, transformative encounters in the realm of sensation.[13]

To Contemplate the Instant of the World

Deleuze credits painter Paul Cézanne with the term "sensation," which names a way for painting to go beyond illustrative and figurative functions.[14] There is sensation, Deleuze explains, when a sensible form blurs the distinction between subject and object by acting on both:

> At one and the same time I *become* in the sensation and something *happens* through the sensation, one through the other, one in the other. And at the limit, it is the same body which, being both subject and object, gives and receives the sensation. As a spectator, I experience the sensation only by entering the painting, by reaching the unity of the sensing and the sensed.[15]

Sensation therefore exceeds the identification of objects by a separate cognizing subject (favored by the dynamic of standing in front of a

---

11. In this sense the flower treatise in *Água Viva* appears as a complement to a short story of Lispector's, where a woman falls into a timeless state of contemplation before a bouquet of roses, followed by contemplating their absence, which leaves a hole inside her and the ability "to imitate them within herself," as if she had, indeed, contracted their singularity. See "A imitação da Rosa" ("The Imitation of the Rose") in *Laços de Família* (Lisboa: Relógio d'Água Editores, 2013), 45.

12. Deleuze, Cours Vincennes–St. Denis: "Crible Et Infini" 17/03/1987. *Les cours de Gilles Deleuze*. Available online: www.webdeleuze.com/textes/142

13. Or "affect" (here "glory" or "joy"), as Deleuze states in his work on Whitehead. See also Deleuze and Guattari, *What is Philosophy?*, trans. Hugh Tomilson (London & New York: Verso, 2015).

14. Sensation operates through "the Figure" or "sensible form" rather than the other way to bypass figuration: "abstract form." Deleuze, *FB*, 34.

15. Deleuze, 35.

painting) in order to seize the body in a double function of giving and receiving that *Água Viva*—which sees itself all at once as a work of painting, music, and writing—knows intimately. To view a Cézanne, or a Francis Bacon, as discussed in chapter 2, is to enter it, and to lose the distinction between "one's body" and the painted body on the canvas. *Água Viva*'s "de natura florum"[16] is announced with "I shall speak of the sadness of flowers so as to feel more the order of whatever exists," and begins with the concise sentence "I want to paint a rose."[17] To read the floral treatise is to contract each blossom's uniqueness.

In *L'œil et l'esprit*, Maurice Merleau-Ponty poetically describes Cézanne's insistence on depicting Mount Sainte Victoire as an effort to "paint the instant of the world."[18] This beautiful formula draws not only on the paintings, but also on the dialogues that Joachim Gasquet wrote, in an attempt to give as true an account as possible of his actual conversations on painting with his friend Paul Cézanne, who says: "Il y a une minute du monde qui passe. La peindre dans sa réalité! Et tout oublier pour cela. Devenir elle-même. Être alors la plaque sensible."[19] Cézanne's thoughts imply that we are usually missing the passing minute of the world, as we inhabit our "self" or our "story," which involves a work of memory in charge of preserving some form of identity across time. The passing minute of the world "in its reality" is something else, impersonal, independent from one's own story or the story of a place. In order to grasp it in its reality, rather than mine, it would be necessary "to become that minute" ("devenir cette minute"), Cézanne says, pinpointing the crucial, constitutive factor in any instance of what Deleuze and Guattari will later call "a becoming." Indeed, if the process of becoming raises a long list of hyphenated terms—becoming-mad, becoming-animal, becoming-woman, becoming-imperceptible, becoming-vegetable—it is because time seized "as such" or "in itself" is sheer multiplicity and change, without a stable entity on which these transformations would occur. When Cézanne says that becoming the instant amounts to being the "sensitive plate," or the

16. Lispector, 55.

17. Lispector, 51–52.

18. Maurice Merleau-Ponty, *L'œil et l'esprit* (Paris: Gallimard, 1964), 23.

19. Gasquet, *Conversations avec Cézanne*, ed. P.M. Doran (Paris: Macula, 1978), 113. "There's a minute of the world that is passing. To paint it in its reality! And to forget everything for that. To become that minute. To then be the sensitive photographic plate."

surface on which the passing minute of the world is at once (in Deleuze's formulation) "sensing and sensed," he evokes the neutrality and accuracy of a photographic plate as a registration medium.

If accessing the instant of the world in its own reality comes at the cost of "forgetting everything," one may wonder whether and how this forgetting that unravels identities could sustain an ethics of relation, especially considering the artworks this book has examined so far, where reading becomes a labor of receiving the work's opaque language, of accepting the unconscious transmission it proposes. Writing on Cézanne and the exigency of the artwork, Maurice Blanchot mentions that Cézanne missed his mother's burial, since he was too absorbed in his painting and resolved to "ne pas perdre une journée" (not miss a day) of painting.[20] Cézanne's gesture does make him seem oblivious to everything, unable, in his passion for painting and the determination not to miss the instant of the world, to care about the life and death of others, at least in according to what social obligations recognize as manifestations of care. Is this what forgetting everything else amounts to? Can an aesthetic clinic fully bear sensation's consequences, such as this "forgetting everything to become the passing minute of the world"? Is "becoming that passing minute" opposed to care?

We have seen that this aesthetic clinic resists any traditional sense of "cure" (related to the word "care") in which treatment would seek to eradicate symptoms in order to restore homeostasis or "aesthetic indifference," as Freud writes.[21] Yet the interactions that the experiments in the aesthetic clinic propose, and their links to the dynamic in the clinical frame of psychoanalysis brought attention to their quest for a mode of relation beyond ipseity and familiarity, where, instead, the uncanny stranger within could meet the uncanny stranger in the other.[22]

20. Maurice Blanchot, *Le livre à venir* (Paris: Gallimard, 1959), 46. The anecdote evokes Dora's second dream, where she misses her father's funeral and calmly stays in her room, reading.

21. Freud cites Fechner. Freud, *SE* XVIII: 9. Like Deleuze, Freud understands "aesthetic" here as "relating to sensation or perception," the Standard Edition suggests (Freud, 9, n1).

22. This other care operates in Bourgeois' reflective body in *Arch of Hysteria* (1993), or in the site for the viewer's body within *Precious Liquids* (1992). Clark's clinic beyond the limits of art, Duras' *Césarée*, where sculpted bodies replace actors, and Calle's photographs of others' unseen, untranslatable pain, and of the world that disappeared with the fall of communism, are other instances.

This care would intervene in the world—in the symbolic understood not as an established realm of norms, but instead as an experimental site, grounded on inherited lack, of social coexistence. What about cosmological or environmental coexistence? If one "forgets everything" to become the instant of the world passing, say, over Mt. St. Victoire, are relation and care discarded?

In a word, no. But when reorganized in the aesthetic clinic, relation and care themselves lose their recognizable appearance, as sensible forms also do. Aesthetic experience is about a mode of attention (which implies care and relation) undetermined by the need to understand or morally approve of an object or situation; furthermore, it is ignited precisely by a shock that suspends these operations of the mind, introducing something unknown. One can describe the kind of aesthetic experience Cézanne's wish invites us to fathom as a decentering of perspective that requires the painter to give up his or her own point of view over the world, and its correlative sense of time, to release an impersonal, yet distinct reality in the making. To paint the instant of the world, the painter must not only gain access to it but also make it visible on the canvas, at least to those receptive to it and willing, like Cézanne, to surrender some control over their organized perception.

This deposition of mastery is also fundamental to the transformation poetry undergoes in Cézanne's time, with Mallarmé's *Crisis of Verse*, whose relevance to the two main contemporary works in question here I begin to show here. One reads in the groundbreaking critical-poetic essay that the poet's elocution is replaced by a different operation:

> L'œuvre pure implique la disparition élocutoire du poëte, qui cède l'initiative aux mots, par le heurt de leur inégalité mobilisés; ils s'allument de reflets réciproques comme une virtuelle traînée de feux sur des pierreries, remplaçant la respiration perceptible en l'ancien souffle lyrique ou la direction personnelle enthousiaste de la phrase.[23]

23. Mallarmé, *Oeuvres Complètes* (Paris: La Pléiade, 1945), 366. Hereafter cited as OC. "The pure work implies the disappearance of the poet as speaker, who yields the initiative to words, mobilized by the clash of their ordered inequalities; they light each other up through reciprocal reflections, like a virtual swooping of fire across precious stones, replacing the perceptible respiration in the former lyric breath, or the enthusiastic personal directing of the sentence." *Divagations*. Trans. Barbara

In the crisis Mallarmé confronts, verse seems ignited on its own, then, beyond the poet's breath, or intention; an instant of the *word* emerges like the instant of the *world* Cézanne pursued without the painter's self to direct eye and hand. The Mallarmean crisis of verse has to do with a sudden glimpse of the Cézannian instant of the world; the two intersect in the realm of sensation where images and words gain a different, nonrepresentational, nondiscursive function, releasing their intensive powers on each other such that they "light each other up." Sensation's two distinctive traits are present here: direct transmission bypasses the poet's intention, while its incessant passage across different levels emerges as that "virtual swooping of fire across precious stones."

Something close too, but even more subtle than the impression of the flashing instant on the photographic plate, or the virtual swooping of fire across precious stones, is emphasized by both Lispector and Horn through water's qualities. Its solubility, for instance, models the processes of contraction, *captar*, and care or "looking after the world" ("tomar conta do mundo"). A "first principle" to the pre-Socratics, water cuts across different kinds of life, taking vastly different shapes and effects, according to the other qualities it encounters in each case. Horn seems to take this protean solubility as a creative principle of her own practice, as her recurrent inclusion of other authors' and artists' words, lines, and traits in her works makes evident.[24] Horn is familiar with Lispector and with *Água Viva* in particular, which, as mentioned earlier, inhabited two of Horn's projects in 2004.

In both *Rings of Lispector* and *Seventeen Paradoxes*, Horn cites the following passage, from the first translation of *Água Viva* into English, *The Stream of Life*: "What I tell you is never what I tell you but something else. Capture this thing that escapes me and yet I live off of it and am

Johnson (Cambridge, MA: Belknap, 2007), 208. Johnson's translations in my essay are modified in reference to Mary Ann Caws' translation.

24. Horn cites not only Lispector, but also, in other projects, Franz Kafka and Emily Dickinson, for instance, and she includes other artists and writers, such as Louise Bourgeois, Anne Carson, Hélène Cixous, and John Waters (*Wonderwater: Alice Offshore*, 2003). For an analysis of Horn's strategies therein, of contagion and alliance with regard to hysteria and the aesthetic clinic, see my "Alice in Wonderwater: Hysteria, Femininity, and Alliance in Clinical Aesthetics," *Deleuze and the Schizoanalysis of Feminism: Alliances and Allies*, ed. Janae Sholtz and Cheri Carr (London: Bloomsbury, 2019), 227–244.

on the surface of brilliant darkness."[25] The phrase is here concerned not so much with assigning or discerning meaning, but instead with prompting an attunement to the irreducible singularity of something unnamed. Or perhaps its name is an oxymoron like the "brilliant darkness" in the mystical theology of Pseudo-Dionysius,[26] on the edge of language, on "the surface" where it escapes "me" and meaning, an outlet into the Cosmos. In *Água Viva* the phrase Horn inlays on the rubber floor constitutes a kind of refrain, like a hummed tune that floats up on the text, and it relates to silence as the force that needs to be heard, received by the reader. Its first iteration is this:

> Ouve-me, ouve o silêncio. O que te falo nunca é o que te falo mas sim outra coisa. Capta essa coisa que me escapa e no entanto vivo dela e estou à tona da brilhante escuridão.[27]

A request to activate the work of *captar* is present both here, and in the next passage's version:

> Ouve-me, ouve meu silencio. O que falo nunca é o que falo e sim outra coisa. Quando digo "águas abundantes" estou falando da força de corpo nas águas do mundo. Capta essa outra coisa de que na verdade falo porque eu mesma não posso.[28]

Deleuze and Guattari find that, at its best, a refrain attains the Cosmos, "harnessing forces"[29] that are nonvisible and nonsonorous in themselves

25. Roni Horn, *Rings of Lispector (Agua Viva)* (Hauser & Wirth Steidl, 2005), np.

26. See Pseudo-Dionysius, *The Complete Works* (Mahwah, New Jersey: Paulist Press, 1988). *The Mystical Theology* 997 A-B: "Where the mysteries of God's Word/ lie simple, absolute and unchangeable / in the brilliant darkness of a hidden silence."

27. Lispector, *AV*, 14. "Hear me, hear the silence. What I tell you is never what I tell you but yes something else. Receive [*capta*] that thing that escapes me and yet I live from it and I am on the surface brilliant darkness."

28. Lispector, 28. "Hear me, hear my silence. What I say is never what I say and yes something else. When I say "abundant waters" I'm speaking of the force of body in the waters of the world. Receive [*capta*] that other thing that I truly speak of because I myself cannot."

29. Deleuze and Guattari, *ATP*, 342. In French, Deleuze and Guattari write "capter des forces," which relates to the word *captar*, whose conceptual specificity I have pointed out. In "De la ritournelle," this verb "capter" relates to electronic reception

in a visual or sonorous material. In this refrain from *Água Viva*, a reader's support is necessary in order for the text to perform its scintillations (to quote Mallarmé), yet it is a reader capable of hearing a silence and of sensing something that escapes the speaker and, in fact, meaning. Repetition is a key strategy to unhinge readers from meaning. Horn therefore experiments with aesthetic modes of reading that follow the text's constraints. One stands and walks around, looking down at the floor in *Rings of Clarice Lispector*'s rubber tiles covering a room, to follow the texts' winding shapes in different directions, which prompt, for instance, to upside-down and mirror-reading. With words, the text calls for an encounter that bypasses what can be said, approaching the realm we discussed in previous chapters as that of the letter and feminine jouissance, and, at the beginning of this chapter, as *lalangue*. By creatively citing *Água Viva*, Horn's piece also relays the call to another, unknown reader. A force is felt in this call and it requires an unprecedented act of reading that takes a unique form at each encounter between that "other thing" that escapes the voice, and some "other thing" at work somewhere in the reader too, also escaping the territory covered by "I, myself," yet at her very own core. Hélène Cixous, for instance, takes the role of reader in the installation, which she considers as an attempt to "translate 'the intangible' without touching it."[30]

However, *Vatnasafn/Library of Water*, located in Stykkishólmur, Iceland, does not directly refer to *Água Viva*. In spite of the connection between the two authors' titles, which include, simply, the word 'water' in different languages, a general description of *Vatnasafn/Library of Water* projects may not initially leave one with the obvious sense of its direct relation to Lispector's *Água Viva*. Yet Horn returns, in the 2007 library, to the techniques in *Rings of Lispector* (2004): in both pieces, a rubber tile floor scattered with words in Futura Bold typeface needs to be read by walking around the room the floor covers. Like a strange, expansive signature, this formal repetition indicates an important connection,

of signals and other sonorous processes made possible with the synthesizer. They take the composer Edgar Varèse as an example for this operation, and oppose it to the work of *Grund* and territory, insofar as they take this synthetic operation to deterritorialized elements of different sorts. See MP, 343–345.

30. This point is made in the publication of a catalogue for the work, featuring an essay by Hélène Cixous, who knows Lispector's *Água Viva* well. "Faire voir le *jamaisvu*" in Horn, *Rings of Lispector*, 33.

regarding a rethinking of the ground-figure relationship with the force of time, as the end of this chapter will show. I would like to argue that the *Vatnasafn/Library* is closely tied to Lispector's poetic meditation in terms of the instant of the world, and that a look at them together brings forth their far-reaching consequences for the aesthetic clinic, as a clinic crucially concerned with a certain work of reading—as contemplation, contraction, or *captar*.

The Now-Instant

Água Viva is a quasi-plotless novel, one that tries to relate the impassioned passing of instants directly: "Esses instantes que decorrem no ar que respiro: em fogos de artifício eles espocam mudos no espaço"[31] and where "the next instant is the unknown." To approach the fire of instants, Lispector indeed explores the interplay of words Mallarmé described, lighting each other up without the poet's direction. In *Água Viva*, the narrating voice takes on the delicate task of transmitting this scintillation to the reader without breaking its movement through a possessive gesture. "I direct nothing. Not even my own words," one reads.[32] "Entende-me:" "Understand me," the voice pleads, "escrevo-te uma onomatopéia, convulsão da linguagem. Transmito-te não uma historia mas apenas palavras que vivem do som."[33] The phrase resonates, indeed, with the perspective of sensation Deleuze underscores through Francis Bacon's "no story to tell" and Cézanne's "to forget everything," adding a paradoxical element, in addressing its reader directly, to plead for "understanding," of a different sort. This "I" does not, of course, transcend the writing; it only emerges at the level of the text, as an effect of that interplay of words and convulsion of language. And it suggests these conditions apply as well to the "you" it addresses. Because of this ephemeral meeting of an "I" and a "you" breathing together throughout a sequence of instants, Lispector thought it appropriate for this text to be defined as a novel (*romance*). In fact, a better translation of the term, more literal, would be "romance."

31. Lispector, *AV*, 9. "Those instants that elapse in the air I breathe: in fireworks they mutely explode in space."

32. Lispector, 27.

33. Lispector, 25. "I write you an onomatopoeia, convulsion of language. I transmit to you not a story but only words that live on sound."

On the one hand, Lispector presents an experimental text exclusively interested in "o instante-jà" (the now-instant) that unleashes an encounter with life's perpetual dynamic of birth and death, figured, for example, by "um pirilampo que acende e apaga, acende e apaga" (a firefly that goes on and off, on and off),[34] and by fireworks exploding mutely in space, and with the limits of meaning and its convulsive effects, on which more later. On the other hand, Horn's *Vatnasafn/Library of Water* is a public installation with a materially visible commentary on global warming, located in a remote, sparsely populated coast where the weather plays a central role in the life of the local community. Of course the instant of the world as landscape today is, in an important sense, one endangered by humans. In order to examine *Vatnasafn/Library of Water* in May 2009, I surely had to add to the CO2 footprint by traveling to Stykkishólmur with a research grant. Additionally, as we know, at the particular moment of my visit, the world economy had just crashed a few months earlier, and Iceland was particularly affected by the financial crisis. And yet awareness of those factors in that moment and the present one does not, as such, give access to the instant of the world in the rigorous terms of sensation Cézanne's, Mallarmé's, and Lispector's works propose. The aesthetic mode of attention required to access the now-instant is not synonymous with a critical awareness of human impact on the environment and on the social under late capitalism. To plunge into an aesthetic mode of attention to the passing minute of the world is, Cézanne said, to forget everything else, and thus to remember, for once, what is perpetually forgotten while everything else is kept in mind, under utilitarian, moral, and even critical viewpoints built on oppositional dialectics. But then, in accessing the passing minute there is, rather than disregard for the ground and site where human and nonhuman life occur, an encounter with the dimension of becoming, or one might also say, of crisis, as I will show.

Rendre le Temps Sensible

Deleuze formalized Cézanne's claim on the passing minute of the world, when he stated: "rendre le Temps sensible en lui-même, tâche commune au peintre, au musicien, parfois à l'écrivain" (to render Time sensible in

34. Lispector, 15.

itself . . . [is] the task common to the musician, the painter, and sometimes the writer).[35] This is no trivial or casual task within the aesthetics Deleuze puts forth, but instead the ultimate sensation that an artist can grapple with. In sensation, "each quality constitutes a field that stands on its own without ceasing to interfere with the others (the 'pathic' moment)."[36] How does Time stand on its own in the "pathic moment"? Endorsing here phenomenologists Maurice Merleau-Ponty and Henri Maldiney, who before him explored Cézanne's work, Deleuze sees in this liberation of qualities "the basis for every possible aesthetic."[37] Thus, sensation beyond figuration is a problem of releasing the autonomous value of qualities and enduring their effects. Such effects are somatic, psychical, conceptual, temporal, and cosmological.

Lispector, who in *Água Viva* undoubtedly pursues the task of "rendering Time sensible in itself," seems to know the musician and painter are after this, too. The epigraph by abstract painter Michel Seuphor is about the spiritual goal of nonrepresentational painting, concerned with "les royaumes incommuniqués de l'esprit" (the incommunicable kingdoms of the spirit);[38] moreover, comparisons of writing to painting and to music abound throughout the text. Sometimes the writing voice laments the slowness of words, when compared to painting in the attempt at grasping the now-instant. Sometimes the writing, initially declared "a string quartet," becomes an *adagio* for a while, and sometimes the writing voice reports on being transfigured by the music she hears.[39] As for Horn, her *Vatnasafn/Library of Water*, as well as her insistent return to words in many of her projects, in particular to modernist literary

35. Deleuze, *Francis Bacon: Logique de la sensation* (Paris: Seuil, 2002), 63; (*FB* 64).

36. Deleuze, *FB*, n1, 178.

37. Deleuze, 178. If Cézanne and French phenomenology offer instances of this process, Bacon and Deleuze continue this tradition, insisting on sensation's performance of a direct transmission, without "a story to tell," and on its incessant passage across different "levels" and "domains" that causes "deformations of the body," so prominent in Bacon's canvases. See *FB*, 36.

38. The full epigraph by Michel Seuphor reads: "There must be a kind of painting totally free of the dependence on the figure—or object—which, like music, illustrates nothing, tells no story, and launches no myth. Such painting would simply evoke the incommunicable kingdoms of the spirit, where dream becomes thought, where line becomes existence.

39. Lispector, *AV*, 18–19.

texts, show that she finds a specific literary function of words that adds to what visual and spatial artforms make possible. This function, aligned with the Mallarmean word, seeks, too, to make Time sensible in itself. To Lispector and Horn, I find, such a undertaking is inseparable from a certain ethics of care that activates the processes of *captar*, contemplation, and looking after the world in the transmission of sensation.

With *Água Viva* and *Vatnasafn/Library of Water* I'd like to show, for one, that Deleuze's claim about *le temps* needs to be read at once as *time, temperature, and weather*. It is no mere accident that all three phenomena are referred to as "le temps" in French. Horn and Lispector, engaging yet other languages and media, highlight the important fact that, when approached from the perspective of sensation—as Deleuze and Guattari, Mallarmé, Cézanne, and French phenomenology do, to different extents—the problem of "Time" involves meteorology, thermodynamics, and temperament. Second, to make time felt is an interstitial experience and experiment (as with *temps*, we have noted that the French language condenses these two words in *expérience*). Making time sensible is a task that brings the writer to the limits of language and the painter or plastic artist to search for words; both meet at a nondiscursive intersection of

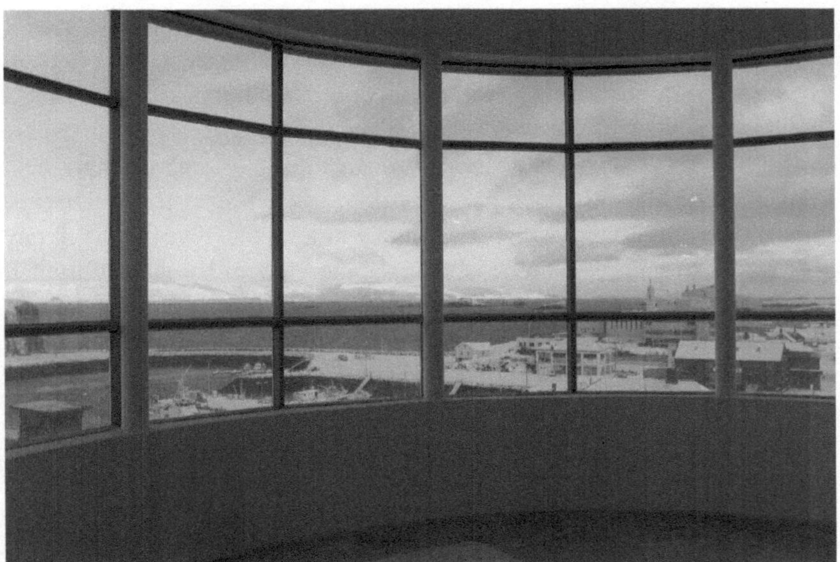

Figure 6.1. *Vatnasafn/Library of Water*, Roni Horn, 2007 (View of the harbor from the library). Photo: Roni Horn. Courtesy of Artangel and the artist.

word and figure.[40] Moreover, making time sensible logically implies the transmission of sensation *to a reader*, and this symptomatic reader is crucial to the aesthetic clinic.

Vatnasafn/Library of Water comments on global warming by proposing a reflection on the link between humans and the weather. Facing the harbor where fishing and ferry boat trips to the West Fjords take place, the installation was set up in 2007 in a building that, in fact, had served as the town's public library, until they had the fortunate problem of not being able to fit their holdings in that space. Today, as a result of Horn's intervention, this former library holds a collection of water brought in from twenty-four glaciers around the country into large glass columns that stand distributed across the library's main room from floor to ceiling, a collection of adjectives in English and Icelandic that refer to both weather conditions and human moods, inlaid on rubber floor tiles in this same room, and a collection of local individuals' accounts on the weather in their lives. Horn emphasizes the fact that the weather plays a major role in the town of Stykkishólmur, just as water matters everywhere in Iceland.

Talking about the weather is commonly considered impersonal in a superficial sense; one talks about the weather to avoid personal or serious subjects. But the weather, of course, can be serious life-and-death business; the instant of the world passing over the St. Victoire for Cézanne is a crucial issue. At *Vatnasafn/Library of Water*, Horn offers an extraordinary landscape; its water collection highlights the fact that a simultaneous view of the twenty-four glaciers in the library is impossible to the human eye, and it does so through a play of multiplying reflections of these glass columns of each other, as well as of the waterscape surrounding the library, which the large windows make visible to library visitors. Furthermore, even an encompassing view of the library itself is impossible, for it cannot be grasped by abstracting it from the seascape, the weather, and the specificity of each passing instant of the world, and each of its passing visitors.

Inside the library, *Água Viva* shows more clearly that its title also evokes environmental phenomena—not only a running water stream;

40. Deleuze acknowledges this in Bacon's statements about his painting having "no story to tell" and "nothing to represent," by referring to Bacon's painted bodies as "figures" after Jean-François Lyotard, whose *Discours, Figure* he cites at the beginning of the essay. The latter's concept of the figural is grounded in Freud's work.

the ocean tide under the full moon is colloquially called "águas vivas" in Brazilian Portuguese, and this term also commonly refers to "jellyfish." It has to do with making *le Temps* sensible, and it emphasizes the paradox of enclosing "água viva" in the confines of a book, which is also present in Horn's gesture with the glacial waters in the library. In both cases, the result is rather that water floods the limits, advancing a different reading practice, where entering the work is unavoidable. I will thus have to accept my momentary condition of immersion in these waters by offering my own account of visiting Horn's *Library of Water*, in order to provide an inevitably partial reading. This will be the reading, or the revisiting, with *Água Viva* in hand, of a moment of reading in the library.

To the Lighthouse

It should have occurred to me that this library might not be open at regular hours in the month of May, just before the tourist season begins. On my first morning in Stykkishólmur, I got up and walked across town to the top of the low hill where *Vatnasafn/Library of Water* stands, facing the sea with its lighthouse windows. I must have walked around its perimeter twice, looking for an entrance while taking photographs of the scene, under a clear blue sky in a kind of daylight whose brightness was unusual to me. I was already in awe after the bus trip from Reykjavik to the town, during which I saw landscapes of volcanoes, sheep farms on hills, glaciers, turquoise pools and waterfalls, and the sea, before it got to be midnight, without getting dark. Trees were rare, of course, and there was nothing close to a crowd. In the two days I spent there, I'm quite sure I interacted with no more than six people, and didn't see too many more. For someone like me, born and raised among more than twenty million people in Mexico City, this was a perfect illustration of the word "exotic."

Probably at the second stroll around the empty 1950s building I started thinking what a shame it would be to have made it all the way to this site and only get to peek at the installation from outside. I have since somewhat improved my planning skills, and have learned to make sure I don't show up to these overseas research sessions unexpectedly. But you must understand that when one grows up in Mexico City, one learns that it is useless to plan too much, that announcing one's ETA is practically an automatic jinx, and that the art of improvisation and

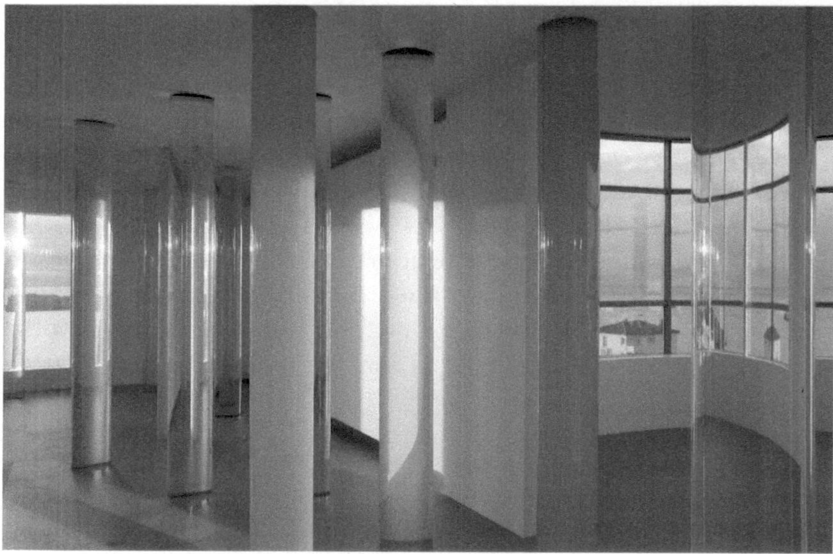

Figure 6.2. *Vatnasafn/Library of Water*, Roni Horn, 2007. Commissioned and produced by Artangel. 24 floor-to-ceiling glass columns (12" dia. × 118" each) filled with water from unique glacial sources. Rubber floor tiles 1.5" thick, with rubber inlaid adjectives in English and Icelandic. 1,500 ft. Photograph: Stefan Altenburger. Courtesy of Artangel and the artist.

determination often yields better encounters. I was still a graduate student when I took this research trip. It has taken me all my graduate education and professional life in the United States to operate according to next month's and next year's calendar, promptly announcing that I will be ten minutes late.

The huge glass window offered ample view of what was kept inside, and yet the viewpoint was not quite right. I wasn't sure why not; the glass wall prevented me, of course, from walking around the room to read all of the rubber tiles, but I had a sense that there was more to the difference, and that it was not merely a practical problem of visibility. To my relief, a woman then climbed up the little hill and greeted me. She was the town librarian, who had spotted me from the new library nearby. She was in charge of the *Library of Water* and would have expected an appointment for my visit at this time of year. In any case, she invited me in, took the time to show me around, and after I explained my purpose of studying this library for a project in art and literary criticism, she entrusted me with the library collections, leaving me alone for as long as I wanted, while she got back to work at the new public library. Her receptiveness seemed faithful to Horn's statement that for this artwork she had imagined "a lighthouse where the viewers become the light."[41] One cannot stop the light from entering through all the glass in this building. I could not know, before entering, what becoming the light would be like.

In the backroom I found the collection called testimonies by community members, where each told a story about their particular relationship to the weather. Horn entitled it *Weather Reports You*, aptly inverting the usual subject–object positions. How, I wondered, does weather report "me," a foreigner in this town? On one of this room's walls, I noticed, hung an archive for the water extraction and installation processes that led to the installation in the main room, hydrographical maps of Iceland, and the library's floor plans. In the larger, main room, facing the harbor, was *Water, Selected*: the twenty-four columns of melted glacial waters, and *You Are the Weather*, made up of one hundred adjectives in Icelandic and English that sprinkled the rubber tiles covering this room's floor. This composition of water, words, glass, rubber, and light, I thought, is what I have come all the way to this town to view and read.

Weather-Appropriate Reading

It was interesting to find myself completely alone in this library, even though Horn had proposed this project to the town mayor as a community center. In addition to the installations, the emptied-out space would be repurposed for the people to gather for recitals, chess classes, a film club. An artist's residence was set up on the lower floor of the two-story building, but I didn't cross paths with the resident, either. Instead of other humans, these traces of human life and its various modes of relating to the environment surrounded me. And yet, unlike the risk of not going inside the library, the absence of other people did not make the visit useless. In fact, solitude helped me to notice that this particular scene one steps into welcomes and emphasizes a multiplicity of modes of attention, reading, and dwelling. This freedom, suggested from the

41. Cited in Lingwood, "Journey to the Library," 17.

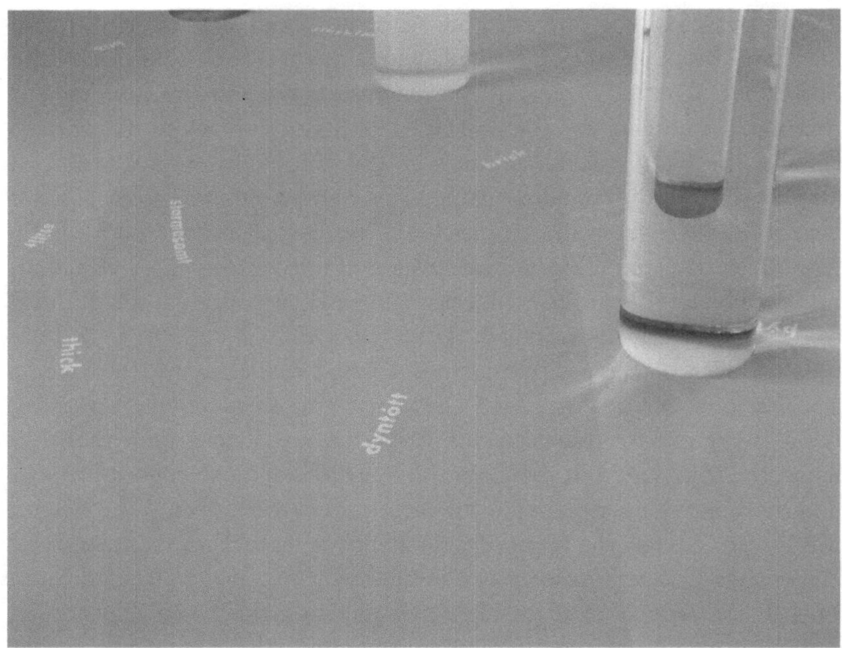

Figure 6.3. *Vatnasafn/Library of Water*, Roni Horn, 2007. Commissioned and produced by Artangel. Photograph: Stefan Altenburger. Courtesy of Artangel and the artist.

outset in the site's bilingual name *Vatnasafn/Library of Water*, in fact distinguishes this installation from other instances of a contemporary artform that can force a single perspective on its participant.[42]

Guattari in *The Three Ecologies* points to the different ecological domains of environment, social relations, and human subjectivity (in this order for Guattari) that together form "an ethico-political articulation" or "*ecosophy*."[43] Horn's installation speaks to these three ecologies, to whose articulation sensation proves essential. The becoming and the event that sensation simultaneously unleashes involve a direct encounter, not only with one's own and others' "Thingly" dimension, as we have noted in

42. For an analysis of the position of installation art with regard to ideology and aesthetic autonomy see Juliane Rebentisch, *Aesthetics of Installation Art* (Berlin: Sternberg Press, 2012).

43. Félix Guattari, *The Three Ecologies*, ed. Ian Pindar and Paul Sutton (London: Continuum, 2005), 28.

the previous experiments, but also with the world in Cézanne's sense, or with what Deleuze and Guattari call "the Cosmos," to think "the encounter between worlds rather than remaining within an enclosure of one's own world."[44]

Raising awareness about humans' relationship and responsibility to the environment is one of *Vatnasafn/Library of Water*'s various important points, and if it is efficient in this regard, it is perhaps less by its direct commentary on the melting glaciers than by sheltering viewers and inviting them to spend time among the water columns, even forgetting about them or about the water's provenance. One is allowed and even invited to be in that space without "contemplating it," in an intentional way at least, and instead, for example, remain focused on playing chess with a fellow visitor. In this situation one ceases to be the viewer of the artwork with a privileged, distanced perspective in order to become a part of the scenario. And in giving up the external standpoint as the only possibility for critical thought, replaced by the constraint to share space inside the artwork with the glacial water, the artwork removes humans from the position underlying global warming and other environmental problems: one of mastery over their surroundings. In emptying out this typical position of mastery to expose it, the work exerts a critical function and points out the critical situation, the crisis and pressure of time that the viewer is in, together with the fast-melting glaciers, the situation that has turned them into precious elements to be collected and encased behind glass. But one is in a library after all, and one might, instead of forgetting about the artwork, choose to interact with this multipurpose

44. Janae Sholtz, *The Invention of a People: Heidegger and Deleuze on Art and the Political* (Edinburgh: Edinburgh University Press, 2015), 126. Sholtz points out that this concern is already present in the late Heidegger as "the planetary," a development from the creative tension between world and earth which imply disclosure and concealment in his earlier work. Deleuze and Guattari's "chaosmosis" fuels Verena Andermatt Conley's work on ecopolitics and the ethics of care, since it offers a way to think unpredictable transformations across various human and nonhuman environments. Conley has compellingly shown that this ecopolitics and ethics presuppose consideration of the world we inhabit. She examines the spatial turn in French philosophy as grounding a political ecology and a care of the possible. This spatial turn, she proposes, would shift emphasis away from time, or at least away from time exclusively. Verena Andermatt Conley, *Spatial Ecologies* (Liverpool: Liverpool University Press, 2012), 2. See also Conley, "The Care of the Possible," *Cultural Politics*, 12.3 (2016): 339–354. The vantage point of sensation, however, shows the relevance of caring about "making time sensible."

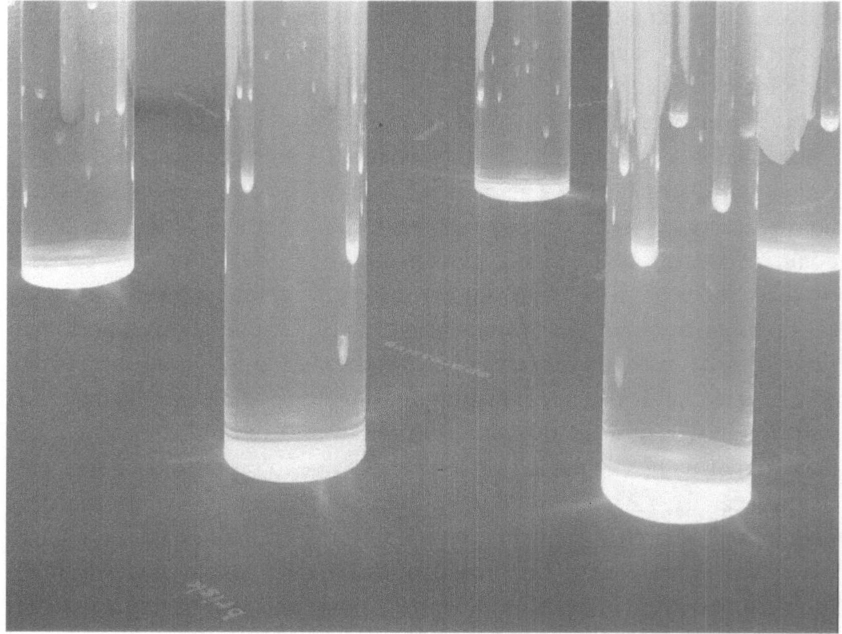

Figure 6.4. *Vatnasafn/Library of Water*, Roni Horn, 2007. Commissioned and produced by Artangel. Photograph: Stefan Altenburger. Courtesy of Artangel and the artist.

site as a reader, and in this role something *beside* the work's commentary on global warming might come forth, no less engaged with the environment, or with the encounters or intersections of ecologies, as Guattari would say. This role of reader cannot restore mastery over the work, since the work calls for its own mode of reading, and thus to read is to accept the work's unique constraints, without a guarantee of mastering anything. The place remains, after all, known as a library. In adapting to the library's strangeness, one's own strangeness might emerge too, since, first of all, how is one to read water?

The main room is covered by a 1,500-square-foot rubber floor made of large square tiles, where the inlaid, bilingual collection of words features adjectives usually applied to both weather conditions and to temperament and moods of individuals: "bright," "calm," "kyrrt," "mollulegur," "sunny," "glettið," "brisk." The attention it draws to different languages reminds me of the fact I mentioned earlier, that in French one would say "le temps" and "le tempérament" for weather and temperament, two words from related Latin origins (*tempus* and *attemperare*). The floor's title, *You Are the Weather (Iceland)* echoes the one hundred portraits of the girl I described earlier in this chapter, whose installation along four walls reveals transformations in mood and weather that defy the stabilization of identity and body image. The affirmation "You Are the Weather" that gives this element of the library its title, together with the variations in human and atmospheric states indicated, invite one to consider one's body as a site of fluctuating intensities that may contradict and harmonize with each other, taking over sporadically, like the changes in light, temperature, and water do in this world. At stake is the Body without Organs this book has considered with regard to the subject of the drives and sublimation.

The schizoanalysts ask: "what is the individuality of a day, a season, or an event?"[45] In the medieval concept of *Haecceity* proposed by Duns Scotus, Deleuze and Guattari found an expression for nonqualitative modes of individuation. Sheer, impersonal, and at once singular becomings, *Haecceities* are differences that, rather than pointing to the thing's "whatness" or *quidditas*, which is subject to generalization, go further than specific form to mark an absolutely distinct "thisness," *haec*. They enable the idea of a quivering yet distinct individuation of accidental forms with their own temporalities and intensities. Such sensible forms are no longer subordinated to a substance, a thing, a person and especially not to a subject understood as the *stable* underlying foundation of a life form.

> A season, a winter, a summer, an hour, a date have a perfect individuality lacking nothing, even though this individuality is different from that of a thing or a subject. They are haecceities in the sense that they consist entirely of relations of movement and rest between molecules or particles, capacities to affect and be affected. When demonology expounds upon the diabolical art of local movements and transports of affect, it also notes the importance of rain, hail, wind, pestilential air, or air polluted by noxious particles, favorable conditions for these transports.[46]

The examples this passage lists—from "a season" to "an hour" to "hail" and "polluted air"—are all constitutive of *le temps* in its singularity, and

45. Deleuze and Guattari, *ATP*, 253.

46. Deleuze and Guattari, 261.

one is invited to approach them beyond the role of qualifying a subject's experience, an object, or a situation. They are viewed as molecular relations of different speeds and transmissive capacities (in terms of "demonological transports of affect"[47])—and not according to a standardized measure, not even according to someone's perspective.

It's not by chance that examples of haecceities in *A Thousand Plateaus*—Federico García Lorca's "A las cinco de la tarde" (five in the evening) or Michel Tournier's "meteors"—come from literature *and* insist on meteorology, thermodynamics, and on floating time rather than chronology, a criterion that corresponds to substantive modes of individuation. In fact, the haecceity, I believe, is fundamentally an aesthetic problem of *making Time sensible in itself*, which Deleuze later considered central to musician, painter, and "sometimes the writer," as previously mentioned. If he also found this "rendre le Temps sensible" to be a task "beyond all measure or cadence,"[48] it is because *le Temps* here is not subordinated to something or someone else. Deleuze thus investigated, with Guattari and beyond, two different temporalities: Chronos and Aeon.

> *Aeon:* the indefinite time of the event, the floating line that knows only speeds and continually divides that which transpires into an already-there that is at the same time not-yet-here, a simultaneous too-late and too-early, a something that is both going to happen and has just happened. *Chronos:* the time of measure that situates things and persons, develops a form, and determines a subject.[49]

Aeonic time, to which haecceities or sensations belong, enjoys the strangely simultaneous not-yet and already that escapes the present of

47. Earlier in this chapter of *A Thousand Plateaus* the schizoanalysts consider *The Hammer of Witches*, a Medieval Inquisition manual, to examine in different cases the status of becoming-animal and of the transformations it involves for individual bodies. Becoming-animal is thus not about humans that turn into werewolves, for instance. Yet the manual's affirmation that there are nonetheless pacts between the Devil and witches, which can involve the devil taking over animal bodies, allows the schizoanalysts to raise the issue of "transporting accidents and affects" across bodies of different species. It is this liberation of the accident and affect, or intensity, that they then define as "an individual, a Haecceity, that enters into composition with other degrees, other intensities . . ." (253).

48. Deleuze, *FB*, 64.

49. Deleuze and Guattari, *ATP*, 262.

ordinary consciousness, allows the schizoanalysts to insist that the artwork's sensation "preserves and is preserved in itself," such that a sculpture's pose, for instance, is maintained "for five thousand years, a gesture that no longer depends on whoever made it."[50]

To Deleuze and Guattari, "the artist's greatest difficulty is to make [the artwork] *stand up on its own*," that is, according to its own logic, "which exceeds any lived."[51] It's certainly possible, and common, to ignore Aeon and organize life within the time of measure, just as it is possible to ignore or reject the unconscious.[52] But if getting the sensation to stand on its own is so difficult to the artist, it is because the intensities that the unconscious and the sensation bear are too much for Chronos, or for what a person can live. Lyotard, prompting a look at the function of expression in tragedy for the development of the psychoanalytic clinic, suggests that, in terms of "a space of desire," "the difference between art and analysis is perhaps no greater than that between the desire to see the desire and the desire to give it expression."[53] The "desire" mobilizing all this involves the fantasy[54] that finds no substitute or place in common language; it cannot as such adapt to Chronos.

Tournier's novel *Les météores* allows the schizoanalysts to highlight the consequences over a subject of opening up to Aeonic time:

> Between the extreme slownesses and vertiginous speeds of geology and astronomy, Michel Tournier places meteorology, where meteors live at our pace: "A cloud forms in the sky like an image in my brain, the wind blows like I breathe, a rainbow spans the horizon for as long as my heart needs to reconcile itself to life, the summer passes like vacation drifts by." But is it by chance that in Tournier's novel this certitude can come only to a twin hero who is deformed and desubjectified, and has acquired a certain ubiquity?[55]

Tournier's beautiful phrase could all too quickly be placed within a romantic framework, in which Nature reflects the transcendental *I* observing

50. Deleuze and Guattari, *What is Philosophy?*, 163.

51. Deleuze and Guattari, 164.

52. On this attitude see Freud's "The Unconscious." *SE* XIV: 166–171.

53. Lyotard, "Principales tendances . . . ," 136.

54. I have discussed fantasy in the first part of this book.

55. Deleuze and Guattari, *ATP*, 261.

it, so the schizoanalysts prevent this with their rhetorical question, insofar as haecceities are not the matter of a subject of consciousness. It is not by chance that "this certitude" happens to the character Paul, a twin, "deformed and desubjectified" by separation from his brother, by travels around the world, and by the loss of an arm and leg. In all these accidents, a kind of passage outside and dissipation of the *I* takes place, beginning with the perception in space of a twin body. To be fit for the sensations and the enunciations that unfold in synchrony with the atmosphere, or that are even inseparable from it ("no one," he thinks regarding another character, "has a greater calling than I to understand your destiny where the meteors, the elements, and your heart blend inextricably"[56]), the body and "I" must have undergone a transformation. Thus the final chapter of *Les météores*, where the passage cited by the schizoanalysts appears, is called, "L'âme déployée" "the unfurled soul." The subject who encounters the temporality of Aeon unbinds, as a condition for joining this meteorological temps.

To unbind, as Deleuze calls it, following and connecting psychoanalysis and Hume, entails the dissolution of preestablished meaning, form, measure, resemblance. "The sensory-motor scheme breaks down from within," writes Deleuze in *The Time-Image*.[57] A gap opens up; Deleuze, with Kant, calls it the fracture of the *I* by the form of pure, empty time, and it is upon inhabiting it—at the expense of the subject's unity and self-image—that individuations become a matter of interactions of speeds at varying intensities and that what Deleuze calls *rendre le Temps sensible* can take place. The temporality of Aeon implies a direct transmission of intensities, without the detour, or bind, of a self. Without the "story to tell" that comes with repression, *le Temps* cuts across bodies, and the drive's "*tempo*" connects to "le rythme du déroulement météorologique" "the rhythm of meteorological unfolding."[58] Indeed, this sounds like sublimation. Thus Paul, whose left arm and leg have been amputated, notes, after deciding to embrace pain and to recover in it everything he has lost, that he feels the left border of his body spread across the planet "in the vehemence of the meteors"[59] and his final sensation is of the shining sun, which provokes

56. Michel Tournier, *Les météores* (Paris: Gallimard, 1975), 509.

57. Deleuze, *Cinéma 2*, 58.

58. Tournier, *Les météores*, 622.

59. Tournier, 624.

> l'évaporation de la neige *sans aucun dégel*. Au-dessus des masses de neige dures et intactes tremble un brouillard transparent et irisé. La neige devient vapeur sans fondre, sans couler, sans mollir.
>
> Cela s'appelle: sublimation.[60]

On May 19, 2009 (but this is still the calendar of Chronos), around noon, *You Are The Weather (Iceland)* (or was it "me"?) was filled with sunlight, and the tiles' ochre warmed my vision, made it fizz, somehow, between the scattered adjectives and the play of shadows cast by the window frames and parts of my body. I took pictures, slowly pacing around.

The "you" the piece addresses is proposed as a momentary fluctuation in this room. One is, as this "you," a relevant agent in the composition and at the same time decentered, since this role is concerned with how one affects and alters the space among other elements, which means an "objective" and total perception of the piece is unavailable. Sharing the large room with these scattered words, and a view of the harbor, *Water, Selected* also scatters throughout the space its set of glass columns that stand from floor to ceiling, like a translucent Parthenon (figure 6.2). This scattered aspect of the room and the reading constraint it poses reflect Mallarmé's spatialization of the poem in his groundbreaking *Un coup de dés jamais n'abolira le hasard*. But the scattered state of words and their power to light each other up freely was already present, as previously noticed, in his *Crisis of verse* essay, where the encountered "exquisite crisis" is, as it turns out, an effect of a thunderstorm that causes the narrator to seek shelter in a library.

Like throws of the dice, the rays of light thrown onto the rubber surface in *You Are The Weather* keep letting chance in, making the text resonate, vibrate and speak newly each time. Readers in *Vatnasafn/ Library of Water* engage on the same plane with the words they encounter only by moving around and across the room in no particular order or direction, while gazing down, directly or through the glass columns that curve the floor and letters. The physical activity to which participants are invited in order to read prevents a full grasp of the whole text and its unification under any given individual in a position of mastery over

60. Tournier, 625. "The snow's evaporation *without thawing*. Above the hard and intact masses of snow a mist trembles transparent and iridescent. The snow becomes steam without melting, without dripping, without softening. / That is called: sublimation."

its stabilized meaning. Horn sets up these words to affect the scene, landscape, reader, moment in ways unpredictable to her, too, by a strategy of leveling all elements or temporalities down to meet each other as *instant of the world*. In *Crise de vers*, the weather's presence as an uncontrollable, decisive, and constraining factor is noteworthy. The essay reproduces as its first paragraph the beginning of another text from 1895 called *Averses ou critique* (the title plays on "a verse" in English and *averses* ("downpours") in French, and is translated as *Downpours or Criticism*).[61] Mallarmé's reflection on the crisis of verse and the different dimensions of words begins with a languorous turn toward the library because of bad weather:

> Tout à l'heure, en abandon de geste, avec la lassitude que cause le mauvais temps désespérant une après l'autre après-midi, je fis retomber, sans une curiosité mais ce lui semble avoir tout lu voici vingt ans, l'effilé de multicolores perles qui plaque la pluie, encore, au chatoiement des brochures dans la bibliothèque. Maint ouvrage, sous la verroterie du rideau, alignera sa propre scintillation: j'aime comme en le ciel mûr, contre la vitre, à suivre des lueurs d'orage.[62]

"Le mauvais temps" (bad weather) affects the confined author's mood here. Resigned, he enters the library, causing a scintillating effect, as the raindrops reflect on the glass book case and the books in turn shine under the lightning. Given the previous steps in this chapter, it should be clear by now that this is much more than an atmospheric detail, decorating the essay whose famous, main statement diagnoses literature with "une exquise crise, fondamentale" "a fundamental, exquisite crisis." It is in the thunderstorm, under its intermittent glimmer, that another interplay of

61. On Mallarmé's play on weather and verse, see Jacques Derrida, "La double séance II." *La dissemination* (Paris: Seuil, 1972).

62. Mallarmé OC, 364. "A minute ago, dropping my hand, with the lassitude that is caused by one afternoon after another of bad weather, I let fall—without curiosity, though it felt as though I had read everything twenty years ago—the string of multicolored pearls left by the rain, reflected in the glass of a case full of books. Many a work, under the beaded curtain, will align its own illumination: I enjoy following their light, as under a saturated cloud, against the window, one follows storm lights across the sky" (Divagations, 201).

texts and words emerges, beyond the poet's control and, as the author states, disconcerting to the traditional French reader at the end of the nineteenth century. The weather, *le temps*, introduces a shift in the reader facing the literature of "the times."[63] Johnson's translation interestingly makes an explicit comparison between, on the one hand, the books that align their own illumination under "the beaded curtain" of raindrops, and, on the other, "the storm lights across the sky." In the French text, however, the iridescence and play of reflections causes the syntax to lose a clear distinction of domains, too. "Maint ouvrage, sous la verroterie du rideau, alignera sa propre scintillation: j'aime comme en le ciel mûr, contre la vitre, à suivre des lueurs d'orage." By its unusual syntax and shift in focus, from the solid books to the scintillation and lightening, the text performs, indeed, a play of reflections between books and thunderstorm that stands on its own and becomes its own strategy for reading.

Once verse—like a thunderstorm (*averse*)—"breaks," as the text states, the meter, rhythm, and tempo of the French language becomes disjointed, scattered. The crisis in question is a matter of *temps* as well, in more than one way, then. The state of "la parole" "the word/speech" (perhaps a particular kind of weather) that Mallarmé designates as specific to literature at the end of his essay is called "virtual," a subtle "vibrancy" that "emanates" from the oscillation between "meaning and sonority," while the vibrancy released in the literary treatment of language—"un mot total, neuf, étranger à la langue et comme incantatoire" (a total word, new, foreign to the language and as incantatory)—is extremely subtle and almost ungraspable.[64] This is, quite precisely, "expression of the desire," which is without a signifier in language, in figural space as Lyotard discerned it.[65] Approaching this virtual mist calls for a scattering

63. Mallarmé situates this crisis after Victor Hugo, "the giant of verse."

64. Mallarmé, OC, 368.

65. Lyotard mentions Cézanne and Mallarmé as instances of an "effort at transgression" that makes them, alongside Joyce and Picasso, "associated with the advent of desire that constitutes the history of the West, and that leads it to an ever-more-radical criticsm or constraint in poetry or the plastic arts" ("Principales tendances . . . ," 133). This is relevant to think of the genre of *Crise de vers*, between criticism and poetry. Lyotard points out that the spatialization of the poem in *Un coup de dés* "radically deprives articulated language of its prosaic function of communication, revealing in it a power that exceeds it: the power to be "seen" [. . .] to figure and not only to signify." *Discourse, Figure*, trans. Antony Hudek and Mary Lydon (Minneapolis: University of Minnesota Press, 2011), 61.

in space where the vibrancies, emanations, and oscillations between meaning and sound can bounce and shimmer. In Horn's library this bounce and shimmer occur through rubber and glass, while the virtual mist rises through the play between different languages and tempos, to which we now turn, adding *Água Viva* as a twenty-fifth water source and a third language to Horn's *Library*.

In *Vatnasafn/Library of Water* with *Água Viva*

As I had said, "the now-instant," written as a single hyphenated word, is the main, if elusive character in Lispector's *Água Viva.* Necessary to this now-instant is the impersonal attunement of an "it" that, the text suggests, lies within, behind the self-consciousness of "I" and "me":

> Mas há também o mistério do impessoal que é o "it": eu tenho o impessoal dentro de mim e não é corrupto e apodrecível pelo pessoal que às vezes me encharca: mas seco-me ao sol e sou um impessoal de caroço seco e germinativo. Meu pessoal é húmus na terra e vive do apodrecimento. Meu "it" é duro como uma pedra-seixo.[66]

One notices that the impersonal dimension of "the it" sought by the writing voice is her very core. One can say she turns her attention, and the readers', toward an instance of life detached from the person that is perpetuated in the plane of identity, and whose truth is "humus," a component sustained from decomposition. She claims, not that there is a pure *self* to reach, but rather a radically impersonal *it* that cannot be assimilated by *I* (nor by "she" or "he" as the text states later). This "it" with its singular definite article brings to mind, of course, Freud's third-person singular pronoun *es*, which becomes the Latin *id* in the

66. Lispector, *AV*, 28. But there's also the mystery of the impersonal that is the "it": I have the impersonal inside of me and it is not corrupt and perishable by the personal that sometimes stagnates me: but I dry out in the sun and am an impersonal of dry and germinative seed. My personal is humus in the earth and it lives from putrefaction. My "it" is hard like a pebble.

English translation and means "it."[67] The impersonal "it" this passage from *Água Viva* highlights would clear the view, then, and the passage through impersonal Time or the world in its own reality, rather than my own.

The "it" is also a kind of refrain in the text, spinning words to the point where meaning collapses: "A trascendência dentro de mim é o "it" vivo e mole e tem o pensamento que uma ostra tem."[68] This provocation of not only figuring transcendence as a humble oyster, but of even considering the kind of thought an oyster might have exposes its reader to an irreducible opacity of almost formless life.[69] All this to tell us the exact nature of an essential "it" behind thought. As the addressed "you," the reader is sought also on this living, soft, formless plane. The plane of "it" is necessary in *Água Viva* because it is nothing else than *time made sensible*: "It é elemento puro. É material do instante do tempo."[70] Not just time, not just the instant, but the *material* of the instant of time, which defies all form and measure.

The correlation of "it" to becoming (or the now-instant) involves some complications. First, it turns on its head the traditional philosophical and religious distinction between the finite or "perishable" order Lispector's passage points to, on the one hand, and its eternal counterpart, distributed in body and soul, respectively. The writing voice's nonperishable part is not "I" but instead "it," located in the reverse side of thought, rather than in self-consciousness. Furthermore, this nonperishable "it" is not outside time in the way the soul is in Platonist and Christian theories. It may be instead closer to the timelessness of the unconscious, as described by Freud, who uses this terminology to insist that unconscious processes are not ordered according to a time sequence, "not altered by the passage of time" (*SE* XIV, 187). But if this leads to understanding the "it" as a

---

67. As noted in chapter 3, Freud himself gleans "it" for his topology of the psyche from Groddeck, who wrote *The Book of the It*. Freud, *SE* XIX: 23.

68. Lispector, 28. "The transcendence inside me is the living and soft 'it' and has the thought that an oyster has."

69. This is the dimension of the letter for Lacan, distinct from that of the signifier, as explained in chapters 4 and 5. It is not a metaphor, but a letter that resists symbolization.

70. Lispector, 32. "*It* is pure element. It is material of the instant of time."

cluster of immutable traces concerned with disparate moments,[71] then "it" could seem incompatible with the perspective of incessant change expressed by becoming. Yet not only does Freud himself highlight the inadequacy of the spatial comparison, inasmuch as the psyche is not spatial; in his 1915 presentation of the characteristics of the unconscious, he discusses, just before introducing timelessness, the mobility of the "cathectic intensities," through the processes of condensation and displacement.[72] Perhaps the schizoanalysts' distinction between an "experimental" and a "fixed" unconscious[73] implies, above all, a different concept of time to the Aristotelian one; the unconscious, then, is less "timeless" than detached from historicism and chronology, and one could instead say, with Lyotard, that it is "omnitemporal."[74] A glimpse at this experimental unconscious engages the process of sublimation, where the intensities of the "it" can take on some kind of sensible form without repression, and where this contact with sensible forms continues the production of the unconscious rather than expressing a content already there. At the extreme point invoked by Cézanne, of "becoming that minute itself," there is no longer a division between "it" and the world in its own reality. If Kant defines Time as "the form of interiority," in the experimental unconscious a Möbian topology is instead necessary, to conceive of "it" in terms of extimacy, which is at work in "becoming."

Água Viva as "jellyfish" comes to mind again, upon reading *Água Viva's* suggestion that "it" has the thought of an oyster. For, the transparent, amorphous, gelatinous life form made up almost entirely of water suggests the materiality and texture of the *it*, all while remaining untouchable, at least not touchable without burning consequences.[75] In *Vatnasafn/Library of Water*, stillness highlights the human eye's inadequacy to notice the

71. Or as a city where different moments coexist, as Freud suggests in his comparison of the mind to Rome, in *Civilization and its Discontents*.

72. Freud, *SE* XIV: 186.

73. Deleuze and Guattari, *ATP*, 2.

74. Jean-François Lyotard, *Discourse, figure*, 337.

75. In her weekly chronicle of January 29, 1972, Lispector relates a dream that may have given *Água Viva* its name, of an untouchable jellyfish, painfully gliding on the table, where the narrator sees her "essential deformation." "A Geleia Viva Como Placenta" (The living jellyfish like placenta), in *A Descoberta do Mundo*. Rio de Janeiro: Rocco, 1999. Many of *Água Viva's* passages come directly from this weekly chronicle.

slow, gigantic geological time of glaciers and their incessant movement, even as this time, due to human activity in the industrialized world, has suddenly accelerated. Thus in Horn's work one is invited to take a step after Tournier's human and meteorological synchrony, which had left the slowness of geology and the speed of astronomy at a remove from Paul's unfurling in the atmosphere. Yes, geological time is too slow for the human eye, but it can still be made sensible, and even lodge itself inside a human building. Perhaps it can be made sensible as something other than an alarming sign of catastrophe.[76] Within the glass columns, this acceleration is dramatically brought to a standstill. At least to the human eye . . . but now the eye begins to see time flickering everywhere. A parallel gesture is made in *Água Viva*: "Parei para tomar água fresca: o copo neste instante-jà é de grosso cristal facetado e com milhares de fáiscas de instantes. Os objetos são tempo parado?"[77] Here the flow of writing recounts its own breaks (which would otherwise remain unknown to the reader) while considering objects from the perspective of differential speeds or temporalities, as Deleuze and Guattari say "relations of movement and rest." The strategy of narrating an absence from the act of writing, in other words, a silence irreducible to meaning, followed by describing a glass of water within or as a now-instant leads to seeing the "cut crystal with thousands of sparks of instants," a scintillating vision that seems amenable or correlative to the figural work Mallarmé and Horn undertake, too. Such a vision precipitates the question of objects being nothing but stopped time, actually, bringing forth, as Horn's *Water Selected* does, the dimension of haecceities that our usual mode of perception excludes. Correlative to the interaction of sensible qualities independent from an object in sensation, and to sensation at the cost of a unified body image, is a concept of time no longer supported by stable identities of subjects (as selves) or objects.

In *Água Viva* this observation of stopped time is placed in direct contrast to the idea of pulsing time, since the passage continues: "Continua a lua cheia. Relógios pararam e o som de um carrilhão rouco escorre pelo muro. Quero ser enterrada com o relógio no pulso para

76. As Briony Fer notes, the installation refuses "to make water a symbol of the earth's catastrophic future any more than it is possible to hold on to the traditional view of water as a symbol of purity." "Storm of the Eye," 29.

77. Lispector, AV, 40. "I stopped to drink cool water: the glass at this now-instant is of thick cut crystal and with thousands of sparks of instants. Are objects halted time?"

que na terra algo possa pulsar o tempo."[78] The full moon's carrying on reminds us that it is the force producing the ebb and flow of this text named *Água Viva*, which, as mentioned earlier in this chapter, is not only "living water" and "jellyfish," but also a name for high ocean tide under the full moon. The text depends on another distant but powerful force, just like its "I" depends on a listening "you." With this stoppage of clocks and the bells' hoarse, dripping sensation, a thought of death arises for the writing voice. How is one to read this wish to be buried with a watch on her wrist, to keep time pulsing underground, beyond her life as a writing "I"? The wish is not for self-preservation for this "I" that knows its fictional status. In a way, the text, read later by "you," is such a watch that keeps pulsing with the reader's participation. The repeated contrast of stopping and continuing on in this passage has the function of inviting its reader to inhabit the differential relation of "now-instants" with the writer. And with the earth, and its nonpulsed time, another "you" into which the body will dissolve.

Stopped time, or still-life as Horn sets it up in the glass columns, also appears in high contrast to the quick, volatile time of weather changes that are especially striking in the region, as well as to the seasons, which in Iceland, neighboring the Arctic Circle, entail radical shifts in the intensity and duration of light and darkness in a day. By such "relations of movement and rest," the *Library of Water* and *Água Viva* shift our focus toward haecceities. My view was of almost noon, in a day of almost twenty-four-hour daylight.

Anamorphic Mirrors

As I said earlier, visitors in *Vatnasafn/Library of Water* may inhabit the place and read in multiple ways. In every case, the sensation of *temps* it fosters cannot be a conscious subject's inner sense; the sensation results from the encounters between different temporalities that are stressed here. The rubber floor's words invoke human participants' *temps*, in the time of reading and as variations in temperament; they resonate with the variations in light, of the day or night outside, and of the refractions produced

78. Lispector, 40. "The moon is still full. Clocks stopped and the sound of hoarse bells drips down the wall. I want to be buried with a watch on my wrist so that in the earth something can pulse time."

by the glass columns. The time I spent alone inside *Vatnasafn/Library of Water* that sunny morning in May made me realize that its visitors do not merely enter into the space of the work. Instead, like everything within that space, our bodies, reflected on the curved transparent columns, are also deformed. Our position with regard to the landscape is not that of the privileged human figure supported by a background, as our vertical bodies slip between the panes holding glacial water in the room and the window panes displaying the ocean and town. One becomes part of a scene where the distinction between indoors and outdoors, land and sea seems to dissolve (figure 6.2). One's own point of view on the place is exceeded here, as the transparency of glass makes inside and outside permeable to each other while producing reflections, repetitions, and deformations that shatter the work of representation that privileges the viewer and only allows us to capture the world as something external to a self. All these effects in *Vatnasafn/Library of Water* contribute to unsettling the everyday mode of individuation concerned with subjects and objects, releasing, precisely, the dimension of haecceities Lispector's text foregrounds in a glass of water's thousand sparks of time.

Água Viva devotes several passages to the theme of the mirror, whose mystery, the writing voice announces, she wants to either paint or speak of with words. As an instrument mysterious to the narrator due to its infinity of reflections and its emptiness, and which she associates with "frozen, hardened water," a mirror is scarcely an object.[79] Like a jellyfish or an oyster, it can do more than simply present us with the image of ourselves with which we are most familiar, and bring us close to haecceities; the challenge the mirror poses to the narrator (and the reader) is that of seeing, painting, or writing the mirror without seeing one's own image—in other words, seeing the "living mirror" itself, in its sheer, neutral emptiness and silence:

> Ao pintá-lo precisei de minha própria delicadeza para não atravessá-lo com minha imagem, pois espelho em que eu me veja já sou eu, só espelho vazio é que é o espelho vivo. Só uma pessoa muito delicada pode entrar no quarto vazio onde há um espelho vazio, e com tal leveza, com tal ausência de si mesma, que a imagem não marca. Como prêmio, essa pessoa

79. Lispector, 70.

> delicada terá então penetrado num dos segredos invioláveis das coisas: viu o espelho propriamente dito.[80]

I remember having an impulse of lying down on my stomach on the rubber floor during my solitary visit in the Library of Water. No one was watching. I lay down. At the time, I had thought of this impulse as a wish for more tactile contact, since my feet were sensing the cushioned texture of rubber as I walked around. In her account of exploring *Rings of Lispector*, which as I said also features rubber tiles with inlaid fragments from *Água Viva*, Cixous features a dialogue between her and Roni around the choice of rubber. "Rubber says Roni—'changes your relationship to the world,'" reports Cixous, and "'reflects your presence, is affected by your presence,'" to which Cixous responds "It yields and does not betray. L'elasticité du corps amoureux" ("the elasticity of the body in love").[81]

Perhaps, however, it may have been more about trying not to fill the room with my deformed reflection. Briony Fer states, from her experience in the *Library*, that "this is an anamorphosis in three dimensions, our own reflections caught and stretched and mangled in it."[82] The fact that, through their curvature, the water columns offer anamorphic reflections that multiply had an uncanny effect on me. I am reminded of Freud's story, in "The Uncanny," of encountering a strange man at the door of his train compartment, to then realize that it was "his own" unsettling image in the door's mirror.[83] As a visual interruption of a representational way of looking, the anamorphosis and the multiplication of one's image undermine the "I"'s image, causing a self-estrangement that may unleash the visitors' playfulness, and also possibly anxiety. I wonder whether I tried to hide from the anamorphic images to escape this uncanniness.

80. Lispector, 72. "When painting it I needed my own delicateness in order not to cross it with my own image, since a mirror in which I see myself is already I, only an empty mirror is what the living mirror is. Only a very delicate person can enter the empty room where there is an empty mirror, and with such lightness, with such absence of self, that her image leaves no mark. As a prize, that delicate person will then have penetrated one of the inviolable secrets of things: she saw the mirror itself."

81. Cixous, "Faire voir le *jamaisvu*," 29.

82. Fer, "Storm of the Eye," 30.

83. See Freud, *SE* XVII: 248, n1. See a commentary on this anecdote in Zupančič's *The Shortest Shadow: Nietzsche's Philosophy of the Two* (Cambridge, MA & London: MIT Press, 2003), 14; and uncanny anamorphosis in Iversen, *Beyond Pleasure*, chapter 2.

Especially since I had no companions to become distracted and absorbed with during my visit. Or whether I had tried to dive close to letters and words for shelter from the overwhelming task of reading water directly. But I also agree with Fer that "what it feels like to be there is precisely not to be able to place language in a simple opposition to sensation."[84] At least it is part of what it feels like. Or had I lain down, instead, in an attempt to see the room for itself, like Lispector's empty mirror or Cézanne's instant of the world? Surely this attitude is different from escaping the anamorphic mirrors out of anxiety. In the first case I would be defending myself against whatever strangeness might surface on the anamorphic mirrors reflecting my distorted and multiplied image. In the second case I would be hoping that these scattered words could provide me with reassuring signification, rather than drowning me in a sea of free flowing adjectives that signification ties back to a person or a thing, making some of them impossible to appear simultaneously.[85] In the third case, I would be following a gesture modeled by the artwork, aligning my body to the horizontality of its field of scattered words, lying still like the encased water, and in doing this, I would perhaps not so much be escaping the scene, but instead be wanting to find out what its uncanniness can tell us if we endure it. I would be trying not to turn the room into my own, while letting my body receive it, "captar," as the rubber floor received my body. The uncanniness did not go away; the rubber yielded; I must have laughed to myself.

I've been wondering "whether" this or that. The conjunction, although it sounds quite right in this context, is a logical simplifier that fails to cover the event. Maybe it was all of these things together, like the disparate adjectives spread across the floor, an odd effect of the weather. This is completely plausible, especially in Iceland, according to *Les météores*. When its protagonist Paul thinks, as cited earlier, that "no one has a greater calling than I to understand your destiny where the meteors, the elements, and your heart blend inextricably,"[86] he is in Iceland, hearing about another man's inability to get past the great glacier

84. Fer, "Storm of the Eye," 24.

85. My colleague David Castillo has sowed this possibility with the observation that, in lying down on my stomach, rather than my back, there could be a resistance or rebellion against the traditional position in the psychoanalytic scene as analysand, and its feminized passivity.

86. Tournier, *Les météores*, 509.

Vatnajökull, which he faces as his weekly circuit's turning point, on a weekly tour taking tourists around the island. This man dreams of not turning back having reached the glacier, to thus break out of a vicious circle that keeps him from marrying the Icelandic woman who led him to this lifestyle, and from returning with her to Arles, his hometown in France. The tale could easily enter Sophie Calle's collection of pain, discussed in the previous chapter. Here the vicissitude of the drive is in part shaped by the giant glacier, and by six-month-long days and nights that have replaced the seasons, as this man explains to Paul, the foreigner. In my case, the almost-twenty-four-hour daylight, the rubber's gentle cushion and the sheets of glass that brought the outdoors indoors and vice versa, unmediated by another human presence had had something to do with my own impulse to end up on the floor.

Deleuze notes that the strategy Goya and Redon use in their painting to release the monster, as abstract line, is to "raise up the ground and dissolve the form."[87] To allow "the ground to rise to the surface" is to accept that "it is there, staring at us, but without eyes."[88] This thought is very consonant with Lacan's in his discussion on the gaze. Deleuze explains that the forms of Self and I are vulnerable on this rising ground related to individuation (haecceity and not identity), as an operation that "involves fields of fluid intensive factors"[89] and precedes forms. The danger of this is that it makes room, not only for artworks such as Goya's or Redon's, but also for "stupidity" (bêtise), which Deleuze shows to be a "specifically human" problem with consequences such as the rise of the "tyrant," when it remains unrecognized: "Stupidity is neither the ground nor the individual, but rather this relation in which individuation brings the ground to the surface without being able to give it form (this ground rises by means of the I, penetrating deeply into the possibility of thought and constituting the unrecognized in every recognition)."[90] If the ground is the unthought, then it is vitally important to notice how it is nonetheless playing a part in thought.

87. Deleuze, *DR*, 28–29.

88. Deleuze, 152.

89. Deleuze, 152.

90. Deleuze, 152.

> The individual distinguishes itself from [the ground]. But [the ground] does not distinguish itself, continuing rather to cohabit with that which divorces itself from it. It is the indeterminate, but the indeterminate in so far as it continues to embrace determination, as the soil does the shoe. Animals are in a sense forewarned against this ground, protected by their explicit forms. Not so for the I and the Self, undermined by the fields of individuation which work beneath them, defenseless against a rising of the ground which holds up to them a distorted or distorting mirror in which all presently thought forms dissolve.[91]

If the determinations of the ground, the soil that embraces the shoe, are only "grasped by a thought that contemplates and invents them separated from their living form, floating on this barren ground," then "everything becomes violence on this passive ground."[92] The ground rose to the rubber surface in *Vatnasfn/Library of Water*, and it was not barren. Its cylindrical mirrors distorted our bodies. Its rubber floor did not stomp on my body like the sole of a shoe against the ground. In these gestures the work sharply criticized human stupidity, restoring through anamorphoses a sensibility for the burgeoning field of individuation, for the drive that was the condition for both stupid tyranny and for the very different, delicate work of "captar," which I now understood involved "giving form" as Horn had done here, without imposing one's own distorted self-recognition. Sensation is one of these ways of giving form, where the condition of real experience "forms an intrinsic genesis, not an extrinsic conditioning."[93]

Lying on this library's floor, I did not feel at all encased like still water but rather spilled and, like the adjectives on the floor, unhinged from a noun. Much like this moment in *Água Viva*: "Vou-te fazer uma confissão: estou um pouco assustada. É que não sei aonde me levará esta minha liberdade. Não é arbitraria nem libertina. Mas estou

91. Deleuze, 152.

92. Deleuze, 198.

93. Deleuze, 154.

solta."[94] Unbound. Within the uncommon mode of individuation of haecceties, I noticed, there's a difference between dwelling in its atmosphere and noticing the shift in which the uncanny, anamorphic effect decenters us,[95] where one confronts the living mirror, which could only reflect the now-instant in its neutrality. The latter is the clinical aim of the aesthetic, and it necessarily pushes the experience beyond pleasure, where the self is bound. While *Vatnasafn/Library of Water* can orchestrate the instant of the world and of the word with the uncontrollable elements of its visitors and the weather, the visitors themselves, as *quid*, are not the haecceity. Still, in the library they "become the light," as Roni wished. That Lispector's now-instant and Horn's instant of the world are, as I assert, interstitial entails, then, that they only take place in the decentering of perspective, as Alenka Zupančič eloquently explains of Nietzsche's event of thought or philosophical act. To read living water, in *Vatnasafn/Library of Water*, in *Água Viva*, is this decentering movement. In Lispector's words, the now-instant takes place "in that almost":

> A vida obliqua? Bem sei que há um desencontro leve entre as coisas, elas quase se chocam, há desencontro entre os seres que se perdem uns aos outros entre palavras que quase não dizem mais nada. Mas quase nos entendemos nesse leve desencontro, nesse quase que é a única forma de suportar a vida em cheio, pois um encontro brusco face a face com ela nos assustaria, espaventaria os seus delicados fios de tela de aranha.[96]

The Shortest Shadow is the title of Zupančič's book on Nietzsche because it refers to "noon" in *Thus Spoke Zarathustra* as "the moment when One

94. Lispector, *AV*, 31. "I've got a confession to make: I'm a little frightened. For I don't know where my freedom will lead me. It is neither arbitrary nor libertine. But I am unbound."

95. In her discussion of truth as a shift of perspective in Nietzsche, Alenka Zupančič convincingly insists that truth is not in the new perspective that emerges, but instead in the shift itself, and that this allows us "to think the decentering as such" (*The Shortest Shadow*, 115).

96. Lispector, *AV*, 64. "Oblique life? I am well aware that there is a slight detachment between things, they almost collide, there is a detachment among the beings that lose one another amongst words that almost don't say anything more. But we almost understand one another in this light discord, in this almost that is the only way to stand full life, since a sudden face-to-face encounter with it would frighten us, scare off its delicate spider's web threads."

turns to Two."[97] She shows that this most subtle event, at once "the moment of a break or split" and "the stillest hour" whose decentering is no less powerful for that, has the status of an internal limit. Its taking place is immanent and impossible to evaluate according to any external measure, as Deleuze had proposed about the condition of real experience forming an intrinsic genesis. To, as Zupančič says, "activate this precise point," of the inner limit when the gaze emerges "as the potential locus of creation"[98] is what the aesthetic clinic seeks.

In Stykkyshólmur I had no other plans for the rest of the day, and no one was rushing me or delaying me. Still, it was time to leave. Filled with this library's silence, I was ready for the outdoor sounds, and I wished to overhear local conversations I would not understand, in Icelandic, which, as Selma, the local tourist guide, explains to Paul in *Les météores*, has not changed much since it was brought by the Vikings in the ninth and tenth centuries, and is to the Scandinavian languages what Classic Latin is to the Romance languages.[99] Later I would turn to *Água Viva*, since now it felt like I had never quite read it before. But before picking up the book, I would just let the day happen to me. "Be the weather." I would swim in the public swimming pool and watch the tiny bubbles fizz against my skin from the Icelandic sulfuric water, and stand by the bay to see the ferry to Flatey leave the dock without me. It was almost noon.

97. Zupančič, *The Shortest Shadow*, 8.

98. Zupančič, 8.

99. Tournier, *Les météores*, 506.

Works Cited

Adams, Parveen. *The Emptiness of the Image*. New York: Routledge, 1995.

André, Serge. *Que veut-une femme?* Paris: Navarin, 1986.

Apollon, Willy. "Féminité dites-vous?" *Savoir: Revue de psychanalyse et d'analyse culturelle* 2.1 (May 1995): 15–45.

———. "Four Seasons in Femininity or Four Men in a Woman's Life." *Topoi* 12 (1993): 101–115.

———. "From the Cultural Construction to Desire." Schema from the GIFRIC Training Seminar "The Clinic of the Symptom." June 5–9, 2017.

———. "From Symptom to Fantasy." In *After Lacan: Clinical Practice and the Subject of the Unconscious*. Albany: State University of New York Press, 2002, 127–140.

———. "The Quest of Desire against the Montage." Lecture Notes on GIFRIC Training Seminar, "The Clinic of the Dream." June 7, 2016.

———. "The Untreatable." Translated by Steven Miller. *UMBR(a). Incurable* (2006): 23–39.

Apollon, Willy, Danielle Bergeron, and Lucie Cantin. *After Lacan: Clinical Practice and the Subject of the Unconscious*. Albany: State University of New York Press, 2002.

Aragon, Louis, and André Breton. "Le cinquantenaire de l'hystérie 1878–1928." *La Révolution surréaliste* (March 15, 1928): 20–22.

Artaud, Antonin. *Pour en finir avec le jugement de Dieu*. Paris: K Éditeur, 1948.

Assoun, Paul-Laurent. *Le pervers et la femme*. Paris: Anthropos, 1989.

Bal, Mieke. "Autotopography: Louise Bourgeois as Builder." *Biography*. 25.1 (2002): 180–202.

———. *Louise Bourgeois' Spider: The Architecture of Art-Writing*. Chicago: University of Chicago Press, 2001.

Barillaud, Sylvie, Pierre-André Boutang, and Jacques Mény. *Jean-Jacques Annaud tourne L'amant*. Renn Productions. 1992. www.dailymotion.com/video/xiuvoq

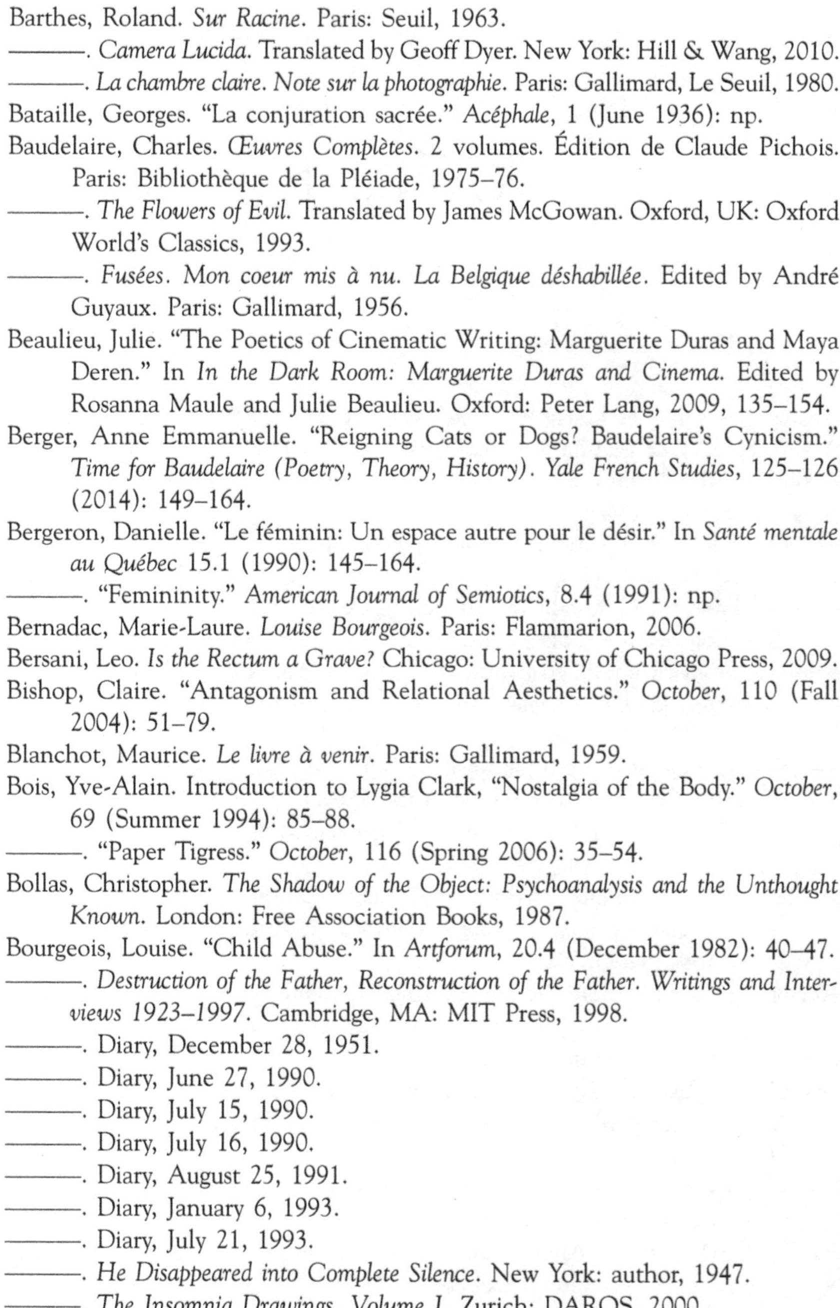

Barthes, Roland. *Sur Racine*. Paris: Seuil, 1963.

———. *Camera Lucida*. Translated by Geoff Dyer. New York: Hill & Wang, 2010.

———. *La chambre claire. Note sur la photographie*. Paris: Gallimard, Le Seuil, 1980.

Bataille, Georges. "La conjuration sacrée." *Acéphale*, 1 (June 1936): np.

Baudelaire, Charles. *Œuvres Complètes*. 2 volumes. Édition de Claude Pichois. Paris: Bibliothèque de la Pléiade, 1975–76.

———. *The Flowers of Evil*. Translated by James McGowan. Oxford, UK: Oxford World's Classics, 1993.

———. *Fusées. Mon coeur mis à nu. La Belgique déshabillée*. Edited by André Guyaux. Paris: Gallimard, 1956.

Beaulieu, Julie. "The Poetics of Cinematic Writing: Marguerite Duras and Maya Deren." In *In the Dark Room: Marguerite Duras and Cinema*. Edited by Rosanna Maule and Julie Beaulieu. Oxford: Peter Lang, 2009, 135–154.

Berger, Anne Emmanuelle. "Reigning Cats or Dogs? Baudelaire's Cynicism." *Time for Baudelaire (Poetry, Theory, History)*. *Yale French Studies*, 125–126 (2014): 149–164.

Bergeron, Danielle. "Le féminin: Un espace autre pour le désir." In *Santé mentale au Québec* 15.1 (1990): 145–164.

———. "Femininity." *American Journal of Semiotics*, 8.4 (1991): np.

Bernadac, Marie-Laure. *Louise Bourgeois*. Paris: Flammarion, 2006.

Bersani, Leo. *Is the Rectum a Grave?* Chicago: University of Chicago Press, 2009.

Bishop, Claire. "Antagonism and Relational Aesthetics." *October*, 110 (Fall 2004): 51–79.

Blanchot, Maurice. *Le livre à venir*. Paris: Gallimard, 1959.

Bois, Yve-Alain. Introduction to Lygia Clark, "Nostalgia of the Body." *October*, 69 (Summer 1994): 85–88.

———. "Paper Tigress." *October*, 116 (Spring 2006): 35–54.

Bollas, Christopher. *The Shadow of the Object: Psychoanalysis and the Unthought Known*. London: Free Association Books, 1987.

Bourgeois, Louise. "Child Abuse." In *Artforum*, 20.4 (December 1982): 40–47.

———. *Destruction of the Father, Reconstruction of the Father. Writings and Interviews 1923–1997*. Cambridge, MA: MIT Press, 1998.

———. Diary, December 28, 1951.

———. Diary, June 27, 1990.

———. Diary, July 15, 1990.

———. Diary, July 16, 1990.

———. Diary, August 25, 1991.

———. Diary, January 6, 1993.

———. Diary, July 21, 1993.

———. *He Disappeared into Complete Silence*. New York: author, 1947.

———. *The Insomnia Drawings, Volume I*. Zurich: DAROS, 2000.

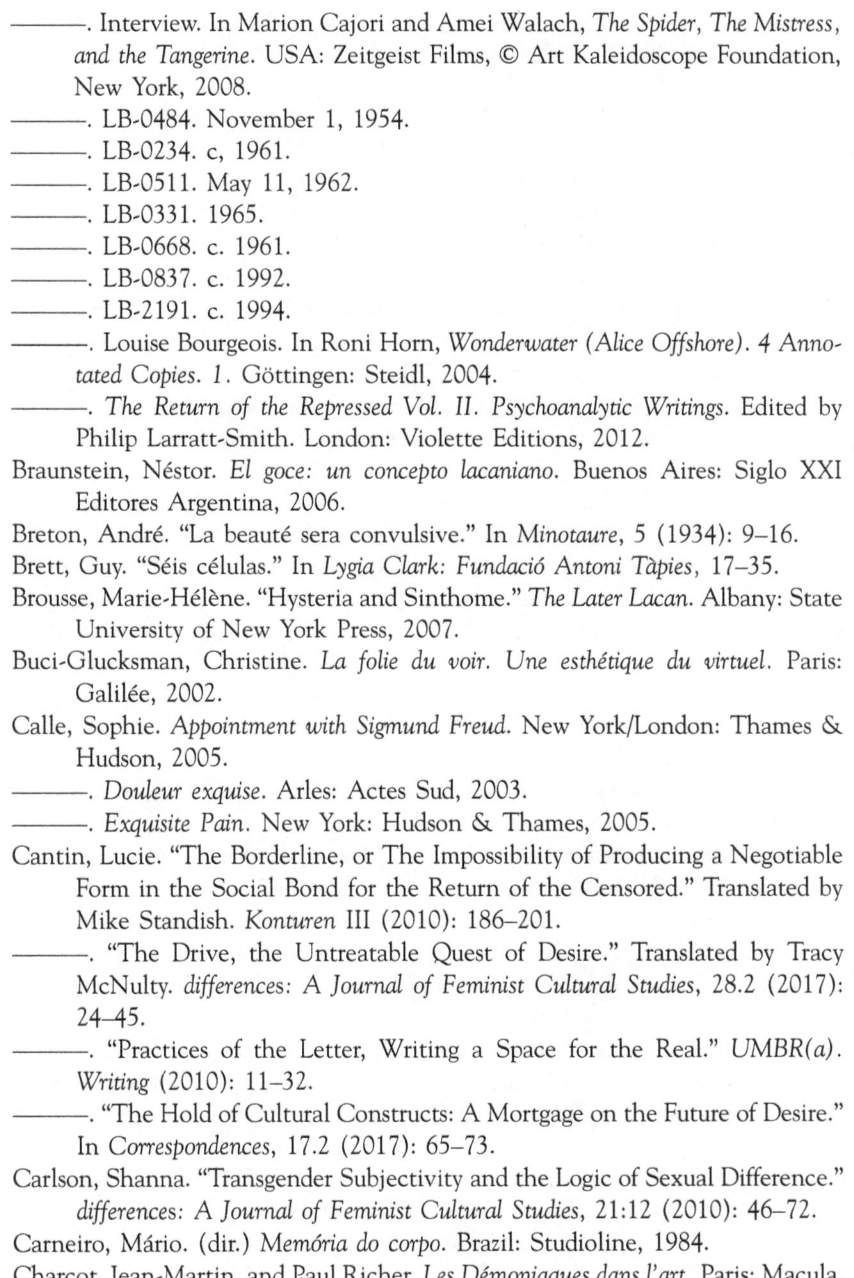

———. Interview. In Marion Cajori and Amei Walach, *The Spider, The Mistress, and the Tangerine*. USA: Zeitgeist Films, © Art Kaleidoscope Foundation, New York, 2008.

———. LB-0484. November 1, 1954.

———. LB-0234. c, 1961.

———. LB-0511. May 11, 1962.

———. LB-0331. 1965.

———. LB-0668. c. 1961.

———. LB-0837. c. 1992.

———. LB-2191. c. 1994.

———. Louise Bourgeois. In Roni Horn, *Wonderwater (Alice Offshore). 4 Annotated Copies. 1*. Göttingen: Steidl, 2004.

———. *The Return of the Repressed Vol. II. Psychoanalytic Writings*. Edited by Philip Larratt-Smith. London: Violette Editions, 2012.

Braunstein, Néstor. *El goce: un concepto lacaniano*. Buenos Aires: Siglo XXI Editores Argentina, 2006.

Breton, André. "La beauté sera convulsive." In *Minotaure*, 5 (1934): 9–16.

Brett, Guy. "Séis células." In *Lygia Clark: Fundació Antoni Tàpies*, 17–35.

Brousse, Marie-Hélène. "Hysteria and Sinthome." *The Later Lacan*. Albany: State University of New York Press, 2007.

Buci-Glucksman, Christine. *La folie du voir. Une esthétique du virtuel*. Paris: Galilée, 2002.

Calle, Sophie. *Appointment with Sigmund Freud*. New York/London: Thames & Hudson, 2005.

———. *Douleur exquise*. Arles: Actes Sud, 2003.

———. *Exquisite Pain*. New York: Hudson & Thames, 2005.

Cantin, Lucie. "The Borderline, or The Impossibility of Producing a Negotiable Form in the Social Bond for the Return of the Censored." Translated by Mike Standish. *Konturen* III (2010): 186–201.

———. "The Drive, the Untreatable Quest of Desire." Translated by Tracy McNulty. *differences: A Journal of Feminist Cultural Studies*, 28.2 (2017): 24–45.

———. "Practices of the Letter, Writing a Space for the Real." *UMBR(a). Writing* (2010): 11–32.

———. "The Hold of Cultural Constructs: A Mortgage on the Future of Desire." In *Correspondences*, 17.2 (2017): 65–73.

Carlson, Shanna. "Transgender Subjectivity and the Logic of Sexual Difference." *differences: A Journal of Feminist Cultural Studies*, 21:12 (2010): 46–72.

Carneiro, Mário. (dir.) *Memória do corpo*. Brazil: Studioline, 1984.

Charcot, Jean-Martin, and Paul Richer. *Les Démoniaques dans l'art*. Paris: Macula, 1984.

Cimaise: Art et Architecture Actuels, 173 (November–December 1984): 29–48.
Cixous, Hélène. "Faire voir le *jamaisvu*." In *Rings of Clarice Lispector*. Göttingen: Hauser & Wirth Steidl, 2005.
Clark, Lygia. "L'art c'est le corps." *Preuves: cahiers mensuels du Congrès pour la liberté et la culture*, 13 (1973): 143–145.
———. "Caminhando." In *Lygia Clark*. Fundació Antoni Tàpies, 151–152.
———. "Capturar um fragmento de tempo suspenso." In *Lygia Clark*. Fundació Antoni Tàpies, 187–188.
———. "Do ato." In *Lygia Clark*. Fundació Antoni Tàpies, 164–165.
———. "Da supressão do objeto (Anotações)," 1975. In *Lygia Clark*. Fundació Antoni Tàpies, 264–269.
———. "Nós somos os propositores," In *Lygia Clark*. Fundació Antoni Tàpies, 233.
———. "O vazio-pleno." In *Lygia Clark* Fundació Antoni Tàpies, 111–113.
———. "Rencontre avec des psychothérapeutes." In Rolnik and Diserens, *De l'œuvre à l'événement*, 59–61.
———. Writings by Lygia Clark (1956–59; 1960–63; 1968–mid-1980s). *The Abandonment of Art 1948–1988*. New York: Museum of Modern Art, 2014.
Clark, Lygia, Ferreira Gullar, and J. Ribamar. *Lygia Clark*. Rio de Janeiro: FUNARTE, 1980.
Conley, Verena Andermatt. *Spatial Ecologies*. Liverpool: Liverpool University Press, 2012.
———. "The Care of the Possible." *Cultural Politics* 12.3 (2016): 339–354.
Copjec Joan. *Read My Desire: Lacan Against the Historicists*. London & New York: Verso, 2015.
———. *Imagine There's No Woman: Ethics and Sublimation*. Cambridge, MA & London: MIT Press, 2002.
Crone, Rainer, and Petrus Graf Schaesberg, *Louise Bourgeois: The Secret of the Cells*. New York, Munich, and London: Prestel, 2011.
David-Ménard, Monique. *Hysteria from Freud to Lacan*. Translated by Catherine Porter. Ithaca, NY: Cornell University Press, 1989.
de la Torre, Shanna. *Sex for Structuralists: The NonOedipal Logics of Femininity and Psychosis*. New York: Palgrave, 2018.
Decker, Hannah. *Freud, Dora, and Vienna*. New York: The Free Press, 1992.
Deleuze, Gilles. *Cinéma 2: L'image-temps*. Paris: Les Éditions de Minuit, 1985.
———. *Coldness and Cruelty*. Translated by Jean McNeil. New York: Zone Books, 1989.
———. Cours Vincennes–St. Denis: Crible Et Infini 17/03/1987. *Les cours de Gilles Deleuze*. Available online at www.webdeleuze.com/textes/142
———. *Difference and Repetition*. Translated by Paul Patton. London: Continuum, 2001.
———. *Expressionism in Philosophy: Spinoza*. Translated by Martin Joughin. New York: Zone Books, 1990.

———. *Francis Bacon: The Logic of Sensation*. Translated by Daniel W. Smith. London and New York: Continuum, 2003.

———. *Francis Bacon: Logique de la sensation*. Paris: Seuil, 2002.

———. *Logic of Sense*. Translated by Mark Lester. New York: Columbia University Press, 1990.

———. *Nietzsche et la philosophie*. Paris: PUF, 1962.

———. *Proust et les signes*. Paris: PUF, 2003.

Deleuze, Gilles; Félix Guattari. *Anti-Oedipus*. Translated by Robert Hurley, Mark Seem, and Helen R. Lane. London: Continuum, 2004.

———. *A Thousand Plateaus*. Translated by Brian Massumi. Minneapolis & London: University of Minnesota Press, 1987.

———. *Kafka: Pour une littérature mineure*. Paris: Les Éditions de Minuit, 1975.

———. *What is Philosophy?* Translated by Hugh Tomilson. London & New York: Verso, 2015.

Delvaux, Martine. "Sophie Calle: No Sex." *Contemporary French and Francophone Studies*, 10.4 (December 2006): 425–435.

Derrida, Jacques. *Éperons: Les Styles de Nietzsche*. Paris: Flammarion, 1978.

———. "La double séance." In *La dissemination*. Paris: Seuil, 1972, 199–317.

Didi-Huberman, Georges. *Devant l'image: Question posée aux fins d'une histoire de l'art*. Paris: Les Éditions de Minuit, 1990.

———. *Invention of Hysteria: Charcot and the Iconography of the Salpêtrière*. Translated by Alisa Hartz. Cambridge, MA & London: MIT Press, 2003.

Dolar, Mladen. "'I Shall Be with You on Your Wedding Night': Lacan and the Uncanny." *October*, 58 (Autumn 1991): 5–23.

Du Bellay, Joachim. *Les regrets; précédé de Les Antiquités de Rome et suivi de La défense et l'illustration de la langue française*. Edited by Samuel S. de Sacy. Paris: Gallimard, 1975.

Duras, Marguerite. *L'amant*. Paris: Les Éditions de Minuit, 1984.

———. *Césarée; Les mains négatives; Aurélia Steiner; Aurelia Steiner*. Paris: Benoît Jacob, 1979. DVD.

———. *Emily L*. Paris: Les Éditions de Minuit, 1987.

———. *Hiroshima mon amour*. Paris: Gallimard, 1959.

———. *Le navire Night; Césarée; Les mains négatives*. Paris: Mercure de France, 2001.

———. *Le ravissement de Lol V. Stein*. Paris: Gallimard, 1964.

———. *La vie matérielle*. Paris: Folio, 1987.

Duras, Marguerite, and Dominique Noguez. *La couleur des mots*. Paris: Benoît Jacob, 2001.

Ettinger, Bracha. "Art as the Transport-Station of Trauma." *Bracha Lichtenberg Ettinger: Artworking 1985–1999*. Brussels: Palais des Beaux-arts, Ghent: Ludion, 2000.

———. "Fascinance and the Girl-to-m/Other Matrixial Feminine Difference." *Psychoanalysis and the Image*. Edited by Griselda Pollock. Oxford, UK: Blackwell, 2006, 60–92.

Ettinger, Bracha, and Kyoko Gardiner "Affectuous Encounters: Feminine Matrixial Encounters in Duras/Resnais' *Hiroshima mon amour*." In *PostGender: Gender, Sexuality and Performativity in Japanese Culture*. Edited by Ayelet Zohar. Newcastle-upon-Tyne: Cambridge Scholars Publishing, 2009, 251–274.

Fédida, Pierre. *L'absence*. Paris: Gallimard, 1978.

———. "Ne pas être en repos avec les mots." Interview with Suely Rolnik. In Rolnik and Diserens. *De l'œuvre à l'événement*, 69–70.

Fer, Briony. "Lygia Clark and the Problem of Art." In *The Abandonment of Art. 1948–1988*. New York: Museum of Modern Art, 2014.

———. "Storm of the Eye." In *Vatnasafn/Library of Water*. London/Göttingen: Artangel/Steidl, 2009, 22–31.

Fink, Bruce. "Jouissance and Knowledge." In *Reading Seminar XX: Lacan's Major Work on Love, Knowledge, and Feminine Sexuality*. Edited by Suzanne Barnard and Bruce Fink. Albany: State University of New York Press, 2002, 21–45.

France, Marie de. *Lais*. Translated by Philippe Walter. Paris: Gallimard, 2000.

Freud, Sigmund. *The Standard Edition of the Complete Psychological Works of Sigmund Freud*. Translated by James Strachey, in collaboration with Anna Freud. Assisted by Alix Strachey and Alan Tyson. London: Vintage, 2001.

SE II. "On the Psychichal Mechanism of Hysterical Phenomena: Preliminary Communication," 1–17.

SE IV. "II: The method of interpreting dreams: An analysis of a specimen dream." *The Interpretation of Dreams*, 96–121.

SE VII. "Fragment of an Analysis of a Case of Hysteria," 3–122.

SE IX. "Some General Remarks on Hysterical Attacks," 227–234.

SE XI. "Five Lectures on Psychoanalysis," 3–55.

SE XIII. "The Moses of Michelangelo," 211–238.

SE XIV. "On Narcissism," 67–102.

SE XIV. Instincts and Their Viscissitudes," 109–140.

SE XIV. "The Unconscious," 159–215.

SE XIV. "A Mythological Parallel to a Visual Obsession," 337–338.

SE XVI. "Lecture XVII: The Sense of Symptoms." 257–272.

SE XVI. "Lecture XXIII: The Paths to the Formation of Symptoms," 358–377.

SE XVII. "From the History of an Infantile Neurosis," 3–122.

SE XVII. "The Uncanny," 218–256.

SE XVIII. *Beyond the Pleasure Principle*, 3–64.

SE XIX. *The Ego and the Id*, 3–59.

SE XXI. *Civilization and its Discontents*, 59–145.

SE XXII. "Femininity," 112–135.

SE XXIII. "Analysis Terminable and Interminable," 216–253.

———. *The Complete Letters of Sigmund Freud to Wilhelm Fliess, 1887–1904*. Translated and edited by Jeffrey Moussaieff Masson. Cambridge: Belknap, 1985.

Gasquet, Joachim. *Conversations avec Cézanne*. Edited by P.M. Doran. Paris: Macula, 1978.

Gherovici, Patricia. *Please Select Your Gender. From the Invention of Hysteria to the Democratizing of Transgenderism*. New York: Routledge, 2011.

———. "Anxious? Castration Is the Solution!" *Psychoanalytic Inquiry* 38.1 (2018): 83–90.

Gil, José. "Ouvrir le corps." In Rolnik and Diserens, *De l'œuvre à l'événement*, 63–66.

Gratton, Johnnie. "Experiment and Experience in the Phototextual Projects of Sophie Calle." In *Women's Writing in Contemporary France: New Writers, New Literatures in the 1990s*. Edited by G. Rye and M. Worton. Manchester & New York: Manchester University Press, 2002, 157–170.

Guattari, Félix. *The Three Ecologies*. Translated by Ian Pindar and Paul Sutton. London: Continuum, 2005.

Gullar, Ferreira. "Theory of the Non-object." Translated by Michael Asbury. *Cosmopolitan Modernisms*. Edited by Kobena Mercer. Cambridge, MA: MIT Press, 2005.

Harari, Roberto. *El Sujeto Descentrado: Una presentación del psicoanálisis*. Lumen: Buenos Aires, 2008.

Herkenhoff, Paulo. "Lygia Clark." In *Lygia Clark*. Fundació Antoni Tàpies, 36–57.

Hoens, Dominiek. "When Love is the Law: On *The Ravishing of Lol V. Stein*." *UMBR(a)* (2005), 105–116.

Hooke, Robert. "Observation XVIII. Of the *Schematisme or Texture* of Cork, and of the Cells and Pores of some other frothy Bodies." In *Micrographia, or Some Physiological Descriptions of Minute Bodies Made by Magnifying Glasses with Observations and Inquiries Thereupon*. London: John Martin James Allestry, 1664.

Horn, Roni. *Another Water*. Zurich: Scalo, 2000.

———. *Rings of Clarice Lispector*. Göttingen: Hauser & Wirth Steidl, 2005.

Iversen, Margaret. *Beyond Pleasure: Freud, Lacan, Barthes*. University Park, PA: Pennsylvania State University Press, 2007.

———. "The World Without a Self: Edward Hopper and Chantal Ackermann." *Art History* (September 2018): 742–760.

Jones, Ernest. *Sigmund Freud. Years of Maturity (1901–1919)*. Volume II. New York: Basic Books, 1955.

Jordan, Shirley Ann. "Exhibiting Pain: Sophie Calle's *Douleur Exquise*." *French Studies: A Quarterly Review*, 61.2 (April 2007): 196–208.

Jottkandt, Sigi. "Signifier and Letter in Kierkegaard and Lacan." *UMBR(a). Writing* (2010): 101–114.

Kaltenbeck, Franz. "Sublimation and Symptom." *Art: Sublimation or Symptom*. Edited by Parveen Adams. London: Karnac, 2003, 103–121.

Kay, Sarah, and Simon Gaunt, *The Troubadours: An Introduction*. Cambridge, UK: Cambridge University Press, 1999.

Klossowski, Pierre. *Nietzsche et le cercle vicieux*. Paris: Mercure, 1969.

———. "Nietzsche, le polythéisme et la parodie." *Revue de métaphysique et de morale*, 63.2/3 (April–September 1958): 325–348.

Kofman, Sarah. *L'enfance de l'art*. Paris: Galilée, 1985.

———. *L'énigme de la femme: La femme dans les textes de Freud*. Paris: Galilée, 1980.

Krauss, Rosalind. Introduction. In *Bachelors*. Cambridge, MA & London: MIT Press, 1999.

———. "Louise Bourgeois: Portrait of the Artist as Fillette." In *Bachelors*. Cambridge, MA & London: MIT Press, 1999.

———. "Objet partiel." In *Louise Bourgeois*. Directed by Marie-Laure Bernadac and Jonas Storsve. Paris: Editions du Centre Pompidou, 2008.

Krauss, Rosalind, and Yve-Alain Bois. *L'informe: Mode d'emploi*. Paris: Éditions du Centre Pompidou, 1999.

Kuspit, Donald. "Louise Bourgeois in Psychoanalysis with Henry Lowenfeld." *Louise Bourgeois: The Return of the Repressed. Vol. I*. Edited by Philip Larratt-Smith. London: Violette, 2012.

Lacan, Jacques. *The Four Fundamental Concepts of Psychoanalysis*. Translated by Alan Sheridan. New York: W.W. Norton, 1981.

———. "The Function and the Field of Speech and Language in Psychoanalysis." *Écrits*. Translated by Bruce Fink. New York: W.W. Norton & Co., 2006, 197–268.

———. "Hommage fait à Marguerite Duras, du ravissement de Lol V. Stein." In *Autres Écrits* Paris: Seuil, 2001, 191–197.

———. "L'instance de la lettre dans l'inconscient." In *Ecrits I*. Paris: Seuil, 1999, 490–526.

———. *La logique du fantasme*, Session 14, March 8, 1967. Unpublished.

———. "Préface à l'édition anglaise du *Séminaire XI*." (1976). In *Autres Écrits* Paris: Seuil, 2001.

———. "Radiophonie." In *Autres Écrits*. Paris: Seuil, 2001.

———. *Le Séminaire Livre III: Les psychoses*. Paris: Seuil, 1981.

———. *Le Séminaire Livre VII: L'éthique de la psychanalyse*. Paris: Seuil, 1986.

———. *Le Séminaire Livre VIII (1960–1961): Le transfert*. Paris: Seuil, 2001.

———. *Le Séminaire Livre XX: Encore*. Paris: Seuil, 1975.

———. *Le Séminaire Livre XXIII: Le sinthome*. Paris: Seuil, 2005.

———. "Subversion of the Subject and Dialectic of Desire in the Freudian Unconscious." In *Écrits*. New York: W.W. Norton & Co., 2006, 671–702.

———. *Télévision*. Paris: Seuil, 1973.

Landman, Claude. "Le noeud du fantasme." *La revue lacanienne*, 6.1 (2010): 27–35.

Leiris, Michel. *Francis Bacon, Full Face and In Profile*. Translated by John Weightman. New York: Rizzoli, 1983.

Leszkowicz, Pawel. "In Search of Lost Space. A la recherche de l'espace perdu." In *Louise Bourgeois. Geometry of Desire*. Warsaw: National Gallery of Art Zachęta, 2003.

Lingwood, James. "Journey to the Library of Water." *Roni Horn: Vatnasafn/ Library of Water*. Edited by Lingwood and Van Noord. Göttingen: Art Angel/Steidl, 2009, 14–19.

Lispector, Clarice. *Água Viva*. Rio de Janeiro: Rocco, 1973.

———. "A Geleia Viva Como Placenta." In A *Descoberta do Mundo*. Rio de Janeiro: Rocco, 1999, 402–403.

———. *Laços de Família*. Lisboa: Relógio d'Água Editores, 2013.

———. *A maçã no escuro*. Rio de Janeiro: Nova Fronteira, 1981.

Lorz, Julienne. "From the Bell Jar to the Cage: The Developmental Path of Louise Bourgeois's Cells." In *Louise Bourgeois, Structures of Existence: The Cells*. Munich: Haus der Kunst, 2015.

Louise Bourgeois: Structures of Existence; The Cells. Press Release. Guggenheim Bilbao, March 18–September 4, 2016.

Lygia Clark: De l'oeuvre à l'événement. Edited by Suely Rolnik and Corinne Diserens. Nantes: Musée de Beaux Arts, 2005.

Lygia Clark. Barcelona: Fundació Antoni Tàpies; Marseille: MAC, galeries contemporaines des Musées de Marseille; Porto: Fundação de Serralves; Bruxelles: Société des Expositions du Palais de Beaux-Arts, Réunion des Musées Nationaux, 1998.

Lyon-Wall, Scott. "Ventouse," *Louise Bourgeois*. Directed by Marie-Laure Bernadac and Jonas Storsve. Paris: Editions du Centre Pompidou, 2008.

Lyotard, Jean-François. *Discourse, Figure*. Translated by Antony Hudek and Mary Lydon. Minneapolis: University of Minnesota Press, 2011.

———. "Principales tendances actuelles de l'étude psychanalytique des expressions artistiques et littéraires." In *Dérive à partir de Freud et Marx*. Paris: Galilée, 1974.

MacCannell, Juliet Flower. *The Hysteric's Guide to The Future Female Subject*. Minneapolis: University of Minnesota Press, 2000.

———. *The Regime of the Brother*. London & New York: Routledge, 1991.

———. "Death Drive in Venice: Sophie Calle as Guide to the Future of Cities." *a: A Journal of Culture and the Unconscious*, 11.1 (2002): 55–78.

———. "Jouissance Between the Clinic and the Academy: The Analyst and Woman." *Qui Parle*, 9.2 (1996): 105–125.

Macel, Christine "Lygia Clark: At the Border of Art." In *Lygia Clark. The Abandonment of Art 1948–1988*. New York: Museum of Modern Art, 2014, 252–261.

Mallarmé, Stéphane. "Crise de vers." *Oeuvres Complètes*. Paris: La Pléiade, 1945.
———. "Crisis of Verse." *Divagations*. Translated by Barbara Johnson. Cambridge, MA: Belknap, 2007.
———. *Selected Poetry and Prose*. Edited by Mary Ann Caws. New York: New Directions, 1982.
Marguerite Duras. www.marguerite-duras.com/L-amant.php
McNulty, Tracy. *The Hostess: Hospitality, Femininty, and The Expropriation of Identity*. Minneapolis: University of Minnesota Press, 2007.
———. *Wrestling with the Angel: Experiments in Symbolic Life*. New York: Columbia University Press, 2014.
———. "Enabling Constraints: Toward an Aesthetics of Symbolic Life." In *UMBR(a). Writing* (2010): 35–63.
Merleau-Ponty, Maurice. *L'oeil et l'esprit*. Paris: Gallimard, 1964.
Millot, Catherine. "Why Writers?" In *UMBR(a). Writing* (2010): 65–75.
Milner, Marion. *On Not Being Able to Paint*. New York: Routledge, 2010.
Moncayo, Raul. *Lalangue, Sinthome, Jouissance, and Nomination: A Reading Companion to Lacan's Seminar XXIII*. London: Karnac, 2017.
Morel, Geneviève. "A Young Man without an Ego: A Study on James Joyce and the Mirror Stage." *Art: Sublimation or Symptom*. Edited by Parveen Adams. London: Karnac, 2003, 123–145.
Museu de Imagens do Inconsciente. www.museuimagensdoinconsciente.org.br/#index
Negrete, Fernanda. "Acts of Love and Unconscious Savoir in Marguerite Duras' Writing." *S Journal of the Circle for Lacanian Ideology Critique*, 12 (2019).
———. "Alice in Wonderwater: Hysteria, Femininity, and Alliance in Clinical Aesthetics." In *Deleuze and the Schizoanalysis of Feminism: Alliances and Allies*. Edited by Janae Sholtz and Cheri Lynn Carr. London: Bloomsbury, 2019: 227–244.
———. "Approaching Impersonal Life with Clarice Lispector." *Humanities*, 7:55 (2018). doi:10.3390/h7020055
———. "Duras' *Césarée* and the Subject of Love." In *CR: The New Centennial Review*, 15.3 (2015): 167–199.
Neilli, René. *L'érotique des troubadours classiques*. Paris: Bibliothèque Méridionale, 1963.
Nietzsche, Friedrich. *The Basic Writings of Nietzsche*. Translated by Walter Kaufmann. New York: Modern Library, 2000.
———. *The Gay Science*. Translated by Walter Kaufmann. New York: Vintage, 1974.
Nixon, Mignon. *Fantastic Reality: Louise Bourgeois and a Story of Modern Art*. Cambridge, MA and London: MIT Press, 2005.
Nobus, Dany. "The Poetic Wisdom of Psychoanalysis: On the Trail of Lacan's New Signifier." Lecture for the Center for the Study of Psychoanalysis and Culture, State University of New York at Buffalo, 3/1/17.

Pedrosa, Mário, "The Vital Need for Art." In *Mário Pedrosa: An Anthology*. Gloria Ferreira, Mário Pedrosa, and Paulo Herkenhoff. Translated by Stephen Berg. New York: MOMA, 2016.

Peppiat, Michael. *Francis Bacon: Anatomy of an Enigma*. New York: Farrar, Straus and Giroux, 1996.

Pollock, Griselda. *After-affects / After-images: Trauma and Aesthetic Transformation in the Virtual Feminist Museum*. Manchester: Manchester University Press, 2013.

Price, Rachel. *The Object of the Atlantic*. Evanston, IL: Northwestern University Press, 2014.

PROATV. "Cómo Louise Bourgeois hizo 'Arch of Hysteria' con Jerry Gorovoy como modelo." Interview on the exhibit *Louise Bourgeois: The Return of the Repressed*, Buenos Aires, Argentina, March 19–June 19, 2011. www.youtube.com/watch?v=Zh6B3QzJeyo

Proust, Marcel. *A la recherche du temps perdu*, II. Paris: Pléiade, 1954.

———. *A la recherche du temps perdu*, III. Paris: Pléiade, 1954.

———. *Le temps retrouvé*: *A la recherche du temps perdu*, VII. Paris: Gallimard, 1990.

———. *Remembrance of Things Past*, II. Translated by Moncrieff and Kilmartin. New York: Vintage, 1982.

———. *Time Regained*. Translated by C.K. Scott. London: Vintage, 2000.

———. *The Captive*. Translated by C.K. Scott. London: Vintage, 2001.

Pseudo-Dionysius the Areopagite, *The Complete Works*. Mahwah, New Jersey: Paulist Press, 1988.

Rabaté, Jean-Michel. *Jacques Lacan: Psychoanalysis and the Subject of Literature*. New York: Palgrave, 2001.

———. "Kallos Anti-Bathos? (From Calle to Freud, Lacan, and Back)" *On Bathos. Literature, Art, Music*. Edited by Sara Crangle and Peter Nicholls. London/New York: Continuum, 2010.

Racine, Jean. *Berenice*. In *Oeuvres complètes 1*. Paris: La Pléiade, 1950.

Rebentisch, Juliane. *Aesthetics of Installation Art*. Berlin: Sternberg Press, 2012.

Rivera, Tania. "L'espace, le sujet, la psychanalyse, l'art contemporain et l'oeuvre de Lygia Clark." *Psychologie Clinique*, 34 (2012): 81–94.

Rolnik, Suely. "The Body's Contagious Memory: Lygia Clark's Return to the Museum" Translated by Rodrigo Nunes. *transversal—eipcp multilingual webjournal*. https://transversal.at/transversal/0507/rolnik/en

———. "Memória do corpo contamina museu." *Concinnitas*, 9.1.12 (July 2008): 15–27.

———. "Molding a Contemporary Soul: The Empty-Full of Lygia Clark." In *The Experimental Exercise of Freedom*. Edited by Susan Martin and Alma Ruiz. Los Angeles: MOCA, 1999.

Rose, Jacqueline. *Sexuality in the Field of Vision*. London: Verso, 1986.

Rosenwach Tank. www.rosenwachtank.com/about.php

Roubaud, Jacques. *Les troubadours: Anthologie bilingue*. Paris: Seghers, 1971.

Samuels, Maurice. "Baudelaire's Boulevard Spectacle: Seeing Through 'Les yeux des pauvres.'" *Time for Baudelaire (Poetry, Theory, History)*. *Yale French Studies*, 125–126 (2014): 167–182.

Schuster, Aaron. *The Trouble with Pleasure: Deleuze and Psychoanalysis*. Cambridge, MA and London: MIT Press, 2016.

Sholtz, Janae. *The Invention of a People: Heidegger and Deleuze on Art and the Political*. Edinburgh: Edinburgh University Press, 2015.

Soler, Colette. *Lacan Reading Joyce*. New York: Routledge, 2018.

———. *Lacan: The Unconscious Reinvented*. Translated by Esther Faye and Susan Schwartz. London, UK: Karnak, 2014.

Stendhal, *Scarlet and Black*. Translated by Margaret Shaw. London: Penguin, 1953.

Tournier, Michel. *Les météores*. Paris: Gallimard, 1975.

Trésor de la Langue Française informatisé: http://atilf.atilf.fr

Verhaeghe, Paul. *Does the Woman Exist? From Freud's Hysteric to Lacan's Feminine*. Translated by Marc du Ry. New York: Other Press, 1999.

Virgili, Fabrice. *La France "virile": Des femmes tondues à la Libération*. Paris: Payot, 2000.

Voruz, Véronique. "Psychoanalysis at the Time of the Post-human: Insisting on the Outside-Sense." *Paragraph* 33.3 (2010): 423–443.

Voruz, Véronique, and Bogdan Wolf. Preface. In *The Later Lacan*. Albany: State University of New York Press, 2007, vii–xvii.

Walusinski, Olivier. "The Girls of the Salpêtrière." *Hysteria: The Rise of an Enigma*. Edited by J. Bogousslavsky. Basel: Karger, 2014: 65–77.

———. "Les filles de la Salpêtrière." *Frontiers of Neurology and Neuroscience*, 33 (2014): 1–10.

Wanderley, Lula. *O dragão posou no espaço*. Rio de Janeiro: Rocco, 2002.

———. "A restruturação do Selfie." *Concinnitas*, 17.2.29 (June 2017): np.

Webster, Jamieson. *Conversion Disorder: Listening to the Body in Psychoanalysis*. New York: Columbia University Press, 2018.

Wilson, Daniel. "Freud's Lamarckian Clinic." In *Psychoanalysis and Inheritance*. Edited by James Godley and Joel Goldbach. Albany: State University of New York Press, 2018.

———. "Writing the Drive: From Freud's Theory of Bisexuality to Wittgenstein and the Limits of Language." *differences: A Journal of Feminist Cultural Studies*, 28.2 (2017): 65–85.

Winnicot, Donald W. *Playing and Reality*. London & New York: Routledge, 2005.

Winocour, Alice. *Augustine*. Paris, France: ARP Sélection, 2012.

Woolf, Virginia. *A Room of One's Own*. Orlando, FL: Harcourt, 2005.

Zupančič, Alenka. *The Shortest Shadow: Nietzsche's Philosophy of the Two*. Cambridge, MA & London: MIT Press, 2003.

———. *What IS Sex?* Cambridge, MA: MIT Press, 2017.

Index

www.ingramcontent.com/pod-product-compliance
Lightning Source LLC
LaVergne TN
LVHW040200080826
844660LV00001B/54

* 9 7 8 1 4 3 8 4 8 0 2 1 3 *